TABLE OF CONTENTS

Sliding Mask

Exam Tips:

1. Read each question carefully before looking at the possible answers.

2. After formulating an answer, determine which of the choices most nearly corresponds with that answer. It should completely answer the question.

3. Answer each question according to the latest regulations and procedures. You will receive credit if the regulations or procedures have changed. Computerized exams may be updated as regulations and procedures change.

4. There is only one answer that is correct and complete. The other answers are either incomplete or are derived from popular misconceptions.

5. If you do not know the answer to a question, try not to spend too much time on it. Continue with those you can answer. Then, return to the unanswered or difficult questions.

6. Unanswered questions will be counted as incorrect.

7. On calculator problems, select the answer nearest your solution. If you have solved it correctly, your answer will be closer to the correct answer than the other choices.

FAA AIRMAN KNOWLEDGE
PRIVATE PILOT
TEST GUIDE

ii

Jeppesen

Published in the United States of America
Jeppesen
55 Inverness Drive East, Englewood, CO 80112-5498
www.jeppesen.com

Cover Photos
Diamond airplane in flight courtesy of Diamond Aircraft Industries

ISBN 978-0-88487-059-3

Jeppesen
55 Inverness Dr. East
Englewood, CO 80112-5498
Web Site: www.jeppesen.com
Email: Captain@jeppesen.com
Copyright © Jeppesen
All Rights Reserved. Published 1992-2009, 2014, 2015
Printed in the United States of America

PREFACE

Thank you for purchasing this Private Pilot FAA Airman Knowledge Test Guide. This test guide will help you understand the answers to the test questions so you can take the FAA knowledge test with confidence. The test guide contains the FAA Private Pilot airplane test questions. Included are the correct answers and explanations, along with study references. Explanations of why the other choices are wrong are included where appropriate. Questions are organized by topic, with explanations conveniently located to the right side of each question. You can use the unique sliding mask to cover up the answers and test yourself. Full-color figures identical to those you will see on the FAA test are included together in Appendix 1 and 2 in the back of the book. Please note that this test guide is intended to supplement your instructor-led flight and ground training—it is not a stand-alone learning tool.

THE JEPPESEN TRAINING PHILOSOPHY

Flight training in the developing years of aviation was characterized by the separation of academics from flight training in the aircraft. For years, ground and flight training were not integrated. Students would consult a large number of books on different subjects, written by different authors, which resulted in a general lack of continuity in training material. The availability of **Jeppesen Training Products** changes this situation with professionally-integrated training materials that incorporate extensive research on teaching theory and on how adults learn most effectively. Some of the Jeppesen design features are:

- Objectives and completion standards included in every lesson.
- Teaching of complex skills using the **building block principle**.
- Incorporation of **meaningful repetition.** Each necessary concept or skill is presented several times throughout the instructional program.

You will find these features in Jeppesen syllabi, textbooks, videos, computer-assisted training (CAT), exercises, exams, and in this test guide. When these elements are combined with an instructor's class discussion and the skills learned in the simulator and airplane, you have an ideal integrated training system, with all materials coordinated.

People tend to retain about 10% of what they read, 20% of what they hear, 30% of what they see, and 50% of what they hear and see together. These retention figures can be increased to as high as 90% by including active learning methods. Active learning includes exercises, stage exams, student/instructor discussions, CAT, and practice in a simulator or airplane.

Levels of learning include rote, understanding, application, and correlation. One of the major drawbacks with test preparation courses that concentrate only on passing the test is that they focus on rote learning, the lowest level of learning. Jeppesen's approach raises the standard by challenging students to learn at the application and correlation levels. Our materials are challenging and motivating, maximizing knowledge and skill retention. More than 3 million pilots have learned to fly using our materials, which include:

TEXTBOOKS — Jeppesen pilot and maintenance training textbooks and e-books contain the answers to many of the questions you may have as you begin your training program. They are based on the **study/review** concept of learning. This means detailed material is presented in an uncomplicated way, then important points are summarized through the use of bold type and color. For best results, study the textbook as an integral part a coordinated package of materials. The textbook is the central component for academic study and is cross-referenced to video and CAT presentations.

ONLINE COURSES — Available for private, instrument, and commercial students, these engaging training courses teach you the academic knowledge needed for your pilot certificate or rating in straightforward, no-nonsense presentations. Strategic use of animation helps you understand concepts beyond what you can learn by just reading about them. Built-in maneuvers lessons show an animated overview of each maneuver, plus pilot's-eye videos that put you in the cockpit with an instructor. It is your best possible preparation prior to actual flight lessons.

VIDEOS — You can also purchase ground school DVDs that contain generous amounts of in-flight video and animated graphics. The DVDs complement the content in the textbook and online course, enabling you to review and reinforce essential concepts presented in the textbook.

SUPPORT COMPONENTS — Supplementary items include training syllabi, stage and end-of-course exams, CDs, FAR/AIM manuals or e-books, the *FARs Explained* book, these airman knowledge test guides, practical test study guides, question banks and airman knowledge testing supplements, the *Aviation Weather* textbook, the student record folder, computer, plotter, and logbook. Jeppesen Sanderson's training products are the most comprehensive pilot training materials available. In conjunction with your instructor, they help you prepare for the FAA exam and practical test; and, more importantly, they help you become a more proficient and safe pilot.

You can purchase our products and services through your Jeppesen dealer. For product, service, or sales information go to **www.jeppdirect.com.** If you have comments, questions, or need explanations about any component of our GFD Training System, we are prepared to offer assistance at any time. Contact us directly at: **TrainingServices@ Jeppesen.com**. You can also contact Jeppesen at the following addresses.

> Jeppesen
> 55 Inverness Drive East
> Englewood, CO 80112-5498
> 1-800-621-JEPP
> 303-799-9090

If you are in Europe, Africa, or the Middle East, contact us at:

Jeppesen & Co., GmbH
Frankfurter Strasse 233
63263 Neu-Isenburg, Germany
Tel: 011-49-6102-5070
Fax: 011-49-6102-507-999

UPDATES OF FAA QUESTIONS — You can obtain free updates for the FAA questions in this test guide by visiting Jeppesen's web site. These updates are generally valid within one year of book publication; if you are using an older test guide, the web site may not update all questions that have changed since the book was printed.

To find Test Prep Updates, go to **www.jeppesen.com/testprep.**

LATEST INFORMATION REGARDING AIRMAN KNOWLEDGE TESTS

In order to prevent students from memorizing the answers to the tests, the FAA randomizes the order of the answer choices to most questions in their knowledge tests. In addition, the FAA publishes only selected questions from their database, limiting the number of questions available to the public. Therefore, you might see questions on your knowledge test that are worded differently than those in this guide. This Jeppesen question bank contains the questions published on the FAA web site plus additional questions that should help you pass your airman knowledge test. If you are able to answer the questions in this guide, then you can reasonably expect to have the required knowledge to pass the FAA Knowledge Test.

Jeppesen has never encouraged its students to memorize answers to FAA questions. We provide comprehensive, no-nonsense study material that teaches you what you need to know to answer the test questions correctly. Our test prep materials always tell you why the correct answer is correct and, if it is not obvious, why the other answers are incorrect. When answering each FAA question, carefully read and evaluate each answer choice and choose the correct answer based on what you know from your study, not from that answer's position or wording.

INTRODUCTION

The Private Pilot FAA Airman Knowledge Test Guide is designed to help you prepare for the Private Pilot Knowledge Test. It covers FAA exam material that applies to airplanes, including pertinent Federal Aviation Regulations (FARs). Questions pertaining to rotorcraft, gliders, balloons, powered-lift, and airships are not included.

We recommend that you use this test guide in conjunction with the Guided Flight Discovery (GFD) Pilot Training System. The test guide is organized like the GFD Private Pilot Textbook, with eleven chapters and distinctive sections within each chapter. Questions are covered in the test guide generally in the same sequence as the material in the textbook. References to applicable page numbers in the textbook are included along with the answers. A separate chapter (Chapter 12) in the test guide is devoted to FAR questions and answers.

Within the chapters, each section contains a brief introduction. FAA test questions appear in the left column and answers and explanations are in the right column. Below is an example of a typical reference for a question.

[1]	[2]	[3]	[4]	[5]	[6]
4-59	**PLT016**	**4-59.**	**Answer C.**	**GFDPP 4-47**	**AIM**

(FAA Question)   *(Explanation of FAA Question)*

[1] Jeppesen designated test guide question number. The first number is the chapter where the question is located in the test guide. In most cases, this corresponds to the chapter in the GFD textbook. The second number is the question number within the chapter. This number may or may not be in sequential order. In this example, the question is in chapter 4 of the test guide and it is the 59th question.

[2] The FAA learning statement code. You can find a complete list of learning statements with learning statement codes in Appendix 3.

[3] The Jeppesen test guide number is repeated in the right hand column above the explanation.

[4] Correct answer to the question, in this case answer C is correct.

[5] The location where the question is covered in the GFD textbook. In this case, the question is covered on page 4-47 in the GFD Private Pilot Textbook.

[6] Abbreviation for the FAA or other authoritative source document. In this case, the reference is the Aeronautical Information Manual (AIM). Abbreviations used in the test guide are as follows:

AC	—	Advisory Circulars
A/FD	—	Airport/Facility Directory
AFH	—	Airplane Flying Handbook, FAA-H-8083-3A
AIM	—	Aeronautical Information Manual
ASI-SA##	—	Air Safety Institute (AOPA) Safety Advisor (By Number)
AW	—	Aviation Weather, AC 00-6A
AWS	—	Aviation Weather Services, AC 00-45
FAR	—	Federal Aviation Regulation

GFDIC	—	Guided Flight Discovery Instrument/Commercial Textbook
GFDPP	—	Guided Flight Discovery Private Pilot Textbook
IAP	—	Instrument Approach Procedure
IFH	—	Instrument Flying Handbook, FAA-H-8083-15
IPG	—	Instrument Procedures Guide (Jeppesen)
IPH	—	Instrument Procedures Handbook, FAA·H-8083·16
NAVWEPS	—	Aerodynamics for Naval Aviators
PHB	—	Pilot's Handbook of Aeronautical Knowledge, FAA-H-8083-25
RMH	—	Risk Management Handbook, FAA-H-8083-2
WBH	—	Aircraft Weight and Balance Handbook, FAA-H-8083-1
TERPS	—	U.S. Standard for Terminal Instrument Procedures

Below the reference line is the FAA question in the left column and the explanation in the right column. The explanation includes the correct answer followed by an explanation of why the answer is correct and if needed, why the other answers are wrong. In some cases, the incorrect answers are not explained. Examples include instances where the answers are calculated, or when the explanation of the correct answer obviously eliminates the wrong answers.

The answers in this test guide are based on official reference documents and, in our judgment, are the best choices of the available answers. Some questions that were valid when the FAA test was developed might no longer be appropriate due to ongoing changes in regulations or official operating procedures. The computer test that you take can be updated at any time. Therefore, when taking the FAA test, it is important to answer the questions according to the latest regulations or official operating procedures.

Three appendices from the FAA test materials are included in the back of the test guide. Appendix 1 provides legends from the appropriate airman knowledge testing supplement. These are an important resource for answering questions about charts and the *Airport/Facility Directory*; remember to look in the legends if you don't know the answer and remember that these legends will be available during your actual test. Appendix 2 contains the figures from the appropriate airman knowledge testing supplement that are needed to answer questions that refer to figures. Appendix 3 contains the FAA Learning Statement Codes and Learning Statements.

HOW TO PREPARE FOR THE FAA TEST
It is important to realize that to become a safe, competent pilot, you need more than just the academic knowledge required to pass a test. For a comprehensive ground training program, we recommend a structured ground school with a qualified flight or ground instructor. An organized course of instruction will help you complete the course in a timely manner, and you will be able to have your questions answered. The additional instruction will be beneficial in your flight training.

Regardless of whether you are in a structured ground training program, you will find this test guide is an excellent training aid to help you prepare for the FAA airman knowledge test. The test guide contains all of the airplane questions as they are presented in the FAA computerized test format. By reviewing the questions and studying the GFD Pilot Training materials, you should be well equipped to take the test.

You will also benefit more from your study if you test yourself as you proceed through the test guide. Cover the answers in the right-hand column, read each question, and choose what you consider the best answer. A sliding mask is provided for this purpose. Move the sliding mask down and read the answer and explanation for that question. You might want to mark the questions you miss for further study and review prior to taking the exam.

The sooner you take the exam after you complete your study, the better. This way, the information will be fresh in your mind, and you will be more confident when you actually take the FAA test.

WHO CAN TAKE THE TEST
When you are ready to take the FAA airman knowledge test, you must present evidence that you have completed the appropriate ground instruction or a home study course. This proof may be in the form of a graduation certificate from a pilot training course, a written statement, or a logbook entry by a certified ground or flight instructor. Although you are encouraged to obtain ground instruction, a home study course may be used. If you cannot provide one of the above documents, you may present evidence of a completed home study course to an FAA aviation safety inspector

for approval.

You also must provide evidence of a permanent mailing address, appropriate identification, and proof of your age. The identification must include a current photograph, your signature, and your residential address, if different from your mailing address. You may present this information in more than one form of identification, such as a driver's license, government identification card, passport, alien residency (green) card, or a military identification card.

WHAT IS A RECREATIONAL PILOT

The recreational pilot certificate was intended for those who are willing to limit their flying to a basic, single-engine aircraft with no more than 180 horsepower and stay within 50 NM of their home airport. Mainly because of the 50 NM limitation, very few people found the recreational pilot certificate to be practical. The number of applicants for recreational pilot certificates is very close to zero. Therefore we have removed all recreational pilot questions from this test guide. If you are interested in an easier pilot certificate than the private pilot certificate, we suggest checking out the sport pilot requirements in FAR 61, Subpart J (FAR 61.301 - FAR 61.327). The sport pilot certificate allows you to fly certain light, two-place aircraft during daylight hours and does not have the 50 NM limitation.

GENERAL INFORMATION — FAA COMPUTER TESTS

Detailed information on FAA computer testing is contained in FAA Order 8080.6, Conduct of Airman Knowledge Tests. This FAA order provides guidance for Flight Standards District Offices (FSDOs) and personnel associated with organizations that are participating in, or are seeking to participate in, the FAA Computer-Assisted Airman Knowledge Testing Program. You also may refer to FAA Order 8700.1, General Aviation Operations Inspector's Handbook, for guidance on computer testing by 14 CFR Parts 141 and 142 pilot schools that hold examining authority.

As an applicant, you don't need all of the details contained in FAA Orders, but you will be interested in some of the general information about computer testing facilities. A **Computer Testing Designee (CTD)** is an organization authorized by the FAA to administer FAA airman knowledge tests via the computer medium. A **Computer Testing Manager (CTM)** is a person selected by the CTD to serve as manager of its national computer testing program. A **Testing Center Supervisor (TCS)** is a person selected by the CTM, with FAA approval, to administer FAA airman knowledge tests at approved testing centers. The TCS is responsible for the operation of the testing center. A **Special Test Administrator (STA)** is a person selected by a CTD to administer FAA airman knowledge tests in unique situations and remote or isolated areas. A test proctor is a properly trained and qualified person, appointed by a TCS, authorized to administer FAA airman knowledge tests.

CTDs are selected by the FAA's Airman Testing Standards Branch. Those selected may include companies, schools, universities, or other organizations that meet specific requirements. For example, they must clearly demonstrate competence in computer technology, centralized database management, national communications network operation and maintenance, national facilities management, software maintenance and support, and technical training and customer support. They must provide computer-assisted testing, test administration, and data transfer service on a national scale. This means they must maintain a minimum of 20 operational testing centers geographically dispersed throughout the United States. In addition, CTDs must offer operational hours that are convenient to the public. An acceptable plan for test security is also required.

TEST MATERIALS, REFERENCE MATERIALS, AND AIDS

You are allowed to use aids, reference materials, and test materials within specified guidelines, provided the actual test questions or answers are not revealed. All models of aviation-oriented computers, regardless of manufacturer, may be used, including hand-held computers designed expressly for aviation use, and also small electronic calculators that perform arithmetic functions. Simple programmable memories, which allow addition to, subtraction from, or retrieval of one number from the memory, are acceptable. Simple functions such as square root or percent keys are also acceptable.

In addition, you may use any reference materials provided with the test. You will find that these reference materials are the same as those in your test guide. They include a printed airman knowledge testing supplement with the legend data and the applicable figures. You also may use scales, straight-edges, protractors, plotters, navigation computers, log sheets, and, as already mentioned, electronic or mechanical calculators that are directly related to the test. Permanently inscribed manufacturer's instructions on the front and back of these aids, such as, formulas, conversions, regulations, signals, weather data, holding pattern diagrams, frequencies, weight and balance formulas, and ATC procedures, are permissible.

WHAT TO EXPECT ON A COMPUTER TEST

Computer testing centers are required to have an acceptable method for the online registration of test applicants during normal business hours. They must provide a dual method, for example, keyboard, touch screen, or mouse, for answering questions. Features that must be provided also include an introductory lesson to familiarize you with computer testing procedures, the ability to return to a test question previously answered (for the purpose of review or answer changes), and a suitable display of multiple-choice and other question types on the computer screen in one frame. Other required features include a display of the time remaining for the completion of the test, a "HELP" function which permits you to review test questions and optional responses, and provisions for your test score on an Airman Knowledge Test Report.

On computer tests, the selection of questions is done for you, and you will answer the questions that appear on the screen. You will be given a specific amount of time to complete the test, which is based on past experience with others who have taken the exam. If you are prepared, you should have plenty of time to complete the test. After you begin the test, the screen will show you the time remaining for completion. When taking the test, keep the following points in mind:

1. Answer each question in accordance with the latest regulations and procedures. If the regulation or procedure has recently changed, you will receive credit for the affected question. However, these questions will normally be deleted or updated on the FAA computerized exams.

2. Read each question carefully before looking at the possible answers. You should clearly understand the problem before attempting to solve it.

3. After formulating an answer, determine which of the alternatives most nearly corresponds with that answer. The answer chosen should completely resolve the problem.

4. From the answers given, it may appear that there is more than one possible answer; however, there is only one answer that is correct and complete. The other answers are either incomplete or are derived from popular misconceptions.

5. Make sure you select an answer for each question. Questions left unanswered will be counted as incorrect.

6. If a certain question is difficult for you, it is best to proceed to other questions. After you answer the less difficult questions, return to those which were unanswered. The FAA computerized test format helps you identify unanswered questions, as well as those questions you wish to review.

7. When solving a calculator problem, select the answer nearest your solution. The problem has been checked with various types of calculators; therefore, if you have solved it correctly, your answer will be closer to the correct answer than the other choices.

8. Generally, the test results will be available almost immediately. Your score will be recorded on an Airman Knowledge Test Report form. [Figure A]

U.S. DEPARTMENT OF TRANSPORTATION
Federal Aviation Administration
Airman Knowledge Test Report

NAME: Jeffrey Scott   APPLICANT ID: 123456789

EXAM: Private Pilot-Airplane   EXAM ID: 90121120070468013

EXAM DATE: 12/11/2007   EXAM SITE: ABS80102

SCORE: 75%   GRADE: PASS   TAKE: 1

Below are learning statement codes which represent learning statements for incorrectly answered questions. For code descriptions, refer to the Learning Statement Reference Guide for Airman Knowledge Testing on the Internet: **www.faa.gov/education_research/testing/airmen/media/LearningStatementReferenceGuide.pdf** .

A single code may represent more than one incorrect response.

PLT012 PLT023 PLT090 PLT091 PLT141 PLT161 PLT173 PLT263 PLT366 PLT369 PLT420 PLT446 PLT447 PLT514

DO NOT LOSE THIS REPORT   (emboss here)

(Place red stamp above here)

EXPIRATION DATE: 12/31/2009

- -

Authorized instructor's statement. (If applicable)

On_____(date) I gave the above named applicant _____ hours of additional instruction in each subject area shown to be deficient and consider the applicant competent to pass the test.

Last _____ Initial _____ Cert. No. _____ Type _____
(Print clearly)

Signature _____

FRAUDULENT ALTERATION OF THIS FORM BY ANY PERSON IS A BASIS FOR SUSPENSION OR REVOCATION OF ANY CERTIFICATES OR RATINGS HELD BY THAT PERSON.

ISSUED BY: Computer Assisted Testing Service, CATS (01/06)

FEDERAL AVIATION ADMINISTRATION

Figure A. This sample Airman Knowledge Test Report shows the applicant's test results. Take 1 indicates this is the first time the applicant has taken this test. Learning statement codes for incorrect answers are included in the report, and an additional instruction section is included in the last part.

The Airman Knowledge Test Report includes learning statement codes for incorrect answers. To determine the knowledge area in which a particular question was incorrectly answered, compare the learning statement codes on this report to those in Appendix 1.

Computer testing designees must provide a way for applicants, who challenge the validity of test questions, to enter comments into the computer. The test proctor should advise you, if you have complaints about test scores, or specific test questions, to write directly to the appropriate FAA office. In addition to comments, you will be asked to respond to a critique form which may vary at different computer testing centers. The TCS must provide a method for you to respond to critique questions projected on the computer screen.

---

1. Did the test administration personnel give you an adequate briefing on testing procedures?

2. Was the "sign-on" accomplished efficiently?

3. Did you have any difficulty reading the computer presentation of test questions?

4. Was the test supplementary material (charts, graphs, tables, etc.) presented in a usable manner?

5. Did you have any difficulty using the "return to previous question for review" procedure?

6. Was the testing room noise level distracting?

7. Did you have adequate work space?

8. Did you have adequate lighting?

9. What is your overall evaluation of the computer testing experience?
   a. Unsatisfactory.
   b. Poor.
   c. Satisfactory.
   d. Highly satisfactory.
   e. Outstanding.

Figure B. Critique forms used at different computer testing centers may vary. This sample form contains typical questions.

RETESTING AFTER FAILURE
The applicant shall surrender the previous test report to the test proctor prior to retesting. The original test report shall be destroyed by the test proctor after administering the retest. The latest test taken will reflect the official score.

14 CFR section 61.49 says an applicant may apply for retesting after receiving additional training and an endorsement from an authorized instructor who has determined the applicant has been found competent to pass the test.

WHERE TO TAKE THE FAA TEST
Almost all testing is now administered via computer at FAA-designated test centers. As indicated, these CTDs are located throughout the U.S. You can expect to pay a fee and the cost varies at different locations. The following is a listing of the approved computer testing designees at the time of publication of this test guide.

Computer Assisted Testing Service (CATS)
www.catstest.com/
1-800-947-4228
Outside U.S. (650) 259-8550

PSI Testing
www.psiexams.com
1-800-211-2754

DISCOVERING AVIATION

This chapter of the Jeppesen *Private Pilot* Textbook discusses the beginnings of aviation, both as a craft and as your own pursuit. You will also read about the human factors that go into conducting every flight.

Each chapter and section in this *Private Pilot FAA Airmen Knowledge Test Guide* directly corresponds to the same chapter and section in *Private Pilot* Textbook, part of the Guided Flight Discovery Pilot Training System. The textbook, also available as an eBook, explores in depth each topic presented in this guide, and covers many areas not tested in your knowledge test. This additional information is vital to your private pilot preparation, and you will be expected to demonstrate understanding of this knowledge on your practical test.

SECTION A — PILOT TRAINING

Throughout history, we have dreamed about achieving the freedom and power of flight. We have looked to the sky, marveled at the birds, and wondered what it must be like to escape the bonds of earth to join them.

THE HISTORY OF FLIGHT

Leonardo daVinci, one of history's greatest intellects, pondered the mysteries of flight as early as the 15th century, with fully developed drawings and schematics for making flight possible for humans. From these origins, we continued our quest for flight. The Mongolfier brothers designed the first lighter-than-air vehicle, a balloon that made its first flight in 1783. Otto Lillienthal answered with the first heavier-than-air craft: a glider, in the years between 1881 and 1896. Orville and Wilbur Wright achieved the first powered, sustained, and controlled airplane flights in history, in 1903 at Kitty Hawk.

Aviation firsts didn't end with that initial airplane. Amelia Earhart and Charles Lindbergh made Atlantic crossings within the next 30 years. With the impetus of World War II driving technology, jet flight and supersonic flight evolved quickly. And then humans reached into space when Neil Armstrong and Edwin Aldrin stepped onto the moon. The Space Shuttle program made space flight practically routine, and soon private spacecraft will take tourists into space. Air travel has largely replaced buses and trains, and new technology could make supersonic flight affordable, making world travel easy and practical. The second hundred years should prove even more exciting than the first.

THE TRAINING PROCESS

In the early days, learning to fly was accomplished by trial and error. Although you might never encounter the same obstacles and hazards faced by the early aviators, becoming a pilot still presents a challenge that requires hard work and dedication. However, the time, energy, and money that you invest in flying will yield countless rewards.

The Federal Aviation Administration oversees all regulatory aspects of flight, and they govern the process by which you will receive your private pilot certificate. You could start training at a fixed-base operator (FBO) at your local airport or you might train through the military. No matter where you fly, you will pass through three phases of flight training—presolo, cross-country and test preparation—in addition to the ground training that supplements your training in the air. Along the way, you will acquire the flight hours necessary to meet the requirements of the certificate.

1-1   PLT371
With respect to the certification of airmen, which is a category of aircraft?

A– Gyroplane, helicopter, airship, free balloon.

B– Airplane, rotorcraft, glider, lighter-than-air.

C– Single-engine land and sea, multiengine land and sea.

1-1. Answer B. GFDPPM 1-18, FAR 1.1
Airmen are certificated according to five categories of aircraft: airplane, rotorcraft, glider, lighter-than-air, and a new category, powered lift. Gyroplane and helicopter are classes of aircraft within the rotorcraft category. Airship and balloon are classes of aircraft within the lighter-than-air category. Single-engine land and sea and multiengine land and sea are the four classes within the airplane category.

1-2   PLT371
With respect to the certification of airmen, which is a class of aircraft?

A– Airplane, rotorcraft, glider, lighter-than-air.

B– Single-engine land and sea, multiengine land and sea.

C– Lighter-than-air, airship, hot air balloon, gas balloon.

1-2. Answer B. GFDPPM 1-18, FAR 1.1
Each category of aircraft is broken down into classes. The airplane category is divided into single-engine land and sea, and multi-engine land and sea.

1-3   PLT371
With respect to the certification of aircraft, which is a category of aircraft?

A– Normal, utility, acrobatic.

B– Airplane, rotorcraft, glider.

C– Landplane, seaplane.

1-3. Answer A. GFDPPM 1-20, FAR 1.1
Normal, utility, and acrobatic are three of the categories under which aircraft are certified, based on their construction and use. Airplane, rotorcraft, and glider are categories of aircraft with respect to certification of AIRMEN. Landplane and seaplane are common, but incomplete, descriptions of CLASSES of airplanes based on airmen certification.

1-4   PLT371
With respect to the certification of aircraft, which is a class of aircraft?

A– Normal, utility, acrobatic, limited.

B– Airplane, rotorcraft, glider, balloon.

C– Transport, restricted, provisional.

1-4. Answer B. GFDPPM 1-20, FAR 1.1
As per the definition in FAR 1.1, "class" when used with respect to the certification of aircraft, is a broad grouping of aircraft having similar means of flight, propulsion or landing. These classes include: airplane, rotorcraft, glider, balloon, and powered-lift. In reality, however, class is not used as a designator in aircraft certification.

SECTION B — AVIATION OPPORTUNITIES

One of the unique joys of aviation is that there is always a challenge to be met; a new adventure on which to embark; one more goal to be achieved. A private pilot certificate opens a door to a future of exciting opportunities and endless possibilities. There are no FAA test questions in this section.

NEW AVIATION EXPERIENCES

As soon as you earn your private pilot certificate, new experiences await you; new scenery, new airports, and new responsibilities. You will be able to carry passengers for the first time, and you can fly cross-country to airports that you have not yet explored. As you gain flying experience and confidence, you might want to expand your aviation horizons. The best way to sharpen your abilities, master new skills, and reenergize your enthusiasm for flight is to pursue additional training.

REFRESHER TRAINING

Refresher training maintains your proficiency as a pilot, and keeps you safe. You can stay current and develop your skills at the same time with some different types of flying. If your initial flight training occurred at an airport near sea level, you will find mountain flying is an exciting challenge that tests all areas of your piloting abilities. Aerobatic flying shows you the limits of an airplane's envelope and puts you in control of a thrilling ride. Checkouts in new aircraft, such as tailwheel or high-performance airplanes, will add to your repertoire, and allow you to go places that you could not in the limited-performance aircraft in which you trained.

ORGANIZATIONS

Organizations for pilots abound. Some cover a broad spectrum of pilots, such as the Aircraft Owners and Pilots Association (AOPA). Others target special interests within aviation. The Experimental Aircraft Association (EAA) involves those who are interested in homebuilt, classic and antique aircraft. The Ninety-Nines, International Organization of Women Pilots, provides networking, fellowship and financial aid for female pilots.

ADDITIONAL RATINGS AND CERTIFICATES

A proficient pilot is always learning, and you might decide in the future to pursue additional certificates and ratings. An instrument rating allows you to fly in clouds and low visibility by reference to instruments. A multi-engine rating puts you in command of larger aircraft with more than one engine. If you have ever wanted to land on water, getting a seaplane rating is a great experience. You might try flying other categories of aircraft: rotorcraft, glider and balloon. Upgrade your certificate and level of expertise with a commercial certificate, which allows you to fly for hire. Teaching others to fly can be a next logical step; a flight instructor (CFI) certificate enables you to prepare future pilots. In order to be an airline captain, you must earn an airline transport pilot (ATP) certificate.

AVIATION CAREERS

Highly trained professional pilots use their skills in a variety of fields. Besides flying as an airline pilot, or teaching as a flight instructor, there are as many different jobs available in aviation as your imagination allows.

Air taxi and charter operations fly passengers or cargo during scheduled flights or provide on-call services. Aircraft sales representatives deliver aircraft from the factory to the dealer or from the dealer to the customer, as well as demonstrate aircraft. Land survey and photography services provide businesses and government agencies with information about commercial property, highways, mining operations, and drilling sites. In addition to providing a unique view of metropolitan areas and natural wonders, sightseeing services fly tourists over scenic areas which may be hard to reach by other means. Powerline and pipeline patrol flight operations consist of checking powerlines, towers, and pipelines for damage, as well as transporting repair crews. Air ambulance operations transport patients to health care facilities for specialized treatment. Helicopter pilots with trained paramedics on board carry critically ill or injured persons from accident scenes to hospitals.

SECTION C — INTRODUCTION TO HUMAN FACTORS

There is more to pilot training than acquiring technical knowledge and gaining proficiency in aircraft control. Understanding how your mind and body function when you fly is as important as knowing the operation of your airplane's systems and equipment. The goal of human factors training for pilots is to increase aviation safety by optimizing human performance and reducing human error.

SINGLE-PILOT RESOURCE MANAGEMENT

Approximately 75 percent of all aviation accidents are human factors related. The phrase *human factors related* more aptly describes these accidents than the term pilot error, because it usually is not a single decision made by the pilot, but a string of decisions, that leads to an accident. Single-pilot resource management (SRM) is the art and science of a pilot managing all available resources to ensure that the outcome of a flight is successful. SRM consists of the following six skills:

1. Aeronautical decision making (ADM)
2. Risk management (RM)
3. Task management
4. Situational awareness
5. Controlled flight into terrain awareness
6. Automation management

PILOT IN COMMAND RESPONSIBILITY

As pilot in command, you make the final decisions, and your choices determine the outcome of the flight. You are directly responsible for your own safety, as well as the safety of your passengers. Understanding your own personal limitations is an important part of being a responsible pilot in command.

SITUATIONAL AWARENESS

Situational awareness is the accurate perception of the operational and environmental factors which affect the aircraft, pilot, and passengers during a specific period of time. Maintaining situational awareness requires an understanding of the significance of these factors and their impact on the flight. When you are situationally aware, you have an overview of the total operation and don't fixate on one factor.

AVIATION PHYSIOLOGY

Aviation physiology is the study of the performance and limitations of the body in the flight environment. Most healthy people do not experience any physical difficulties as a result of flying. However, there are some physiological factors which you should be aware of as you begin flight training.

PRESSURE EFFECTS

As the airplane climbs and descends, variations in atmospheric pressure effect many parts of your body. As outside air pressure changes, air trapped in the ears, teeth, sinus cavities, and gastrointestinal tract can cause pain and discomfort. Common associated ailments include ear and sinus block, toothaches, gastrointestinal pain, as well as the after-effects of scuba diving.

MOTION SICKNESS

Motion sickness is caused by the brain receiving conflicting messages about the state of the body. You may experience motion sickness during initial flights, but it generally goes away within the first 10 lessons. Anxiety and stress contribute to motion sickness. Symptoms of motion sickness include general discomfort, nausea, dizziness, paleness, sweating, and vomiting.

STRESS AND FATIGUE

We define stress as the body's response to physical and psychological demands placed upon it. Stress causes the release of chemical hormones (such as adrenaline) into the blood and the acceleration of the metabolism to provide energy to the muscles. In addition, blood sugar, heart rate, respiration, blood pressure, and perspiration all increase. Stress can be caused by fatigue, and fatigue on its own can affect your ability to make timely and wise decisions.

DRUGS

Whether the drug is alcohol, an illicit drug, or an over-the-counter medication, it may affect your ability to safely act as pilot-in-command. Depressants, such as cold medication and alcohol, slow reaction times and decrease your sense of responsibility. Stimulants, like caffeine and appetite suppressants, put you on edge and may cause you to make rash decisions. Hallucinogens, such as some illegal drugs, may have after-effects that last for days or weeks. Consider carefully what the effects any drug you are taking will be on your piloting skill. If in doubt, consult an aviation medical examiner.

1-5   **PLT436**

How soon after the conviction for driving while intoxicated by alcohol or drugs shall it be reported to the FAA, Civil Aviation Security Division?

A— No later than 60 days after the motor vehicle action.

B— No later than 30 working days after the motor vehicle action.

C— Required to be reported upon renewal of medical certificate.

1-5. Answer A. GFDPP 1-66 (FAR 91.15)

According to 91.15, certificated pilots must provide a written report of each motor vehicle action to the FAA not later than 60 days after the action.

AIRPLANE SYSTEMS

CHAPTER 2

SECTION A — AIRPLANES

Although airplanes are designed for a variety of purposes, the basic components of most airplanes are essentially the same. Once the practical aspects of building an airworthy craft are resolved, what ultimately becomes the final model is largely a matter of the original design objectives and aesthetics. In a sense then, airplane design is a combination of art and science.

The aircraft is the composite of many parts. The airframe consists of the fuselage, wings, empennage, trim devices and landing gear. The engine and propeller provide the motion by which the airplane develops lift, and flies. The pilot's operating handbook (POH) is so vital that it is considered to be part of the airplane as well.

2-1   PLT373
Where may an aircraft's operating limitations be found?

A– On the Airworthiness Certificate.

B– In the current, FAA-approved flight manual, approved manual material, markings, and placards, or any combination thereof.

C– In the aircraft airframe and engine logbooks.

2-1. Answer B. GFDPP 2-10 (FAR 91.9)
Operating limits can be found in any of these sources.

2-2   PLT170
To minimize the side loads placed on the landing gear during touchdown, the pilot should keep the

A– direction of motion of the aircraft parallel to the runway.

B– longitudinal axis of the aircraft parallel to the direction of its motion.

C– downwind wing lowered sufficiently to eliminate the tendency for the aircraft to drift.

2-2. Answer B. AFH
Keeping the longitudinal axis parallel to the direction of motion ensures that the main gear will touchdown and roll as designed, parallel to the aircraft's direction of travel. Side loading the gear is not only bad for the aircraft structurally, but can result in the aircraft rolling away from the runway centerline on touchdown.

2-3   PLT377
Where may an aircraft's operating limitations be found if the aircraft has an Experimental or Special light-sport airworthiness certificate?

A– Attached to the Airworthiness Certificate.

B– In the current, FAA-approved flight manual.

C– In the aircraft airframe and engine logbooks.

2-3. Answer A. GFDPP 2-10, FAA Order 8130.2
Operating limitations for experimental aircraft are actually part of Form 8130-7, which is the special airworthiness certificate. As with all airworthiness certificates, this one must be carried in the aircraft, which ensures the operating limitations of an experimental or light sport aircraft are available to the PIC.

SECTION B — POWERPLANT AND RELATED SYSTEMS

Airplanes require a means of thrust in order to achieve enough lift to overcome the effects of gravity. The modern aircraft powerplant still maintains several similarities with its predecessors, including the requirement for precise interaction of the engine, propeller, and other related systems

ENGINES

In order to get the most performance out of your aircraft's engine, you need to know how the combustion process works, and what you can do to maximize the efficiency of its operation.

MIXTURE

- The purpose of adjusting the fuel/air mixture is to decrease fuel flow to compensate for decreased air density.
- Take off at high-elevation airports can require leaning the engine during run-up for best power.
- The mixture must be enriched prior to a descent.

CARBURETORS AND FUEL INJECTION

- The operating principle of float-type carburetors is based on the difference in air pressure between the venturi throat and the air inlet.
- The conditions most favorable to carburetor icing include an outside temperature between 20 and 70 degrees F and high humidity.
- In a normally-aspirated engine with a fixed-pitch propeller, the first indication of carburetor ice is a loss of RPM.
- Applying carburetor heat will: enrichen the fuel/air mixture; decrease engine performance; and cause a temporary decrease in RPM, followed by a gradual increase.
- Float-type carburetors are more susceptible to icing than fuel-injected systems.
- Fuel injection can offer lower fuel consumption, increased horsepower, lower operating temperatures, and longer engine life. The most significant safety advantage is the reduced risk of induction icing.

IGNITION

- The main purpose of a dual ignition system on an aircraft is to provide system redundancy.
- Another advantage of dual ignition systems is improved engine performance.

ABNORMAL COMBUSTION

- If the grade of fuel used in an engine is lower than specified for the engine, it will most likely cause detonation.
- Detonation occurs when the unburned charge in the cylinders explodes instead of burning normally.
- If a pilot suspects detonation during climbout, the initial corrective action is to lower the nose slightly to increase airspeed, which improves cooling.
- The uncontrolled firing of the fuel/air charge in advance of normal spark ignition is known as preignition.

FUEL SYSTEMS

- On aircraft equipped with fuel pumps, running a fuel tank dry before switching tanks is unwise because the engine-driven or electric boost fuel pump may draw air into the fuel system and cause vapor lock.
- Using fuel of a lower-than-specified grade can cause cylinder head and engine oil temperature gauges to exceed their normal operating ranges.
- Fuel of the next higher octane can be substituted if the recommended octane is not available.
- Filling the fuel tanks after the last flight of the day will prevent moisture condensation by eliminating air space in the tanks.

OIL SYSTEMS

- For internal cooling, reciprocating aircraft engines rely on the circulation of lubricating oil.
- An abnormally high oil temperature indication may be caused by the oil level being too low.

COOLING SYSTEMS

- Excessively high engine temperatures will cause loss of power, excessive oil consumption, and possible permanent internal engine damage.
- If the engine oil temperature and cylinder head temperature gauges have exceeded their normal operating range, the pilot may be operating with too much power and the mixture set too lean.
- To aid engine cooling during climb, the pilot can lower the nose, reduce the rate of climb and increase airspeed.
- To cool an engine that is overheating, the pilot can enrich the fuel mixture.

PROPELLERS

The propellers on single-engine airplanes can be divided into two basic types: fixed-pitch and constant-speed.

CONSTANT SPEED

- A constant-speed propeller enables selecting an RPM that results in a blade angle for most efficient performance.
- Engine operation on an aircraft equipped with a constant-speed propeller is conducted with the throttle controlling power output, as registered on the manifold pressure gauge, and the propeller control regulating engine RPM.
- When operating an engine equipped with a constant-speed propeller, the pilot must avoid high manifold pressure setting.

2-4   PLT342
Excessively high engine temperatures will

A— cause damage to heat-conducting hoses and warping of the cylinder cooling fins.

B— cause loss of power, excessive oil consumption, and possible permanent internal engine damage.

C— not appreciably affect an aircraft engine.

2-4. Answer B. GFDPP 2-34, PHB
High temperature can cause detonation and a resulting loss of power, excessive oil consumption, and engine damage, including scoring of the cylinders and damage to pistons, rings, and valves.

2-5   PLT342
If the engine oil temperature and cylinder head temperature gauges have exceeded their normal operating range, the pilot may have been operating with

A— the mixture set too rich.

B— higher-than-normal oil pressure.

C— too much power and with the mixture set too lean.

2-5. Answer C. GFDPP 2-35, PHB
With high power settings and the mixture set too lean, overheating can result. This can be indicated by a high engine oil temperature and cylinder head temperature.

2-6   PLT478
One purpose of the dual ignition system on an aircraft engine is to provide for

A— improved engine performance.

B— uniform heat distribution.

C— balanced cylinder head pressure.

2-6. Answer A. GFDPP 2-24, AFH
Dual ignition systems fire two spark plugs, which improves combustion of the fuel/air mixture and results in slightly more power.

2-7   PLT253

On aircraft equipped with fuel pumps, when is the auxiliary electric driven pump used?

A– In the event engine-driven fuel pump fails.

B– All the time to aid the engine-driven fuel pump.

C– Constantly except in starting the engine.

2-7. Answer A. GFDPP 2-27, PHB

The auxiliary electric pump is a backup for an engine-driven pump. Although labeling, procedures for use, and control switches differ between manufacturers, these auxiliary pumps can cause operational problems if used inappropriately. In some systems, continuous use of both the auxiliary pump and the engine-driven pump can cause an excessively rich mixture. Besides the back-up function, auxiliary pumps are commonly used to provide fuel under pressure for engine starting.

2-8   PLT191

The operating principle of float-type carburetors is based on the

A– automatic metering of air at the venturi as the aircraft gains altitude.

B– difference in air pressure at the venturi throat and the air inlet.

C– increase in air velocity in the throat of a venturi causing an increase in air pressure.

2-8. Answer B. GFDPP 2-18, PHB

The decreased pressure caused by air flowing rapidly through the venturi tube draws fuel from the float chamber.

2-9   PLT191

The basic purpose of adjusting the fuel/air mixture at altitude is to

A– decrease the amount of fuel in the mixture in order to compensate for increased air density.

B– decrease the fuel flow in order to compensate for decreased air density.

C– increase the amount of fuel in the mixture to compensate for the decrease in pressure and density of the air.

2-9. Answer B. GFDPP 2-19, AFH

If fuel flow is not decreased with altitude, the mixture becomes too rich with fuel. Therefore, the fuel mixture must be leaned to maintain the proper fuel/air ratio.

2-10   PLT249

During the run-up at a high-elevation airport, a pilot notes a slight engine roughness that is not affected by the magneto check but grows worse during the carburetor heat check. Under these circumstances, what would be the most logical initial action?

A– Check the results obtained with a leaner setting of the mixture.

B– Taxi back to the flight line for a maintenance check.

C– Reduce manifold pressure to control detonation.

2-10. Answer A. GFDPP 2-19, AFH

In this case, engine roughness is probably caused by the mixture set too rich for the high altitude. When the carburetor heat is turned on, the warmer air entering the carburetor is less dense, and the mixture is further enriched. As a result, the engine roughness increases. The problem can usually be corrected by leaning the mixture.

2-11   PLT249
While cruising at 9,500 feet MSL, the fuel/air mixture is properly adjusted. What will occur if a descent to 4,500 feet MSL is made without readjusting the mixture?

A– The fuel/air mixture may become excessively lean.

B– There will be more fuel in the cylinders than is needed for normal combustion, and the excess fuel will absorb heat and cool the engine.

C– The excessively rich mixture will create higher cylinder head temperatures and may cause detonation.

2-11. Answer A. GFDPP 2-19, AFH
With a decrease in altitude, air density increases. This means you will have to enrich the mixture as you descend, otherwise the fuel/air mixture can become excessively lean.

2-12   PLT190
Which condition is most favorable to the development of carburetor icing?

A– Any temperature below freezing and a relative humidity of less than 50 percent.

B– Temperature between 32 and 50°F and low humidity.

C– Temperature between 20 and 70°F and high humidity.

2-12. Answer C. GFDPP 2-19, PHB
Carburetor icing is most likely between 20° and 70°F in high humidity conditions.

2-13   PLT190
The possibility of carburetor icing exists even when the ambient air temperature is as

A– high as 70°F and the relative humidity is high.

B– high as 95°F and there is visible moisture.

C– low as 0°F and the relative humidity is high.

2-13. Answer A. GFDPP 2-20, PHB
Carburetor icing is most probable between 20° and 70°F with high humidity or visible moisture.

2-14   PLT190
If an aircraft is equipped with a fixed-pitch propeller and a float-type carburetor, the first indication of carburetor ice would most likely be

A– a drop in oil temperature and cylinder head temperature.

B– engine roughness.

C– loss of RPM.

2-14. Answer C. GFDPP 2-21, PHB
The restricted airflow through the carburetor causes an enriched mixture and loss of RPM.

2-15   PLT189
Applying carburetor heat will

A– result in more air going through the carburetor.

B– enrich the fuel/air mixture.

C– not affect the fuel/air mixture.

2-15. Answer B. GFDPP 2-20, 21, PHB
When the carburetor heat is turned on, the warmer air entering the carburetor is less dense, and the mixture is enriched.

2-16   PLT189
What change occurs in the fuel/air mixture when carburetor heat is applied?

A– A decrease in RPM results from the lean mixture.

B– The fuel/air mixture becomes richer.

C– The fuel/air mixture becomes leaner.

2-16. Answer B. GFDPP 2-20, 21, PHB
When the carburetor heat is turned on, the warmer air entering the carburetor is less dense, and the mixture is enriched.

2-17   PLT189
Generally speaking, the use of carburetor heat tends to

A– decrease engine performance.

B– increase engine performance.

C– have no effect on engine performance.

2-17. Answer A. GFDPP 2-21, PHB
Since the warmer air entering the carburetor is less dense, the fuel/air mixture is enriched and power decreases.

2-18   PLT189
The presence of carburetor ice in an aircraft equipped with a fixed-pitch propeller can be verified by applying carburetor heat and noting

A– an increase in RPM and then a gradual decrease in RPM.

B– a decrease in RPM and then a constant RPM indication.

C– a decrease in RPM and then a gradual increase in RPM.

2-18. Answer C. GFDPP 2-21, PHB
When carburetor heat is first applied, the mixture is enriched, and RPM decreases. Then, as the ice melts, airflow into the carburetor increases, leaning the mixture, and RPM increases.

2-19   PLT191
With regard to carburetor ice, float-type carburetor systems in comparison to fuel injection systems are generally considered to be

A– more susceptible to icing.

B– equally susceptible to icing.

C– susceptible to icing only when visible moisture is present.

2-19. Answer A. GFDPP 2-21, PHB
Because fuel injection systems do not have a venturi throat, they are not as susceptible to icing as float-type carburetors.

2-20   PLT250

If the grade of fuel used in an aircraft engine is lower than specified for the engine, it will most likely cause

A– a mixture of fuel and air that is not uniform in all cylinders.

B– lower cylinder head temperatures.

C– detonation.

2-20. Answer C. GFDPP 2-26, PHB

The higher the grade of fuel, the more pressure it can withstand without detonating. Conversely, lower fuel grades are more prone to detonation.

2-21   PLT115

Detonation occurs in a reciprocating aircraft engine when

A– the spark plugs are fouled or shorted out or the wiring is defective.

B– hot spots in the combustion chamber ignite the fuel/air mixture in advance of normal ignition.

C– the unburned charge in the cylinders explodes instead of burning normally

2-21. Answer C. GFDPP 2-25, PHB

Detonation occurs when the fuel/air mixture suddenly explodes in the cylinders instead of burning smoothly.

2-22   PLT115

Detonation may occur at high-power settings when

A– the fuel mixture ignites instantaneously instead of burning progressively and evenly.

B– an excessively rich fuel mixture causes an explosive gain in power.

C– the fuel mixture is ignited too early by hot carbon deposits in the cylinder.

2-22. Answer A. GFDPP-2-25, PHB

Detonation occurs when the fuel/air mixture suddenly explodes in the cylinders instead of burning smoothly. Detonation is caused by excessively lean mixtures while hot spots in the cylinder describes pre-ignition.

2-23   PLT115

If a pilot suspects that the engine (with a fixed-pitch propeller) is detonating during climb-out after takeoff, the initial corrective action to take would be to

A– lean the mixture.

B– lower the nose slightly to increase airspeed.

C– apply carburetor heat.

2-23. Answer B. GFDPP 2-26, PHB

Detonation can occur when the engine overheats. One action to help cool the engine is to increase airspeed, thus increasing the cooling airflow around the engine.

2-24   PLT249
The uncontrolled firing of the fuel/air charge in advance of normal spark ignition is known as

A– combustion.

B– pre-ignition.

C– detonation.

2-24. Answer B. GFDPP 2-26, PHB
Pre-ignition occurs when the fuel/air mixture ignites too soon.

2-25   PLT250
Which would most likely cause the cylinder head temperature and engine oil temperature gauges to exceed their normal operating ranges?

A– Using fuel that has a lower-than-specified fuel rating.

B– Using fuel that has a higher-than-specified fuel rating.

C– Operating with higher-than-normal oil pressure.

2-25. Answer A. GFDPP 2-30, PHB
Lower grade fuels will detonate under less pressure. Using a lower fuel rating than specified can cause excessive engine temperatures.

2-26   PLT250
What type fuel can be substituted for an aircraft if the recommended octane is not available?

A– The next higher octane aviation gas.

B– The next lower octane aviation gas.

C– Unleaded automotive gas of the same octane rating.

2-26. Answer A. GFDPP 2-30, PHB
If the manufacturer's recommendations are followed, the next higher grade of fuel may normally be used.

2-27   PLT250
Filling the fuel tanks after the last flight of the day is considered a good operating procedure because this will

A– force any existing water to the top of the tank away from the fuel lines to the engine.

B– prevent expansion of the fuel by eliminating airspace in the tanks.

C– prevent moisture condensation by eliminating airspace in the tanks.

2-27. Answer C. GFDPP 2-29, PHB)
As the airplane cools overnight, water condenses in the tanks from vapor in the air and enters the fuel. Filling the tanks eliminates the air space and prevents condensation.

2-28   PLT324
For internal cooling, reciprocating aircraft engines are especially dependent on

A– a properly functioning thermostat.

B– air flowing over the exhaust manifold.

C– the circulation of lubricating oil.

2-28. Answer C. GFDPP 2-32, PHB
Engine oil lubricates moving parts, reduces friction, and removes some of the heat from the cylinders.

2-29   PLT324
An abnormally high engine oil temperature indication may be caused by

A– the oil level being too low.

B– operating with a too high viscosity oil.

C– operating with an excessively rich mixture.

2-29. Answer A. GFDPP 2-33, PHB
If the oil level is too low, it can cause high engine oil temperatures.

2-30   PLT342
What action can a pilot take to aid in cooling an engine that is overheating during a climb?

A– Reduce rate of climb and increase airspeed.

B– Reduce climb speed and increase RPM.

C– Increase climb speed and increase RPM.

2-30. Answer A. GFDPP 2-35, PHB
Reducing the rate of climb and increasing airspeed will increase the cooling airflow around the engine.

2-31   PLT342
What is one procedure to aid in cooling an engine that is overheating?

A– Enrichen the fuel mixture.

B– Increase the RPM.

C– Reduce the airspeed.

2-31. Answer A. GFDPP 2-35, PHB
A richer fuel mixture burns at a slightly lower temperature and helps cool the engine.

2-32   PLT342
How is engine operation controlled on an engine equipped with a constant-speed propeller?

A– The throttle controls power output as registered on the manifold pressure gauge and the propeller control regulates engine RPM.

B– The throttle controls power output as registered on the manifold pressure gauge and the propeller control regulates a constant blade angle.

C– The throttle controls engine RPM as registered on the tachometer and the mixture control regulates the power output.

2-32. Answer A. GFDPP 2-38, PHB
The throttle controls the power output of the engine, which is indicated on the manifold pressure gauge. The propeller control changes the pitch of the propeller blades, thus controlling engine RPM, which is indicated on the tachometer.

2-33   PLT350

What is an advantage of a constant-speed propeller?

A– Permits the pilot to select and maintain a desired cruising speed.

B– Permits the pilot to select the blade angle for the most efficient performance.

C– Provides a smoother operation with stable RPM and eliminates vibrations.

2-33. Answer B. GFDPP 2-38, PHB
By selecting the proper blade angle, the pilot can convert a high percentage of engine power into thrust over a wide range of RPM and airspeed combinations. This allows the most efficient performance to be gained from the engine.

2-34   PLT351

A precaution for the operation of an engine equipped with a constant-speed propeller is to

A– avoid high RPM settings with high manifold pressure.

B– avoid high manifold pressure settings with low RPM.

C– always use a rich mixture with high RPM settings.

2-34. Answer B. GFDPP 2-39, PHB
For a given RPM setting, there is a maximum allowable manifold pressure. Generally, high manifold pressures with low RPM should be avoided to prevent internal stress within the engine.

2-35   PLT479

What should be the first action after starting an aircraft engine?

A– Adjust for proper RPM and check for desired indications on the engine gauges.

B– Place the magneto or ignition switch momentarily in the OFF position to check for proper grounding.

C– Test each brake and the parking brake.

2-35. Answer A. GFDPP 2-33, PHB
Immediately after starting an engine, set the proper RPM and check engine gauges for proper indications.

2-36   PLT479

Should it become necessary to handprop an airplane engine, it is extremely important that a competent pilot

A– call "contact" before touching the propeller.

B– be at the controls in the cockpit.

C– be in the cockpit and call out all commands.

2-36. Answer B. GFDPP 2-39, PHB
When hand-propping an airplane, a competent pilot must be at the controls to prevent the airplane from moving and to set the engine controls properly.

2-37   PLT342
Excessively high engine temperatures, either in the air
or on the ground, will

A— increase fuel consumption and may increase power
    due to the increased heat.

B— result in damage to heat-conducting hoses and warp-
    ing of cylinder cooling fans.

C— cause loss of power, excessive oil consumption, and
    possible permanent internal engine damage.

2-37. Answer C. GFDPP 2-34
High temperatures can cause detonation and a resulting loss of power, excessive oil consumption, and engine
damage, including scoring of the cylinders and damage
to piston, rings, and valves.

2-38   PLT254
To properly purge water from the fuel system of an aircraft equipped with fuel tank sumps and a fuel strainer
quick drain, it is necessary to drain fuel from the

A— fuel strainer drain.

B— lowest point in the fuel system.

C— fuel strainer drain and the fuel tank sumps.

2-38. Answer C. GFDPP 2-29, PHB
When the fuel strainer is being drained, water in the tank
may not appear until all the fuel has been drained from
the lines leading to the tank. Therefore, drain enough
fuel from the fuel strainer to be certain that fuel is being
drained from the tank. The amount will depend on the
length of the fuel line from the tank to the drain. Water
may also remain in the fuel tank even after the fuel
strainer has ceased to show any trace of water. This
residual water can be removed only by draining the fuel
tank sump drains.

SECTION C — FLIGHT INSTRUMENTS

Of the instruments located in the airplane cockpit, the indicators which provide information regarding the airplane's attitude, direction, altitude, and speed are collectively referred to as the flight instruments. Traditionally, the flight instruments are sub-divided into categories according to their method of operation.

PITOT-STATIC INSTRUMENTS

The pitot-static system supplies ambient air pressure to operate the altimeter and vertical speed indicator (VSI), and both ambient and ram air to the airspeed indicator.

STANDARD TEMPERATURE AND PRESSURE

- The standard temperature and pressure values for sea level are 15°C and 29.92 inches Hg (1013.2 hPa).

PITOT SYSTEM

- The pitot system provides impact pressure for the airspeed indicator.

V-SPEEDS

- The red line on an airspeed indicator represents never-exceed speed, which is the maximum speed at which the airplane can be operated in smooth air.
- The yellow arc indicates the caution range.
- The green arc denotes the normal operating range, with the bottom of the arc representing the power-off stalling speed in a specified configuration, and the upper limit representing the maximum structural cruising speed.
- The white arc identifies the normal flap operating range. The bottom of the white arc indicates the power-off stall speed in the landing configuration.
- Maneuvering speed is an important airspeed limitation that is not marked on the airspeed indicator.
- The indicated airspeed at which a given airplane stalls in a particular configuration will remain the same, regardless of altitude.

TYPES OF ALTITUDE

- Altimeter setting is the value to which the barometric pressure scale of the altimeter is set so that the altimeter indicates true altitude at field elevation.
- Variations in temperature affect the altimeter, as pressure levels are raised on warm days and the indicated altitude is lower than the true altitude.
- True altitude is the vertical distance of the aircraft above sea level.
- Absolute altitude is the vertical distance of the aircraft above the surface.
- Pressure altitude is the altitude indicated when the barometric pressure scale is set to 29.92.
- Density altitude is the pressure altitude corrected for nonstandard temperature.
- Indicated altitude is the same as true altitude when at sea level under standard conditions.
- Pressure altitude equals true altitude under standard conditions.
- One inch of change of Hg in the altimeter causes 1,000 feet of altitude change in the same direction.
- The aircraft will be lower than indicated when flown into areas of colder than standard air temperature, or lower pressure.
- An increase in ambient temperature will increase the density altitude at a given airport.
- If the pitot tube becomes clogged, the airspeed indicator is affected; if the static vents are clogged, the altimeter, airspeed indicator, and vertical speed indicator are affected.

GYROSCOPIC INSTRUMENTS

Gyroscopic instruments include the turn coordinator, attitude indicator and heading indicator. They operate off of a gyro's tendency to remain rigid in space.

TURN COORDINATOR

- A turn coordinator provides an indication of the aircraft's rate of movement about the yaw and roll axes.

ATTITUDE INDICATOR

- To properly adjust the attitude indicator during level flight, align the miniature airplane to the horizon bar.
- A pilot determines the direction of bank from the attitude indicator by the relationship of the miniature airplane to the deflected horizon bar.

HEADING INDICATOR

- The heading indicator must be periodically realigned with the magnetic compass as the gyro precesses.

MAGNETIC COMPASS

The magnetic compass contains a bar magnet, which swings freely to align with the Earth's magnetic field.

DEVIATION

- Deviation in a magnetic compass is caused by the magnetic fields in the aircraft distorting the lines of magnetic force.

TURNING AND ACCELERATION ERRORS

- In the Northern Hemisphere, a magnetic compass will show a turn toward the west if a right turn is entered from a north heading, and a turn toward the east if a left turn is entered from a north heading. A turn toward the north is indicated if an aircraft is accelerated while on an east or west heading, a turn toward the south if an aircraft is decelerated while on a west heading, and correctly, if the aircraft is on a north or south heading.
- The indications of a magnetic compass in flight are correct only when the aircraft is in straight and level, unaccelerated flight.

2-39   **PLT506**
Which V-speed represents maneuvering speed?

A– V_A.

B– V_{LO}.

C– V_{NE}.

2-39. Answer A. GFDPP 2-53, FAR 1.2
V_A is defined as the design maneuvering speed.

2-40   **PLT166**
If an altimeter setting is not available before flight, to which altitude should the pilot adjust the altimeter?

A– The elevation of the nearest airport corrected to mean sea level.

B– The elevation of the departure area.

C– Pressure altitude corrected for nonstandard temperature.

2-40. Answer B. GFDPP 2-57, FAR 91.121
If unable to obtain a local altimeter setting, you should set the altimeter to the field elevation prior to departure.

2-41   PLT166
Prior to takeoff, the altimeter should be set to which altitude or altimeter setting?

A– The current local altimeter setting, if available, or the departure airport elevation.

B– The corrected density altitude of the departure airport.

C– The corrected pressure altitude for the departure airport.

2-41. Answer A. GFDPP 2-57, FAR 91.121
If unable to obtain a local altimeter setting, you should set the altimeter to the field elevation prior to departure.

2-42   PLT337
If the pitot tube and outside static vents become clogged, which instruments would be affected?

A– The altimeter, airspeed indicator, and turn-and-slip indicator.

B– The altimeter, airspeed indicator, and vertical speed indicator.

C– The altimeter, attitude indicator, and turn-and-slip indicator.

2-42. Answer B. GFDPP 2-61, PHB
The altimeter, the airspeed indicator, and the vertical speed indicator all use static air and would therefore be affected.

2-43   PLT337
Which instrument will become inoperative if the pitot tube becomes clogged?

A– Altimeter.

B– Vertical speed.

C– Airspeed.

2-43. Answer C. GFDPP 2-61, PHB
The airspeed indicator operates by sensing ram air (impact pressure) in the pitot tube.

2-44   PLT337
Which instrument(s) will become inoperative if the static vents become clogged?

A– Airspeed only.

B– Altimeter only.

C– Airspeed, altimeter, and vertical speed.

2-44. Answer C. GFDPP 2-61, PHB
The altimeter, the airspeed indicator, and the vertical speed indicator all use static air and would therefore be affected.

2-45   PLT041
(Refer to figure 3.) Altimeter 1 indicates

A– 500 feet.

B– 1,500 feet.

C– 10,500 feet.

2-45. Answer C. GFDPP 2-55, PHB
The small 10,000' pointer is just beyond the 1, indicating that the altitude is above 10,000 feet. The wide 1,000' pointer is between 0 and 1, which indicates less than 1,000 feet. Finally, the 100' pointer is on 5. The altimeter reading is 10,500 feet.

2-46   PLT041
(Refer to figure 3.) Altimeter 2 indicates

A– 1,500 feet.

B– 4,500 feet.

C– 14,500 feet.

2-46. Answer C. GFDPP 2-55, PHB
The 10,000' pointer is above 1, the 1,000' pointer is above 4, and the 100' pointer is on 5. This indicates an altitude of 14,500 feet.

2-47   PLT041
(Refer to figure 3.) Altimeter 3 indicates

A– 9,500 feet.

B– 10,950 feet.

C– 15,940 feet.

2-47. Answer A. GFDPP 2-55, PHB
The 10,000' pointer is near 1, the 1,000' pointer is above 9, and the 100' pointer is on 5. This indicates the altitude is 9,500 feet.

2-48   PLT041
(Refer to figure 3.) Which altimeter(s) indicate(s) more than 10,000 feet?

A– 1, 2, and 3.

B– 1 and 2 only.

C– 1 only.

2-48. Answer B. GFDPP 2-55, PHB
On Altimeter 1, the small 10,000' pointer is just beyond the 1, indicating that the altitude is above 10,000 feet. The wide 1,000' pointer is between 0 and 1, which indicates less than 1,000 feet. Finally, the 100' pointer is on 5. The altimeter reading is 10,500 feet. On Altimeter 2, the 10,000' pointer is above 1, the 1,000' pointer is above 4, and the 100' pointer is on 5. This indicates an altitude of 14,500 feet. On Altimeter 3, the 10,000' pointer is near 1, the 1,000' pointer is above 9, and the 100' pointer is on 5. This indicates the altitude is 9,500 feet.

2-49   PLT166
Altimeter setting is the value to which the barometric pressure scale of the altimeter is set so the altimeter indicates

A– calibrated altitude at field elevation.

B– absolute altitude at field elevation.

C– true altitude at field elevation.

2-49. Answer C. GFDPP 2-57, AW
When the current altimeter setting is set on the ground, the altimeter reads true altitude of the field, which is the actual height above mean sea level.

2-50   PLT165
How do variations in temperature affect the altimeter?

A– Pressure levels are raised on warm days and the indicated altitude is lower than true altitude.

B– Higher temperatures expand the pressure levels and the indicated altitude is higher than true altitude.

C– Lower temperatures lower the pressure levels and the indicated altitude is lower than true altitude.

2-50. Answer A. GFDPP 2-60, PHB
Because atmospheric pressure levels are raised on warm days, the aircraft will be at a higher altitude than indicated. In other words, the indicated altitude is lower than true altitude.

2-51   PLT023
What is true altitude?

A— The vertical distance of the aircraft above sea level.

B— The vertical distance of the aircraft above the surface.

C— The height above the standard datum plane.

2-51. Answer A. GFDPP 2-57, PHB
True altitude is the actual height (vertical distance) above mean sea level.

2-52   PLT023
What is absolute altitude?

A— The altitude read directly from the altimeter.

B— The vertical distance of the aircraft above the surface.

C— The height above the standard datum plane.

2-52. Answer B. GFDPP 2-58, PHB
Absolute altitude is the height (vertical distance) above the surface.

2-53   PLT023
What is density altitude?

A— The height above the standard datum plane.

B— The pressure altitude corrected for nonstandard temperature.

C— The altitude read directly from the altimeter.

2-53. Answer B. GFDPP 2-56, PHB
Density altitude is found by applying a correction for non-standard temperature to the pressure altitude.

2-54   PLT023
What is pressure altitude?

A— The indicated altitude corrected for position and installation error.

B— The altitude indicated when the barometric pressure scale is set to 29.92.

C— The indicated altitude corrected for nonstandard temperature and pressure.

2-54. Answer B. GFDPP 2-56, PHB
Pressure altitude is the height above the standard datum plane when 29.92 is set in the scale.

2-55   PLT023
Under what condition is indicted altitude the same as true altitude?

A— If the altimeter has no mechanical error.

B— When at sea level under standard conditions.

C— When at 18,000 feet MSL with the altimeter set at 29.92.

2-55. Answer B. GFDPP 2-57, AW
In this situation, both indicated and true altitude would be zero.

2-56   PLT167
If it is necessary to set the altimeter from 29.15 to 29.85, what change occurs?

A— 70-foot increase in indicated altitude.

B— 70-foot increase in density altitude.

C— 700-foot increase in indicated altitude.

2-56. Answer C. GFDPP 2-59, PHB
A one inch change of Hg in the altimeter equals 1,000 feet of altitude change in the same direction. In this case, you increased the altimeter .7 of an inch (29.85 - 29.15 = .7), therefore, the indicated altitude increased 700 feet.

2-57   PLT337
The pitot system provides impact pressure for which instrument?

A— Altimeter.

B— Vertical-speed indicator.

C— Airspeed indicator.

2-57. Answer C. GFDPP 2-61, PHB
The airspeed indicator senses impact pressure to provide an airspeed reading.

2-58   PLT123
As altitude increases, the indicated airspeed at which a given airplane stalls in a particular configuration will

A— decrease as the true airspeed decreases.

B— decrease as the true airspeed increases.

C— emain the same regardless of altitude.

2-58. Answer C. GFDPP 2-55, PHB
Since airspeed indicators are calibrated to read true airspeed only under standard sea level conditions, the indicated airspeed does not reflect lower air density at higher altitudes. As a result, the indicated airspeed of a stall remains the same.

2-59   PLT088
What does the red line on an airspeed indicator represent?

A— Maneuvering speed.

B— Turbulence or rough-air speed.

C— Never-exceed speed.

2-59. Answer C. GFDPP 2-53, PHB
The red line is the never-exceed speed.

2-60   PLT088
(Refer to figure 4.)
What is the full flap operating range for the airplane?

A— 55 to 100 KTS

B— 55 to 208 KTS

C— 55 to 165 KTS

2-60. Answer A. GFDPP 2-52, PHB
The white arc indicates the flap operating range. On this instrument, it is 55 to 100 knots.

2-61   PLT088
(Refer to figure 4.)
What is the caution range of the airplane?

A– 0 to 55 KTS

B– 100 to 165 KTS

C– 165 to 208 KTS

2-61. Answer C. GFDPP 2-52, PHB
The yellow arc indicates the caution range. On this instrument, it is 165 to 208 knots.

2-62   PLT088
(Refer to figure 4.)
The maximum speed at which the airplane can be operated in smooth air is

A– 100 KTS.

B– 165 KTS.

C– 208 KTS.

2-62. Answer C. GFDPP 2-52, PHB
In smooth air, an airplane can be operated in the yellow arc up to the red line, in this case, 208 KTS.

2-63   PLT088
(Refer to figure 4.)
Which marking identifies the never-exceed speed?

A– Upper limit of the green arc

B– Upper limit of the white arc

C– The red radial line

2-63. Answer C. GFDPP 2-52, PHB
The red line is the never-exceed speed, the yellow arc is the caution range, the green arc is the normal operating range, and the white arc is the flap operating range.

2-64   PLT088
(Refer to figure 4.)
Which color identifies the power-off stalling speed in a specified configuration?

A– Upper limit of the green arc.

B– Upper limit of the white arc.

C– Lower limit of the green arc.

2-64. Answer C. GFDPP 2-52, PHB
The lower limit of the green arc represents the power-off stall speed in a specified configuration (usually flaps up, gear retracted).

2-65   PLT088
(Refer to figure 4.)
What is the maximum flaps-extended speed?

A– 58 KTS

B– 100 KTS

C– 165 KTS

2-65. Answer B. GFDPP 2-52, PHB
This is represented by the upper limit of the white arc, which in this case is 100 KTS.

2-66   **PLT088**
(Refer to figure 4.)
Which color identifies the normal flap operating range?

A– The lower limit of the white arc to the upper limit of the green arc.

B– The green arc.

C– The white arc.

2-66. Answer C. GFDPP 2-52, PHB
The white arc indicates the normal flap operating range.

2-67   **PLT088**
(Refer to figure 4.)
Which color identifies the power-off stalling speed with wing flaps and landing gear in the landing configuration?

A– Upper limit of the green arc.

B– Upper limit of the white arc.

C– Lower limit of the white arc.

2-67. Answer C. GFDPP 2-52, PHB
Stall speed with flaps and gear down is represented by the lower limit of the white arc.

2-68   **PLT088**
(Refer to figure 4.)
What is the maximum structural cruising speed?

A– 100 KTS

B– 165 KTS

C– 208 KTS

2-68. Answer B. GFDPP 2-52, PHB
This speed is indicated by the upper limit of the green arc, which in this case is 165 KTS.

2-69   **PLT088**
What is an important airspeed limitation that is not color coded on airspeed indicators?

A– Never-exceed speed.

B– Maximum structural cruising speed.

C– Maneuvering speed.

2-69. Answer C. GFDPP 2-53, PHB
The maneuvering speed of an airplane is not shown on the airspeed indicator. It can be found in the airplane manual or on placards.

2-70   **PLT086**
(Refer to figure 5.)
A turn coordinator provides an indication of the

A– movement of the aircraft about the yaw and roll axes.

B– angle of bank up to but not exceeding 30°.

C– attitude of the aircraft with reference to the longitudinal axis.

2-70. Answer A. GFDPP 2-66, PHB
The turn coordinator senses movement about the vertical axis (yaw) and the longitudinal axis (roll).

2-71   PLT278
(Refer to figure 6.)

The proper adjustment to make on the attitude indicator during level flight is to align the

A– horizon bar to the level-flight indication.

B– horizon bar to the miniature airplane.

C– miniature airplane to the horizon bar.

2-71. Answer C. GFDPP 2-68, PHB
The miniature airplane is adjustable and should be set to match the level flight indication of the horizon bar.

2-72   PLT278
(Refer to figure 6.)

How should a pilot determine the direction of bank from an attitude indicator such as the one illustrated?

A– By the direction of deflection of the banking scale (A).

B– By the direction of deflection of the horizon bar (B).

A– By the relationship of the miniature airplane (C) to the deflected horizon bar (B).

2-72. Answer C. GFDPP 2-66, PHB
As the airplane banks, the relationship between the miniature airplane and the horizon bar depict the direction of turn.

2-73   PLT215
Deviation in a magnetic compass is caused by the

A– presence of flaws in the permanent magnets of the compass.

B– difference in the location between true north and magnetic north.

C– magnetic fields within the aircraft distorting the lines of magnetic force.

2-73. Answer C. GFDPP 2-71, PHB
Metal and electronic components in the aircraft create magnetic fields which distort the lines of magnetic force. This causes deviation errors in the compass readings.

2-74   PLT215
In the Northern Hemisphere, a magnetic compass will normally indicate initially a turn toward the west if

A– a left turn is entered from a north heading.

B– a right turn is entered from a north heading.

C– an aircraft is accelerated while on a north heading.

2-74. Answer B. GFDPP 2-74, PHB
When turning from a northerly heading, the compass initially indicates a turn in the opposite direction. When starting a right turn, toward the east, the compass begins to show a turn to the west.

2-75   PLT215
In the Northern Hemisphere, a magnetic compass will normally indicate initially a turn toward the east if

A– an aircraft is decelerated while on a south heading.

B– an aircraft is accelerated while on a north heading.

C– a left turn is entered from a north heading.

2-75. Answer C. GFDPP 2-74, PHB
When turning from a northerly heading, the compass initially indicates a turn in the opposite direction. When starting a right turn, toward the east, the compass begins to show a turn to the west.

In this question, during a left turn toward the west, the magnetic compass would initially indicate a turn to the east.

2-76 PLT215

In the Northern Hemisphere, a magnetic compass will normally indicate a turn toward the north if

A— a right turn is entered from an east heading.

B— an aircraft is decelerated while on an east or west heading.

C— an aircraft is accelerated while on an east or west heading.

2-76. Answer C. GFDPP 2-73, PHB
Acceleration error is most pronounced on east/west headings. Using the acronym ANDS (Accelerate — North, Decelerate — South), acceleration will show a turn to the north, and deceleration will show a turn to the south.

2-77 PLT215

In the Northern Hemisphere, the magnetic compass will normally indicate a turn toward the south when

A— a left turn is entered from an east heading.

B— a right turn is entered from a west heading.

C— the aircraft is decelerated while on a west heading.

2-77. Answer C. GFDPP 2-73, PHB
Acceleration error is most pronounced on east/west headings. Using the acronym ANDS (Accelerate — North, Decelerate — South), acceleration will show a turn to the north, and deceleration will show a turn to the south.

2-78 PLT215

In the Northern Hemisphere, if an aircraft is accelerated or decelerated, the magnetic compass will normally indicate

A— a turn momentarily.

B— correctly when on a north or south heading.

C— a turn toward the south.

2-78. Answer B. GFDPP 2-73, PHB
Since acceleration and deceleration errors are most pronounced on east/west headings, accelerating or decelerating on a north or south heading will not show much of an error on the magnetic compass.

2-79 PLT215

During flight, when are the indications of a magnetic compass accurate?

A— Only in straight-and-level unaccelerated flight.

B— As long as the airspeed is constant.

C— During turns if the bank does not exceed 18°.

2-79. Answer A. GFDPP 2-74, PHB
Magnetic dip causes turning and acceleration/deceleration errors. For this reason, magnetic compass indications are accurate only in straight-and-level unaccelerated flight.

2-80 PLT206

If the outside air temperature (OAT) at a given altitude is warmer than standard, the density altitude is

A— equal to pressure altitude.

B— lower than pressure altitude.

C— higher than pressure altitude.

2-80. Answer C. GFDPP 2-56, 57, PHB
When the OAT is warmer than standard, the density altitude (DA) is higher than pressure altitude.

2-81   PLT173

What are the standard temperature and pressure values for sea level?

A– 15°C and 29.92 inches Hg.

B– 59°C and 1013.2 millibars.

C– 59°F and 29.92 millibars.

2-81. Answer A. GFDPP 2-51, PHB

The standard atmosphere is a temperature of 15°C (59°F) and 29.92" Hg (1013.2 millibars).

2-82   PLT173

If a pilot changes the altimeter setting from 30.11 to 29.96, what is the approximate change in indication?

A– Altimeter will indicate .15 inches Hg higher.

B– Altimeter will indicate 150 feet higher.

C– Altimeter will indicate 150 feet lower.

2-82. Answer C. GFDPP 2-59, PHB

Each .1" change on the altimeter setting equates to about 100 feet. In this case, the change is .15 lower, or 150 feet.

2-83   PLT023

Under which condition will pressure altitude be equal to true altitude?

A– When the atmospheric pressure is 29.92 inches Hg.

B– When standard atmospheric conditions exist.

C– When indicated altitude is equal to the pressure altitude.

2-83. Answer B. GFDPP 2-57, AW

Pressure altitude equals true altitude when standard atmospheric conditions exist. When nonstandard conditions exist, true altitude will not equal pressure altitude.

2-84   PLT023

Under what condition is pressure altitude and density altitude the same value?

A– At sea level, when the temperature is 0°F.

B– When the altimeter has no installation error.

C– At standard temperature.

2-84. Answer C. GFDPP 2-56, PHB

Since density altitude is pressure altitude corrected for nonstandard temperature, DA and PA are equal only at standard temperature.

2-85   PLT041

If a flight is made from an area of low pressure into an area of high pressure without the altimeter setting being adjusted, the altimeter will indicate

A– the actual altitude above sea level.

B– higher than the actual altitude above sea level.

C– lower than the actual altitude above sea level.

2-85. Answer C. GFDPP 2-59, AW

The aircraft will be at a higher true (actual) altitude above sea level than is indicated. In other words, the altimeter will indicate lower than the actual altitude.

Section C — Flight Instruments

2-86   PLT041
If a flight is made from an area of low pressure into an area of high pressure without the altimeter setting being adjusted, the altimeter will indicate

A– lower than the actual altitude above sea level.

B– higher than the actual altitude above sea level.

C– the actual altitude above sea level.

2-86. Answer B. GFDPP 2-59, AW
Remember, "from high to low, look out below." In other words, the aircraft will be at a lower true (actual) altitude than indicated, so the altimeter indicates higher than actual.

2-87   PLT165
Under what condition will true altitude be lower than indicated altitude?

A– In colder than standard air temperature.

B– In warmer than standard air temperature.

C– When density altitude is higher than indicated altitude.

2-87. Answer A. GFDPP 2-60, AW
When the air is colder than standard, the aircraft's actual (true) altitude will be lower than indicated.

2-88   PLT165
Which condition would cause the altimeter to indicate a lower altitude than true altitude?

A– Air temperature lower than standard.

B– Atmospheric pressure lower than standard.

C– Air temperature warmer than standard.

2-88. Answer C. GFDPP 2-60, AW
When the air is colder than standard, the aircraft's actual (true) altitude will be lower than indicated. In this question, the air temperature is warmer than standard, so indicated altitude will be lower than actual (true) altitude.

2-89   PLT023
Which factor would tend to increase the density altitude at a given airport?

A– An increase in barometric pressure.

B– An increase in ambient temperature.

C– A decrease in relative humidity.

2-89. Answer B. GFDPP 2-56, AW
When the air is colder than standard, the aircraft's actual (true) altitude will be lower than indicated.

In this question, the air temperature is warmer than standard, so indicated altitude will be lower than actual (true) altitude.

2-90   PLT215
The angular difference between true north and magnetic north is

A– magnetic deviation.

B– magnetic variation.

C– compass acceleration error.

2-90. Answer B. GFDPP 2-70, 9-11, PHB
Magnetic variation occurs because the earth's magnetic poles do not coincide with its geographic poles, and a magnetic compass aligns with the magnetic poles. You can determine local magnetic variation by referencing the isogonic lines on aeronautical charts, which are represented by dashed magenta lines.

2-91   PLT215
In the Northern Hemisphere, a magnetic compass will normally indicate a turn toward the north if

A– a left turn is entered from a west heading.

B– an aircraft is decelerated while on an east or west heading.

C– an aircraft is accelerated while on an east or west heading.

2-91. Answer C. GFDPP 2-73, PHB
An acronym to easily remember acceleration errors is ANDS (Accelerate North Decelerate South). Acceleration errors occur primarily due the counter weights added to offset magnetic dip.

2-92   PLT215
What should be the indication on the magnetic compass as you roll into a standard rate turn to the right from a south heading in the Northern Hemisphere?

A– The compass will initially indicate a turn to the left.

B– The compass will indicate a turn to the right, but at a faster rate than is actually occurring.

C– The compass will remain on south for a short time, then gradually catch up to the magnetic heading of the airplane.

2-92. Answer B. GFDPP 2-74, PHB
A turn from a southerly heading, results in a compass indication in the correct direction, but leading the actual heading. Various compass errors arise due to magnetic dip and from the compass counter weights added to off-set dip.

2-93   PLT215
When converting from true course to magnetic heading, a pilot should

A– subtract easterly variation and right wind correction angle.

B– add westerly variation and subtract left wind correction angle.

C– subtract westerly variation and add right wind correction angle.

2-93. Answer B. GFDPP 2-70, PHB
Remember, "East is least, West is best" to recall that easterly variation is subtracted and westerly is added. This calculation is often performed in conjunction with wind correction calculations using the formula:

TC ± WCA = TH ± VAR = MH ± DEV = CH

When using the wind side of a flight computer, add wind correction if your wind dot is to the right of the centerline, and subtract if it's to the left. You can easily visualize this by remembering that compass headings decrease as you turn left, so a correction to the left requires that you subtract the correction angle.

2-94   PLT215
Deviation error of the magnetic compass is caused by

A– northerly turning error.

B– certain metals and electrical systems within the aircraft.

C– the difference in location of true north and magnetic north.

2-94. Answer B. GFDPP 2-71, PHB
Metal and electronic components in the aircraft create magnetic fields which distort the lines of magnetic force. This causes deviation errors in the compass readings.

CHAPTER 3

AERODYNAMIC PRINCIPLES

SECTION A — FOUR FORCES OF FLIGHT

Understanding what makes an airplane fly begins with learning the four forces of flight.

- The four forces that act on an aircraft in flight are lift, weight, thrust and drag.
- The forces acting on an airplane are in equilibrium when the aircraft is in unaccelerated flight.
- During straight-and-level flight, lift equals weight, and thrust equals drag.

CRITICAL ANGLE OF ATTACK

The angle between the chord line and the relative wind is the angle of attack.

FLAPS

- One of the main functions of flaps during an approach is to increase the angle of descent without increasing the airspeed.
- Flaps enable the pilot to make steeper approaches to a landing without increasing airspeed.

WEIGHT

The angle of attack at which an airplane wing stalls will remain the same regardless of gross weight.

GROUND EFFECT

- Ground effect is the result of the interference of the surface of the Earth with the airflow patterns about an airplane.
- As a result of ground effect, induced drag decreases, and any excess speed at the point of flare may cause considerable floating.
- Ground effect may result in becoming airborne before reaching recommended takeoff speed.

3-1   PLT247

The four forces acting on an airplane in flight are

A– lift, weight, thrust, and drag.

B– lift, weight, gravity, and thrust.

C– lift, gravity, power, and friction.

3-1. Answer A. GFDPP 3-2, AFH

In normal (nonacrobatic) flight conditions, lift is the upward force created by airflow over and under the wings. Weight, caused by the downward pull of gravity, opposes lift. Thrust is the forward force which propels the airplane, and drag is the retarding force opposing thrust.

3-2   PLT247

When are the four forces that act on an airplane in equilibrium?

A– During unaccelerated flight.

B– When the aircraft is accelerating.

C– When the aircraft is at rest on the ground.

3-2. Answer A. GFDPP 3-3, AFH

In straight-and-level, unaccelerated flight, the four forces are in equilibrium. Lift equals weight, and thrust equals drag.

3-3   PLT168

(Refer to figure 1.) The acute angle A is the angle of

A– incidence.

B– attack.

C– dihedral.

3-3. Answer B. GFDPP 3-5, PHB

The angle between the chord line and the relative wind is the angle of attack.

3-4   PLT168

The term "angle of attack" is defined as the angle between the

A– chord line of the wing and the relative wind

B– airplane's longitudinal axis and that of the air striking the airfoil.

C– airplane's center line and the relative wind.

3-4. Answer A. GFDPP 3-4, PHB

The angle of attack is the angle between the chord line of the wing and the relative wind.

3-5   PLT247

What is the relationship of lift, drag, thrust, and weight when the airplane is in straight-and-level flight?

A– Lift equals weight and thrust equals drag.

B– Lift, drag, and weight equal thrust.

C– Lift and weight equal thrust and drag.

3-5. Answer A. GFDPP 3-3, AFH

Assuming the airplane is not accelerating, thrust equals drag, and lift equals weight.

3-6   PLT473

One of the main functions of flaps during approach and landing is to

A– decrease the angle of descent without increasing the airspeed.

B– permit a touchdown at a higher indicated airspeed.

C– increase the angle of descent without increasing the airspeed.

3-6. Answer C. GFDPP 3-12, AFH

Because flaps increase lift, induced drag is also increased, thus allowing a steeper angle of descent without increasing airspeed.

3-7   PLT473

What is one purpose of wing flaps?

A– To enable the pilot to make steeper approaches to a landing without increasing the airspeed.

B– To relieve the pilot of maintaining continuous pressure on the controls.

C– To decrease wing area to vary the lift.

3-7. Answer A. GFDPP 3-12, AFH

Flaps increase both lift and induced drag, allowing a steeper descent without increasing airspeed.

3-8   PLT168

The angle of attack at which an airplane wing stalls will

A– increase if the CG is moved forward.

B– change with an increase in gross weight.

C– remain the same regardless of gross weight.

3-8. Answer C. GFDPP 3-6, FTP

The critical angle of attack (angle of attack at which an airplane stalls) is determined by the lift coefficient of a particular wing configuration. An airplane will stall when the critical angle of attack is exceeded, regardless of weight or airspeed.

3-9   PLT131

What is ground effect?

A– The result of the interference of the surface of the Earth with the airflow patterns about an airplane.

B– The result of an alteration in airflow patterns increasing induced drag about the wings of an airplane.

C– The result of the disruption of the airflow patterns about the wings of an airplane to the point where the wings will no longer support the airplane in flight.

3-9. Answer A. GFDPP 3-18, AFH

When flying close to the ground, the airflow around an airplane is altered by interference with the surface of the earth. The resulting ground effect reduces the induced drag on the airplane.

3-10   PLT131

Floating caused by the phenomenon of ground effect will be most realized during an approach to land when at

A– less than the length of the wingspan above the surface.

B– twice the length of the wingspan above the surface.

C– a higher-than-normal angle of attack.

3-10. Answer A. GFDPP 3-18, AFH

Ground effect becomes noticeable when the height of the airplane above the ground is less than the length of the wingspan.

3-11   PLT131

What must a pilot be aware of as a result of ground effect?

A– Wingtip vortices increase creating wake turbulence problems for arriving and departing aircraft.

B– Induced drag decreases; therefore, any excess speed at the point of flare may cause considerable floating.

C– A full stall landing will require less up elevator deflection than would a full stall when done free of ground effect.

3-11. Answer B. GFDPP 3-18, AFH

Since ground effect decreases induced drag, the airplane tends to float while excess speed bleeds off.

3-12   PLT131
Ground effect is most likely to result in which problem?

A— Setting to the surface abruptly during landing.

B— Becoming airborne before reaching recommended takeoff speed.

C— Inability to get airborne even though airspeed is sufficient for normal takeoff needs.

3-12. Answer B. GFDPP 3-18, AFH
The decreased induced drag while in ground effect allows the airplane to become airborne at a lower airspeed. This may fool you into thinking the airplane is capable of flying at the lower airspeed when you climb out of ground effect.

3-13   PLT025
Which statement relates to Bernoulli's principle?

A— For every action there is an equal and opposite reaction.

B— An additional upward force is generated as the lower surface of the wing deflects air downward.

C— Air traveling faster over the curved upper surface of an airfoil causes lower pressure on the top surface.

3-13. Answer C. GFDPP 3-4
Bernoulli's principle, from Swiss mathematician, Daniel Bernoulli, simply states that as the velocity of a fluid (including air), increases, its internal pressure decreases.

3-14   PLT168
The angle between the chord line of an airfoil and the relative wind is known as the angle of

A— lift.

B— attack.

C— incidence.

3-14. Answer B. GFDPP 3-5
In addition to knowing the relationship of relative wind and angle of attack, remember that angle of attack is not an angle that is relative to the horizon or the aircraft's pitch in relationship to the ground. For example, the critical angle of attack, at which a wing will always stall, can occur in any flight attitude.

3-15   PLT236
Changes in the center of pressure of a wing affect the aircraft's

A— lift/drag ratio.

B— lifting capacity.

C— aerodynamic balance and controllability.

3-15. Answer C. GFDPP 3-4, PHB
A wing's center of pressure moves forward and back with changing angles of attack (forward for high angles and back for lower). This movement changes the position of the air loads on the wing, which results in changes to an airplane's aerodynamic balance and controllability.

SECTION B — STABILITY

- Although no airplane is completely stable, all airplanes must have desirable handling characteristics.
- An aircraft that is inherently stable will require less effort to control.

LONGITUDINAL STABILITY

- Longitudinal stability in an airplane involves the pitching motion or tendency of the aircraft to move about its lateral axis.

LOCATION OF THE CG

- The location of the CG, with respect to the center of lift, determines the longitudinal stability of the airplane.
- An airplane loaded with the CG aft of the approved CG range will be difficult to recover from a stalled condition.
- Loading an aircraft to the most aft CG will cause the airplane to be less stable at all speeds.

HORIZONTAL STABILIZER

When power is reduced, and the controls are not adjusted, an aircraft pitches nose down because the downwash on the elevators from the propeller slipstream is reduced and elevator effectiveness is reduced.

STALLS

The inherent stability of an airplane is particularly important as it relates to the aircraft's ability to avoid stalls and spins. Familiarization with the causes and effects of stalls is especially important during flight at slow airspeeds, such as during takeoff and landing, where the margin above the stall speed is small.

SPINS

- The aircraft must be placed in a stalled condition in order to spin.
- During a spin, both wings are stalled.

3-16   **PLT213**

An airplane said to be inherently stable will

A— be difficult to stall.

B— require less effort to control.

C— not spin.

3-16. Answer B. GFDPP 3-22, PHB

An airplane that is inherently stable tends to return to its original attitude after it has been displaced, and is therefore easier to control.

3-17   **PLT213**

What determines the longitudinal stability of an airplane?

A— The location of the CG with respect to the center of lift.

B— The effectiveness of the horizontal stabilizer, rudder, and rudder trim tab.

C— The relationship of thrust and lift to weight and drag.

3-17. Answer A. GFDPP 3-26, PHB

The longitudinal stability of an airplane is determined primarily by the location of the center of gravity (CG) in relation to the center of lift.

3-18   PLT351

What causes an airplane (except a T-tail) to pitch nosedown when power is reduced and controls are not adjusted?

A– The CG shifts forward when thrust and drag are reduced.

B– The downwash on the elevators from the propeller slipstream is reduced and elevator effectiveness is reduced.

C– When thrust is reduced to less than weight, lift is also reduced and the wings can no longer support the weight.

3-18. Answer B. GFDPP 3-30, PHB

At higher power settings, in airplanes other than T-tail designs, the propeller slipstream causes a greater downward force on the horizontal stabilizer. When power is reduced, this downward force on the tail is also reduced, and the nose pitches down.

3-19   PLT240

An airplane has been loaded in such a manner that the CG is located aft of the aft CG limit. One undesirable flight characteristic a pilot might experience with this airplane would be

A– a longer takeoff run.

B– difficulty in recovering from a stalled condition.

C– stalling at higher-than-normal airspeed.

3-19. Answer B. GFDPP 3-28, AFH

With a CG aft of the rear CG limit, the airplane becomes tail heavy and unstable in pitch because the horizontal stabilizer is less effective. This condition makes it difficult, if not impossible, to recover from a stall or spin.

3-20   PLT240

Loading an airplane to the most aft CG will cause the airplane to be

A– less stable at all speeds.

B– less stable at slow speeds, but more stable at high speeds.

C– less stable at high speeds, but more stable at low speeds.

3-20. Answer A. GFDPP 3-28, AFH

In an airplane loaded to the aft CG limit, the horizontal stabilizer is less effective, causing the airplane to be less stable at all speeds.

3-21   PLT245

In what flight condition must an aircraft be placed in order to spin?

A– Partially stalled with one wing low.

B– In a steep diving spiral.

C– Stalled.

3-21. Answer C. GFDPP 3-39, AFH

An airplane must be stalled before a spin can develop.

3-22   PLT245

During a spin to the left, which wing(s) is/are stalled?

A– Both wings are stalled.

B– Neither wing is stalled.

C– Only the left wing is stalled.

3-22. Answer A. GFDPP 3-39, AFH

In a spin, both wings are stalled but in a spin to the left, the left wing is more stalled.

SECTION C — AERODYNAMICS OF MANEUVERING FLIGHT

The extent to which an airplane can perform a variety of maneuvers is primarily a matter of design and a measure of its overall performance. Although aircraft design and performance may differ, the aerodynamic forces acting on any maneuvering aircraft are essentially the same. Understanding the aerodynamics of maneuvering flight can help you perform precise maneuvers while keeping your airplane within its design limitations.

TORQUE

Torque effect is greatest at low airspeeds, high power settings and high angles of attack.

P-FACTOR

- P-factor is the result of the propeller blade descending on the right, and producing more thrust than the ascending blade on the left.
- P-factor is most pronounced at high angles of attack.

LIFT/DRAG RATIO

Establishing the proper glide attitude and airspeed is critical to ensure the best possibility of reaching a suitable landing area.

HORIZONTAL COMPONENT OF LIFT

The horizontal component of lift is what makes an airplane turn.

LOAD FACTOR

Load factor is the ratio of the load supported by the airplane's wings to the actual weight of the aircraft and its contents.

IN TURNS

- Turns increase the load factor on an airplane, as compared to straight-and-level flight.
- The amount of excess load that can be imposed on an airplane depends on its speed.
- At 60 degrees of bank, 2 Gs are required to maintain level flight. To determine how much weight the airplane's wing structure must support, multiply the airplane's weight by the number of Gs.

IN STALLS

During an approach to a stall, an increased load factor will cause the airplane to stall at a higher airspeed.

MANEUVERING SPEED

V_A is defined as maneuvering speed.

3-23   PLT243

In what flight condition is torque effect the greatest in a single-engine airplane?

A— Low airspeed, high power, high angle of attack.

B— Low airspeed, low power, low angle of attack.

C— High airspeed, high power, high angle of attack.

3-23. Answer A. GFDPP 3-47, PHB

Torque effect is greatest at low airspeeds, high power settings, and high angles of attack.

3-24   PLT243

The left turning tendency of an airplane caused by P-factor is the result of the

A— clockwise rotation of the engine and the propeller turning the airplane counter-clockwise.

B— propeller blade descending on the right, producing more thrust than the ascending blade on the left.

C— gyroscopic forces applied to the rotating propeller blades acting 90° in advance of the point the force was applied.

3-24. Answer B. GFDPP 3-49, PHB

P-factor, or asymmetric propeller loading, normally occurs at a high angle of attack. The descending propeller blade on the right side takes a larger "bite" of the air, and produces more thrust than the ascending blade on the left. The result is a left turning tendency of the airplane.

3-25   PLT243

When does P-factor cause the airplane to yaw to the left?

A— When at low angles of attack.

B— When at high angles of attack.

C— When at high airspeeds.

3-25. Answer B. GFDPP 3-49, PHB

P-factor is most pronounced at high angles of attack, which cause the descending propeller blade to produce more thrust.

3-26   PLT309

(Refer to figure 2.)

If an airplane weighs 2,300 pounds, what approximate weight would the airplane structure be required to support during a 60° banked turn while maintaining altitude?

A— 2,300 pounds.

B— 3,400 pounds.

C— 4,600 pounds.

3-26. Answer C. GFDPP 3-60, PHB

At 60 degrees of bank, 2 Gs are required to maintain level flight. This means that the airplane's wing structure must support twice the airplane's weight, or 2,300 × 2 = 4,600 pounds.

3-27   PLT309

(Refer to figure 2.)

If an airplane weighs 3,300 pounds, what approximate weight would the airplane structure be required to support during a 30° banked turn while maintaining altitude?

A— 1,200 pounds.

B— 3,100 pounds.

C— 3,960 pounds.

3-27. Answer C. GFDPP 3-60, PHB

The load factor for 30 degrees of bank is 1.154, or about 1.2. The airplane weight (3,300) multiplied by the load factor (1.2) is 3,960 pounds which the wing structure must support.

3-28 PLT309
(Refer to figure 2.)

If an airplane weighs 4,500 pounds, what approximate weight would the airplane structure be required to support during a 45° banked turn while maintaining altitude?

A– 4,500 pounds.

B– 6,750 pounds.

C– 7,200 pounds.

3-28. Answer B. GFDPP 3-60, PHB
At 45 degrees of bank the load factor is 1.414, or approximately 1.5, the wing loading would be 4,500 × 1.5, or 6,750 pounds.

3-29 PLT311
The amount of excess load that can be imposed on the wing of an airplane depends upon the

A– position of the CG.

B– speed of the airplane.

C– abruptness at which the load is applied.

3-29. Answer B. GFDPP 3-63, PHB
The amount of excess load that can be imposed on an airplane depends on its speed. If abrupt control movements or strong gusts are applied at low airspeeds, the airplane will stall before the load becomes excessive. At higher airspeeds, the increased airflow causes a greater lifting capacity. A sudden control input or gust at a high airspeed may result in an excessive load factor beyond safe limits.

3-30 PLT310
Which basic flight maneuver increases the load factor on an airplane as compared to straight-and-level flight?

A– Climbs.

B– Turns.

C– Stalls.

3-30. Answer B. GFDPP 3-60, PHB
In a level turn, lift must be increased to compensate for the loss of vertical lift as well as overcome centrifugal force. Since the wings must support not only the airplane's weight, but also the load imposed by centrifugal force, the load factor is greater than 1 G.

3-31 PLT242
What force makes an airplane turn?

A– The horizontal component of lift.

B– The vertical component of lift.

C– Centrifugal force.

3-31. Answer A. GFDPP 3-56, PHB
In a turn, lift has both a vertical and a horizontal component. The horizontal component of lift, which is also referred to as centripetal force, opposes centrifugal force and causes the airplane to turn.

3-32 PLT018
During an approach to a stall, an increased load factor will cause the airplane to

A– stall at a higher airspeed.

B– have a tendency to spin.

C– be more difficult to control.

3-32. Answer A. GFDPP 3-61, PHB
Stall speed increases in proportion to load factor. Added G-forces cause an airplane to stall at an airspeed higher than the normal 1 G airspeed.

3-33 PLT219
Select the four flight fundamentals involved in maneuvering an aircraft.

A– Aircraft power, pitch, bank, and trim.

B– Starting, taxiing, takeoff, and landing.

C– Straight-and-level flight, turns, climbs, and descents.

3-33. Answer C. AFH
All controlled flight consists of one of the four fundamental maneuvers or some combination of them.

THE FLIGHT ENVIRONMENT

SECTION A — SAFETY OF FLIGHT

Maintaining the safety of flight is your number one priority as a pilot. Some safety issues apply to every flight, such as collision avoidance and maintaining minimum safe altitudes. Other safety considerations only apply in certain situations; for example, taxiing in wind, flight over hazardous terrain, and effective exchange of flight controls with your instructor. As pilot in command, you need to consider the factors which can affect your flight and take the appropriate actions to ensure safety.

VISUAL SCANNING

- The most effective method of scanning for other aircraft for collision avoidance during daylight hours is to use a series of short, regularly spaced eye movements to search each 10-degree section.
- An aircraft on a collision course with your aircraft will show little relative movement.
- Haze reduces visibility, making objects appear to be farther away than they really are.
- When climbing or descending VFR along an airway, execute gentle banks left and right for continuous scanning of the airspace.
- Prior to beginning each maneuver, make clearing turns to scan the entire area for other traffic.

RIGHT-OF-WAY

- An aircraft in distress has right-of-way over all other aircraft.
- When two aircraft are converging, the aircraft on the right has right-of-way.
- The least maneuverable aircraft has the right-of-way: a glider has right-of-way over an airship, airplane or rotorcraft.
- An aircraft that is towing or refueling another has the right-of-way over other engine-driven aircraft.
- When aircraft are approaching head-on, each shall give way to the right.
- When two or more aircraft are approaching the airport with the intention of landing, the one at the lower altitude has the right-of-way.

MINIMUM SAFE ALTITUDES

- Except for conducting a normal takeoff or landing, the pilot must maintain enough altitude to allow for an emergency landing in the event of an engine failure, without creating an undue hazard to people or property on the surface.
- Pilots must maintain at least 500 feet between their aircraft and any person, vessel, vehicle or structure on the surface.
- If you aren't able to obtain a local altimeter setting before departing, set the altimeter to the local field elevation.

TAXIING IN WIND

- When taxiing with a quartering tailwind, the aileron should be down on the side from which the wind is blowing.
- When taxiing with a quartering headwind, the aileron should be up on the side from which the wind is blowing.
- A quartering tailwind is the most critical wind condition to a tricycle-gear, high-wing airplane.

4-1   PLT414
Which aircraft has the right-of-way over all other air traffic?

A– A balloon.

B– An aircraft in distress.

C– An aircraft on final approach to land.

4-1. Answer B. GFDPP 4-6, FAR 91.113C
An aircraft in distress has the right-of-way over all other aircraft.

4-2   PLT414
What action is required when two aircraft of the same category converge, but not head-on?

A– The faster aircraft shall give way.

B– The aircraft on the left shall give way.

C– Each aircraft shall give way to the right.

4-2. Answer B. GFDPP 4-6, FAR 91.113
The aircraft on the right has the right-of-way and the aircraft on the left shall give way.

4-3   PLT414
Which aircraft has the right-of-way over the other aircraft listed?

A– Glider.

B– Airship.

C– Aircraft refueling other aircraft.

4-3. Answer A. GFDPP 4-7, FAR 91.113
In general, the least maneuverable aircraft normally has the right-of-way. A glider has the right-of-way over an airship, airplane, or rotorcraft. An aircraft that is towing or refueling another aircraft has the right-of-way over all other engine-driven aircraft (but not a glider).

4-4   PLT414
An airplane and an airship are converging. If the airship is left of the airplane's position, which aircraft has the right-of-way?

A– The airship.

B– The airplane.

C– Each pilot should alter course to the right.

4-4. Answer A. GFDPP 4-7, FAR 91.113
In general, the least maneuverable aircraft normally has the right-of-way. A glider has the right-of-way over an airship, airplane, or rotorcraft. An aircraft that is towing or refueling another aircraft has the right-of-way over all other engine-driven aircraft (but not a glider).

Since an airship is less maneuverable than an airplane, the airship has the right-of-way.

4-5   PLT414
Which aircraft has the right-of-way over the other aircraft listed?

A– Airship.

B– Aircraft towing other aircraft.

C– Gyroplane.

4-5. Answer B. GFDPP 4-7, FAR 91.113
An aircraft towing or refueling another aircraft has the right-of-way over all other engine-driven aircraft.

4-6   PLT414

What action should the pilots of a glider and an airplane take if on a head-on collision course?

A– The airplane pilot should give way to the left.

B– The glider pilot should give way to the right.

C– Both pilots should give way to the right.

4-6. Answer C. GFDPP 4-6, FAR 91.113

When any aircraft are approaching each other head-on, both pilots should alter their course to the right. For aircraft approaching head-on, the FARs do not make a distinction between aircraft categories.

4-7   PLT414

When two or more aircraft are approaching an airport for the purpose of landing, the right-of-way belongs to the aircraft

A– that has the other to its right.

B– that is the least maneuverable.

C– at the lower altitude, but it shall not take advantage of this rule to cut in front of or to overtake another.

4-7. Answer C. GFDPP 4-8, FAR 91.113

When two or more aircraft are approaching an airport for landing, the one at the lower altitude has the right-of-way, but you should not use this rule to cut in front of another aircraft.

4-8   PLT430

Except when necessary for takeoff or landing, what is the minimum safe altitude for a pilot to operate an aircraft anywhere?

A– An altitude allowing, if a power unit fails, an emergency landing without undue hazard to persons or property on the surface.

B– An altitude of 500 feet above the surface and no closer than 500 feet to any person, vessel, vehicle, or structure.

C– An altitude of 500 feet above the highest obstacle within a horizontal radius of 1,000 feet.

4-8. Answer A. GFDPP 4-8, FAR 91.119

Except for a normal takeoff and landing, you must maintain enough altitude to allow an emergency landing in the event of an engine failure without undue hazard to people or property on the surface.

4-9   PLT430

Except when necessary for takeoff or landing, what is the minimum safe altitude required for a pilot to operate an aircraft over congested areas?

A– An altitude of 1,000 feet above any person, vessel, vehicle, or structure.

B– An altitude of 500 feet above the highest obstacle within a horizontal radius of 1,000 feet.

C– An altitude of 1,000 feet above the highest obstacle within a horizontal radius of 2,000 feet.

4-9. Answer C. GFDPP 4-8, FAR 91.119

The minimum safe altitude required over a congested area is 1,000 feet above any obstacle within a horizontal radius of 2,000 feet of the aircraft.

4-10   PLT430
Except when necessary for takeoff or landing, what is the minimum safe altitude for a pilot to operate an aircraft over other than a congested area?

A– An altitude allowing, if a power unit fails, an emergency landing without undue hazard to persons or property on the surface.

B– An altitude of 500 feet AGL, except over open water or a sparsely populated area, which requires 500 feet from any person, vessel, vehicle, or structure.

C– An altitude of 500 feet above the highest obstacle within a horizontal radius of 1,000 feet.

4-10. Answer B. GFDPP 4-8, FAR 91.119
The minimum safe altitude required is 500 feet AGL, except over open water or a sparsely populated area, which requires 500 feet from any person, vessel, vehicle, or structure.

4-11   PLT430
Except when necessary for takeoff or landing, an aircraft may not be operated closer than what distance from any person, vessel, vehicle, or structure?

A– 500 feet.

B– 700 feet.

C– 1,000 feet.

4-11. Answer A. GFDPP 4-8, FAR 91.119
The words person, vessel, vehicle, or structure apply for operations over a sparsely populated or open water area, and the distance is 500 feet.

4-12   PLT485
When taxiing with strong quartering tailwinds, which aileron positions should be used?

A– Aileron down on the downwind side.

B– Ailerons neutral.

C– Aileron down on the side from which the wind is blowing.

4-12. Answer C. GFDPP 4-9, AFH
With a quartering tailwind, the aileron should be down on the side from which the wind is blowing in order to prevent the wind from flowing under the wing and lifting it.

4-13   PLT485
Which aileron positions should a pilot generally use when taxiing in strong quartering headwinds?

A– Aileron up on the side from which the wind is blowing.

B– Aileron down on the side from which the wind is blowing.

C– Ailerons neutral.

4-13. Answer A. GFDPP 4-9, AFH
To counteract the lifting tendency of a quartering headwind, the aileron should be up on the side from which the wind is blowing.

4-14   **PLT485**

Which wind condition would be most critical when taxiing a nosewheel equipped high-wing airplane?

A– Quartering tailwind.

B– Direct crosswind.

C– Quartering headwind.

4-14. Answer A. GFDPP 4-11, AFH

A tricycle-gear, high-wing airplane is most susceptible to a quartering tailwind because a strong airflow beneath the wing and horizontal stabilizer can lift the airplane and tip or nose it over.

4-15   **PLT485**

(Refer to figure 9, Area A.) How should the flight controls be held while taxiing a tricycle-gear equipped airplane into a left quartering headwind?

A– Left aileron up, elevator neutral.

B– Left aileron down, elevator neutral.

C– Left aileron up, elevator down.

4-15. Answer A. GFDPP 4-11, AFH

While taxiing a tricycle-gear airplane in a quartering headwind, the aileron should be up on the side from which the wind is blowing, and the elevator neutral to prevent any lifting force on the tail. In this case, the wind is from the left, so the left aileron should be up.

4-16   **PLT485**

(Refer to figure 9, Area B.) How should the flight controls be held while taxiing a tailwheel airplane into a right quartering headwind?

A– Right aileron up, elevator up.

B– Right aileron down, elevator neutral.

C– Right aileron up, elevator down.

4-16. Answer A. GFDPP 4-11, AFH

In a tailwheel airplane, the aileron is held up on the upwind side, and the elevator is held up to prevent the tail from lifting. Since the tail of most tailwheel airplanes is lower than the nose while taxiing, a strong headwind blowing on a neutral or down elevator could cause the tail to rise.

4-17   **PLT485**

(Refer to figure 9, Area C.) How should the flight controls be held while taxiing a tailwheel airplane with a left quartering tailwind?

A– Left aileron up, elevator neutral.

B– Left aileron down, elevator neutral.

C– Left aileron down, elevator down.

4-17. Answer C. GFDPP 4-11, AFH

For a quartering tailwind, the controls are held the same for both tailwheel and tricycle-gear airplanes. Ailerons are down on the side from which the wind is blowing. The elevator is down to prevent the wind from lifting the tail.

4-18   **PLT194**

Prior to starting each maneuver, pilots should

A– check altitude, airspeed, and heading indications.

B– visually scan the entire area for collision avoidance.

C– announce their intentions on the nearest CTAF.

4-18. Answer B. GFDPP 4-6, AIM

To ensure you can see other aircraft which may be blocked by blindspots, make clearing turns and scan the area.

4-19   PLT125
What procedure is recommended when climbing or descending VFR on an airway?

A– Execute gentle banks, left and right for continuous visual scanning of the airspace.

B– Advise the nearest FSS of the altitude changes.

C– Fly away from the centerline of the airway before changing altitude.

4-19. Answer A. GFDPP 4-5, AIM
Because of potential traffic on airways, it is important to scan. Making shallow turns allows you to compensate for blindspots.

4-20   PLT194
What effect does haze have on the ability to see traffic or terrain features during flight?

A– Haze causes the eyes to focus at infinity.

B– The eyes tend to overwork in haze and do not detect relative movement easily.

C– All traffic or terrain features appear to be farther away than their actual distance.

4-20. Answer C. GFDPP 4-4, AIM
Since haze reduces visibility, objects are closer than they appear.

4-21   PLT194
The most effective method of scanning for other aircraft for collision avoidance during daylight hours is to use

A– regularly spaced concentration on the 3-, 9-, and 12-o'clock positions.

B– a series of short, regularly spaced eye movements to search each 10-degree sector.

C– peripheral vision by scanning small sectors and utilizing offcenter viewing.

4-21. Answer B. GFDPP 4-3, AIM
The eyes are able to focus clearly only on a small area, approximately 10°, so a series of short eye movements is most effective.

4-22   PLT194
Which technique should a pilot use to scan for traffic to the right and left during straight-and-level flight?

A– Systematically focus on different segments of the sky for short intervals.

B– Concentrate on relative movement detected in the peripheral vision area.

C– Continuous sweeping of the windshield from right to left.

4-22. Answer A. GFDPP 4-3, AIM
The eyes are able to focus clearly only on a small area, approximately 10°, so a series of short eye movements is most effective.

4-23   PLT194
How can you determine if another aircraft is on a collision course with your aircraft?

A– The other aircraft will always appear to get larger and closer at a rapid rate.

B– The nose of each aircraft is pointed at the same point in space.

C– There will be no apparent relative motion between your aircraft and the other aircraft.

4-23. Answer C. GFDPP 4-3, AIM
A lack of relative movement can indicate that the two aircraft are moving toward one another on a collision course.

4-24   PLT194
Most midair collision accidents occur during

A– hazy days.

B– clear days.

C– cloudy nights.

4-24. Answer B. GFDPP 4-2, AFH
Year after year, NTSB reporting indicates that most midair collisions occur near an airport in daytime VFR weather.

4-25   PLT119
The Aeronautical Information Manual (AIM) specifically encourages pilots to turn on their landing lights when operating below 10,000 feet, day or night, and especially when operating

A– in Class B airspace.

B– in conditions of reduced visibility.

C– within 15 miles of a towered airport.

4-25. Answer B. AIM
The FAA's voluntary pilot safety program, Operation Lights On, encourages pilots to turn on their landing lights when operating below 10,000 feet, day or night, especially within 10 miles of any airport; also in conditions of reduced visibility and in areas where flocks of birds can be expected, such as coastal areas, lake areas, and around trash dumps.

4-26   PLT208
When executing an emergency approach to land in a single-engine airplane, it is important to maintain a constant glide speed because variations in glide speed

A– increase the chances of shock cooling the engine.

B– assure the proper descent angle is maintained until entering the flare.

C– nullify all attempts at accuracy in judgment of gliding distance and landing spot.

4-26. Answer C. GFDPP, AFH
Maintain a constant gliding speed because variations of gliding speed nullify all attempts at accuracy in judgment of gliding distance and the landing spot. Factors such as altitude, obstructions, wind direction, landing direction, landing surface and gradient, and landing distance requirements of the airplane will determine the pattern and approach procedures to use.

SECTION B — AIRPORTS

Each day, aircraft takeoff and land at private grass strips, busy international airports and every type of field in between. Whether most of your flying is out of your local airport or you frequently journey to new destinations, an airport will never be unfamiliar territory once you learn the basic procedures for operating in the terminal environment.

RUNWAY LAYOUT
- Runway numbers correspond to the magnetic direction and are rounded to the nearest 10 degrees, with the last zero dropped out.

SEGMENTED CIRCLES
- Traffic pattern indicators on the segmented circle show the final and base legs to various runways on the airport. The wind cone or sock in the center gives current wind direction.

RUNWAY MARKINGS
- At many airports, the area before a displaced threshold may be used for taxi and takeoff.
- Landings should be made after the displaced threshold.
- A closed runway is marked with Xs painted on its surface at each end.

AIRPORT LIGHTING

BEACON
- When an airport's beacon is on during the daytime, it usually means that the weather is below basic VFR minimums (ceiling less than 1000 feet and/or visibility is less than 3 miles).
- A military airport beacon alternates two quick flashes of white with one green flash.

VISUAL GLIDESLOPE INDICATORS
- Pilots should fly at or above the glide path when approaching an airport with a VASI installed.
- A slightly high indication on a precision approach path indicator shows three white lights and one red.
- A below glideslope indication on a tri-color VASI is red.
- An above glideslope indication on a tri-color VASI is amber.
- Green is the indication on a tri-color VASI for being on the glide path.
- A pulsating approach slope indicator provides a pulsating red light when below the glide path. Pulsating white is above glide path, and steady white is on the glide path.
- On a two-bar VASI, red over white indicates you are on the glide slope. White over white is above the glide slope, and red over red is below the glide slope.

TAXIWAY LIGHTS
- Taxiway edge lights are blue.

PILOT-CONTROLLED LIGHTING
At airports with a three-step pilot-controlled lighting system, seven clicks of the microphone will set the lights on high intensity. Five clicks turns the lights to medium, and three turns the lights to low.

- At airports with a three-step pilot-controlled lighting system, seven clicks of the microphone will set the lights on high intensity. Five clicks turns the lights to medium, and three turns the lights to low.

AIRPORT OPERATIONS

- Local airport advisory (LAA) service is operated within 10 statute miles of an airport where a control tower is not operating but where a flight service station (FSS) is located on the airport. The FSS provides a complete local airport advisory service to arriving and departing aircraft.

- Pilots should state their position on the airport when calling the tower for takeoff from a runway intersection.

- At controlled airports, air traffic control can clear a pilot to land and hold short. Pilots may accept such a clearance if the pilot-in-command determines that the aircraft can safely land and stop within the available landing distance (ALD).

- Student pilots or pilots who are not familiar with LAHSO should not participate in the program.

- The pilot-in-command has the final authority to accept or decline any land-and-hold-short clearance. Pilots should decline a LAHSO clearance if they determine that the clearance compromises safety.

4-27   PLT147
While operating in class D airspace, each pilot of an aircraft approaching to land on a runway served by a visual approach slope indicator (VASI) shall

A— maintain a 3° glide until approximately 1/2 mile to the runway before going below the VASI.

B— maintain an altitude at or above the glide slope until a lower altitude is necessary for a safe landing.

C— stay high until the runway can be reached in a power-off landing.

4-27. Answer B. GFDPP 4-33, FAR 91.129
The VASI glide path provides safe obstruction clearance to the runway. Therefore, the pilot should fly at or above the glide path.

4-28   PLT147
When approaching to land on a runway served by a visual approach slope indicator (VASI), the pilot shall

A—maintain an altitude that captures the glide slope at least 2 miles downwind from the runway threshold.

B—maintain an altitude at or above the glide slope.

C—remain on the glide slope and land between the two-light bar.

4-28. Answer B. GFDPP 4-33, FAR 91.129
The VASI glide path provides safe obstruction clearance to the runway. Therefore, the pilot should fly at or above the glide path.

4-29   PLT147
Which approach and landing objective is assured when the pilot remains on the proper glidepath of the VASI?

A— Runway identification and course guidance.

B— Safe obstruction clearance in the approach area.

C— Lateral course guidance to the runway.

4-29. Answer B. GFDPP 4B, AIM
Remaining on the proper glidepath ensures obstruction clearance in the approach area.

4-30   PLT141
Airport taxiway edge lights are identified at night by

A–white directional lights.
B–blue omnidirectional lights.
C–alternate red and green lights.

4-30. Answer B. GFDPP 4-35, AFH
Taxiway edge lights are blue.

4-31   PLT147
A slightly high glide slope indication from a precision approach path indicator is

A–four white lights.
B–three white lights and one red light.
C–two white lights and two red lights.

4-31. Answer B. GFDPP 4-34, AIM
A slightly high indication on a precision approach path indicator shows three white lights and one red light.

4-32   PLT147
A below glide slope indication from a tri-color VASI is

A–a red light signal.
B–a pink light signal.
C–a green light signal.

4-32. Answer A. GFDPP 4-33, AIM
A below glide slope indication on a tri-color VASI is red.

4-33   PLT147
An above glide slope indication from a tri-color VASI is

A–a white light signal.
B–a green light signal.
C–an amber light signal.

4-33. Answer C. GFDPP 4-33, AIM
Amber is the color used for an above glide slope indication. White is not used in a tri-color VASI, and green is the indication for being on the glide path.

4-34   PLT147
An on glide slope indication from a tri-color VASI is

A–a white light signal.
B–a green light signal.
C–an amber light signal.

4-34. Answer B. GFDPP 4-33, AIM
Amber is the color used for an above glide path indication. White is not used in a tri-color VASI, and green is the indication for being on the glide path.

4-35   PLT147
A below glide slope indication from a pulsating approach slope indicator is a

A–pulsating white light.

B–steady white light.

C–pulsating red light.

4-35. Answer C. GFDPP 4-34, AIM
A pulsating approach slope indicator provides a pulsating red light when below glide slope.

4-36   PLT147
(Refer to figure 48.) Illustration A indicates that the aircraft is

A–below the glide slope.

B–on the glide slope.

C–above the glide slope.

4-36. Answer B. GFDPP 4-33, AIM
A red over white indication is on glide slope.

4-37   PLT147
(Refer to figure 48.) VASI lights as shown by illustration C indicate that the airplane is

A–off course to the left.

B–above the glide slope.

C–below the glide slope.

4-37. Answer B. GFDPP 4-33, AIM
A white over white indication is above glide slope.

4-38   PLT147
(Refer to figure 48.) While on final approach to a runway equipped with a standard 2-bar VASI, the lights appear as shown by illustration D. This means that the aircraft is

A–above the glide slope.

B–below the glide slope.

C–on the glide slope.

4-38. Answer B. GFDPP 4-33, AIM
A red over red indication is below the glide slope.

4-39   PLT145
To set the high intensity runway lights on medium intensity, the pilot should click the microphone seven times, then click it

A– one time within four seconds.

B– three times within three seconds.

C– five times within five seconds.

4-39. Answer C. GFDPP 4-36, AIM
At airports with three-step pilot-controlled runway lighting system, seven clicks turns all the lights on to the maximum intensity. Five clicks turns the lights to medium.

4-40   PLT141
An airport's rotating beacon operated during daylight hours indicates

A–there are obstructions on the airport.

B–that weather at the airport located in Class D airspace is below basic VFR weather minimums.

C–the Air Traffic Control tower is not in operation.

4-40. Answer B. GFDPP 4-31, AIM
When the airport beacon is on during the daytime, it usually means that the ceiling is less than 1,000 feet and/or the visibility is less than three statute miles (below basic VFR minimums).

4-41   PLT141
A military air station can be identified by a rotating beacon that emits

A–white and green alternating flashes.

B–two quick, white flashes between green flashes.

C–green, yellow, and white flashes.

4-41. Answer B. GFDPP 4-33, AIM
A military airport beacon has two quick flashes of white light between green flashes.

4-42   PLT141
How can a military airport be identified at night?

A–Alternate white and green light flashes.

B–Dual peaked (two quick) white flashes between green flashes.

C–White flashing lights with steady green at the same location.

4-42. Answer B. GFDPP 4-32, AIM
A military airport beacon has two quick flashes of white light between green flashes.

4-43   PLT141
(Refer to figure 49.) That portion of the runway identified by the letter A may be used for

A–landing.

B–taxiing and takeoff.

C–taxiing and landing.

4-43. Answer B. GFDPP 4-24, AIM
At many airports, the area prior to a displaced threshold may be used for taxi and takeoff (and rollout after landing).

4-44   **PLT141**

The "yellow demarcation bar" marking indicates

A– runway with a displaced threshold that precedes the runway.

B– a hold line from a taxiway to a runway.

C– the beginning of available runway for landing on the approach side.

4-44. Answer A. GFDPP 4-25, AIM

This double bar delineates a runway with a displaced threshold from a blast pad, stopway or taxiway that precedes the runway.

4-45   **PLT141**

(Refer to Figure 66, Item E.) This sign is a visual clue that

A– confirms the aircraft's location to be on taxiway "B."

B– warns the pilot of approaching taxiway "B."

C– indicates "B" holding area is ahead.

4-45. Answer A. GFDPP 4-28, AIM

A taxiway location sign has a black background with a yellow border and yellow letter(s) inscribed in the center. The yellow letter designates the taxiway on which the aircraft is located.

4-46   **PLT141**

(Refer to Figure 66, Item F.) This sign confirms your position on

A– runway 22.

B– routing to runway 22.

C– taxiway 22.

4-46. Answer A. AIM

A runway location sign has a black background with a yellow border and yellow runway number inscribed in the center. The yellow number designates the runway on which the aircraft is located.

4-47   PLT077
(Refer to figure 49.) According to the airport diagram, which statement is true?

A–Runway 30 is equipped at position E with emergency arresting gear to provide a means of stopping military aircraft.

B–Takeoffs may be started at position A on Runway 12, and the landing portion of this runway begins at position B.

C–The takeoff and landing portion of Runway 12 begins at position B.

4-47. Answer B. GFDPP 4-24, AIM
At many airports, the area prior to a displaced threshold may be used for taxi and takeoff (and rollout after landing).

Landings may be made after the displaced threshold at position "B."

4-48   PLT077
(Refer to figure 49.) What is the difference between area A and area E on the airport depicted?

A–"A" may be used for taxi and takeoff; "E" may be used only as an overrun.

B–"A" may be used for all operations except heavy aircraft landings; "E" may be used only as an overrun.

C–"A" may be used only for taxiing; "E" may be used for all operations except landings.

4-48. Answer A. GFDPP 4-24, 25, AIM
At many airports, the area prior to a displaced threshold may be used for taxi and takeoff (and rollout after landing).

Area "E" is a blastpad/stopway, and because of its pavement strength cannot support continuous operations, but may be used as an overrun.

4-49   PLT077
(Refer to figure 49.) Area C on the airport depicted is classified as a

A–stabilized area.

B–multiple heliport.

C–closed runway.

4-49. Answer C. GFDPP 4-25, AIM
A closed runway is depicted by Xs.

4-50   PLT141
(Refer to Figure 65.) Which marking indicates a vehicle lane?

A– A.

B– C.

C– E.

4-50. Answer B. GFDPP 4B AIM
Lanes for ground vehicles look something like a road painted on the airport surface.

4-51 PLT141
(Refer to Figure 66, Item A) From the cockpit, this marking confirms the aircraft to be

A– on a taxiway, about to enter runway zone.

B– on a runway, about to clear.

C– near an instrument approach clearance zone.

4-51. Answer A. AIM
This sign is a runway holding position sign, which is located at the holding position on taxiways that intersect a runway or on runways that intersect other runways.

4-52 PLT141
(Refer to figure 50.) The arrows that appear on the ends of the north/south runway indicate that these areas

A–may be used only for taxiing.

B–is usable for taxiing, takeoff, and landing.

C–cannot be used for landing, but may be used for taxiing and takeoff.

4-52. Answer C. GFDPP 4-24, AIM
At many airports, the area prior to a displaced threshold may be used for taxi and takeoff (and rollout after landing).

4-53 PLT141
The numbers 9 and 27 on a runway indicate that the runway is oriented approximately

A–009° and 027° true.

B–090° and 270° true.

C–090° and 270° magnetic.

4-53. Answer C. GFDPP 4-17, AIM
Runway numbers correspond to the magnetic, not true, direction, and are rounded to the nearest 10°, with the last zero omitted.

4-54 PLT077
(Refer to figure 50.) Select the proper traffic pattern and runway for landing.

A–Left-hand traffic and Runway 18.

B–Right-hand traffic and Runway 18.

C–Left-hand traffic and Runway 22.

4-54. Answer B. GFDPP 4-17, AIM
The wind indicates a landing should be made to the south, and the segmented circle shows right-hand traffic for Runway 18.

4-55 PLT077
(Refer to figure 50.) If the wind is as shown by the landing direction indicator, the pilot should land on

A–Runway 18 and expect a crosswind from the right.

B–Runway 22 directly into the wind.

C–Runway 36 and expect a crosswind from the right.

4-55. Answer A. GFDPP 4-20, AIM
The wind is from the southwest, so a landing on Runway 18 would provide both a headwind component and a crosswind from the right.

4-56   PLT039
(Refer to figure 51.) The segmented circle indicates that the airport traffic is

A–left-hand for Runway 18 and right-hand for Runway 36.

B–right-hand for Runway 9 and left-hand for Runway 27.

C–left-hand for Runway 36 and right-hand for Runway 18.

4-56. Answer C. GFDPP 4-21, AIM
The segmented circle indicates left-hand traffic for Runway 36, and right-hand traffic for Runway 18.

4-57   PLT039
(Refer to figure 51.) The traffic patterns indicated in the segmented circle have been arranged to avoid flights over an area to the

A–south of the airport.

B–north of the airport.

C–southeast of the airport.

4-57. Answer C. GFDPP 4-21, AIM
Since the traffic pattern for the north-south runway is west of the field, and the pattern for the east-west runway is north of the field, there should be no flights southeast of the airport.

4-58   PLT039
(Refer to figure 51.) The segmented circle indicates that a landing on Runway 26 will be with a

A–right-quartering headwind.

B–left-quartering headwind.

C–right-quartering tailwind.

4-58. Answer A. GFDPP 4-21, AIM
Since the wind cone shows wind from the northwest, a landing to the west will provide a right-quartering headwind.

4-59   PLT039
(Refer to figure 51.) Which runway and traffic pattern should be used as indicated by the wind cone in the segmented circle?

A– Right-hand traffic on Runway 18.

B– Left-hand traffic on Runway 36.

C– Right-hand traffic on Runway 9.

4-59. Answer B. GFDPP 4-21, AIM
With wind from the northwest, landing on Runway 36 would provide a quartering headwind.

4-60   **PLT140**
Who should not participate in the Land and Hold Short Operations (LAHSO) program?

A–Recreational pilots only.

B–Military pilots.

C–Student pilots.

4-60. Answer C. GFDPP 4-30, AIM
Student pilots or pilots not familiar with LAHSO should not accept LAHSO clearances. Recreational and military pilots have no limitations, provided they are familiar with the LAHSO program.

4-61   **PLT140**
Who has final authority to accept or decline any land and hold short (LAHSO) clearance?

A–Pilot-in-command.

B–Owner/operator.

C–Second-in-command.

4-61. Answer A. GFDPP 4-30, AIM
The pilot in command (PIC) has the final authority to accept or decline any LAHSO clearances. The PIC should decline a LAHSO clearance if he/she determines it will compromise safety.

4-62   **PLT140**
When should pilots decline a land and hold short (LAHSO) clearance?

A–When it will compromise safety.

B–Only when the tower operator concurs.

C–Pilots can not decline clearance.

4-62. Answer A. GFDPP 4-30, AIM
The pilot in command (PIC) has the final authority to accept or decline any LAHSO clearances. The PIC should decline a LAHSO clearance if he/she determines it will compromise safety.

4-63   **PLT078**
Where is the "Available Landing Distance" (ALD) data published for an airport that utilizes Land and Hold Short Operations (LAHSO) published?

A– Special Notices section of the Airport Facility Directory (A/FD).

B– 14 CFR Part 91, General Operating and Flight Rules.

C– Aeronautical Information Manual (AIM).

4-63. Answer A. GFDPP 4-30, AIM
ALD data is published in the special notices section of the Airport/Facility Directory (A/FD) and in the U.S. Terminal Procedures Publications.

4-64   **PLT140**
What is the minimum visibility for a pilot to receive a land and hold short (LAHSO) clearance?

A–3 nautical miles

B–3 statute miles.

C–1 statute mile.

4-64. Answer B. AIM
Pilots should only receive a LAHSO clearance when there is a minimum ceiling of 1,000 feet and 3 statute miles visibility.

4-65   PLT141
When approaching taxiway holding lines from the side with the continuous lines, the pilot

A– may continue taxiing.

B– should not cross the lines without ATC clearance.

C– should continue taxiing until all parts of the aircraft have crossed the lines.

4-65. Answer B. GFDPP 4-26, AIM
When approaching a taxiway hold line from the side with the continuous (solid) line at a towered airport, pilots should not cross the hold line without ATC clearance. At a non-towered airport, stop and check for traffic before crossing any hold line.

4-66   PLT141
The numbers 8 and 26 on the approach ends of the runway indicate that the runway is orientated approximately

A– 008° and 026° true.

B– 080° and 260° true.

C– 080° and 260° magnetic.

4-66. Answer C. GFDPP 4-17, PHB
Runway numbers indicate the runway's MAGNETIC direction to the nearest 10 degrees. Runway 8 (really 080) would have a magnetic direction of approximately 080°, and 26 would be approximately 260° magnetic.

4-67   PLT150
The recommended entry position to an airport traffic pattern is

A– 45° to the base leg just below traffic pattern altitude.

B– to enter 45° at the midpoint of the downwind leg at traffic pattern altitude.

C– to cross directly over the airport at traffic pattern altitude and join the downwind leg.

4-67. Answer B. GFDPP 4-18, PHB
The recommended standard left-hand traffic pattern specifies a 45° entry at the midpoint of the runway on the downwind leg.

4-68   PLT141
What is the purpose of the runway/runway hold position sign?

A– Denotes entrance to runway from a taxiway.

B– Denotes area protected for an aircraft approaching or departing a runway.

C– Denotes intersecting runways.

4-68. Answer A. GFDPP 4-28, AFH
The runway/runway hold position sign displays the headings of the runway in white letters on a red background. It is a mandatory instruction sign that is equivalent, and usually coexistent, with a hold short taxiway marking.

4-69   PLT141
What does the outbound destination sign identify?

A– Identifies entrance to the runway from a taxiway.

B– Identifies direction to take-off runways.

C– Identifies runway on which an aircraft is located.

4-69. Answer B. PHB, AIM
An outbound destination sign displays black text on a yellow background, and a vertical black arrow. These signs always have an arrow showing the direction of the taxing route to that destination.

4-70   PLT435
If a control tower and an FSS are located on the same airport, which function is provided by the FSS during those periods when the tower is closed?

A– Automatic closing of the IFR flight plan.

B– Approach control services.

C– Airport Advisory Service.

4-70. Answer C. AIM
Local Airport Advisory (LAA) service is one of several airport advisory/information services operated within 10 statute miles of an airport where a control tower is not operating but where a flight service station (FSS) is located on the airport. At such locations, the FSS provides a complete local airport advisory service to arriving and departing aircraft. During periods of fast-changing weather the FSS will automatically provide Final Guard (wind/altimeter monitoring service) from the time the aircraft reports "on-final" or "taking-the-active- runway" until the aircraft reports "on-the-ground" or "airborne."

Flight service stations do not provide air traffic control services, such as automatically closing flight plans and approach control.

4-71   PLT222
When should pilots state their position on the airport when calling the tower for takeoff?

A– When visibility is less than 1 mile.

B– When parallel runways are in use.

C– When departing from a runway intersection.

4-71. Answer C. AIM
The tower assumes you are at the end of the runway unless you tell them the intersection. For example: "Centennial Tower, Cessna 5-2-3-8-Kilo, at intersection Alpha-3, Runway 3-5-right, ready for takeoff."

SECTION C — AERONAUTICAL CHARTS

Maps are essential in turning imaginary excursions into actual trips. Aeronautical charts are maps which provide a detailed portrayal of an area's topography and include aeronautical and navigational information. Before you learn about the specific features and symbology of aeronautical charts, you need to understand some basic concepts which apply to representations of the earth's surface on maps.

LATITUDE AND LONGITUDE

In the United States, latitude increases as you travel north, and longitude increases as you travel west. Each tick mark on the sectional chart represents one minute of latitude or longitude.

SECTIONAL CHARTS

A blue segmented circle on a sectional chart depicts Class D airspace.

CHART SYMBOLS

Refer to figures.

4-72   PLT064
(Refer to figure 21.)
(Area 3) Determine the approximate latitude and longitude of Currituck County Airport.

A– 36°24'N - 76°01'W.

B– 36°48'N - 76°01'W.

C– 47°24'N - 75°58'W.

4-72. Answer A. GFDPP 4-41, PHB
This airport is located northeast of the number "3." Starting near the top of the chart excerpt, near number "1" find the labels for the 37° latitude line and the 76° longitude line. That means the latitude line through the middle of the picture is 36°30'N. Count down the tick marks—one minute per tick mark—until abeam Currituck County Airport at 36°24'N. At one tick mark west of the 76° longitude line, the airport's longitude is 76°01'W.

4-73   PLT064
(Refer to figure 22.)
(Area 2) Which airport is located at approximately 47°21'30"N latitude and 101°01'30"W longitude?

A– Poleschook.

B– Washburn.

C– Johnson

4-73. Answer B. GFDPP 4-41, PHB
Note that the 48° latitude line crosses the top third of the chart. The latitude line along the bottom third is 30' less, or 47°30'N. Count down 9-1/2 tick marks (minutes) for 47°21'30"N. Because the airport's longitude is more than 101°W, move to the left of the 101° line 1-1/2 tick marks to arrive at 101°01'30"W. This intersection is at Washburn Airport (5C8).

4-74   PLT064
(Refer to figure 22.)
(Area 2) The CTAF/MULTICOM frequency for Garrison Airport is

A– 123.0 MHz.

B– 122.8 MHz

C– 122.9 MHz.

4-74. Answer C. GFDPP 4-47, AIM
The frequency next to the CTAF symbol (the letter "C" in a dark circle) is the multicom frequency of 122.9.

4-75 **PLT064**
(Refer to figure 23 and 32.)
(Area 2) At Coeur D'Alene, which frequency should be used as a Common Traffic Advisory Frequency (CTAF) to self-announce position and intentions?

A– 122.05 MHz.

B– 122.1/108.8 MHz.

C– 122.8 MHz.

4-75. Answer C. GFDPP 4-47, AIM
In this example, the airport data block located near Coeur D'Alene airport lists 122.8 as the CTAF frequency that should be used to self-announce your position and your intentions. In addition, the Airport/Facility Directory excerpt specifies 122.8 as both the CTAF and UNICOM frequency.

4-76 **PLT064**
(Refer to figure 23 and 32.)
(Area 2) At Coeur D'Alene, which frequency should be used as a Common Traffic Advisory Frequency (CTAF) to monitor airport traffic?

A– 122.05 MHz.

B– 122.8 MHz.

C– 135.075 MHz

4-76. Answer B. GFDPP 4-47, AIM
At non-towered airports, the CTAF frequency is used to self-announce position or intentions. The Airport/Facility Directory lists the CTAF/Unicom Frequency as 122.8 MHz. The CTAF symbol on the sectional chart is beside the frequency of 122.8 MHz.

4-77 **PLT064-**
(Refer to figure 23 and 32.)
(Area 2) What is the correct UNICOM frequency to be used at Coeur D'Alene to request fuel?

A– 122.1/108.8 MHz.

B– 122.8 MHz.

C– 135.075 MHz.

4-77. Answer B. GFDPP 4-47, AIM
Use the Unicom/CTAF frequency of 122.8 to request fuel, transportation, or other airport information of a general nature.

4-78 **PLT064**
(Refer to figure 26.)
(Area 3) If Dallas Executive Tower is not in operation, which frequency should be used as a Common Traffic Advisory Frequency (CTAF) to monitor airport traffic?

A– 122.95 MHz.

B– 126.35 MHz.

C– 127.25 MHz.

4-78. Answer C. GFDPP 4-47, AIM
Because the tower frequency, designated "CT - 127.25" is next to the CTAF symbol, the CTAF frequency is the tower frequency.

4-79   PLT064
(Refer to figure 27.)
(Area 4) The CTAF/UNICOM frequency at Jamestown
Airport is

A– 118.425 MHz.

B– 122.2 MHz.

C– 123.0 MHz.

4-79. Answer C. GFDPP 4-47, AIM
The CTAF symbol is next to the frequency 123.0.

4-80   PLT064
(Refer to figure 27.)
(Area 5) What is the CTAF/UNICOM frequency at
Barnes County Airport?

A– 118.725 MHz.

B– 122.8 MHz.

C– 1490 kHz.

4-80. Answer B. GFDPP 4-47, AIM
The CTAF symbol is next to the UNICOM frequency
122.8. 118.725 is the frequency for obtaining weather
conditions from the automated surface observing system
(ASOS) and 1490 kHz is an AM radio station.

4-81   PLT376
Refer to figure 27.)
(Area 3) When flying over Arrowwood National
Wildlife Refuge, a pilot should fly no lower than

A– 2,000 feet AGL.

B– 2,500 feet AGL.

C– 3,000 feet AGL.

4-81. Answer A. GFDPP 4-44, AIM
Pilots are requested to maintain a minimum of 2,000 feet
above National Wildlife Refuges.

4-82   PLT064
(Refer to figure 22.)
On what frequency can a pilot receive Hazardous
Inflight Weather Advisory Service (HIWAS) in the vicin-
ity of area 1?

A– 122.0 MHz.

B– 118.725 MHz.

C– The Minot VOR frequency.

4-82. Answer C. GFDPP 4-48, Chart Legend
The circled "H" in the corner of the Minot VORTAC
indicates that weather information (HIWAS) is available
over the VOR frequency, which is 117.1 MHz.

4-83   PLT064
(Refer to figure 21.)
(Area 5) The CAUTION box denotes what hazard to
aircraft?

A– Unmarked balloon on cable to 3,008 feet MSL.

B– Unmarked balloon on cable to 3,008 feet AGL.

C– Unmarked blimp hangers at 308 feet MSL.

4-83. Answer A. GFDPP 4-51, Chart Legend
The CAUTION box indicates an unmarked balloon on a
cable to 3,008 feet MSL.

4-84   PLT064
(Refer to figure 21.)

(Area 2) The flag symbol at Lake Drummond represents a

A– compulsory reporting point for the Norfolk Class C Airspace.

B– compulsory reporting point for Hampton Roads Airport.

C– visual checkpoint used to identify position for initial callup to Norfolk Approach Control.

4-84. Answer C. GFDPP 4-51, Chart Legend
The flag represents a visual checkpoint used to identify your position for approach control. Since the flag is 22 nautical miles southwest of Norfolk International Airport, it can be assumed that the checkpoint is used when contacting Norfolk Approach.

4-85   PLT064
(Refer to figure 21.)
(Area 2) The elevation of the Chesapeake Regional Airport is

A– 19 feet.

B– 23 feet.

C– 55 feet.

4-85. Answer A. GFDPP 4-47, Chart Legend
The elevation is the first number listed before the runway information. In this case, it is 19 feet.

4-86   PLT064
(Refer to figure 21, area 1.) The NALF Fentress (NFE) Airport is in what type of airspace?

A– Class C.

B– Class E.

C– Class G.

4-86. Answer B. GFDPP 4C, Chart Legend
NFE is outside the solid magenta lines delineating the Norfolk Class C airspace, but inside a dashed magenta circle indicating Class E airspace.

4-87   PLT012
(Refer to figure 22.)
The terrain elevation of the light tan area between Minot (area 1) and Audubon Lake (area 2) varies from

A– sea level to 2,000 feet MSL.

B– 2,000 feet to 2,500 feet MSL.

C– 2,000 feet to 2,700 feet MSL.

4-87. Answer B. GFDPP 4-43, Chart Legend
The colored scale shows that the tan area represents terrain above 2,000 feet MSL. In addition, the legend states that the contour interval is 500 feet. Between Minot and Audubon Lake, there are no contour lines in the tan area, which indicates there is no terrain above 2,500 feet. A check of the airports in this area shows their elevations are all less than 2,500 feet. In addition, tower heights in MSL minus their AGL heights all yield base elevations less than 2,500 feet.

4-88   PLT064
(Refer to figure 22.)
Which public use airports depicted are indicated as having fuel?

A— Minot Intl. (area 1).

B— Minot Intl. (area 1) and Mercer County Regional Airport (area 3).

C— Mercer County Regional Airport (area 3) and Garrison (area 2).

4-88. Answer A. GFDPP 4-46, Chart Legend
Tick marks around an airport symbol indicate that fuel is available.

4-89   PLT064
(Refer to figure 24.)
The flag symbols at Statesboro Bullock County Airport, Claxton-Evans County Airport, and Ridgeland Airport are

A— airports with special traffic patterns.

B— outer boundaries of Savannah Class C airspace.

C— visual checkpoints to identify position for initial callup prior to entering Savannah Class C airspace.

4-89. Answer C. GFDPP 4-47, Chart Legend
The flag symbols represent checkpoints used to identify the aircraft position for Approach Control. In this case, they are visual checkpoints used when contacting Savannah Approach Control.

4-90   PLT064
(Refer to figure 24.)
(Area 3) What is the height of the lighted obstacle approximately 6 nautical miles southwest of Savannah International?

A— 1,534 feet MSL.

B— 1,549 feet AGL.

C— 1,549 feet MSL.

4-90. Answer C. GFDPP 4-51, Chart Legend
About 6 nautical miles southwest of the center of Savannah International airport is a lighted obstacle with its elevation marked as 1,549 (1,534). The first number is height in MSL, and the number in parentheses is height AGL.

4-91   PLT064
(Refer to figure 24.)
(Area 3) The top of the group obstruction approximately 11 nautical miles from the Savannah VORTAC on the 010° radial is

A— 455 feet AGL.

B— 455 feet MSL.

C— 549 feet MSL.

4-91. Answer B. GFDPP 4-51, Chart Legend
This group is labeled "stacks." At 11 NM, it is just outside the VOR compass rose. When only one number is printed, not in parenthesis, it is the MSL altitude.

4-92   PLT064
(Refer to figure 25.)
(Area 1) What minimum altitude is necessary to verti-cally clear the obstacle on the northeast side of Airpark East Airport by 500 feet?

A– 1,010 feet MSL.
B– 1,273 feet MSL.
C– 1,283 feet MSL.

4-92. Answer B. GFDPP 4-51, Chart Legend
In other than congested areas, you must clear obstacles by 500 feet. Add 500 feet to the obstacle elevation of 773 feet MSL.

4-93   PLT064
(Refer to figure 25.)
(Area 2) What minimum altitude is necessary to ver-tically clear the obstacle on the southeast side of Winnsboro Airport by 500 feet?

A– 823 feet MSL.
B– 1,013 feet MSL.
C– 1,403 feet MSL.

4-93. Answer C. GFDPP 4-51, Chart Legend
Here, the FARs require 500 feet of obstacle clearance. Add 500 feet to the obstacle elevation of 903 feet MSL

4-94   PLT101
(Refer to figure 26
(Area 2) The control tower frequency for Addison Airport is

A– 122.95 MHz.
B– 126.0 MHz.
C– 133.4 MHz

4-94. Answer B. GFDPP 4-47, Chart Legend
The tower frequency at Addison Airport is 126.0 as indicated by the letters "CT."

4-95   PLT101
(Refer to figure 26.)
(Area 8) What minimum altitude is required to fly over the Cedar Hill TV towers in the congested area east of Joe Pool Lake?

A– 2,731 feet MSL.
B– 3,049 feet MSL.
C– 3,549 feet MSL.

4-95. Answer C. GFDPP 4-51, FAR 91.119
Because this is a congested area, add 1,000 feet to the elevation of the highest obstacle. The highest elevation (height) of these towers is 2,549 feet MSL (1,731 feet AGL), so the minimum altitude would be 3,549 feet MSL.

4-96   PLT064
(Refer to figure 26.)
(Area 5) The navigation facility at Dallas-Ft. Worth International (DFW) is a

A– VOR.

B– VORTAC.

C– VOR/DME.

4-96. Answer C. GFDPP 4-48, Chart Legend
This symbol appears immediately south of the runways at DFW. According to Legend 1, a hexagon surrounded by a square is a VOR/DME symbol.

4-97   PLT064
Pilots flying over a national wildlife refuge are requested to fly no lower than

A– 1,000 feet AGL.

B– 2,000 feet AGL.

C– 3,000 feet AGL.

4-97. Answer B. GFDPP 4-44, AIM
Pilots should fly no lower than 2,000 feet AGL over a national wildlife area.

4-98   PLT064
Which is true concerning the blue and magenta colors used to depict airports on Sectional Aeronautical Charts?

A– Airports with control towers underlying Class A, B, and C airspace are shown in blue, Class D and E airspace are magenta.

B– Airports with control towers underlying Class C, D, and E airspace are shown in magenta

C– Airports with control towers underlying Class B, C, D, and E airspace are shown in blue.

4-98. Answer C. GFDPP 4-46
Airports with control towers are depicted in blue on sectional charts.

4-99   PLT064
Which statement about longitude and latitude is true?

A– Lines of longitude are parallel to the Equator.

B– Lines of longitude cross the Equator at right angles.

C– The 0° line of latitude passes through Greenwich, England.

4-99. Answer B. GFDPP 4-40
Lines of longitude connect the poles, and therefore, are perpendicular to the equator.

SECTION D — AIRSPACE

To efficiently manage the large amount of air traffic that traverses the sky each day, the airspace above the United States is divided into several classes. In each airspace class, specific rules apply. For example, there are VFR weather minimums which you must maintain. In some areas, you need to communicate with ATC and comply with pilot certification and aircraft equipment requirements. In addition, the airspace over the United States includes special use and other airspace areas where certain restrictions apply or specific ATC services are provided.

CLASS G AIRSPACE

- VFR flight in Class G (uncontrolled) airspace requires 1 mile of visibility and clear of clouds.
- Night VFR in Class G requires 3 miles visibility, and 500 feet below, 1,000 feet above and 2,000 feet horizontal distance from clouds.

CONTROLLED AIRSPACE

- Below 10,000 feet MSL in Class C, D and E airspace, the cloud clearances are 500 feet below, 1,000 feet above and 2,000 feet horizontal. Flight visibility is 3 statute miles. Above 10,000 feet MSL in Class C, D and E airspace, the cloud clearances are 1 mile horizontal and 1,000 feet above and below. Flight visibility is 5 statute miles.
- An operable 4096-code or Mode S transponder with an encoding altimeter is required in Class A, Class C and within 30 NM of a primary Class B airport (within 10,000 feet of the surface).
- Federal airways are considered Class E airspace; the same minimums apply. They extend four nautical miles on each side of the airway centerline. Altitudes normally include 1,200 AGL up to 17,999 feet MSL.

CLASS D AIRSPACE

- VFR flight minimums in Class D airspace are 3 s.m. visibility and 1000 feet ceiling. Airspace becomes Class D only when there is an operating control tower.
- Two-way radio communications are required for taking off and landing at an airport with an operating control tower.
- When approaching Class D airspace, you must contact the primary airport's control tower.
- When departing a non-towered satellite airport, you must contact the primary airport's control tower as soon as practicable after takeoff.
- The lateral dimensions of Class D airspace are based on the instrument procedures for which the controlled airspace is established.

CLASS C AIRSPACE

- Two-way communications must be established with approach control before entering Class C airspace.
- Two way radio communications and an operable 4096-code transponder with an encoding altimeter are required for operating in Class C airspace.
- Class C airspace usually consists of a 5 NM radius core surface area that extends from the surface up to 4,000 feet above the primary airport elevation, and a 10 NM radius shelf area that extends from 1,200 feet up to 4,000 feet above the airport elevation. An "outer area" extends to 20 NM from the airport, where radar service is available, but contact with ATC is not required.

CLASS B AIRSPACE

- A pilot must have either a private pilot certificate, or a student pilot certificate with a logbook endorsement from an appropriately rated instructor.
- Two-way radio communication must be established, and a clearance granted, before the pilot enters Class B airspace.
- Class B day VFR minimums are 3 miles visibility and clear of clouds.

CLASS A AIRSPACE

*   The altimeter must be set to 29.92 at and above 18,000 feet MSL.
*   VFR flight is prohibited in Class A airspace.

SPECIAL VFR

*   A special VFR clearance allows the pilot to operate VFR within Class D airspace when the visibility is at least 1 mile and the aircraft can remain clear of clouds.
*   To operate under special VFR at night you must have a current instrument rating, and the airplane must be equipped for instrument flight.
*   Special VFR for fixed-wing aircraft is not authorized at airports with "No Special VFR" written over the airport identification name.

SPECIAL USE AIRSPACE

*   Special use airspace serves to confine certain flight activities and to place limitations on aircraft operations which are not part of these activities.
*   All pilots flying within an alert area are equally responsible for collision avoidance.
*   MOAs signify high density military training activities.
*   When operating VFR in an MOA, pilots should exercise extreme caution when military training is being conducted.
*   Warning areas often contain hazards such as aerial gunnery and guided missiles.
*   Pilots may fly through a restricted area only with the controlling agency's authorization.

MILITARY TRAINING ROUTES

*   IR designates an IFR military training route, where aircraft may fly at speeds in excess of 250 knots.
*   When the route is a three digit number, the route contains one or more sections above 1,500 feet AGL.

4-100   PLT040
(Refer to figure 27, Area 2.) The day VFR visibility and cloud clearance requirements to operate over the town of Cooperstown, after departing and climbing out of the Cooperstown Airport at or below 700 feet AGL are

A– 3 miles and clear of clouds.

B– 1 mile and 1,000 feet above, 500 feet below, and 2,000 feet horizontally from clouds.

C– 1 mile and clear of clouds.

4-100. Answer C. FAR 91.155
This area is inside a magenta shaded ring, meaning that Class E airspace begins at 700 feet AGL. Below 700 feet AGL, the minimums for Class G airspace apply.

4-101   PLT161
Unless otherwise specified, Federal Airways include that Class E airspace extending upward from

A– 700 feet above the surface up to and including 17,999 feet MSL.

B– 1,200 feet above the surface up to and including 17,999 feet MSL.

C– the surface up to and including 18,000 feet MSL.

4-101. Answer B. GFDPP 4-60, AIM
Federal Airways normally begin at 1,200 feet AGL and extend up to, but not including, 18,000 feet MSL.

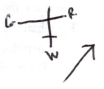

4-102   PLT162
The width of a Federal Airway from either side of the centerline is

A– 4 nautical miles.

B– 6 nautical miles.

C– 8 nautical miles.

4-102. Answer A. GFDPP 4D, AIM
A Federal airway is normally 8 NM wide (4 NM each side of the centerline).

4-103   PLT163
Normal VFR operations in Class D airspace with an operating control tower require the ceiling and visibility to be at least

A– 1,000 feet and 1 mile

B– 1,000 feet and 3 miles

C– 2,500 feet and 3 miles

4-103. Answer B. GFDPP 4-82, FAR 91.155
In order to operate in Class D airspace, the VFR visibility minimum is three statute miles. In addition, the ceiling must be at least 1,000 feet.

4-104   PLT163
At what altitude shall the altimeter be set to 29.92, when climbing to cruising flight level?

A– 14,500 feet MSL.

B– 18,000 feet MSL.

C– 24,000 feet MSL.

4-104. Answer B. GFDPP 4-71, FAR 91.121
To standardize altimeter settings in Class A airspace, all pilots are required to set their altimeters to 29.92 at and above 18,000 feet MSL.

4-105   PLT040
A blue segmented circle on a Sectional Chart depicts which class airspace?

A– Class B

B– Class C

C– Class D

4-105. Answer C. GFDPP 4-79, Chart Legend
Class D airspace is designated on sectional charts by a blue segmented circle. Class B airspace is indicated by a solid blue line. Class C airspace is designated by a solid magenta line.

4-106   PLT163
Airspace at an airport with a part-time control tower is classified as Class D airspace only

A— when the weather minimums are below basic VFR.

B— when the associated control tower is in operation.

C— when the associated Flight Service Station is in operation.

4-106. Answer B. GFDPP 4-62, AIM
In order for airspace to be classified as Class D there must be an operating control tower.

4-107   PLT434
Unless otherwise authorized, two-way radio communications with Air Traffic Control are required for landings or takeoffs.

A— at all tower controlled airports regardless of weather conditions.

B— at all tower controlled airports only when weather conditions are less than VFR.

C— at all tower controlled airports within Class D airspace only when weather conditions are less than VFR.

4-107. Answer A. GFDPP 4-63, FAR 91.129
When operating at an airport where a control tower is in operation, you must be in radio contact with ATC whether or not VFR conditions exist.

4-108   PLT434
Two-way radio communication must be established with the Air Traffic Control facility having jurisdiction over the area prior to entering which class airspace?

A— Class C

B— Class E

C— Class G

4-108. Answer A. GFDPP 4-65, FAR 91-130
You must establish two-way communications prior to entering a Class C airspace area, and maintain it while operating within the Class C airspace.

4-109   PLT434
What minimum radio equipment is required for operation within Class C airspace?

A— Two-way radio communications equipment and a 4096-code transponder.

B— Two-way radio communications equipment, a 4096-code transponder, and DME.

C— Two-way radio communications equipment, a 4096-code transponder, and an encoding altimeter.

4-109. Answer C. GFDPP 4-65, FAR 91.130, 91.215
To operate in a Class C airspace area, you are required to have both a two-way radio and a 4096-code transponder with encoding altimeter.

4-110 PLT161
What minimum pilot certification is required for operation within Class B airspace?

A– Recreational Pilot Certificate.

B– Private Pilot Certificate or Student Pilot Certificate with appropriate logbook endorsements.

C– Private Pilot Certificate with an instrument rating.

4-110. Answer B. GFDPP 4-65, FAR 91.131
To operate in a Class B airspace area, a pilot must hold a private pilot certificate. However, within certain Class B airspace areas, student pilot operations may be conducted after receiving specific training and a logbook endorsement from an authorized flight instructor.

4-111 PLT161
What minimum pilot certification is required for operation within Class B airspace?

A– Private Pilot Certificate or Student Pilot Certificate with appropriate logbook endorsements.

B– Commercial Pilot Certificate.

C– Private Pilot Certificate with an instrument rating.

4-111. Answer A. GFDPP 4-65, FAR 91.131
To operate in a Class B airspace area, a pilot must hold a private pilot certificate. However, within certain Class B airspace areas, student pilot operations may be conducted after receiving specific training and a logbook endorsement from an authorized flight instructor.

4-112 PLT161
What minimum radio equipment is required for VFR operation within Class B airspace?

A– Two-way radio communications equipment and a 4096-code transponder.

B– Two-way radio communications equipment, a 4096-code transponder, and an encoding altimeter.

C– Two-way radio communications equipment, a 4096-code transponder, an encoding altimeter, and a VOR or TACAN receiver.

4-112. Answer B. GFDPP 4-65, FAR 91.131
VFR operations within Class B airspace areas require a two-way radio and a 4096-code transponder with an encoding altimeter.

4-113 PLT161
An operable 4096-code transponder and Mode C encoding altimeter are required in

A– Class B airspace and within 30 miles of the Class B primary airport.

B– Class D airspace.

C– Class E airspace below 10,000 feet MSL.

4-113. Answer A. GFDPP 4-65, FAR 91.131
A 4096-code transponder with an encoding altimeter is required for operations within a Class B airspace area. It is not required in Class D airspace or Class E airspace below 10,000 feet MSL.

4-114 PLT161
In which type of airspace are VFR flights prohibited?

A– Class A
B– Class B
C– Class C

4-114. Answer A. GFDPP 4-71, FAR 91.135
Only IFR operations are allowed in Class A airspace. VFR flights are allowed in Class B and C airspace if authorized by ATC.

4-115   PLT434

During operations within controlled airspace at altitudes of less than 1,200 feet AGL, the minimum horizontal distance from clouds requirement for VFR flight is

A— 1,000 feet.

B— 1,500 feet.

C— 2,000 feet.

4-115. Answer C. GFDPP 4-82, FAR 91.155

In controlled airspace, other than Class B, below 10,000 feet, it does not matter whether you are above or below 1,200 feet AGL. The VFR cloud clearance is 2,000 feet horizontal.

4-116   PLT016

What minimum visibility and clearance from clouds are required for VFR operations in Class G airspace at 700 feet AGL or below during daylight hours?

A— 1 mile visibility and clear of clouds.

B— 1 mile visibility, 500 feet below, 1,000 feet above, and 2,000 feet horizontal clearance from clouds.

C— 3 miles visibility and clear of clouds.

4-116. Answer A. GFDPP 4-82, FAR 91.155

For VFR flight in uncontrolled or class G airspace below 1,200 feet during daytime, you are only required to have 1 mile visibility and remain clear of clouds.

4-117   PLT016

What minimum flight visibility is required for VFR flight operations on an airway below 10,000 feet MSL?

A— 1 mile.

B— 3 miles.

C— 4 miles.

4-117. Answer B. GFDPP 4-82, FAR 91.155

Since an airway is Class E airspace, the minimum visibility below 10,000 feet MSL is 3 statute miles.

4-118   PLT163

The minimum distance from clouds required for VFR operations on an airway below 10,000 feet MSL is

A— remain clear of clouds.

B— 500 feet below, 1,000 feet above, and 2,000 feet horizontally.

C— 500 feet above, 1,000 feet below, and 2,000 feet horizontally.

4-118. Answer B. GFDPP 4-82, FAR 91.155

The VFR cloud clearances for Class E airspace apply. Below 10,000 feet MSL, you must remain 500 feet below, 1,000 feet above, and 2,000 feet horizontally.

4-119   PLT163
During operations within controlled airspace at altitudes of more than 1,200 feet AGL, but less than 10,000 feet MSL, the minimum distance above clouds requirement for VFR flight is

A– 500 feet.

B– 1,000 feet.

C– 1,500 feet.

4-119. Answer B. GFDPP 4-82, FAR 91.155
Below 10,000 feet MSL in Class C and D Airspace, the cloud clearances are 500 feet below, 1,000 feet above, and 2,000 feet horizontal. In Class B airspace, however, the cloud clearance is just "clear of clouds."

4-120   PLT163
VFR flight in controlled airspace above 1,200 feet AGL and below 10,000 feet MSL requires a minimum visibility and vertical cloud clearance of

A– 3 miles, and 500 feet below or 1,000 feet above the clouds in controlled airspace.

B– 5 miles, and 1,000 feet below or 1,000 feet above the clouds at all altitudes.

C– 5 miles, and 1,000 feet below or 1,000 feet above the clouds only in Class A airspace.

4-120. Answer A. GFDPP 4-82, FAR 91.155
Below 10,000 feet MSL in Class C and D Airspace, the cloud clearances are 500 feet below, 1,000 feet above, and 2,000 feet horizontal. In Class B airspace, however, the cloud clearance is just "clear of clouds."

4-121   PLT163
During operations outside controlled airspace at altitudes of more than 1,200 feet AGL, but less than 10,000 feet MSL, the minimum flight visibility for VFR flight at night is

A– 1 mile.

B– 3 miles.

C– 5 miles.

4-121. Answer B. GFDPP 4-82, FAR 91.155
In Class G airspace at these altitudes, night VFR operations require 3 miles visibility.

4-122   PLT163
Outside controlled airspace, the minimum flight visibility requirement for VFR flight above 1,200 feet AGL and below 10,000 feet MSL during daylight hours is

A– 1 mile.

B– 3 miles.

C– 5 miles.

4-122. Answer A. GFDPP 4-82, FAR 91.155
In Class G airspace at these altitudes, night VFR operations require 3 miles visibility.

In uncontrolled airspace below 10,000 feet MSL and above 1,200 feet AGL, required daytime visibility is 1 mile.

4-123   PLT163
During operations outside controlled airspace at altitudes of more than 1,200 feet AGL, but less than 10,000 feet MSL, the minimum distance below clouds requirement for VFR flight at night is

A– 500 feet.

B– 1,000 feet.

C– 1,500 feet.

4-123. Answer A. GFDPP 4-82, FAR 91.155
At night, in uncontrolled airspace below 10,000 feet MSL (both above and below 1,200 feet AGL), the VFR cloud clearance is 500 feet below.

4-124   PLT163
The minimum flight visibility required for VFR flights above 10,000 feet MSL and more than 1,200 feet AGL in controlled airspace is

A– 1 mile.

B– 3 miles.

C– 5 miles.

4-124. Answer C. GFDPP 4-82, FAR 91.155
At or above 10,000 feet MSL and above 1,200 feet AGL, the required visibility is 5 statute miles, whether in controlled or uncontrolled airspace.

4-125   PLT163
For VFR flight operations above 10,000 feet MSL and more than 1,200 feet AGL, the minimum horizontal distance from clouds required is

A– 1,000 feet.

B– 2,000 feet.

C– 1 mile.

4-125. Answer C. GFDPP 4-82, FAR 91.155
Whether in controlled or uncontrolled airspace at these altitudes, the minimum VFR horizontal distance from clouds is 1 statute mile.

4-126   PLT163
During operations at altitudes of more than 1,200 feet AGL and at or above 10,000 feet MSL, the minimum distance above clouds requirement for VFR flight is

A– 500 feet.

B– 1,000 feet.

C– 1,500 feet.

4-126. Answer B. GFDPP 4-82, FAR 91.155
For VFR flights at these altitudes, whether in controlled airspace or not, you are required to remain 1,000 feet above clouds. The only exception is for daytime operations below 1,200 feet AGL in uncontrolled airspace. In this case it is clear of clouds.

4-127   PLT163
No person may take off or land an aircraft under basic VFR at an airport that lies within Class D airspace unless the

A– flight visibility at that airport is at least 1 mile.

B– ground visibility at that airport is at least 1 mile.

C– ground visibility at that airport is at least 3 miles.

4-127. Answer C. GFDPP 4-63, FAR 91.155
To take off or land under VFR in a Class D airspace area, the ceiling must be at least 1,000 feet and the ground visibility must be at least 3 statute miles. Flight visibility may be used if ground visibility is not available.

4-128   **PLT163**

The basic VFR weather minimums for operating an aircraft within Class D airspace are

A— 500-foot ceiling and 1 mile visibility.

B— 1,000-foot ceiling and 3 miles visibility.

C— clear of clouds and 2 miles visibility.

4-128. Answer B. GFDPP 4-82, FAR 91.155
To take off or land under VFR in a Class D airspace area, the ceiling must be at least 1,000 feet and the ground visibility must be at least 3 statute miles. Flight visibility may be used if ground visibility is not available.

4-129   **PLT163**

A special VFR clearance authorizes the pilot of an aircraft to operate VFR while within Class D airspace when the visibility is

A— less than 1 mile and the ceiling is less than 1,000 feet.

B— at least 1 mile and the aircraft can remain clear of clouds.

C— at least 3 miles and the aircraft can remain clear of clouds.

4-129. Answer B. GFDPP 4-71, FAR 91.157
When authorized by ATC, special VFR allows you to operate with one statute mile visibility as long as you can remain clear of clouds.

4-130   **PLT163**

What is the minimum weather condition required for airplanes operating under special VFR in Class D airspace?

A— 1 mile flight visibility.

B— 1 mile flight visibility and 1,000-foot ceiling.

C— 3 miles flight visibility and 1,000-foot ceiling.

4-130. Answer A. GFDPP 4-71, FAR 91.157
When authorized by ATC, special VFR allows you to operate with one statute mile visibility as long as you can remain clear of clouds.

4-131   **PLT161**

What are the minimum requirements for airplane operations under special VFR in Class D airspace at night?

A— The airplane must be under radar surveillance at all times while in Class D airspace.

B— The airplane must be equipped for IFR and with an altitude reporting transponder.

C— The pilot must be instrument rated, and the airplane must be IFR equipped.

4-131. Answer C. GFDPP 4-72, FAR 91.157
For special VFR at night, you must have a current instrument rating, and the airplane must be equipped for IFR operations.

4-132   PLT161

No person may operate an airplane within Class D airspace at night under special VFR unless the

A— flight can be conducted 500 feet below the clouds.

B— airplane is equipped for instrument flight.

C— flight visibility is at least 3 miles.

4-132. Answer B. GFDPP 4-72, FAR 91.157

For special VFR at night, you must have a current instrument rating, and the airplane must be equipped for IFR operations.

4-133   PLT161

An operable 4096-code or Mode S transponder with an encoding altimeter is required in which airspace?

A— Class A, Class B (and within 30 miles of the Class B primary airport), and Class C.

B— Class D and Class E (below 10,000 feet MSL).

C— Class D and Class G (below 10,000 feet MSL).

4-133. Answer A. GFDPP 4-59, FAR 91.215

A transponder with an encoding transponder is required in Class A, Class B, and Class C airspace.

4-134   PLT161

With certain exceptions, all aircraft within 30 miles of a Class B primary airport from the surface upward to 10,000 feet MSL must be equipped with

A— an operable VOR or TACAN receiver and an ADF receiver.

B— instruments and equipment required for IFR operations.

C— an operable transponder having either Mode S or 4096-code capability with Mode C automatic altitude reporting capability.

4-134. Answer C. GFDPP 4-59, FAR 91.215

An appropriate transponder capable of providing altitude encoding is required to be in use when within 30 miles of a Class B primary airport.

4-135   PLT040

(Refer to figure 26, Area 4) The floor of Class B airspace overlying Hicks Airport (T67) north-northwest of Fort Worth Meacham Field is

A— at the surface

B— 3,200 feet MSL

C— 4,000 feet MSL

4-135. Answer C. GFDPP 4-67, Chart Legend

The altitudes of this portion of the Class B airspace are indicated by "110" over "40." This means the Class B airspace extends from a floor of 4,000 feet MSL up to 11,000 feet MSL.

4-136   PLT040

(Refer to figure 26, Area 2.) The floor of Class B airspace at Addison Airport is

A— at the surface

B— 3,000 feet MSL

C— 3,100 feet MSL

4-136. Answer B. GFDPP 4-67, Chart Legend

The altitudes of this portion of the Class B airspace are indicated by "110" over "30." This means the Class B airspace extends from a floor of 3,000 feet MSL up to 11,000 feet MSL.

4-137   PLT064
(Refer to figure 21, Area 4.) What hazards to aircraft may exist in restricted areas such as R-5302B?

A– Military training activities that necessitate acrobatic or abrupt flight maneuvers.

B– Unusual, often invisible, hazards such as aerial gunnery or guided missiles.

C– High volume of pilot training or an unusual type of aerial activity.

4-137. Answer B. GFDPP 4-75, AIM
Restricted areas have invisible hazards to aircraft, such as artillery firing, aerial gunnery, or guided missiles.

4-138   PLT393
(Refer to figure 27, Area 2.) What hazards to aircraft may exist in areas such as Devils Lake East MOA?

A– Military training activities that necessitate acrobatic or abrupt flight maneuvers.

B– High volume of pilot training or an unusual type of aerial activity.

C– Unusual, often invisible, hazards to aircraft such as artillery firing, aerial gunnery, or guided missiles.

4-138. Answer A. GFDPP 4-74, AIM
Most training activities in a MOA involve acrobatic or abrupt flight maneuvers.

4-139   PLT064
(Refer to figure 22, Area 3.) What type military flight operations should a pilot expect along IR 644?

A– VFR training flights above 1,500 feet AGL at speeds less than 250 knots.

B– IFR training flights above 1,500 feet AGL at speeds in excess of 250 knots.

C– Instrument training flights below 1,500 feet AGL at speeds in excess of 150 knots.

4-139. Answer B. GFDPP 4-77, AIM
IR routes are designed to be flown by military aircraft at speeds often in excess of 250 kts. An IR Route with three letters in the designator (IR 644) indicates one or more segments are above 1,500 feet AGL.

4-140   PLT163
(Refer to figure 23, Area 1.) The visibility and cloud clearance requirements to operate VFR during daylight hours over Sandpoint Airport at 1,200 feet AGL are

A– 1 mile and 1,000 feet above, 500 feet below, and 2,000 feet horizontally from each cloud.

B– 1 mile and clear of clouds.

C– 3 miles and 1,000 feet above, 500 feet below, and 2,000 feet horizontally from each cloud.

4-140. Answer C. GFDPP 4-61, FAR 91.155
The airspace is Class E above 700 feet AGL. The day VFR minimums are 3 miles visibility and 1,000 feet above, 500 feet below, and 2,000 feet horizontally from all clouds.

4-141   PLT163
(Refer to figure 27, Area 2.) The visibility and cloud clearance requirements to operate VFR during daylight hours over the town of Cooperstown between 1,200 feet AGL and 10,000 feet MSL are

A– 3 miles and 1,000 feet above, 500 feet below, and 2,000 feet horizontally from clouds

B– 1 mile and clear of clouds.

C– 1 mile and 1,000 feet above, 500 feet below, and 2,000 feet horizontally from clouds.

4-141. Answer A. GFDPP 4-61, 82, FAR 91.155
Cooperstown is within the Class E airspace of the Cooperstown Airport. The floor of this airspace is 700 feet AGL. Visibility of 3 miles and 1,000 feet above, 500 feet below, and 2,000 feet horizontally from clouds is required to operate VFR in controlled airspace below 10,000 feet MSL.

4-142   PLT161
(Refer to figure 27, Area 1.) Identify the airspace over the town of McHenry.

A– Class G airspace — surface up to but not including 700 feet MSL, Class E airspace — 700 feet to 14,500 feet MSL.

B– Class G airspace — surface up to but not including 1,200 feet AGL, Class E airspace — 1,200 feet AGL up to but not including 18,000 feet MSL.

C– Class G airspace — surface up to but not including 18,000 feet MSL.

4-142. Answer B. GFDPP 4-58, Chart Legend
The lower left corner of the sectional chart excerpt shows a blue shaded area indicating that in the area covered by this chart, Class E airspace extends from 1,200 ft AGL to 18,000 MSL unless otherwise marked.

4-143   PLT040
(Refer to figure 27, Area 6.) The airspace overlying and within 5 miles of Barnes County Airport is

A– Class D airspace from the surface to the floor of the overlying Class E airspace.

B– Class E airspace from the surface to 1,200 feet MSL.

C– Class G airspace from the surface to 700 feet AGL.

4-143. Answer C. GFDPP 4-61, Chart Legend
The magenta shading around the airport indicates that Class E airspace begins at 700 feet AGL. Below 700 feet the airspace is uncontrolled (Class G) airspace. Class D airspace, marked with a blue dashed line around the airport, is not shown anywhere on this chart.

4-144   PLT101
(Refer to figure 26, Area 7.) The airspace overlying Collin County Mc Kinney Airport (TKI) is controlled from the surface to

A– 2,900 feet MSL.

B– 2,500 feet MSL.

C– 700 feet AGL.

4-144. Answer A. GFDPP 4-63, Chart Legend
The controlled airspace this question is referring to is Class D airspace. The top of Class D airspace (MSL) is shown within the square dashed box.

4-145   PLT101
(Refer to figure 26, Area 4.) The airspace directly over-lying Fort Worth Meacham is

A– Class B airspace to 10,000 feet MSL.

B– Class C airspace to 5,000 feet MSL.

C– Class D airspace to 3,200 feet MSL.

4-145. Answer C. GFDPP 4-63, Chart Legend
The blue segmented circle indicates Fort Worth Meacham is located in Class D airspace. The [32] indicates the ceiling of the Class D airspace is 3,200 feet MSL.

4-146   PLT161
(Refer to figure 24, Area 3.) What is the floor of the Savannah Class C airspace at the shelf area (outer circle)?

A– 1,300 feet AGL

B– 1,300 feet MSL

C– 1,700 feet MSL

4-146. Answer B. GFDPP 4-64, AIM
The floor of the shelf area of most Class C airspace is normally approximately 1,200 feet AGL. At Savannah, the 1,200 feet AGL has been rounded up to 1,300 feet MSL (airport elevation is 51 feet) The exact limits in MSL are depicted on the chart ("41/13").

4-147   PLT064
(Refer to figure 21, Area 1.) What minimum radio equipment is required to land and take off at Norfolk International?

A– Mode C transponder and omnireceiver.

B– Mode C transponder and two-way radio.

C– Mode C transponder, omnireceiver, and DME.

4-147. Answer B. GFDPP 4-59, 65, FAR 91.130
The area depicted is Class C airspace. Aircraft operating in Class C airspace must be equipped with a Mode C transponder and pilots are required to maintain two-way radio communications.

4-148   PLT064
(Refer to figure 26.) At which airports is fixed-wing Special VFR not authorized?

A– Fort Worth Meacham and Fort Worth Spinks.

B– Dallas-Fort Worth International and Dallas Love Field.

C– Addison and Redbird.

4-148. Answer B. GFDPP 4-72, Chart Legend
The "NO SVFR" over the airport identification name indicates that fixed-wing special VFR is not authorized.

4-149   PLT064
(Refer to figure 23, Area 3.) The vertical limits of that portion of Class E airspace designated as a Federal Airway over Magee Airport are

A– 1,200 feet AGL to 17,999 feet MSL.

B– 7,500 feetMSL to 17,999 feet MSL.

C– 700 feet MSL to 12,500 feet MSL.

4-149. Answer A. GFDPP 4-60, Chart Legend
Class E airspace includes Federal, or Victor, airways which usually extend to 4 nautical miles on each side of the airway centerline and, unless otherwise indicated, extends from 1,200 feet AGL up to, but not including, 18,000 feet MSL.

4-150   PLT161
The vertical limit of Class C airspace above the primary airport is normally

A— 1,200 feet AGL.
B— 3,000 feet AGL.
C— 4,000 feet AGL.

4-150. Answer C. GFDPP 4-64, AIM
The vertical limit of Class C airspace is 4,000 feet above the primary airport. This is the same for both the inner and outer circles.

4-151   PLT161
The radius of the procedural Outer Area of Class C airspace is normally

A— 10 NM.
B— 20 NM.
C— 30 NM.

4-151. Answer B. GFDPP 4-64, AIM
Class C airspace areas have a procedural outer area not shown on charts. Normally this area extends 20 NM from the primary Class C airspace airport. You may obtain radar services in this area, but are not required to contact ATC to operate here.

4-152   PLT161
Under what condition may an aircraft operate from a satellite airport within Class C airspace?

A— The pilot must file a flight plan prior to departure.
B— The pilot must monitor ATC until clear of the Class C airspace.
C— The pilot must contact ATC as soon as practicable after takeoff.

4-152. Answer C. GFDPP 4-65, FAR 91.130
A pilot must establish two-way communications with ATC as soon as practical after takeoff.

4-153   PLT064
Under what condition, if any, may pilots fly through a restricted area?

A— When flying on airways with an ATC clearance.
B— With the controlling agency's authorization.
C— Regulations do not allow this.

4-153. Answer B. GFDPP 4-75, FAR 91.133
The controlling agency may grant permission to fly through a restricted area.

4-154   PLT064
What action should a pilot take when operating under VFR in a Military Operations Area (MOA)?

A— Obtain a clearance from the controlling agency prior to entering the MOA.
B— Operate only on the airways that transverse the MOA.
C— Exercise extreme caution when military activity is being conducted.

4-154. Answer C. GFDPP 4-74, AIM
Due to the possibility of military training activities, pilots operating in a MOA should use extra caution and be vigilant for military traffic.

4-155   PLT444
Responsibility for collision avoidance in an alert area rests with

A– the controlling agency.

B– all pilots.

C– Air Traffic Control.

4-155. Answer B. GFDPP 4-73, AIM
All pilots flying in an alert area, whether participating in activities or transitioning the area, are equally responsible for collision avoidance.

4-156   PLT161
The lateral dimensions of Class D airspace are based on

A– the number of airports that lie within the Class D airspace.

B– 5 statute miles from the geographical center of the primary airport.

C– the instrument procedures for which the controlled airspace is established.

4-156. Answer C. GFDPP 4-63, AIM
The actual lateral dimensions of Class D airspace varies with each location, but, in general, Class D airspace is based on the instrument procedures for the airports in that area.

4-157   PLT435
A non-tower satellite airport, within the same Class D airspace as that designated for the primary airport, requires radio communications be established and maintained with the

A– satellite airport's UNICOM.

B– associated Flight Service Station.

C– primary airport's control tower.

4-157. Answer C. GFDPP 4-63, FAR 91.129
When approaching Class D airspace, you must contact the primary airport's control tower before entering the airspace. When departing a nontowered satellite airport, contact the controlling tower as soon as practical after takeoff.

4-158   PLT161
Which initial action should a pilot take prior to entering Class C airspace?

A– Contact approach control on the appropriate frequency.

B– Contact the tower and request permission to enter.

C– Contact the FSS for traffic advisories.

4-158. Answer A. GFDPP 4-65, AIM
Prior to entering Class C airspace, you need to establish contact with approach control.

4-159   PLT161
What ATC facility should the pilot contact to receive a special VFR departure clearance in Class D airspace?

A– Automated Flight Service Station.

B– Air Traffic Control Tower.

C– Air Route Traffic Control Center.

4-159. Answer B. GFDPP 4-71, FAR 91.157
The control tower is the ATC facility which issues a special VFR clearance.

4-160   PLT040

Flight through a restricted area should not be accomplished unless the pilot has

A— filed an IFR flight plan.

B— received prior authorization from the controlling agency.

C— received prior permission from the commanding officer of the nearest military base.

4-160. Answer B. GFDPP 4-75, FAR 91.133, AIM

You must receive prior authorization from the controlling agency before operating in a restricted area. If you are operating on an IFR flight plan and ATC clears you through that airspace, then they are acting as the controlling agency and providing you the needed authorization. The FAA is not the controlling agency when the restricted area is "hot" and will not clear you through the airspace at those times.

4-161   PLT162

When a control tower, located on an airport within Class D airspace, ceases operation for the day, what happens to the airspace designation?

A— The airspace designation normally will not change.

B— The airspace remains Class D airspace as long as a weather observer or automated weather system is available.

C— The airspace reverts to Class E or a combination of Class E and G airspace during the hours the tower is not in operation.

4-161. Answer C. GFDPP 4-62, AIM

Class D Airspace exists only when the control tower is operating. When the tower shuts down, you will normally continue to use the tower frequency as a Common Traffic Advisory Frequency (CTAF).

4-162   PLT161

With certain exceptions, Class E airspace extends upward from either 700 feet or 1,200 feet AGL to, but does not include,

A— 10,000 feet MSL.

B— 14,500 feet MSL.

C— 18,000 feet MSL.

4-162. Answer C. GFDPP 4-59

Unless otherwise indicated, E airspace begins at 700 feet or 1,200 feet AGL and continues up to, but not including 18,000 MSL. Notice that the upper limit is defined by MSL, while the lower limit is typically defined by AGL.

4-163   PLT281

Information concerning parachute jumping sites may be found in the

A— NOTAMs.

B— Airport/Facility Directory.

C— Graphic Notices and Supplemental Data.

4-163. Answer B. GFDPP 4-78, PHB

Established parachute sites will be listed in the Airport/Facility Directory. Frequently used sites will also be depicted on aeronautical charts and single events or infrequently used sites will be listed in NOTAMS.

COMMUNICATION AND FLIGHT INFORMATION

SECTION A — RADAR AND ATC SERVICES

Computer-enhanced radar displays have greatly expanded the capabilities of air traffic control, providing you with an extra "crewmember" whenever you fly. This section reviews the various radar and air traffic control facilities in use. Topics include equipment, such as transponders, radar and VHF communication radios, and services available to pilots operating under visual flight rules (VFR).

TRANSPONDER OPERATIONS

- You may not use an ATC transponder unless it has been tested and inspected within the preceding 24 calendar months.
- Avoid inadvertently selecting the transponder codes 7500, 7600, or 7700.
- Unless otherwise required, set the transponder to squawk 1200 when operating under VFR.
- When leaving Class B, C or D airspace and being advised that radar service is terminated, squawk 1200.

VFR RADAR SERVICES

Traffic information is given with respect to the hands of a clock, with the aircraft at the center. The 12 o'clock position is straight ahead, 6 o'clock is directly behind, 3 o'clock is 90 degrees to the right and 9 o'clock 90 is degrees to the left.

TERMINAL VFR RADAR SERVICES

- Basic radar service for VFR aircraft provides traffic advisories and limited vectoring on a workload permitting basis.
- To request VFR radar service and a transponder code, contact ground control or clearance delivery, and request the appropriate radar service.
- A small number of terminal radar service areas (TRSAs) provide sequencing and separation for participating VFR aircraft. Class B and C areas also provide these services, but "participation" is mandatory.

AUTOMATIC TERMINAL INFORMATION SERVICE (ATIS)

Automatic Terminal Information Service (ATIS) is the continuous broadcast of recorded information concerning non-control data in selected high-activity terminal areas.

FLIGHT SERVICE STATIONS (FSS)

The call sign for a flight service station is its name, followed by the word "radio." On initial call-up, provide the aircraft's full call sign, using the phonetic alphabet.

5-1   PLT426

No person may use an ATC transponder unless it has been tested and inspected within at least the preceding

A– 6 calendar months.

B– 12 calendar months.

C– 24 calendar months.

5-1. Answer C. GFDPP 5-4, FAR 91.413

No person may use an ATC transponder unless it has been tested and inspected within at least the preceding 24 calendar months.

5-2   PLT196

Automatic Terminal Information Service (ATIS) is the continuous broadcast of recorded information concerning

A– pilots of radar-identified aircraft whose aircraft is in dangerous proximity to terrain or to an obstruction.

B– nonessential information to reduce frequency congestion.

C– noncontrol information in selected high-activity terminal areas.

5-2. Answer C. GFDPP 5-12

ATIS is broadcast at certain busy airports, and provides noncontrol weather and runway information.

5-3   PLT194

An ATC radar facility issues the following advisory to a pilot flying on a heading of 090°: "TRAFFIC 3 O'CLOCK, 2 MILES, WESTBOUND..." Where should the pilot look for this traffic?

A– East.

B– South.

C– West.

5-3. Answer B. GFDPP 5-8, AIM

Since the pilot is heading east, the 3 o'clock position is to the right, which is south.

5-4   PLT194

An ATC radar facility issues the following advisory to a pilot flying on a heading of 360°: "TRAFFIC 10 O'CLOCK, 2 MILES, SOUTHBOUND..." Where should the pilot look for this traffic?

A– Northwest.

B– Northeast.

C– Southwest.

5-4. Answer A. GFDPP 5-8, AIM

Since the pilot's 12 o'clock position is north, the 10 o'clock position is northwest.

5-5   PLT194
An ATC radar facility issues the following advisory to a pilot during a local flight: "TRAFFIC 2 O'CLOCK, 5 MILES, NORTHBOUND..." Where should the pilot look for this traffic?

A– Between directly ahead and 90° to the left.

B– Between directly behind and 90° to the right.

C– Between directly ahead and 90° to the right.

5-6   PLT194
An ATC radar facility issues the following advisory to a pilot flying north in a calm wind: "TRAFFIC 9 O'CLOCK, 2 MILES, SOUTHBOUND..." Where should the pilot look for this traffic?

A– South.

B– North.

C– West.

5-7   PLT172
Basic radar service in the terminal radar program is best described as

A– mandatory radar service provided by the Automated Radar Terminal System (ARTS) program.

B– safety alerts, traffic advisories, and limited vectoring to VFR aircraft.

C– wind-shear warning at participating airports.

5-8   PLT172
From whom should a departing VFR aircraft request radar traffic information during ground operations?

A– Clearance delivery.

B– Ground control, on initial contact.

C– Tower, just before takeoff.

5-5. Answer C. GFDPP 5-8, AIM
Since the pilot's 12 o'clock is directly ahead, and 3 o'clock is 90° to the right, 2 o'clock is approximately 60° right.

5-6. Answer C. GFDPP 5-8, AIM
The pilot's 12 o'clock is north, so 9 o'clock is left, or west.

5-7. Answer B. GFDPP 5-10, AIM
Basic radar service for VFR aircraft provides safety alerts, traffic advisories, and limited vectoring on a workload-permitting basis. Unlike Class B and Class C service, basic service is not mandatory for VFR aircraft. Wind shear warning is NOT part of the basic radar service. Note: The terminology for radar service has changed to Basic, TRSA, Class C, and Class B.

5-8. Answer B. GFDPP 5-10, AIM
You should request radar traffic information by notifying ground control on initial contact with your request and proposed direction of flight. Clearance delivery is incorrect because normally, it only provides IFR clearances, and it may not be available at all airports. Requesting the service from the tower, just before takeoff, could delay either the departure or availability of the service. Note: The terminology for radar service has changed to Basic, TRSA, Class C, and Class B.

5-9   PLT172
TRSA Service in the terminal radar program provides

A– sequencing and separation for participating VFR aircraft.

B– IFR separation (1,000 feet vertical and 3 miles lateral) between all aircraft.

C– warning to pilots when their aircraft are in unsafe proximity to terrain, obstructions, or other aircraft.

5-9. Answer A. GFDPP 5-10, AIM
TRSA service provides separation between all participating VFR aircraft and all IFR aircraft operating in the TRSA. Pilot participation is urged but not mandatory.

5-10   PLT497
When making routine transponder code changes, pilots should avoid inadvertent selection of which code?

A– 7200.

B– 7000.

C– 7500

5-10. Answer C. GFDPP 5-5, AIM
You should avoid inadvertent selection of transponder codes which may set off false alarms at radar facilities. These codes are: 7500 for hijacking, 7600 for radio communications failure, and 7700 for emergencies.

5-11   PLT497
When operating under VFR below 18,000 feet MSL, unless otherwise authorized, what transponder code should be selected?

A– 1200.

B– 7600.

C– 7700.

5-11. Answer A. GFDPP 5-5, AIM
The transponder code for VFR aircraft is 1200. Aircraft operating above 18,000 feet MSL are in Class A airspace and must have an IFR clearance.

5-12   PLT497
Unless otherwise authorized, if flying a transponder equipped aircraft, a pilot should squawk which VFR code?

A– 1200.

B– 7600.

C– 7700.

5-12. Answer A. GFDPP 5-5, AIM
The transponder code for VFR aircraft is 1200. Aircraft operating above 18,000 feet MSL are in Class A airspace and must have an IFR clearance.

5-13   PLT497
If Air Traffic Control advises that radar service is terminated when the pilot is departing Class C airspace, the transponder should be set to code

A– 0000.

B– 1200.

C– 4096.

5-13. Answer B. GFDPP 5-5, AIM
Since you would then be operating under VFR, the transponder should be set to 1200.

5-14　　　PLT078
(Refer to figure 53.)

Which type radar service is provided to VFR aircraft at Lincoln Municipal?

A– Sequencing to the primary Class C airport and standard separation.

B– Sequencing to the primary Class C airport and conflict resolution so that radar targets do not touch, or 1,000 feet vertical separation.

C– Sequencing to the primary Class C airport, traffic advisories, conflict resolution, and safety alerts.

5-14. Answer C. GFDPP 5-11, AIM
The VFR services provided within a Class C airspace area (formerly ARSA) include: sequencing all arriving aircraft to the primary Class C airport; providing traffic advisories and conflict resolutions between IFR and VFR aircraft so that radar targets do not touch, or 500 feet vertical separation, and between VFR aircraft, traffic advisories and safety alerts.

5-15　　　PLT044
When an air traffic controller issues radar traffic information in relation to the 12-hour clock, the reference the controller uses is the aircraft's

A– true course.

B– ground track.

C– magnetic heading.

5-15. Answer B. GFDPP 5-8, PHB
Controllers can see an aircraft's ground track on radar, but cannot factor in any crab angle applied for wind correction. Pilots should consider this when reacting to ATC traffic advisories.

5-16　　　PLT196
Absence of the sky condition and visibility on an ATIS broadcast indicates that

A– weather conditions are at or above VFR minimums.

B– the sky condition is clear and visibility is unrestricted.

C– the ceiling is at least 5,000 feet and visibility is 5 miles or more.

5-16. Answer C. GFDPP 5-12, AIM
If the ceiling is at least 5,000 feet and visibility is 5 miles or more, reporting of the ceiling/sky condition, visibility, and obstructions to vision is optional.

5-17　　　PLT044
As Pilot in Command of an aircraft, under which situation can you deviate from an ATC clearance?

A– When operating in Class A airspace at night.

B– If an ATC clearance is not understood and in VFR conditions.

C– In response to a traffic alert and collision avoidance system resolution advisory.

5-17. Answer C. GFDPP 3-55, AIM
Pilots who deviate for a resolution advisory must be responding to a TCAS II system. Those pilots must also report the deviation to ATC as soon as possible. Remember that there may be other reasons for deviating from and ATC clearance, since the PIC may deviate from any clearance if such action is necessary to ensure the safety of the flight.

SECTION B — RADIO PROCEDURES

Pilots use standard terminology to ensure that communication between aircraft and ground facilities is smooth and concise. This section covers VHF radio characteristics, common terms and proper phraseology. Coordinated Universal Time (UTC), radio procedures and ground radio facilities are also included.

USING NUMBERS ON THE RADIO

State altitudes as individual numbers, with the word "thousand" included as appropriate. At altitudes of 10,000 feet and above, each digit of the thousands is pronounced, for example "one zero thousand."

COORDINATED UNIVERSAL TIME (UTC)

To convert the local departure or arrival time to UTC, add the hours of difference from the number on the time conversion table. For example, to convert MST to UTC, add 7 hours to MST.

5-18   PLT502

A steady green light signal directed from the control tower to an aircraft in flight is a signal that the pilot

A— is cleared to land.

B— should give way to other aircraft and continue circling.

C— should return for landing.

5-18. Answer A. GFDPP 5-301, FAR 91.125

A steady green light while in flight means you are cleared to land.

5-19   PLT502

Which light signal from the control tower clears a pilot to taxi?

A— Flashing green.

B— Steady green.

C— Flashing white.

5-19. Answer A. GFDPP 5-31, FAR 91.125

While on the ground, a flashing green light means cleared to taxi.

5-20   PLT502

If the control tower uses a light signal to direct a pilot to give way to other aircraft and continue circling, the light will be

A— flashing red.

B— steady red.

C— alternating red and green.

5-20. Answer B. GFDPP 5-31, FAR 91.125

While in flight, a steady red light means give way and continue circling.

5-21   PLT502

A flashing white light signal from the control tower to a taxiing aircraft is an indication to

A– taxi at a faster speed.

B– taxi only on taxiways and not cross runways.

C– return to the starting point on the airport.

5-21. Answer C. GFDPP 5-31, FAR 91.125

A flashing white light while operating on the ground means return to the starting point on the airport.

5-22   PLT502

An alternating red and green light signal directed from the control tower to an aircraft in flight is a signal to

A– hold position.

B– exercise extreme caution.

C– not land; the airport is unsafe.

5-22. Answer B. GFDPP 5-31, FAR 91.125

An alternating red and green signal means the same whether you are in flight or on the ground — exercise extreme caution.

5-23   PLT502

While on final approach for landing, an alternating green and red light followed by a flashing red light is received from the control tower. Under these circumstances, the pilot should

A– discontinue the approach, fly the same traffic pattern and approach again, and land.

B– exercise extreme caution and abandon the approach, realizing the airport is unsafe for landing.

C– abandon the approach, circle the airport to the right, and expect a flashing white light when the airport is safe for landing.

5-23. Answer B. GFDPP 5-31, FAR 91.125

An alternating red and green signal means exercise extreme caution. This is followed by a flashing red signal, which, in flight, means that the airport is unsafe.

5-24   PLT012

(Refer to figure 28.)

An aircraft departs an airport in the eastern daylight time zone at 0945 EDT for a 2-hour flight to an airport located in the central daylight time zone. The landing should be at what coordinated universal time?

A– 1345Z.

B– 1445Z.

C– 1545Z.

5-24. Answer C. GFDPP 5-23, AIM

To convert the local departure time to UTC, add 4 hours (0945 + 4:00 = 1345). Two hours later is 1545Z.

5-25   PLT012

(Refer to figure 28.)

An aircraft departs an airport in the central standard time zone at 0v930 CST for a 2-hour flight to an airport located in the mountain standard time zone. The landing should be at what time?

A– 0930 MST.

B– 1030 MST.

C– 1130 MST.

5-25. Answer B. GFDPP 5-23, AIM

Add 2 hours to the 0930 departure time to find the arrival time of 1130 CST. Since Mountain time is 1 hour earlier than Central, subtract 1 hour, for a landing time of 1030 MST.

5-26   PLT012

(Refer to figure 28.)

An aircraft departs an airport in the central standard time zone at 0845 CST for a 2-hour flight to an airport located in the mountain standard time zone. The landing should be at what coordinated universal time?

A– 1345Z.

B– 1445Z.

C– 1645Z.

5-26. Answer C. GFDPP 5-23, AIM

Departure time (0845) plus 2 hours is 1045 CST. Convert CST to UTC by adding 6 hours, for a landing time of 1645Z.

5-27   PLT012

(Refer to figure 28.)

An aircraft departs an airport in the mountain standard time zone at 1615 MST for a 2-hour 15-minute flight to an airport located in the Pacific standard time zone. The estimated time of arrival at the destination airport should be

A– 1630 PST.

B– 1730 PST.

C– 1830 PST.

5-27. Answer B. GFDPP 5-23, AIM

Add 2:15 to 1615 MST to find the arrival time of 1830 MST. Since Pacific time is one hour earlier than MST, the arrival time is 1730 PST.

5-28   PLT012

(Refer to figure 28.)

An aircraft departs an airport in the Pacific standard time zone at 1030 PST for a 4-hour flight to an airport located in the central standard time zone. The landing should be at what coordinated universal time?

A– 2030Z.

B– 2130Z.

C– 2230Z.

5-28. Answer C. GFDPP 5-23, AIM

Add 4 hours to 1030 PST to find the arrival time of 1430 PST. To convert PST to UTC, add 8 hours. The landing time is 2230Z.

5-29   **PLT012**
(Refer to figure 28.)

An aircraft departs an airport in the mountain standard time zone at 1515 MST for a 2-hour 30-minute flight to an airport located in the Pacific standard time zone. What is the estimated time of arrival at the destination airport?

A– 1645 PST.

B– 1745 PST.

C– 1845 PST.

5-29. Answer A. GFDPP 5-23, AIM
Add 2:30 to 1515 MST to find the arrival time of 1745 MST. Convert MST to PST by subtracting 1 hour. The answer is 1645 PST.

5-30   **PLT064**
(Refer to figure 21.)

(Area 3) What is the recommended communications procedure for a landing at Currituck County Airport?

A– Transmit intentions on 122.9 MHz when 10 miles out and give position reports in the traffic pattern.

B– Contact Elizabeth City FSS for airport advisory service.

C– Contact New Bern FSS for area traffic information.

5-30. Answer A. GFDPP 5-25, AIM
The CTAF symbol is next to the frequency of 122.9. The normal procedure is to transmit intentions when 10 miles out and give position reports in the pattern.

5-31   **PLT064**
(Refer to figure 27.)

(Area 2) What is the recommended communication procedure when inbound to land at Cooperstown Airport?

A– Broadcast intentions when 10 miles out on the CTAF/MULTICOM frequency, 122.9 MHz.

B– Contact UNICOM when 10 miles out on 122.8 MHz.

C– Circle the airport in a left turn prior to entering traffic.

5-31. Answer A. GFDPP 5-25, AIM
The CTAF/MULTICOM frequency, 122.9, is depicted next to the CTAF symbol. Pilots should broadcast intentions on this frequency when 10 miles from the field.

5-32   **PLT204**
When flying HAWK N666CB, the proper phraseology for initial contact with McAlester AFSS is

A– "MC ALESTER RADIO, HAWK SIX SIX SIX CHARLIE BRAVO, RECEIVING ARDMORE VORTAC, OVER."

B– "MC ALESTER STATION, HAWK SIX SIX SIX CEE BEE, RECEIVING ARDMORE VORTAC, OVER."

C– "MC ALESTER FLIGHT SERVICE STATION, HAWK NOVEMBER SIX CHARLIE BRAVO, RECEIVING ARDMORE VORTAC, OVER."

5-32. Answer A. GFDPP 5-21, AIM
The callsign for a flight service station is its name, followed by the word "radio." The aircraft's full callsign should be given, using the phonetic alphabet.

5-33   PLT204
The correct method of stating 4,500 feet MSL to ATC is

A– "FOUR THOUSAND FIVE HUNDRED."

B– "FOUR POINT FIVE."

C– "FORTY-FIVE HUNDRED FEET MSL."

5-33. Answer A. GFDPP 5-22, AIM
Altitudes should be stated as individual numbers with the word hundreds or thousands added as appropriate. In this case, 4,500 feet should be read as "FOUR THOUSAND FIVE HUNDRED."

5-34   PLT204
The correct method of stating 10,500 feet MSL to ATC is

A– "TEN THOUSAND, FIVE HUNDRED FEET."

B– "TEN POINT FIVE."

C– "ONE ZERO THOUSAND, FIVE HUNDRED."

5-34. Answer C. GFDPP 5-22, AIM
See explanation for Question 5-33. In addition, for altitudes at and above 10,000 feet MSL, each digit of the thousands is pronounced, so that 10,500 becomes "ONE ZERO THOUSAND FIVE HUNDRED."

5-35   PLT435
Prior to entering an Airport Advisory Area, a pilot should

A– monitor ATIS for weather and traffic advisories.

B– contact approach control for vectors to the traffic pattern.

C– contact the local FSS for airport and traffic advisories.

5-35. Answer C. GFDPP 5-24, AIM
A local nonautomated FSS provides airport and traffic advisories for an Airport Advisory Area.

5-36   PLT150
If the aircraft's radio fails, what is the recommended procedure when landing at a controlled airport?

A– Observe the traffic flow, enter the pattern, and look for a light signal from the tower.

B– Enter a crosswind leg and rock the wings.

C– Flash the landing lights and cycle the landing gear while circling the airport.

5-36. Answer A. GFDPP 5-31, AIM
To avoid conflicts and cause the least disruption in the traffic flow, determine the landing direction, and enter the pattern. Watch the tower for a light signal and acknowledge by rocking the wings. At night, acknowledge by flashing the landing or navigation lights.

5-37   PLT044
After landing at a tower-controlled airport, when should the pilot contact ground control?

A– When advised by the tower to do so.

B– Prior to turning off the runway.

C– After reaching a taxiway that leads directly to the parking area.

5-37. Answer A. GFDPP 5-28, AIM
The tower will normally instruct you to exit the runway and contact ground control.

5-38   PLT502

If instructed by ground control to taxi to Runway 9, the pilot may proceed

A– via taxiways and across runways to, but not onto, Runway 9.

B– to the next intersecting runway where further clearance is required.

C– via taxiways and across runways to Runway 9, where an immediate takeoff may be made.

5-38. Answer A. GFDPP 5-27, AIM
A clearance to taxi to a runway allows the pilot to proceed to that runway and cross any intersecting runways.

5-39   PLT402
When activated, an emergency locator transmitter (ELT) transmits on

A– 118.0 and 118.8 MHz.

B– 121.5 and 243.0 MHz.

C– 123.0 and 119.0 MHz.

5-39. Answer B. GFDPP 5-33, AIM
The frequencies used for ELTs are the emergency frequencies of 121.5 MHz (VHF) and 243.0 MHz (UHF).

5-40   PLT402
When must the battery in an emergency locator transmitter (ELT) be replaced (or recharged if the battery is rechargeable)?

A– After one-half the battery's useful life.

B– During each annual and 100-hour inspection.

C– Every 24 calendar months.

5-40. Answer A. GFDPP 5-34, FAR 91.207
The ELT battery must be replaced or recharged after one-half the battery's useful life.

5-41   PLT402
When may an emergency locator transmitter (ELT) be tested?

A– Anytime.

B– At 15 and 45 minutes past the hour.

C– During the first 5 minutes after the hour.

5-41. Answer C. GFDPP 5-34, AIM
To prevent false alerts, ELT testing should be conducted only during the first 5 minutes after any hour.

5-42   PLT402
Which procedure is recommended to ensure that the emergency locator transmitter (ELT) has not been activated?

A– Turn off the aircraft ELT after landing.

B– Ask the airport tower if they are receiving an ELT signal.

C– Monitor 121.5 before engine shutdown.

5-42. Answer C. GFDPP 5-34, AIM
By monitoring 121.5, you will be able to hear the ELT signal if it has been activated.

5-43   PLT370
An ATC clearance provides

A– priority over all other traffic.

B– adequate separation from all traffic.

C– authorization to proceed under specified traffic conditions in controlled airspace.

5-43. Answer C. GFDPP 5-26, AIM
A clearance is authorization from ATC to operate under specific conditions in controlled airspace.

5-44   PLT078
(Refer to figure 53.)

When approaching Lincoln Municipal from the west at noon for the purpose of landing, initial communications should be with

A– Lincoln Approach Control on 124.0 MHz.

B– Minneapolis Center on 128.75 MHz.

C– Lincoln Tower on 118.5 MHz.

5-44. Answer A. GFDPP 5-26, A/FD
The communications section of the Airport/Facility Directory indicates that the airport is in Class C airspace (formerly ARSA), and that you should contact approach control. When west of the airport (170° – 349°), the frequency to use is 124.0. To confirm that Lincoln Approach Control is operational at noon, check the hours of operation.

5-45   PLT078
(Refer to figure 53.)

What is the recommended communications procedure for landing at Lincoln Municipal during the hours when the tower is not in operation?

A– Monitor airport traffic and announce your position and intentions on 118.5 MHz.

B– Contact UNICOM on 122.95 MHz for traffic advisories.

C– Monitor ATIS for airport conditions, then announce your position on 122.95 MHz.

5-45. Answer A. GFDPP 5-23, A/FD
The CTAF frequency is listed as 118.5, and is used when the tower is not in operation. Standard procedures are to monitor airport traffic and announce your position on CTAF.

5-46   PLT435
As standard operating practice, all inbound traffic to an airport without a control tower should continuously monitor the appropriate facility from a distance of

A– 25 miles.

B– 20 miles.

C– 10 miles.

5-46. Answer C. GFDPP 5-25, AIM
In addition to monitoring a CTAF within 10 miles when inbound or outbound from a non-towered airport, pilots should also make an initial call to announce their intention if they plan to land at the airport. They should then report on each leg of the pattern.

SECTION C — SOURCES OF FLIGHT INFORMATION

Aviation publications exist to aid you in planning a flight, many available online. These resources include the Aeronautical Information Manual (AIM), Airport/Facility Director (A/FD), Federal Aviation Regulations, advisory circulars, Jeppesen Pilot Resource Services, and Notices to Airmen.

AIRPORT/FACILITY DIRECTORY

*   Nonstandard traffic patterns are included in the remarks following the runway data for each runway.
*   Information regarding parachute jumping is also listed in the Airport/Facility Directory.

ADVISORY CIRCULARS

*   FAA advisory circulars may be ordered directly from the Government Printing Office.
*   FAA advisory circulars (ACs) that relate to certain subject matters are identified by numeric codes. Those pertaining to airmen are issued under subject number 60 (example AC 60-22). Airspace ACs are issued under subject number 70. ATC and General Operations ACs are issued under subject number 90.

5-47   PLT435
(Refer to figure 23.)

(Area 2) For information about the parachute jumping and glider operations at Silverwood Airport, refer to

A– notes on the border of the chart.

B– the Airport/Facility Directory.

C– the Notices to Airmen (NOTAM) publication.

5-47. Answer B. GFDPP 5-39, Chart Legend
The Airport/Facility Directory includes information about parachute jumping areas.

5-48   PLT116
FAA advisory circulars (some free, others at cost) are available to all pilots and are obtained by

A– distribution from the nearest FAA district office.

B– ordering those desired from the Government Printing Office.

C– subscribing to the Federal Register.

5-48. Answer B. GFDPP 5-46, PHB
You can order advisory circulars from the Government Printing Office or obtain them free from the FAA web site. FAA district offices do not stock advisory circulars for sale to the public. The Federal Register contains notices of proposed rulemaking and final rules, but does not contain advisory circulars.

5-49   PLT078
(Refer to figure 53.)

Where is Loup City Municipal located with relation to the city?

A– Northeast approximately 3 miles.

B– Northwest approximately 1 mile.

C– East approximately 10 miles.

5-49. Answer B. GFDPP 5-38, A/FD
The first line of the A/FD includes the distance and direction from the associated city. The entry 1 NW indicates that the airport is 1 mile northwest of the city.

5-50   PLT078
(Refer to figure 53.)

The landing distance available on Rwy 17 at Lincoln Airport is

A– 5,400 feet.

B– 5,800 feet.

C– 8,286 feet.

5-50. Answer A. AF/D Legend.
The landing distance available (LDA) appears under Runway Declared Distance Information. For Rwy 17, it is 5,400 feet.

5-51   PLT078
(Refer to figure 53.)

The landing distance available on Rwy 32 at Lincoln Airport is

A– 7,816 feet.

B– 8,286 feet.

C– 8,649 feet.

5-51. Answer A. AF/D Legend.
The landing distance available (LDA) appears under Runway Declared Distance Information. For Rwy 32, it is 7,816 feet.

5-52   PLT078
(Refer to figure 53.)

Traffic patterns in effect at Lincoln Municipal are

A– to the right on Runway 17L and Runway 35L; to the left on Runway 17R and Runway 35R.

B– to the left on Runway 17L and Runway 35L; to the right on Runway 17R and Runway 35R.

C– to the right on Runways 14-32.

5-52. Answer B. GFDPP 5-38, A/FD
Remarks following the runway data for each runway include nonstandard traffic patterns. Left-hand patterns are used if not otherwise stated. Right-hand traffic is noted for Runway 17R and Runway 35R. Left traffic is used for Runways 17L, 35L, 14, and 32.

5-53   PLT116
FAA advisory circulars containing subject matter specifically related to Airmen are issued under which subject number?

A– 60.

B– 70.

C– 90.

5-53. Answer A. GFDPP 5-45, AC 00-2
Advisory circulars relating to Airmen are issued under subject number 60.

5-54   **PLT116**
FAA advisory circulars containing subject matter specifically related to Air Traffic Control and General Operations are issued under which subject number?

A– 60.

B– 70.

C– 90.

5-54. Answer C. GFDPP 5-45, AC 00-2
Advisory circulars relating to Air Traffic Control and General Operations are issued under subject number 90.

5-55   **PLT323**
What information is contained in the Notices to Airmen Publication (NTAP)?

A– Current NOTAM (D) and FDC NOTAMs.

B– All current NOTAMs.

C– Current Airport/Facility Directory information and FDC NOTAMs.

5-55. Answer A. GFDPP 5-47, AIM
The Notices to Airmen Publication (NTAP) contains all current NOTAM(D)s and FDC NOTAMs (except FDC NOTAMs for temporary flight restrictions) available for publication.

CHAPTER 6

METEOROLOGY FOR PILOTS

SECTION A — BASIC WEATHER THEORY

Weather touches every aspect of flight. As pilots we are inextricably linked to the weather. In this section, we'll look at the basic framework of weather theory and its significance to flight operations. Subject areas include the atmosphere, circulation/pressure, temperature and moisture. In addition to the *Private Pilot Manual*, you may wish to consult Jeppesen's *Aviation Weather*.

ATMOSPHERIC CIRCULATION

Atmospheric circulation refers to the movement of air relative to the earth's surface.

TEMPERATURE

Every physical process of weather is accompanied by, or is the result of, a heat exchange.

ATMOSPHERIC PRESSURE

Unequal heating of the Earth's surface causes variations in altimeter settings between weather reporting points.

FRICTIONAL FORCE

Below 2000 feet AGL, friction with the Earth's surface deflects the wind, making the winds at the surface generally different from the winds aloft.

LOCAL WIND PATTERNS

Convective circulation patterns associated with sea breezes are caused by cool, dense air moving inland from over the water.

6-1   PLT512
What causes variations in altimeter settings between weather reporting points?

A– Unequal heating of the Earth's surface.

B– Variation of terrain elevation.

C– Coriolis force.

6-1. Answer A. GFDPP 6-7, AW
Temperature changes cause variations in air pressure and density. Because the earth's surface is heated unevenly, altimeter settings will be different between weather stations.

6-2   PLT516

The wind at 5,000 feet AGL is southwesterly while the surface wind is southerly. This difference in direction is primarily due to

A– stronger pressure gradient at higher altitudes.

B– friction between the wind and the surface.

C– stronger Coriolis force at the surface.

6-2. Answer B. GFDPP 6-9, AW
Above 2,000 feet AGL, wind flows along isobars. Below that altitude, friction with the earth's surface deflects the wind.

6-3   PLT494

Convective circulation patterns associated with sea breezes are caused by

A– warm, dense air moving inland from over the water.

B– water absorbing and radiating heat faster than the land.

C– cool, dense air moving inland from over the water.

6-3. Answer C. GFDPP 6-11, AW
During the day, land surfaces become warmer than the adjacent water surfaces. This warms the air above the land causing the air to rise. The rising air is replaced by the inland flow of cooler, denser air located over the water. As the warm air flows over the water it cools and descends. This starts the cycle all over again. During the night, the process is reversed as the land cools off faster than the water.

SECTION B — WEATHER PATTERNS

Weather patterns clue you into trends that directly affect your flying. Grasping the movement of weather patterns will aid you greatly during all of your flights. This section covers atmospheric stability, cloud types, air masses, and fronts.

ATMOSPHERIC STABILITY

- Stability of the air can be measured by its actual lapse rate.
- A characteristic of stable air is the presence of stratiform clouds.
- When moist, stable air flows upslope, you can expect the formation of stratus type clouds.
- Characteristics of unstable air include turbulence and good surface visibility.

TEMPERATURE INVERSIONS

- A temperature inversion most often denotes an increase in temperature as altitude is increased.
- The most frequent type of ground or surface-based temperature inversion is that which is produced by terrestrial radiation on a clear, relatively still night.
- The weather conditions that can be expected beneath a low-level temperature inversion layer when the relative humidity is high are smooth air, poor visibility, fog, haze or low clouds.
- A temperature inversion is associated with a stable layer of air.

MOISTURE

The processes by which moisture is added to unsaturated air are evaporation and sublimation.

DEWPOINT

- The dewpoint is the temperature to which the air must be cooled in order to become saturated.
- The amount of water vapor which air can hold depends on the air temperature.

FROST

- If the temperature of the collecting surface is at or below the dewpoint of the adjacent air, and the dewpoint is below freezing, frost will form.
- Frost on the wings affects takeoff performance by disrupting the smooth flow of air over the airfoil, adversely affecting its lifting capacity. Frost may prevent the airplane from becoming airborne at normal takeoff speed. Frost is considered a hazard to flight for this reason.

CLOUDS

- Cloud bases can be estimated by using a lapse rate of 4.5 degrees per 1000 feet and the temperature/dewpoint spread. Divide the temperature/dewpoint spread by the lapse rate to find the height of the cloud bases above the surface, in thousands of feet.
- Clouds, fog or dew will always form when water vapor condenses.

TYPES

Clouds are divided into four families according to their height range. These are low clouds, middle clouds, high clouds, and clouds with vertical development.

NIMBUS

The suffix "nimbus," used in naming clouds, denotes a rain cloud.

STRATUS

Stratus clouds form when moist, stable air flows upslope.

FOG

- If the temperature/dewpoint spread is small and decreasing, and the temperature is above freezing, fog or low clouds are likely to develop.
- Radiation fog forms as warm, moist air lies over flatland areas on clear, calm nights.
- Advection fog forms when a warm air mass moves inland from the coast in winter.
- Advection fog and upslope fog depend upon wind in order to exist.
- Low-level turbulence can occur, and icing can become hazardous in steam fog.

CLOUDS WITH VERTICAL DEVELOPMENT

Clouds with extensive vertical development and associated turbulence can be expected when an unstable airmass is forced upward.

PRECIPITATION

Precipitation can range from light rain that is easy to fly through, to freezing rain that poses a serious hazard to all types of aircraft, even those with de-ice and anti-ice equipment.

TYPES

The presence of ice pellets at the surface is evidence that there is a temperature inversion with freezing rain at a higher altitude.

AIRMASSES

Airmasses are large-scale parcels of air that have a set of characteristics (i.e. moist, unstable) that distinguishes them from one another.

CLASSIFICATIONS

- Characteristics of a moist, unstable airmass are cumuliform clouds and showery precipitation.
- A stable airmass generally contains smooth air.

FRONTS

The boundary between two different airmasses is referred to as a front.

FRONTAL DISCONTINUITIES

- One of the most easily recognizable discontinuities across a front is a change in temperature.
- One weather phenomenon which will always occur when flying across a front is a change in the wind direction.

FRONTAL WEATHER

Steady precipitation preceding a front is an indication of stratiform clouds with little or no turbulence.

6-4   PLT134
How will frost on the wings of an airplane affect takeoff performance?

A– Frost will disrupt the smooth flow of air over the wing, adversely affecting its lifting capability.

B– Frost will change the camber of the wing, increasing its lifting capability.

C– Frost will cause the airplane to become airborne with a higher angle of attack, decreasing the stall speed.

6-4. Answer A. GFDPP 6-20, PHB
Frost disrupts the smooth airflow over the wing and can cause early separation of the airflow, resulting in a loss of lift.

6-5   PLT512
Every physical process of weather is accompanied by, or is the result of, a

A– movement of air.

B– pressure differential.

C– heat exchange.

6-5. Answer C. GFDPP 6-19, AW
Every physical process of weather such as heating, cooling, evaporation, and condensation, is caused by, or is the result of, a heat exchange.

6-6   PLT512
A temperature inversion would most likely result in which weather condition?

A– Clouds with extensive vertical development above an inversion aloft.

B– Good visibility in the lower levels of the atmosphere and poor visibility above an inversion aloft.

C– An increase in temperature as altitude is increased.

6-6. Answer C. GFDPP 6-17, AW
Normally, temperature decreases with altitude. During an inversion, cooler air is trapped beneath a warmer layer of air. Therefore, temperature increases with altitude.

6-7   PLT512
The most frequent type of ground or surface-based temperature inversion is that which is produced by

A– terrestrial radiation on a clear, relatively still night.

B– warm air being lifted rapidly aloft in the vicinity of mountainous terrain.

C– the movement of colder air under warm air, or the movement of warm air over cold air.

6-7. Answer A. GFDPP 6-18, AW
An inversion commonly forms on clear, cool nights when the ground radiates heat and cools faster than the overlying air.

6-8   PLT512
Which weather conditions should be expected beneath a low-level temperature inversion layer when the relative humidity is high?

A— Smooth air, poor visibility, fog, haze, or low clouds.

B— Light wind shear, poor visibility, haze, and light rain.

C— Turbulent air, poor visibility, fog, low stratus type clouds, and showery precipitation.

6-8. Answer A. GFDPP 6-17, AW
Low-level temperature inversions normally occur in stable, smooth air, with poor visibility due to trapped pollutants which are commonly referred to as condensation nuclei. In addition, high humidity tends to cause formation of fog and low clouds.

6-9   PLT512
What is meant by the term "dewpoint"?

A— The temperature at which condensation and evaporation are equal.

B— The temperature at which dew will always form.

C— The temperature to which air must be cooled to become saturated.

6-9. Answer C. GFDPP 6-20, AW
When air is cooled to its dewpoint, it can hold no more moisture, and is said to be saturated.

6-10   PLT512
The amount of water vapor which air can hold depends on the

A— dewpoint.

B— air temperature.

C— stability of the air.

6-10. Answer B. GFDPP 6-19, AW
The amount of moisture in the air primarily depends on the temperature. For example, warm air can hold more moisture than cool air.

6-11   PLT512
Clouds, fog, or dew will always form when

A— water vapor condenses.

B— water vapor is present.

C— relative humidity reaches 100 percent.

6-11. Answer A. GFDPP 6-22, AW
Condensation occurs when water vapor changes to liquid form. Examples are when water vapor changes to clouds, fog, or dew.

6-12   PLT512
What are the processes by which moisture is added to unsaturated air?

A— Evaporation and sublimation.

B— Heating and condensation.

C— Supersaturation and evaporation.

6-12. Answer A. GFDPP 6-19, AW
Evaporation occurs when liquid water changes to water vapor. Sublimation is the changing of ice directly to water vapor. Both processes add moisture to the air.

6-13   PLT512
Which conditions result in the formation of frost?

A– The temperature of the collecting surface is at or below freezing when small droplets of moisture fall on the surface.

B– The temperature of the collecting surface is at or below the dewpoint of the adjacent air and the dewpoint is below freezing.

C– The temperature of the surrounding air is at or below freezing when small drops of moisture fall on the collecting surface.

6-13. Answer B. GFDPP 6-20, AW
When the dewpoint of the surrounding air is below freezing, and the collecting surface is at or below the dewpoint, water vapor sublimates directly into ice crystals or frost instead of condensing into dew.

6-14   PLT512
The presence of ice pellets at the surface is evidence that there

A– are thunderstorms in the area.

B– has been cold frontal passage.

C– is a temperature inversion with freezing rain at a higher altitude.

6-14. Answer C. GFDPP 6-27, AW
Due to a temperature inversion, a warm layer of air is aloft and keeps the rain in liquid form. As the rain falls through colder air, it begins to freeze, finally turning into ice pellets. Ice pellets always indicate freezing rain at a higher altitude. Ice pellets can form under various conditions, and do not necessarily indicate thunderstorms.

6-15   PLT512
What measurement can be used to determine the stability of the atmosphere?

A– Atmospheric pressure.

B– Actual lapse rate.

C– Surface temperature.

6-15. Answer B. GFDPP 6-17, AW
The stability of air refers to its resistance to displacement upward or downward; it is determined by the actual lapse rate. Lapse rate generally refers to the decrease in temperature with an increase in altitude. A high lapse rate tends to indicate unstable air, and a low lapse rate is an indicator of stability in the atmosphere.

6-16   PLT512
What would decrease the stability of an air mass?

A– Warming from below.

B– Cooling from below.

C– Decrease in water vapor.

6-16. Answer A. GFDPP 6-16, AW
Stability is altered by a change in the lapse rate of an air mass. Warming from below or cooling from above will increase the lapse rate and make the air less stable.

6-17   PLT512
What is a characteristic of stable air?

A– Stratiform clouds.

B– Unlimited visibility.

C– Cumulus clouds.

6-17. Answer A. GFDPP 6-23, AW
There is very little vertical development of clouds in stable air, and stratiform clouds and poor visibility are typical. Cumulus clouds and good visibility are indicators of unstable air.

6-18   PLT512
Moist, stable air flowing upslope can be expected to

A– produce stratus type clouds.

B– cause showers and thunderstorms.

C– develop convective turbulence.

6-19   PLT512
If an unstable air mass is forced upward, what type clouds can be expected?

A– Stratus clouds with little vertical development.

B– Stratus clouds with considerable associated turbulence.

C– Clouds with considerable vertical development and associated turbulence.

6-20   PLT512
What feature is associated with a temperature inversion?

A– A stable layer of air.

B– An unstable layer of air.

C– Chinook winds on mountain slopes.

6-21   PLT512
What is the approximate base of the cumulus clouds if the surface air temperature at 1,000 feet MSL is 70°F and the dewpoint is 48°F?

A– 4,000 feet MSL.

B– 5,000 feet MSL.

C– 6,000 feet MSL.

6-22   PLT512
At approximately what altitude above the surface would the pilot expect the base of cumuliform clouds if the surface air temperature is 82°F and the dewpoint is 38°F?

A– 9,000 feet AGL.

B– 10,000 feet AGL.

C– 11,000 feet AGL.

6-18. Answer A. GFDPP 6-23, AW
Stratus clouds are produced in stable air. When moist air flows upslope it cools to its saturation point, and clouds are formed.

6-19. Answer C. GFDPP 6-25, AW
Clouds with extensive vertical development are formed when unstable air is lifted. These cumulus type clouds are associated with moderate to severe turbulence.

6-20. Answer A. GFDPP 6-17, AW
Temperature inversions occur in stable air. Inversions cannot form in unstable air. As Chinook winds descend, the temperature rises. This is the opposite of an inversion (cooler air under a warmer layer). In the U.S., the typical example of Chinook winds is the downslope, easterly flow from the Rocky Mountains.

6-21. Answer C. GFDPP 6-20, AW
Cloud bases can be estimated by using a lapse rate of 4.5°F per 1,000 feet and the temperature/dewpoint spread (70 − 48 = 22). Divide 22 by 4.5 to find the approximate cloud base in thousands of feet. In this case, the cloud bases will be 4,889 (22 ÷ 4.5 × 1,000) feet above the surface, or rounded to 5,000 feet. Since the surface is 1,000 feet MSL, the cloud base should be approximately 6,000 feet MSL.

6-22. Answer B. GFDPP 6-20, AW
Cloud bases can be estimated by using a lapse rate of 4.5°F per 1,000 feet and the temperature/dewpoint spread.

6-23 **PLT512**
What are characteristics of a moist, unstable air mass?

A– Cumuliform clouds and showery precipitation.

B– Poor visibility and smooth air.

C– Stratiform clouds and showery precipitation.

6-23. Answer A. GFDPP 6-29, AW
Cumuliform clouds are indicative of unstable air. These clouds normally produce showery, not continuous, precipitation. Poor visibility, smooth air, and stratiform clouds are characteristic of stable air.

6-24 **PLT512**
What are characteristics of unstable air?

A– Turbulence and good surface visibility.

B– Turbulence and poor surface visibility.

C– Nimbostratus clouds and good surface visibility.

6-24. Answer A. GFDPP 6-29, AW
The lifting motion of unstable air produces turbulence. Clouds and pollutants are not trapped as they are in stable layers of air, and good visibility is typical with unstable air. Poor surface visibility and nimbostratus clouds are typical of stable air masses.

6-25 **PLT511**
A stable air mass is most likely to have which characteristic?

A– Showery precipitation.

B– Turbulent air.

C– Smooth air.

6-25. Answer C. GFDPP 6-29, AW
Stable air resists the lifting motion that is associated with turbulence, and is typically smooth. Showery precipitation and turbulent air are characteristics of unstable air.

6-26 **PLT192**
The suffix "nimbus," used in naming clouds, means

A– a cloud with extensive vertical development.

B– a rain cloud.

C– a middle cloud containing ice pellets.

6-26. Answer B. GFDPP 6-22, AW
The word "nimbus" is the Latin word for rainstorm or cloud, and is used today to designate rain clouds, such as cumulonimbus or nimbostratus.

6-27 **PLT192**
Clouds are divided into four families according to their

A– outward shape.

B– height range.

C– composition.

6-27. Answer B. GFDPP 6-22, AW
Clouds are also grouped by families according to their altitudes (height range). The four families are low, middle, high, and clouds with extensive vertical development.

6-28 **PLT511**
The boundary between two different air masses is referred to as a

A– frontolysis.

B– frontogenesis.

C– front.

6-28. Answer C. GFDPP 6-30, AW
The boundary area where two air masses of different properties meet is called a front.

6-29   PLT511
One of the most easily recognized discontinuities across a front is

A– a change in temperature.

B– an increase in cloud coverage.

C– an increase in relative humidity.

6-29. Answer A. GFDPP 6-31, AW
Since a front is the boundary between air masses of differing temperatures, one of the easiest ways to recognize frontal passage is the change in temperature.

6-30   PLT511
One weather phenomenon which will always occur when flying across a front is a change in the

A– wind direction.

B– type of precipitation.

C– stability of the air mass.

6-30. Answer A. GFDPP 6-31, AW
A shift in wind direction always occurs across a front.

6-31   PLT511
Steady precipitation preceding a front is an indication of

A– stratiform clouds with moderate turbulence.

B– cumuliform clouds with little or no turbulence.

C– stratiform clouds with little or no turbulence.

6-31. Answer C. GFDPP 6-23, 32, AW
Steady precipitation, stratiform clouds, and little or no turbulence are all typical of stable air.

6-32   PLT226
What situation is most conducive to the formation of radiation fog?

A– Warm, moist air over low, flatland areas on clear, calm nights.

B– Moist, tropical air moving over cold, offshore water.

C– The movement of cold air over much warmer water.

6-32. Answer A. GFDPP 6-23, AW
On clear, calm nights in flat areas, radiation fog forms when moist air cools to its dewpoint. Ground fog is a form of radiation fog.

6-33   PLT226
If the temperature/dewpoint spread is small and decreasing, and the temperature is 62°F, what type weather is most likely to develop?

A– Freezing precipitation.

B– Thunderstorms.

C– Fog or low clouds.

6-33. Answer C. GFDPP 6-22, AW
When the temperature/dewpoint spread decreases to zero, the likely result is the condensation of water vapor into visible moisture, such as fog or low clouds.

6-34   PLT226

In which situation is advection fog most likely to form?

A– A warm, moist air mass on the windward side of mountains.

B– An air mass moving inland from the coast in winter.

C– A light breeze blowing colder air out to sea.

6-34. Answer B. GFDPP 6-23, AW

On clear, calm nights in flat areas, radiation fog forms when moist air cools to its dewpoint. Ground fog is a form of radiation fog.

When warmer air moves inland, advection fog is likely to form.

6-35   PLT226

What types of fog depend upon wind in order to exist?

A– Radiation fog and ice fog.

B– Steam fog and ground fog.

C– Advection fog and upslope fog.

6-35. Answer C. GFDPP 6-23, AW

On clear, calm nights in flat areas, radiation fog forms when moist air cools to its dewpoint. Ground fog is a form of radiation fog.

When warmer air moves inland, advection fog is likely to form.

6-36   PLT226

Low-level turbulence can occur and icing can become hazardous in which type of fog?

A– Rain-induced fog.

B– Upslope fog.

C– Steam fog.

6-36. Answer C. GFDPP 6-23, AW

Steam fog is formed by cold, dry air moving over warmer water. As the water particles evaporate and rise, they often freeze and fall back into the water. Icing and low-level turbulence can result

SECTION C — WEATHER HAZARDS

As a pilot, you can combine knowledge of the weather with respect for what it can do to avoid flying in the most hazardous conditions. This section covers such hazards as thunderstorms, turbulence, icing and restrictions to visibility, addressing cause, as well as hazardous effects.

THUNDERSTORMS

- Cumulonimbus clouds have the greatest turbulence.
- The conditions necessary for the formation of cumulonimbus clouds are a lifting action and unstable, moist air.
- Thunderstorms are formed when high humidity, lifting force and unstable conditions combine.

TYPES

- Thunderstorms which generally produce the most intense hazard to aircraft are squall line thunderstorms.
- A non-frontal, narrow band of active thunderstorms that often develops ahead of a cold front is known as a squall line.

LIFE CYCLE

- The cumulus stage of a thunderstorm is associated with a continuous updraft.
- The mature stage of a thunderstorm begins with precipitation beginning to fall.
- Thunderstorms reach their greatest intensity during the mature stage.
- The dissipating stage is characterized predominantly by downdrafts.

HAZARDS

- If there is thunderstorm activity in the vicinity of an airport at which you plan to land, you can expect to encounter wind-shear turbulence during the landing approach.
- Lightning is always associated with thunderstorms.

TURBULENCE

- Upon encountering severe turbulence, the pilot should attempt to maintain a level flight attitude.
- Towering cumulus clouds indicate convective turbulence.

WAKE TURBULENCE

- Wingtip vortices are created only when an aircraft is developing lift.
- The greatest vortex strength occurs when the generating aircraft is heavy, clean and slow.
- Wingtip vortices created by a large aircraft tend to sink below the aircraft that is generating the turbulence.
- When taking off or landing at an airport where heavy aircraft are operating, one should be particularly alert to the hazards of wingtip vortices because this turbulence tends to sink into the flight path of the aircraft operating below the aircraft generating the turbulence.
- The wind condition that requires maximum caution when avoiding wake turbulence on landing is a light, quartering tailwind.

MOUNTAIN WAVE TURBULENCE

- An almond or lens-shaped cloud which appears stationary, but which may contain winds of up to 50 knots or more, is referred to as a lenticular cloud.
- Crests of standing mountain waves may be marked by stationary, lens-shaped clouds known as standing lenticular clouds.
- Possible mountain wave turbulence could be anticipated when winds of 40 knots or greater blow across a mountain ridge, when the air is stable.

WIND SHEAR

- Wind shear can occur at all altitudes, in all directions.
- Hazardous wind shear may be expected in areas of low-level temperature inversion, frontal zones and clear air turbulence.
- A pilot can expect a wind shear zone in a temperature inversion whenever the wind speed at 2000 to 4000 feet above the surface is at least 25 knots.

ICING

- Visible moisture is necessary for the formation of in-flight structural icing.
- Areas of freezing rain create the environment in which structural icing is most likely to have the highest accumulation rate.

6-37   PLT192
An almond or lens-shaped cloud which appears stationary, but which may contain winds of 50 knots or more, is referred to as

A— an inactive frontal cloud.

B— a funnel cloud.

C— a lenticular cloud.

6-37. Answer C. GFDPP 6-50, AW
Lenticular clouds are the lens-shaped clouds that form at the crests of mountain waves.

6-38   PLT192
Crests of standing mountain waves may be marked by stationary, lens-shaped clouds known as

A— mammatocumulus clouds.

B— standing lenticular clouds.

C— roll clouds.

6-38. Answer B. GFDPP 6-50, AW
Lenticular clouds are the lens-shaped clouds that form at the crests of mountain waves.

6-39   PLT192
What clouds have the greatest turbulence?

A— Towering cumulus.

B— Cumulonimbus.

C— Nimbostratus.

6-39. Answer B. GFDPP 6-42, AW
Cumulonimbus clouds, which form thunderstorms and tornadoes, produce the most severe turbulence.

6-40   PLT192
What cloud types would indicate convective turbulence?

A— Cirrus clouds.

B— Nimbostratus clouds.

C— Towering cumulus clouds.

6-40. Answer C. GFDPP 6-45, AW
Towering cumulus clouds are formed by convective currents, caused by rising heated air. These rising air currents cause convective turbulence.

6-41   PLT518
Possible mountain wave turbulence could be anticipated when winds of 40 knots or greater blow

A– across a mountain ridge, and the air is stable.

B– down a mountain valley, and the air is unstable.

C– parallel to a mountain peak, and the air is stable.

6-41. Answer A. GFDPP 6-50, AW
Mountain waves are formed when strong winds (40 knots or greater) flow across a barrier, such as a mountain ridge. When the air is stable, the flow is laminar, or layered, and creates a series of waves. Unstable air that is forced upward tends to continue rising, often creating thunderstorms.

6-42   PLT518
Where does wind shear occur?

A– Only at higher altitudes.

B– Only at lower altitudes.

C– At all altitudes, in all directions.

6-42. Answer C. GFDPP 6-51, AW
Wind shear can occur at middle and high altitudes near thunderstorms or the jet stream, and near the ground in the vicinity of thunderstorms or temperature inversions. The shear can be either vertical or horizontal.

6-43   PLT518
When may hazardous wind shear be expected?

A– When stable air crosses a mountain barrier where it tends to flow in layers forming lenticular clouds.

B– In areas of low-level temperature inversion, frontal zones, and clear air turbulence.

C– Following frontal passage when stratocumulus clouds form indicating mechanical mixing.

6-43. Answer B. GFDPP 6-50, 51, AW
Wind shear can be found above a temperature inversion when the surface air is cold and calm, and the warmer layer above it is moving at 25 knots or more. Since frontal zones are identified by a shift in the wind, wind shear can be expected. Clear air turbulence can be associated with either vertical or horizontal wind shear.

6-44   PLT518
A pilot can expect a wind-shear zone in a temperature inversion whenever the windspeed at 2,000 to 4,000 feet above the surface is at least

A– 10 knots.

B– 15 knots.

C– 25 knots.

6-44. Answer C. GFDPP 6-51, AW
A temperature inversion with light surface winds may form near the surface on a clear night. You can expect a shear zone in the inversion if the winds at 2,000 to 4,000 feet are 25 knots or more.

6-45   PLT274
One in-flight condition necessary for structural icing to form is

A– small temperature/dewpoint spread.

B– stratiform clouds.

C– visible moisture.

6-45. Answer C. GFDPP 6-53, AW
Structural icing requires two conditions to form: (1) visible moisture, such as rain or cloud droplets, and (2) temperature of the aircraft surface must be at or below freezing. A small temperature/dewpoint spread may be present without visible moisture. Stratiform clouds are not the only cloud types in which icing can occur.

6-46   PLT274

In which environment is aircraft structural ice most likely to have the highest accumulation rate?

A— Cumulus clouds with below freezing temperatures.

B— Freezing drizzle.

C— Freezing rain.

6-46. Answer C. GFDPP 6-53, AW

The rate of structural ice accumulation is usually the highest in freezing rain below a frontal surface. As the rain falls through air with temperatures below freezing it becomes supercooled. The supercooled drops freeze on impact with the large water droplets, and heavy rain accelerates the build up.

6-47   PLT274

Why is frost considered hazardous to flight?

A— Frost changes the basic aerodynamic shape of the airfoils, thereby decreasing lift.

B— Frost slows the airflow over the airfoils, thereby increasing control effectiveness.

C— Frost spoils the smooth flow of air over the wings, thereby decreasing lifting capability.

6-47. Answer C. GFDPP 6-20, AW

Frost disrupts the smooth airflow over the wing and can cause early separation of the airflow, resulting in a loss of lift.

6-48   PLT274

How does frost affect the lifting surfaces of an airplane on takeoff?

A— Frost may prevent the airplane from becoming air-borne at normal takeoff speed.

B— Frost will change the camber of the wing, increasing lift during takeoff.

C— Frost may cause the airplane to become airborne with a lower angle of attack at a lower indicated air-speed.

6-48. Answer A. GFDPP 6-20, AW

Frost disrupts the smooth airflow over the wing and can cause early separation of the airflow, resulting in a loss of lift.

By disrupting the airflow over the wings, frost can pre-vent an airplane from becoming airborne at the normal takeoff speed.

6-49   PLT192

The conditions necessary for the formation of cumulo-nimbus clouds are a lifting action and

A— unstable air containing an excess of condensation nuclei.

B— unstable, moist air.

C— either stable or unstable air.

6-49. Answer B. GFDPP 6-38,42, AW

Three conditions are normally required for the formation of cumulonimbus clouds. These are lifting action, insta-bility, and moisture.

6-50   PLT495

What feature is normally associated with the cumulus stage of a thunderstorm?

A— Roll cloud.

B— Continuous updraft.

C— Frequent lightning.

6-50. Answer B. GFDPP 6-40, AW

In the early, or cumulus, stage of a thunderstorm, con-tinuous updrafts cause the cloud to build upwards.

6-51   PLT495
Which weather phenomenon signals the beginning of the mature stage of a thunderstorm?

A– The appearance of an anvil top.

B– Precipitation beginning to fall.

C– Maximum growth rate of the clouds.

6-51. Answer B. GFDPP 6-41, AW
The mature stage of a thunderstorm begins when the rain drops grow too large to be supported by the updrafts, and precipitation begins to fall.

6-52   PLT271
The destination airport has one runway, 08-26, and the wind is calm. The normal approach in calm wind is a left hand pattern to runway 08. There is no other traffic at the airport. A thunderstorm about 6 miles west is beginning its mature stage, and rain is starting to reach the ground. The pilot decides to

A– fly the pattern to runway 08 since the storm is too far away to affect the wind at the airport.

B– fly the normal pattern to runway 08 since the storm is west and moving north and any unexpected wind will be from the east or southeast toward the storm.

C– fly an approach to runway 26 since any unexpected wind due to the storm will be westerly.

6-52. Answer C. GFDPP 6C, AW
The outflow from a mature thunderstorm west of the airport could create significant winds from the west. If landing on Runway 08, the aircraft could experience a dangerous sheer to a tailwind. Landing to the west, on Runway 26, is the best choice. In addition, a Runway 26 traffic pattern is on the east side of the airport, farther away from the storm.

6-53   PLT495
What conditions are necessary for the formation of thunderstorms?

A– High humidity, lifting force, and unstable conditions.

B– High humidity, high temperature, and cumulus clouds.

C– Lifting force, moist air, and extensive cloud cover.

6-53. Answer A. GFDPP 6-38, AW
Three conditions are normally required for the formation of cumulonimbus clouds. These are lifting action, instability, and moisture.

As moist, unstable air is lifted, it builds cumulonimbus clouds, which form thunderstorms.

6-54   PLT495
During the life cycle of a thunderstorm, which stage is characterized predominately by downdrafts?

A– Cumulus.

B– Dissipating.

C– Mature.

6-54. Answer B. GFDPP 6-41, AW
As moist, unstable air is lifted, it builds cumulonimbus clouds, which form thunderstorms.

The mature stage of a thunderstorm begins when the rain drops grow too large to be supported by the updrafts, and precipitation begins to fall.

As a thunderstorm dissipates, updrafts weaken and downdrafts become predominate.

6-55   PLT495
Thunderstorms reach their greatest intensity during the

A– mature stage.

B– downdraft stage.

C– cumulus stage.

6-55. Answer A. GFDPP 6-41, AW
Thunderstorms are most violent during the mature stage, with strong updrafts and downdrafts, severe turbulence, lightning, heavy rain, hail, strong surface winds, and gust fronts.

6-56   PLT495
Thunderstorms which generally produce the most intense hazard to aircraft are

A– squall line thunderstorms.

B– steady-state thunderstorms.

C– warm front thunderstorms.

6-56. Answer A. GFDPP 6-39, AW
Squall lines often contain severe steady-state thunderstorms and present the most hazardous conditions to aircraft.

6-57   PLT495
A nonfrontal, narrow band of active thunderstorms that often develop ahead of a cold front is known as a

A– prefrontal system.

B– squall line.

C– dry line.

6-57. Answer B. GFDPP 6-39, AW
Squall lines are a narrow band of thunderstorms that often develop ahead of a cold front.

6-58   PLT495
If there is thunderstorm activity in the vicinity of an airport at which you plan to land, which hazardous atmospheric phenomenon might be expected on the landing approach?

A– Precipitation static.

B– Wind-shear turbulence.

C– Steady rain.

6-58. Answer B. GFDPP 6-50, AW
In the vicinity of thunderstorms, hazardous wind-shear turbulence should always be expected.

6-59   PLT501
Upon encountering severe turbulence, which flight condition should the pilot attempt to maintain?

A– Constant altitude and airspeed.

B– Constant angle of attack.

C– Level flight attitude.

6-59. Answer C. GFDPP 6-44, AW
If entering severe turbulence, the best procedure is to slow to a speed not faster than maneuvering airspeed and maintain a constant level flight attitude. Variations in airspeed and altitude should be expected and tolerated.

6-60   PLT495
Which weather phenomenon is always associated with a thunderstorm?

A– Lightning.

B– Heavy rain.

C– Hail.

6-60. Answer A. GFDPP 6-43, AW
Because thunder is caused by lightning, the name thunderstorm implies that lightning is always associated with a thunderstorms.

6-61   PLT509
Wingtip vortices are created only when an aircraft is

A– operating at high airspeeds.

B– heavily loaded.

C– developing lift.

6-61. Answer C. GFDPP 6-47, PHB
Any time an aircraft is developing lift, air flows over the wingtip to form wingtip vortices.

6-62   PLT509
The greatest vortex strength occurs when the generating aircraft is

A– light, dirty, and fast.

B– heavy, dirty, and fast.

C– heavy, clean, and slow.

6-62. Answer C. GFDPP 6-47, PHB
Heavy aircraft, in a clean configuration, flying at low airspeeds with high angles of attack, generate the strongest vortices.

6-63   PLT509
Wingtip vortices created by large aircraft tend to

A– sink below the aircraft generating turbulence.

B– rise into the traffic pattern.

C– rise into the takeoff or landing path of a crossing runway.

6-63. Answer A. GFDPP 6-47, PHB
Wingtip vortices tend to sink below the flight path of the aircraft which generated them.

6-64   PLT509
When taking off or landing at an airport where heavy aircraft are operating, one should be particularly alert to the hazards of wingtip vortices because this turbulence tends to

A— rise from a crossing runway into the takeoff or landing path.

B— rise into the traffic pattern area surrounding the airport.

C— sink into the flight path of aircraft operating below the aircraft generating the turbulence.

6-64. Answer C. GFDPP 6-47, PHB
Wingtip vortices tend to sink below the flight path of the aircraft which generated them.

6-65   PLT509
The wind condition that requires maximum caution when avoiding wake turbulence on landing is a

A— light, quartering headwind.

B— light, quartering tailwind.

C— strong headwind.

6-65. Answer B. GFDPP 6-47, PHB
A light, quartering tailwind is the most hazardous because it can move the upwind vortex over the runway and forward into the landing zone.

6-66   PLT509
When landing behind a large aircraft, the pilot should avoid wake turbulence by staying

A— above the large aircraft's final approach path and landing beyond the large aircraft's touchdown point.

B— below the large aircraft's final approach path and landing before the large aircraft's touchdown point.

C— above the large aircraft's final approach path and landing before the large aircraft's touchdown point.

6-66. Answer A. GFDPP 6-47, PHB
Because wake turbulence tends to sink, an aircraft that is a large aircraft should stay above the large aircraft's flight path and land beyond its touchdown point.

6-67   PLT509
When departing behind a heavy aircraft, the pilot should avoid wake turbulence by maneuvering the aircraft

A– below and downwind from the heavy aircraft.

B– above and upwind from the heavy aircraft.

C– below and upwind from the heavy aircraft.

6-67. Answer B. GFDPP 6-47, PHB
Because wake turbulence tends to sink and drift downwind, an aircraft should stay above and upwind of the preceding aircraft.

6-68   PLT509
When landing behind a large aircraft, which procedure should be followed for vortex avoidance?

A– Stay above its final approach flight path all the way to touchdown.

B– Stay below and to one side of its final approach flight path.

C– Stay well below its final approach flight path and land at least 2,000 feet behind.

6-68. Answer A. GFDPP 6-47
Vortices (wake turbulence) are generated at an airplane's wingtips whenever the wings are producing lift. Wingtip vortices tend to sink below the flight path of the generating airplane. Therefore, remaining above the glide path and landing beyond the touchdown point of a large airplane is a recommended practice to avoid wake turbulence.

6-69   PLT509
How does the wake turbulence vortex circulate around each wingtip?

A– Inward, upward, and around each tip.

B– Inward, upward, and counterclockwise.

C– Outward, upward, and around each tip.

6-69. Answer C. GFDPP 6-47, PHB
Wake turbulence vortices are a by-product of lift. They move outward, upward and around each wingtip.

CHAPTER 7

INTERPRETING WEATHER DATA

SECTION A — THE FORECASTING PROCESS

Pilots depend on reliable weather predictions. These are generated through a complex process involving both observers and intricate computer programs. Covered in this section are forecasting methods and the accuracy and limitations of those methods. Although no FAA questions on the knowledge exam pertain to this section, this information is critical to your general knowledge as a safe pilot.

SECTION B — PRINTED REPORTS AND FORECASTS

By learning to interpret printed weather reports and forecasts, you will add much to your ability to picture the weather patterns that affect your flying.

PRINTED WEATHER REPORTS

Printed weather reports give information that reflects actual conditions.

METARS

- Winds on an aviation routine weather report are referenced to true north.
- Peak gusts on an aviation routine weather report are denoted by a number following a "G" after the wind direction and base speed.
- Cloud heights or visibility into an obscuration are reported with three digits in hundreds of feet. Visibility is reported in statute miles and is indicated by the abbreviation "SM."
- For aviation purposes, ceiling is defined as the height above the Earth's surface of the lowest broken or overcast layer or vertical visibility into an obscuration.
- The definition of VFR is a visibility of at least 3 miles and a ceiling of at least 1,000 feet.
- The remarks section of a METAR is used to report weather considered significant to aircraft operations. The contraction "RMK" precedes the remarks.

PIREPS

- In a PIREP, identified by the letters "UA," sky condition is designated by the letters "SK," followed by the base and top of each cloud layer.
- The wind direction and velocity in a PIREP are shown as "WV" and the direction and speed, with the last digit of the wind direction dropped.
- The ceiling is the lowest layer reported as broken, overcast, or obscured.
- Turbulence is reported in a PIREP as "TB" followed by an intensity designation, such as "SVR," "MDT," or "LGT." The altitude of the turbulence layer is also reported.
- Icing is reported in a PIREP after the letters "IC." This is followed by the intensity of the icing, and the altitude of the layers in which it was encountered.

PRINTED WEATHER FORECASTS

Printed weather forecasts are a useful tool in planning ahead for a flight and predicting potential weather at your destination.

TAFS

- TAFs are usually valid for a 24-hour period and are scheduled four times a day (0000Z, 0600Z, 1200Z and 1800Z). The six-digit issuance date/time group is followed by the valid date/time group.
- In a TAF, the abbreviation "SHRA" stands for rain showers.
- A gradual change in the weather is prefaced by the abbreviation "BECMG" and the Zulu time during which the weather is forecast to change- i.e. "BECMG 1012" would mean that the weather change is expected to happen between 1000Z and 1200Z. The time frame is followed by the change expected, such as "3 SM" would mean the visibility is forecast to change to 3 statute miles.
- When rapid changes in the forecast are expected (usually within one hour), the code "FM" is used. When the abbreviation "VRB" appears before the wind speed, the wind is expected to be variable at that speed.
- A change group is used when a significant, lasting change to the weather conditions is forecast during the valid time.
- Wind blocks read as follows: wind direction comes first, followed by speed, and then any gust factor expected. Ceilings are given by the amount of coverage, followed by the cloud base height, in hundreds of feet.

- The code "NSW" means that no significant weather change is forecast to occur.
- Cumulonimbus clouds are the only cloud type included in the TAFs.

AVIATION AREA FORECASTS (FAs)

- Area forecasts cover the expected general weather conditions over several states. They are useful in determining the forecast weather at airports without a dedicated terminal forecast.
- The outlook for a specific period of time is marked by the abbreviation "OTLK" followed by the date and Zulu time. For example, the block "042300-050500" stands for the period between 2300Z on the 4th day of the month, to 0500Z on the 5th day of the month.
- To determine the freezing level and area of probable icing aloft, refer to Inflight Aviation Weather Advisories. Area forecasts alone do not contain freezing levels and areas of probable icing, however, they are supplemented by Airmets and Sigmets (Inflight Aviation Weather Advisories) which do contain freezing levels and areas of probable icing.
- The section of the area forecast titled "SIG CLDS AND WX" contains a summary of cloudiness and weather significant to flight operations broken down by states or other geographical areas. Obstructions to vision, such as IFR conditions and fog, are included in this section.
- The HAZARDS section lists hazards to aviation, such as turbulence and icing, for selected areas.

WINDS AND TEMPERATURES ALOFT FORECASTS (FDs)

- The first two digits represent the wind direction in relation to true north. The next two digits are the speed. Temperatures follow the wind block. Note that temperatures are assumed negative above 24,000 feet.
- Winds of 100 to 199 knots have 50 added to the direction. For example, when there is a wind direction above 360, subtract 50 to get a reasonable wind direction, and add 100 to the listed wind speed.
- When the term "light and variable" is used in reference to a winds aloft forecast, the coded group and wind speed is 9900 and less than 5 knots.

SEVERE WEATHER REPORTS AND FORECASTS

Severe weather reports and forecasts alert pilots to hazardous flight conditions, both potential and actual.

AIRMETS

AIRMETs are issued as a warning of weather conditions particularly hazardous to small, single-engine aircraft.

SIGMETS

- SIGMETs are issued as a warning of weather conditions hazardous to all aircraft.
- A SIGMET would contain information on severe icing, since it is a hazard to all aircraft.

CONVECTIVE SIGMETS

- Tornadoes, embedded thunderstorms, and hail 3/4 inch or greater in diameter are all weather phenomenon contained within a convective SIGMET.
- When a current convective SIGMET forecasts thunderstorms, those indicated are obscured by massive cloud layers.

7-1   PLT059
(Refer to figure 12.)
Which of the reporting stations have VFR weather?

A– All.

B– KINK, KBOI, and KJFK.

C– KINK, KBOI, and KLAX.

7-2   PLT026
For aviation purposes, ceiling is defined as the height above the Earth's surface of the

A– lowest reported obscuration and the highest layer of clouds reported as overcast.

B– lowest broken or overcast layer or vertical visibility into an obscuration.

C– lowest layer of clouds reported as scattered, broken, or thin.

7-3   PLT059
(Refer to figure 12.)
The wind direction and velocity at KJFK is from

A– 180° true at 4 knots.

B– 180° magnetic at 4 knots.

C– 040° true at 18 knots.

7-4   PLT059
(Refer to figure 12.)
What are the wind conditions at Wink, Texas (KINK)?

A– Calm.

B– 110° at 12 knots, peak gusts 18 knots.

C– 111° at 2 knots, peak gusts 18 knots.

7-5   PLT059
(Refer to figure 12.)
The remarks section for KMDW has RAB35 listed. This entry means

A– blowing mist has reduced the visibility to 1-1/2 SM.

B– rain began at 1835Z.

C– the barometer has risen .35 inches Hg.

7-1. Answer C. GFDPP 7-13, 15, AWS
To answer this question you must know that the definition of VFR is a visibility of at least 3 statute miles and ceiling of at least 1,000 feet. KINK has 15 miles visibility with clear skies, KBOI has 30 miles visibility with a scattered layer at 15,000 feet, and KLAX has 6 miles visibility, with scattered layers at 700 feet and 25,000 feet. Remember, a scattered layer does not consititute a ceiling.

7-2. Answer B. GFDPP 7-15, AWS
According to Aviation Weather Services, AC 00-45D, a ceiling is defined as the lowest broken or overcast layer, or vertical visibility into an obscuration.

7-3. Answer A. GFDPP 7-11, 12, AWS
The wind at KJFK is shown as 18004KT. This means the wind is from 180 degrees at 04 knots. Winds on an aviation routine weather report are referenced to true north.

7-4. Answer B. GFDPP 7-11, 12, AWS
The winds at KINK are shown as 11012G18KT. The direction is 110 degrees, and the velocity is 12 knots, with peak gusts of 18 knots.

7-5. Answer B. GFDPP 7-16, AWS
The remarks section of a METAR is used to report weather considered significant to aircraft operations. According to AC 00-45D, the contraction "RMK" precedes remarks. Included are the beginning and ending times of certain weather phenomena. In this case, "RA" is the abbreviation for rain and "B35" indicates the rain began at thirty-five minutes past the hour, or 1835Z.

7-6   PLT059
(Refer to figure 12.)

What are the current conditions depicted for Chicago Midway Airport (KMDW)?

A– Sky 700 feet overcast, visibility 1-1/2SM, rain.

B– Sky 7000 feet overcast, visibility 1-1/2SM, heavy rain.

C– Sky 700 feet overcast, visibility 11, occasionally 2SM, with rain.

7-6. Answer A. GFDPP 7-13, 14, 16, AWS
Cloud heights or the vertical visibility into an obscuration are reported with three digits in hundreds of feet. Visibility is reported in statute miles and is indicated by the abbreviation "SM." In this case, the METAR from KMDW indicates Midway has visibility of 1-1/2 miles and the sky is overcast at 700 feet. The "RA" indicates precipitation in the form of rain.

7-7   PLT061
(Refer to figure 14.)

The base and tops of the overcast layer reported by a pilot are

A– 1,800 feet MSL and 5,500 feet MSL.

B– 5,500 feet AGL and 7,200 feet MSL.

C– 7,200 feet MSL and 8,900 feet MSL.

7-7. Answer C. GFDPP 7-17, AWS
In the PIREP, which is identified by the letters, UA, sky cover is designated by the letters, SK, followed by the base and top of each cloud layer. The overcast layer is shown as OVC 072-TOP 089, which means the base is 7,200 feet and the tops are 8,900 feet. Altitudes are MSL unless otherwise noted.

7-8   PLT061
(Refer to figure 14.)

The wind and temperature at 12,000 feet MSL as reported by a pilot are

A– 080° at 21 knots and -7°C.

B– 090° at 21 MPH and -9°F.

C– 090° at 21 knots and -9°C.

7-8. Answer A. GFDPP 7-17, AWS
The ambient temperature and wind velocity appear in the part of the pilot report that says "/TA M7/WV 08021/". All temperatures aloft are given in degrees Celsius, and the "M" indicates temperatures below zero. Wind speed is reported in knots.

7-9   PLT061
(Refer to figure 14.)

If the terrain elevation is 1,295 feet MSL, what is the height above ground level of the base of the ceiling?

A– 505 feet AGL.

B– 1,295 feet AGL.

C– 6,586 feet AGL.

7-9. Answer A. GFDPP 7-17, AWS
The ceiling is the lowest cloud layer reported as broken, overcast, or obscured. In this case, the lowest layer is 1,800 feet broken (MSL). Subtract the ground elevation to find the AGL height (1,800 − 1,295 = 505 feet AGL).

7-10   PLT061
(Refer to figure 14.)

The intensity of the turbulence reported at a specific altitude is

A– moderate from 5,500 feet to 7,200 feet.

B– moderate at 5,500 feet and at 7,200 feet.

C– light from 5,500 feet to 7,200 feet.

7-10. Answer C. GFDPP 7-17, AWS
Turbulence is reported as "/TB LGT 055-072/". This means the turbulence is light between 5,500 and 7,200 feet MSL.

7-11   PLT061
(Refer to figure 14.)

The intensity and type of icing reported by a pilot is

A– light to moderate rime.

B– light to moderate.

C– light to moderate clear.

7-11. Answer A. GFDPP 7-17, AWS
Icing intensity and type is shown in this pilot report (PIREP) as "/IC LGT-MDT RIME/" or light to moderate rime.

7-12   PLT291
From which primary source should information be obtained regarding expected weather at the estimated time of arrival if your destination has no Terminal Forecast?

A– Low-Level Prognostic Chart.

B– Weather Depiction Chart.

C– Area Forecast.

7-12. Answer C. GFDPP 7-20, AWS
The area forecast (FA) is useful to help determine expected weather at airports which do not have terminal forecasts. The low-level prognostic chart is more useful for flight planning several hours before a flight; however, it generally does not provide enough detail for an accurate estimate of destination weather. The weather depiction chart shows general weather conditions and is also useful for flight planning purposes, but it does not show forecast conditions.

7-13   PLT072
(Refer to figure 15.)

What is the valid period for the TAF for KMEM?

A– 1200Z to 1200Z.

B– 1200Z to 1800Z.

C– 1800Z to 1800Z.

7-13. Answer C. GFDPP 7-18, 19, AWS
TAFs are usually valid for a twenty-four hour period and are scheduled four times a day (0000Z, 0600Z, 1200Z, and 1800Z). The six-digit issuance date/time group is followed by the valid date/time group. Therefore, "121720Z 121818" indicates the KMEM TAF was issued on the 12th at 1720 Zulu. This report is valid from 1800 Zulu on the 12th until 1800 Zulu on the 13th.

7-14   PLT072
(Refer to figure 15.)

In the TAF for KMEM, what does "SHRA" stand for?

A– Rain showers.

B– A shift in wind direction is expected.

C– A significant change in precipitation is possible.

7-14. Answer A. GFDPP 7-13, 14, 18, AWS
This group of the TAF, "PROB40 2202 3SM SHRA," indicates there is a forty percent probability, between 2200 Zulu and 0200 Zulu, the visibility will be 3 statute miles with showery precipitation or rain showers. The next entry, "FM0200 35012KT OVC008" indicates, from 0200 Zulu, the wind is expected to be from 350° at 12 knots, but this is not abbreviated by the code "SHRA."

7-15 PLT072
(Refer to figure 15.)

Between 1000Z and 1200Z the visibility at KMEM is forecast to be?

A– 1/2 statute mile.

B– 3 statute miles.

C– 6 statute miles.

7-16 PLT072
(Refer to figure 15.)

What is the forecast wind for KMEM from 1600Z until the end of the forecast?

A– Variable in direction at 6 knots.

B– No significant wind.

C– Variable in direction at 4 knots.

7-17 PLT072
(Refer to figure 15.)

In the TAF from KOKC, the "FM (FROM) Group" is forecast for the hours from 1600Z to 2200Z with the wind from

A– 180° at 10 knots, becoming 200° at 13 knots.

B– 160° at 10 knots.

C– 180° at 10 knots.

7-18 PLT072
(Refer to figure 15.)

In the TAF from KOKC, the clear sky becomes

A– overcast at 2,000 feet during the forecast period between 2200Z and 2400Z.

B– overcast at 200 feet with a 40% probability of becoming overcast at 600 feet during the forecast period between 2200Z and 2400Z.

C– overcast at 200 feet with the probability of becoming overcast at 400 feet during the forecast period between 2200Z and 2400Z.

7-15. Answer B. GFDPP 7-19, AWS
During a specified time period when changes in the weather conditions are forecast, a change group is appended to the forecast. In this case, "BECMG 1012" indicates a change in the weather will occur between 1000Z and 1200Z. The "3SM" indicates the visibility should become 3 statute miles.

7-16. Answer A. GFDPP 7-19, AWS
This part of the forecast reads, "FM1600 VRB06KT P6SM SKC=". From 1600Z until the end of forecast the wind is variable in direction at 6 knots, with visibility greater than 6 miles.

7-17. Answer C. GFDPP 7-19, AWS
Rapid changes in the forecast are indicated by the code "FM" followed by the time the change should occur. 18010KT indicates wind from 180 degrees at 10 knots. "BECMG 2224" means that the next change will be happening gradually from 2200 to 2400Z.

7-18. Answer A. GFDPP 7-19, AWS
When a gradual change in the forecast weather is expected, the becoming (BECMG) change group is used, followed by the beginning and ending times. The TAF from KOKC, "BECMG 2224 20013G20KT 4SM SHRA OVC020" means between 2200Z and 2400Z the weather will gradually change to winds from 200° at 13 knots gusting to 20 knots, 4 miles visibility in rain showers, and overcast skies at 2,000 feet.

7-19   PLT072
(Refer to figure 15.)

During the time period from 0600Z to 0800Z, what visibility is forecast for KOKC?

A– Greater than 6 statute miles.

B– Not forecasted.

C– Possibly 6 statute miles.

7-19. Answer A. GFDPP 7-19, AWS
This section reads, "BECMG 0608 21015KT P6SM SCT040=". This means that between 0600-0800Z, the wind will become 210° at 15 knots, visibility is forecast to be greater than (not possibly) 6 statute miles, and clouds will become scattered at 4,000 feet.

7-20   PLT072
(Refer to figure 15.)

The only cloud type forecast in TAF reports is

A– Nimbostratus.

B– Cumulonimbus.

C– Scattered cumulus.

7-20. Answer B. GFDPP 7-20, AWS
According to AC 00-45E, cumulonimbus clouds are the only cloud type included in TAFs. If cumulonimbus clouds are expected at the airport, the contraction "CB" is appended to the height of the cloud layer to indicate the base of the cumulonimbus cloud.

7-21   PLT291
To best determine general forecast weather conditions covering a flight information region, the pilot should refer to

A– satellite maps.

B– aviation area forecasts.

C–weather depiction charts.

7-21. Answer B. GFDPP 7-20, AWS
An Aviation Area Forecast (FA) covers the expected general weather conditions over several states. The FA also provides information on general weather conditions at airports that are not covered by other weather reports of forecasts.

7-22   PLT081
(Refer to figure 16.)

What is the outlook for the southern half of Indiana after 0700Z?

A– VFR.

B– IFR.

C– Marginal VFR.

7-22. Answer A. GFDPP 7-21, 22, AWS
The last section is the VFR Clouds and Weather Section of the Chicago FA that includes southern Indiana. The outlook period is on the 25th of the month from 0800 to 1400, and for southern Indiana (at the very bottom) the outlook is for VFR. The definition of VFR is no ceiling, or a ceiling greater than 3,000 feet and visibility greater than 5 miles.

7-23   PLT294
To determine the freezing level and areas of probable icing aloft, the pilot should refer to the

A– inflight aviation weather advisories.

B– area forecast.

C– weather depiction chart.

7-23. Answer A. GFDPP 7-22, AWS
Freezing level and icing aloft are contained in inflight weather advisories which include SIGMETs, convective SIGMETs, AIRMETs, alert service weather watch bulletins (AWWs), center weather advisories (CWAs), and urgent PIREPs. These advisories are broadcast via Enroute Flight Advisory Service (EFAS) and Hazardous In-flight Weather Advisory Service (HIWAS).

7-24   **PLT291**

The section of the Area Forecast entitled "VFR CLDS/WX" contains a general description of

A— forecast sky cover, cloud tops, visibility, and obstructions to vision along specific routes.

B— cloudiness and weather significant to flight operations broken down by states or other geographical areas.

C— clouds and weather which cover an area greater than 3,000 square miles and is significant to VFR flight operations.

7-24. Answer C. GFDPP 7-22, AWS

"VFR Clouds and Weather" includes visibility and cloud cover by state or other well-known geographic areas. Specific forecast sections give a general description of clouds and weather which cover an area greater than 3,000 square miles and that are significant to VFR flight operations.

7-25   **PLT081**

(Refer to figure 16.)

What sky condition and visibility are forecast for upper Michigan in the eastern portions after 2300Z?

A— Ceiling 100 feet overcast and 3 to 5 statute miles visibility.

B— Ceiling 1,000 feet overcast and 3 to 5 nautical miles visibility.

C— Ceiling 1,000 feet overcast and 3 to 5 statute miles visibility.

7-25. Answer C. GFDPP 7-22, AWS

In VFR clouds and weather section in the UPR MI LS (upper Michigan, Lake Superior) and ERN PTNS (eastern portions) the ceiling and visibility, after 23Z, are listed as CLG OVC 010 VIS 3-5 SM (Ceiling 1,000 overcast, 3-5 statute miles visibility).

7-26   **PLT081**

(Refer to figure 16.)

The Chicago FA forecast section is valid until the twenty-fifth at

A— 1945Z

B— 0800Z

C— 1400Z

7-26. Answer B. GFDPP 7-21, AWS

In the first line, "CHI" indicates the area for which the FA is valid. The "C" following CHI indicates VFR clouds and weather while the FA indicates what type of forecast message it is. The "241945" indicates the date and time the FA was issued. The next line "SYNOPSIS AND VFR CLDS/WX" states what information is contained in this forecast message. "CLDS/WX VALID UNTIL 250800" means that the forecast section of the FA is valid until the 25th at 0800Z, while the outlook portion is valid from the 25th at 0800Z until the 25th at 1400Z. ND SD NE KS MN IA MO WI LM LS MI LH IL IN KY describes the area for which this FA forecast is valid.

7-27   **PLT081**

(Refer to figure 16.)

What sky condition and type obstructions to vision are forecast for upper Michigan in the western portions from 0200Z until 0500Z?

A— Ceiling becoming 1,000 feet overcast with visibility 3 to 5 statute miles in mist.

B— Ceiling becoming 100 feet overcast with visibility 3 to 5 statute miles in mist.

C— Ceiling becoming 1,000 feet overcast with visibility 3 to 5 nautical miles in mist.

7-27. Answer A. GFDPP 7-21, 22, AWS

Upper Michigan and Lake Superior, western portion is abbreviated UPR MI LS, WRN PTNS. From 02-05Z, the ceiling is becoming 1,000 overcast (OVC 010) and visibility 3-5 statute miles (3-5 SM) with mist (BR).

7-28   PLT067
What is indicated when a current CONVECTIVE SIGMET forecasts thunderstorms?

A– Moderate thunderstorms covering 30 percent of the area.

B– Moderate or severe turbulence.

C– Thunderstorms obscured by massive cloud layers.

7-28. Answer C. GFDPP 7-27, AIM
One of the criteria for issuing a Convective SIGMET is embedded thunderstorms. A Convective SIGMET is issued when level 4 thunderstorms (very strong, not moderate) cover 40 percent (not 30 percent) of an area. Severe or greater turbulence is implied, not moderate or severe.

7-29   PLT067
What information is contained in a CONVECTIVE SIGMET?

A– Tornadoes, embedded thunderstorms, and hail 3/4 inch or greater in diameter.

B– Severe icing, severe turbulence, or widespread dust storms lowering visibility to less than 3 miles.

C– Surface winds greater than 40 knots or thunderstorms equal to or greater than video integrator processor (VIP) level 4.

7-29. Answer A. GFDPP 7-27, AIM
Convective SIGMETs are issued for any of the following phenomena: tornadoes, lines of thunderstorms, embedded thunderstorms, areas of level 4 thunderstorms covering 40 percent of the area, and hail of 3/4 inch or greater in diameter.

7-30   PLT067
SIGMET's are issued as a warning of weather conditions hazardous to which aircraft?

A– Small aircraft only.

B– Large aircraft only.

C– All aircraft.

7-30. Answer C. GFDPP 7-26, AWS
SIGMETs are issued for weather potentially hazardous to all aircraft. An AIRMET advises of weather which is of operational interest to all aircraft, but may be hazardous to aircraft with limited capabilities, such as light single-engine airplanes.

7-31   PLT290
Which in-flight advisory would contain information on severe icing not associated with thunderstorms?

A– Convective SIGMET.

B– SIGMET.

C– AIRMET.

7-31. Answer B. GFDPP 7-26, AWS
A SIGMET advises of weather potentially hazardous to all aircraft, which would include severe icing. A Convective SIGMET is an advisory of especially hazardous thunderstorm activity.

7-32   PLT290
AIRMET's are advisories of significant weather phenomena but of lower intensities than Sigmets and are intended for dissemination to

A– only IFR pilots.

B– all pilots.

C– only VFR pilots.

7-32. Answer B. GFDPP 7-25, AWS
An AIRMET advises of weather that is of operational interest to all aircraft, but may be hazardous to aircraft with limited capabilities, such as light single-engine airplanes.

7-33 **PLT076**
(Refer to figure 17.)
What wind is forecast for STL at 9,000 feet?

A– 230° true at 32 knots.

B– 230° magnetic at 25 knots.

C– 230° true at 25 knots

7-33. Answer A. GFDPP 7-23, AWS
In the Winds and Temperatures Aloft Forecast (FD), directions are relative to TRUE NORTH and rounded to the nearest 10 degrees. The wind information is given as 2332+02. The first two digits represent the wind direction in relation to true north, 230°. The next two digits are the speed, which in this case is 32 knots. The temperature is +2°C.

7-34 **PLT076**
(Refer to figure 17.)
What wind is forecast for STL at 12,000 feet?

A– 230° true at 56 knots.

B– 230° true at 39 knots.

C– 230° magnetic at 56 knots.

7-34. Answer B. GFDPP 7-23, AWS
In the Winds and Temperatures Aloft Forecast (FD), directions are relative to TRUE NORTH and rounded to the nearest 10 degrees. The wind entry for STL at 12,000 feet is 2339–04. The first two digits represent the wind direction, 230° true. The next two digits are the speed, 39 knots. The temperature is –4°C.

7-35 **PLT076**
What values are used for Winds Aloft Forecasts?

A– Magnetic direction and knots.

B– Magnetic direction and miles per hour.

C– True direction and knots.

7-35. Answer C. GFDPP 7-23, AWS
All forecast and ASOS/AWOS-reported winds are given in true direction, and speed is always in knots. The only time wind direction is given in magnetic is when it is provided by the Tower or ATIS.

7-36 **PLT076**
When the term "light and variable" is used in reference to a Winds Aloft Forecast, the coded group and wind-speed is

A– 0000 and less than 7 knots.

B– 9900 and less than 5 knots.

C– 9999 and less than 10 knots.

7-36. Answer B. GFDPP 7-24, AWS
The direction is shown as 99, which means the direction is variable. When the second two digits are listed as 00, the speed is less than 5 knots.

SECTION C — GRAPHIC WEATHER PRODUCTS

Graphic weather products help you grasp the overall weather picture by giving you maps of actual and forecast patterns.

GRAPHIC REPORTS

Graphic weather reports use information gathered from ground observations, weather radar, satellites, and other sources to give you a pictorial view of large-scale weather patterns and trends.

SURFACE ANALYSIS CHART

A stationary front is depicted with rounded warm front symbols on one side and triangular cold front symbols on the opposite side.

WEATHER DEPICTION CHART

- (Refer to figure 18) The shaded area is an area of IFR weather. The symbol with two horizontal lines (=) indicates fog.
- An outlined area enclosed by contour lines without shading indicates marginal VFR weather. The station models on the weather depiction chart give the percentage of cloud coverage. The ceiling is shown below the model in hundreds of feet AGL.

RADAR SUMMARY CHART

- Radar weather reports are of special interest to pilots because they indicate the location of precipitation along with type, intensity and trend.
- (Refer to figure 19) The movement pennant points in the direction of the return's movement. Each barb on the pennant indicates 10 knots, with half barbs being 5 knots.
- The symbol "RW+" denotes a rain shower (RW) with an increasing intensity or new echo (+).
- The top of the precipitation is shown in hundreds of feet MSL.
- The dashed line encloses a severe weather watch area.

GRAPHIC FORECASTS

Graphic forecasts take reported conditions and trends and extrapolate future weather from them, displaying these predictions pictorially.

SIGNIFICANT WEATHER PROGNOSTIC CHART

- The significant weather prognostic charts are best used by a pilot for determining areas to avoid, due to freezing levels and turbulence.
- (Refer to figure 20) A hat-shaped symbol in the upper left-hand panel indicates moderate turbulence. The figure 180 means the turbulence is from the surface up to 18,000 feet.
- (Refer to figure 20) An outlined area shows showery precipitation ahead of a cold front. The symbols indicate thunderstorms and rain showers.
- The movement and direction of an area of high or low pressure is indicated by an arrow, with the speed listed in knots. The underlined two-digit number below the pressure symbol represents the sea level pressure in millibars.
- A dashed line represents the freezing level. Numbers on the edge of the chart show the altitude of the freezing level in hundreds of feet MSL.

7-37   PLT075
(Refer to figure 18.)

What is the status of the front that extends from Nebraska through the upper peninsula of Michigan?

A– Cold.

B– Warm

C– Stationary

7-38   PLT075
(Refer to figure 18.)

The IFR weather in northern Texas is due to

A– low ceilings.

B– dust devils.

C– intermittent rain.

7-39   PLT075
(Refer to figure 18.)

Of what value is the Weather Depiction Chart to the pilot?

A– For determining general weather conditions on which to base flight planning.

B– For a forecast of cloud coverage, visibilities, and frontal activity.

C– For determining frontal trends and air mass characteristics.

7-40   PLT075
(Refer to figure 18.)

The marginal weather in central Kentucky is due to low

A– visibility.

B– ceiling and visibility.

C– ceiling.

7-41   PLT075
(Refer to figure 18.)

What weather phenomenon is causing IFR conditions in central Oklahoma?

A– Low visibility only.

B– Heavy rain Showers.

C– Low Ceilings and visibility.

7-37. Answer A. GFDPP 7-31, AWS
This front is depicted with triangular symbols on the south side of the front. This symbology indicates a cold front. A warm front has rounded symbols on one side of the frontal line, while a stationary front has triangular symbols on one side and rounded symbols on the other.

7-38. Answer A. GFDPP 7-33, AWS
The shaded area in northern Texas is an area of IFR weather. This shaded area indicates a ceiling of less than 1,000 feet AGL and/or visibility of less than 3 s.m. Since the visibility in northern Texas is indicated as 3 s.m. (near the double dash fog symbol), the IFR weather is caused by low ceilings.

7-39. Answer A. GFDPP 7-33, AWS
The weather depiction chart shows a "birds eye" view of general weather conditions over a wide area, and is useful for flight planning purposes by showing areas of adverse weather. It depicts actual weather conditions, and is not a forecast. Although it does show locations of fronts, it does not indicate trends or high and low pressure areas.

7-40. Answer C. GFDPP 7-32, 33, AWS
An area enclosed by non-shaded contour lines indicates marginal VFR weather conditions. This means the visibility is three to five miles and/or the ceiling is 1,000 to 3,000 feet. The station in central Kentucky is reporting 3,000-foot overcast, with no visibility indication (meaning 6 or more miles visibility).

7-41. Answer C. GFDPP 7-32, 33, AWS
The shaded area indicates IFR. In this case, the filled station model in central Oklahoma indicates overcast sky and the "3" below the model indicates 300 foot ceiling. The "2-1/2" to the left of the model indicates IFR visibility of 2-1/2 statute miles. The bracket to the right of the model indicates an automatic weather observation.

7-42   PLT075
(Refer to figure 18.)

According to the Weather Depiction Chart, the weather for a flight from southern Michigan to north Indiana is ceilings

A– 1,000 to 3,000 feet and/or visibility 3 to 5 miles.

B– less than 1,000 feet and/or visibility less than 3 miles.

C– greater than 3, 000 feet and visibility greater than 5 miles.

7-42. Answer C. GFDPP 7-32, 33, AWS
There are no shaded or contoured areas along this route. This indicates VFR areas with a ceiling greater than 3,000 feet and a visibility greater than 5 miles.

7-43   PLT037
Radar weather reports are of special interest to pilots because they indicate

A– location of precipitation along with type, intensity, and cell movement of precipitation.

B– location of precipitation along with type, intensity, and trend.

C– large areas of low ceilings and fog.

7-43. Answer A. GFDPP 7-33, AWS
Radar weather reports show areas of precipitation; type, such as rain showers; intensity, such as light or heavy; and azimuth of movement. Intensity trend is no longer coded on the Radar Weather Report.

7-44   PLT353
What information is provided by the Radar Summary Chart that is not shown on other weather charts?

A– Lines and cells of hazardous thunderstorms.

B– Ceilings and precipitation between reporting stations.

C– Types of clouds between reporting stations.

7-44. Answer A. GFDPP 7-33, 35, AWS
Individual thunderstorm cells as well as lines of thunderstorms are depicted on radar summary charts. Since the radar returns are reflected off precipitation, not clouds, they do not show ceilings or types of clouds.

7-45   PLT063
(Refer to figure 19.)

(Area B) What is the top for precipitation of the radar return?

A– 24,000 feet AGL.

B– 2,400 feet MSL.

C– 24,000 feet MSL.

7-45. Answer C. GFDPP 7-34, AWS
240 indicates the highest precipitation top in the area in hundreds of feet above mean sea level, which in this case is 24,000 feet MSL.

7-46   PLT063
(Refer to figure 19.)

(Area D) What is the direction and speed of movement of the cell?

A— North at 17 knots.

B— South at 17 knots.

C— North at 17 MPH.

7-46. Answer A. GFDPP 7-34, AWS
Cell movement is indicated by an arrow pointing north and a number (17) indicating speed in knots.

7-47   PLT063
(Refer to figure 19.)

(Area E) The top of the precipitation of the cell is

A— 16,000 feet MSL.

B— 25,000 feet MSL.

C— 16,000 feet AGL.

7-47. Answer A. GFDPP 7-34, AWS
160 indicates the highest precipitation top in the area in hundreds of feet above mean sea level, which in this case is 16,000 feet MSL.

7-48   PLT063
What does the heavy dashed line that forms a large rectangular box on a radar summary chart refer to?

A— Severe weather watch area.

B— Areas of hail 1/4 inch in diameter.

C— Areas of heavy rain.

7-48. Answer A. GFDPP 7-34, AWS
Severe weather watch areas are outlined by heavy dashed lines, usually in the form of a large rectangular box. The watch number, if any, is also printed at the bottom of the chart together with the issuance time and expiration time.

7-49   PLT068
(Refer to figure 20.)

How are Significant Weather Prognostic Charts best used by a pilot?

A— For overall planning at all altitudes.

B— For determining areas to avoid (freezing levels and turbulence).

C— For analyzing current frontal activity and cloud coverage.

7-49. Answer B. GFDPP 7-37, AWS
In addition to outlining areas of instrument flight rule (IFR) and marginal visual flight rule (MVFR) weather, these charts include freezing levels and areas of turbulence. Since the significant weather panels are valid from the surface up to 24,000 feet, they are intended for planning flights below this altitude, not all altitudes. These charts do not depict current frontal activity because they are forecasts, not observations. The lower two panels are 12- and 24-hour surface progs and the upper two panels are 12- and 24-hour progs for the surface up to 400 millibars, or approximately 24,000 feet.

7-50   PLT068
(Refer to figure 20.)

Interpret the weather symbol depicted in Utah on the 12-hour Significant Weather Prognostic Chart.

A— Moderate turbulence, surface to 18,000 feet.

B— Base of clear air turbulence, 18,000 feet.

C— Thunderstorm tops at 18,000 feet.

7-50. Answer A. GFDPP 7-38, 39, AWS
On the upper left panel, the symbol indicates moderate turbulence. The notation 180/ means the turbulence is from the surface up to 18,000 feet.

7-51   PLT068
(Refer to figure 20.)

What weather is forecast for the Florida area just ahead of the stationary front during the first 12 hours?

A— Ceiling 1,000 to 3,000 feet and/or visibility 3 to 5 miles with intermittent precipitation.

B— Ceiling 1,000 to 3,000 feet and/or visibility 3 to 5 miles with continuous precipitation.

C— Ceiling less than 1,000 feet and/or visibility less than 3 miles with continuous precipitation.

7-51. Answer B. GFDPP 7-37, 38, AWS
The upper left panel indicates a ceiling 1,000-3,000 feet and/or a visibility of 3-5 miles. This is marginal VFR (MVFR). The dot symbols in the shaded area within the lower left panel indicates continuous rain.

7-52   PLT068
(Refer to figure 20.)

The enclosed shaded area associated with the low pressure system over northern Utah is forecast to have

A— continuous snow.

B— intermittent snow.

C— continuous snow showers.

7-52. Answer A. GFDPP 7-37, 38, AWS
The area is shaded, indicating continuous precipitation. Two snow symbols (**) indicate that this precipitation is continuous snow.

7-53   PLT068
(Refer to figure 20.)

At what altitude is the freezing level over the middle of Florida on the 12-hour Significant Weather Prognostic Chart?

A— 4,000 feet.

B— 12,000 feet.

C— 8,000 feet.

7-53. Answer B. GFDPP 7-37, 38, AWS
The upper left panel contains a dashed green line marked with the number 120, which crosses central Florida. This represents the height of the 12,000 ft freezing level.

SECTION D — SOURCES OF WEATHER INFORMATION

The sources of weather information are as varied as the weather itself. You can divide the information into those products used during preflight and those you would access during your flight for updates. In this section, we look at three types of briefings, and various supplement sources. Many are automated outlets, such as the pilot's automatic telephone weather answering service (PATWAS).

PREFLIGHT WEATHER SOURCES

There are a number of ways of receiving preflight weather information, including television and on-line sources. The Flight Service Station remains a primary source.

FLIGHT SERVICE STATIONS (FSS)

- When telephoning a weather briefing facility for preflight weather information, pilots should state the aircraft identification or the pilot's name. The pilot should also state the intended route, destination, type of aircraft and whether or not they intend to fly VFR only.
- To get a complete weather briefing for the planned flight, the pilot should request a standard briefing.
- The pilot should request an abbreviated briefing to supplement mass-disseminated data, or to update a previous briefing.
- An outlook briefing is the weather briefing provided when the information requested is six or more hours in advance of the proposed departure time. A pilot requesting information for the following morning should ask for an outlook briefing.

IN-FLIGHT WEATHER SOURCES

Often, you will need to receive updated information during a flight. In-flight weather services include the En Route Flight Advisory Service (EFAS) and the Transcribed Weather Broadcast (TWEB).

EN ROUTE FLIGHT ADVISORY SERVICE (EFAS)

- The pilot should expect actual weather information and thunderstorm activity along the route from an EFAS.
- EFAS can be contacted by calling Flight Watch on 122.0.

TRANSCRIBED WEATHER BROADCAST (TWEB)

To obtain a continuous transcribed weather briefing, including winds aloft and route forecasts for a cross-country flight, pilots should monitor a TWEB on an ADF radio receiver or VOR receiver, using appropriate NDB or VOR frequencies.

7-54   PLT513
Individual forecasts for specific routes of flight can be obtained from which weather source?

A– Transcribed Weather Broadcasts (TWEBs).

B– Terminal Forecasts.

C– Area Forecasts.

7-54. Answer A. GFDPP 7-49, AWS
The information in a transcribed weather broadcast (TWEB) varies, but generally it contains route-oriented data.

7-55   PLT513
Transcribed Weather Broadcasts (TWEBs) may be monitored by tuning the appropriate radio receiver to certain

A– airport advisory frequencies.

B– VOR and NDB frequencies.

C– ATIS frequencies.

7-55. Answer B. GFDPP 7-49, AWS
TWEB's are broadcast over certain VOR and NDB frequencies. Airport advisory frequencies are used by an FSS at uncontrolled airports to provide general airport information to pilots. Automatic terminal information service (ATIS) frequencies are used to broadcast recorded airport information.

7-56   PLT513
When telephoning a weather briefing facility for pre-flight weather information, pilots should state

A– the aircraft identification or the pilot's name.

B– true airspeed.

C– fuel on board.

7-56. Answer A. GFDPP 7-44, AWS
Pilots should give their name or the aircraft number, as well as other specific information, to the weather briefer.

7-57   PLT514
To get a complete weather briefing for the planned flight, the pilot should request

A– a general briefing.

B– an abbreviated briefing.

C– a standard briefing.

7-57. Answer C. GFDPP 7-45, AIM
A standard briefing is the most compete type of weather briefing.

7-58   PLT514
Which type weather briefing should a pilot request, when departing within the hour, if no preliminary weather information has been received?

A– Outlook briefing.

B– Abbreviated briefing.

C– Standard briefing.

7-58. Answer C. GFDPP 7-45, AIM
A standard briefing is the most compete type of weather briefing.

7-59   PLT514
Which type of weather briefing should a pilot request to supplement mass disseminated data?

A– An outlook briefing.

B– A supplemental briefing.

C– An abbreviated briefing.

7-59. Answer C. GFDPP 7-46, AIM
A standard briefing is the most compete type of weather briefing.

7-60   PLT514
To update a previous weather briefing, a pilot should request

A– an abbreviated briefing.

B– a standard briefing.

C– an outlook briefing.

7-60. Answer A. GFDPP 7-46, AIM
A standard briefing is the most compete type of weather briefing.

7-61   PLT514
A weather briefing that is provided when the information requested is 6 or more hours in advance of the proposed departure time is

A— an outlook briefing.

B— a forecast briefing.

C— a prognostic briefing.

7-61. Answer A. GFDPP 7-46, AIM
A standard briefing is the most compete type of weather briefing.

7-62   PLT514
When requesting weather information for the following morning, a pilot should request

A— an outlook briefing.

B— a standard briefing.

C— an abbreviated briefing.

7-62. Answer A. GFDPP 7-46, AIM
Assuming this would be 6 or more hours away, the pilot would request an outlook briefing.

7-63   PLT513
To obtain a continuous transcribed weather briefing, including winds aloft and route forecasts for a cross-country flight, a pilot should monitor a

A— VHF radio receiver tuned to an Automatic Terminal Information Service (ATIS) frequency.

B— Transcribed Weather Broadcast (TWEB) on an NDB or a VOR facility.

C— regularly scheduled weather broadcast on a VOR frequency.

7-63. Answer B. GFDPP 7-49, AIM
Transcribed Weather Broadcasts, or TWEBs, can be monitored on many NDB and/or VOR stations. ATIS broadcasts are local airport information only. Scheduled VOR weather broadcasts may also be local only. The answers to this question can be somewhat misleading, since a TWEB can be broadcast over either an NDB (ADF) or a VOR. However, some VORs broadcast only local information and do not include route forecasts. In general, most TWEBs include route information,

7-64   PLT513
What should pilots state initially when telephoning a weather briefing facility for preflight weather information?

A— Tell the number of occupants on board.

B— State their total flight time.

C— Identify themselves as pilots.

7-64. Answer C. GFDPP 7-44, AWS
You should identify yourself as a pilot or student pilot and include concise facts about your flight.

1.   Type of flight VFR or IFR

2.   Aircraft identification or pilot's name

3.   Aircraft type

4.   Departure point

5.   Route of flight

6.   Destination

7.   Altitude

8.   Estimated time of departure

9.   Estimated time enroute or estimated time of arrival

Briefers do not need to know how many hours the pilot has flown. They also do not need to know the number of occupants on board the aircraft; this information will be on the flight plan.

7-65   PLT513
When telephoning a weather briefing facility for pre-flight weather information, pilots should state

A— the full name and address of the formation commander.

B— that they possess a current pilot certificate.

C— whether they intend to fly VFR only.

7-65. Answer C. GFDPP 7-44, AWS
It is important that the briefer knows whether a pilot intends to fly VFR or IFR, so that the information can help the pilot make a go/no-go decision.

7-66   PLT515
How should contact be established with an En Route Flight Advisory Service (EFAS) station, and what service would be expected?

A— Call EFAS on 122.2 for routine weather, current reports on hazardous weather, and altimeter settings.

B— Call flight assistance on 122.5 for advisory service pertaining to severe weather.

C— Call Flight Watch on 122.0 for information regarding actual weather and thunderstorm activity along proposed route.

7-66. Answer C. GFDPP 7-48, AWS
Below FL180, EFAS is contacted on 122.0. Actual weather and thunderstorm activity along the pilot's route is provided.

7-67   PLT515
What service should a pilot normally expect from an En Route Flight Advisory Service (EFAS) station?

A— Actual weather information and thunderstorm activity along the route.

B— Preferential routing and radar vectoring to circum-navigate severe weather.

C— Severe weather information, changes to flight plans, and receipt of routine position reports.

7-67. Answer A. GFDPP 7-47, 48, AWS
Below FL180, EFAS is contacted on 122.0. Actual weather and thunderstorm activity along the pilot's route is provided.

7-68   PLT515
Below FL180, en route weather advisories should be obtained from an FSS on

A— 122.0 MHz.

B— 122.1 MHz.

C— 123.6 MHz.

7-68. Answer A. GFDPP 7-48, AIM
Below FL180, EFAS is contacted on 122.0. Actual weather and thunderstorm activity along the pilot's route is provided.

AIRPLANE PERFORMANCE

SECTION A — PREDICTING PERFORMANCE

Performance describes the effectiveness of an aircraft in doing the jobs for which it was designed. In this section, we'll look at performance speeds, factors affecting performance, and the pilot's operating handbook (POH). Included are typical examples of performance charts and tables.

FACTORS AFFECTING PERFORMANCE

Many outside factors can affect the way your aircraft performs in various situations.

DENSITY ALTITUDE

- If the outside air temperature at a given altitude is warmer than standard, the density altitude is higher than pressure altitude.
- High temperature, high relative humidity, and high density altitude all reduce aircraft takeoff and climb performance.
- (Refer to figure 8.) In order to find the density altitude for given conditions, first find the pressure altitude, using the pressure altitude conversion factor scale and interpolating for the current pressure. Then, find the temperature on the OAT scale at the bottom of the graph and follow its line vertically to where it intersects the pressure altitude line. From this point, follow the horizontal density altitude line to the left scale to find an approximate density altitude.
- Density altitude and pressure altitude are the same value at standard temperature.

TAKEOFF AND LANDING PERFORMANCE

- (Refer to figure 37) To find the headwind and crosswind components, first determine the difference between the runway heading and the wind direction. Then, find the intersection of the degrees line and the wind velocity arc.
- (Refer to figure 37) To find a velocity at an aircraft's maximum crosswind component, begin with the crosswind component at the bottom of the chart. Follow the line up to where it intersects the degree line representing the angle of crosswind. Then, read the wind velocity.
- (Refer to figure 38) To determine the total distance required to land, start at the bottom left side of the chart. Find the OAT and follow the line up to the corresponding pressure altitude. Move right to the reference line and parallel the diagonal guide line downward to intersect the weight line. Move straight across to the next reference line, and parallel the diagonal headwind guide line down to intersect the wind component line. Move straight across to the next reference line and parallel the diagonal obstacle height guide line up to the obstacle given. The landing distance is read on the right side.
- (Refer to figure 39) To determine the landing distance, find the table that corresponds to the temperature and pressure altitudes that most closely resemble the given conditions. If you need to take into account an obstacle, select that distance. Be sure to check additional factors listed at the bottom of the chart, including headwind, nonstandard temperature and surface conditions.
- (Refer to figure 41) To determine takeoff distance, start at the bottom left of the chart, and find the temperature and pressure altitude. Move straight across to the reference line, and follow the guide line down to the given weight. Move across to the next reference line, and follow the headwind guide line down to the given value. Follow the line straight across to the next reference line, and move down to the stated obstacle height. Move parallel to the guide line and read the distance from the right side of the chart. If there is no wind or obstacle, move straight across the corresponding section to the next reference line.

CLIMB PERFORMANCE

- V_X is the best angle of climb, and it provides the greatest gain in altitude over the shortest distance during climb after takeoff.
- V_Y is the best rate of climb, and it provides the greatest gain in altitude over a given period of time.
- An aircraft's operating limitations are found in several places, including the current, FAA-approved flight manual, approved manual material, markings, placards, or any combination thereof.

CRUISE PERFORMANCE

- (Refer to figure 36) To determine the TAS in given conditions, use the left-hand portion of the table, under the appropriate temperature heading. Interpolate between the given pressure altitudes, if necessary, to find the TAS.
- (Refer to figure 36) To determine the expected fuel consumption, first go to the table under the appropriate temperature heading. Go down to the given pressure altitude and read across to find the fuel flow and TAS. Find the time enroute by dividing the distance by the TAS. Multiply the time by the fuel flow.
- (Refer to figure 36) To determine the manifold pressure setting, go to the appropriate temperature heading, and go down to the pressure altitude. Read the MP from the table, noting all RPM values are the same.

8-1   PLT506
Which would provide the greatest gain in altitude in the shortest distance during climb after takeoff?

A– V_Y

B– V_A

C– V_X

8-1. Answer C. GFDPP 8-16, AFH
V_X is the best angle of climb. This gives you the greatest gain in altitude for horizontal distance traveled.

8-2   PLT506
After takeoff, which airspeed would the pilot use to gain the most altitude in a given period of time?

A– V_Y

B– V_X

C– V_A

8-2. Answer A. GFDPP 8-16, AFH
Use V_Y, the best RATE of climb speed, to gain altitude in minimum time when nearby obstacles are not a factor. Use the slower V_X, the best ANGLE of climb speed to gain altitude in minimum horizontal distance and clear obstacles. V_A, maneuvering speed, is not a climb speed.

8-3   PLT127
What effect does high density altitude, as compared to low density altitude, have on propeller efficiency and why?

A– Efficiency is increased due to less friction on the propeller blades.

B– Efficiency is reduced because the propeller exerts less force at high density altitudes than at low density altitudes.

C– Efficiency is reduced due to the increased force of the propeller in the thinner air.

8-3. Answer B. GFDPP 8-19, PHB
Because the air is less dense, there is less airflow through the propeller, and the force and efficiency are reduced.

8-4   **PLT134**
Which combination of atmospheric conditions will reduce aircraft takeoff and climb performance?

A– Low temperature, low relative humidity, and low density altitude.

B– High temperature, low relative humidity, and low density altitude.

C– High temperature, high relative humidity, and high density altitude.

8-4. Answer C. GFDPP 8-8, PHB
High temperatures increase density altitude with a resulting decrease in aircraft performance. In addition, high humidity reduces engine performance.

8-5   **PLT127**
What effect does high density altitude have on aircraft performance?

A– It increases engine performance.

B– It reduces climb performance.

C– It increases takeoff performance.

8-5. Answer B. GFDPP 8-19, PHB
A high density altitude decreases engine performance with a resulting reduction in climb performance.

8-6   **PLT127**
What effect, if any, does high humidity have on aircraft performance?

A– It increases performance.

B– It decreases performance.

C– It has no effect on performance.

8-6. Answer B. GFDPP 8-8, PHB
High humidity reduces engine performance by slightly increasing the density altitude of air entering the engine and retarding smooth burning of the fuel.

8-7   **PLT012**
(Refer to figure 36.)

Approximately what true airspeed should a pilot expect with 65 percent maximum continuous power at 9,500 feet with a temperature of 36°F below standard?

A– 163 KTS.

B– 161 KTS.

C– 158 KTS.

8-7. Answer C. GFDPP 8-22, PHB
Use the left-hand portion of the table, under ISA –36°F. Interpolate between the TAS values for 8,000 feet (157 KTS) and 10,000 feet (160 KTS). The closest answer is 158 KTS.

8-8   **PLT012**
(Refer to figure 36.)

What is the expected fuel consumption for a 1,000-nautical mile flight under the following conditions?

Pressure altitude...8,000 ft

Temperature...22°C

Manifold pressure...20.8 inches Hg.

Wind...Calm.

A– 60.2 gallons.

B– 70.1 gallons.

C– 73.2 gallons.

8-8. Answer B. GFDPP 8-22, PHB
The temperature of 22°C is found on the right-hand portion of the table (ISA + 20°C) at 8,000 feet. Read across to find a fuel flow of 11.5 GPH, and TAS of 164 Knots (use knots because the distance is in nautical miles). Now, find the time enroute by dividing 1,000 NM by 164 knots (Normally you would use groundspeed, but with a calm wind, TAS equals groundspeed.) The time enroute is approximately 6.1 hours. Multiply the time by fuel flow. The total fuel consumption is 70.1 gallons.

8-9   **PLT012**
(Refer to figure 36.)

What fuel flow should a pilot expect at 11,000 feet on a standard day with 65 percent maximum continuous power?

A– 10.6 gallons per hour.

B– 11.2 gallons per hour.

C– 11.8 gallons per hour.

8-9. Answer B. GFDPP 8-22, PHB
Use the center portion of the table for a standard day. You will need to interpolate to find the fuel flow for 11,000 feet which is halfway between 12,000 and 10,000 feet. The answer is 11.2 (11.5 – 10.9 = .6 ÷ 2 =.3 + 10.9 = 11.2).

8-10   **PLT012**
(Refer to figure 36.)

Determine the approximate manifold pressure setting with 2,450 RPM to achieve 65 percent maximum continuous power at 6,500 feet with a temperature of 36°F higher than standard.

A– 19.8 inches Hg.

B– 20.8 inches Hg.

C– 21.0 inches Hg.

8-10. Answer C. GFDPP 8-22, PHB
The RPM is the same for all altitudes. Therefore, to determine what manifold pressure (MP) is required to achieve 65% maximum continuous power, enter the table under ISA + 36°F. The MP for 6,000 feet is 21.0", and for 8,000 feet it is 20.8". The interpolated MP for 6,500 feet is 20.95". The closest answer is 21.0" Hg.

8-11   **PLT013**
(Refer to figure 37.)

What is the headwind component for a landing on Runway 18 if the tower reports the wind as 220° at 30 knots?

A– 19 knots.

B– 23 knots.

C– 26 knots.

8-11. Answer B. GFDPP 8-12, PHB
First, compute the difference between the runway (180°) and the wind (220°). The result is an angle of 40 degrees. Find the intersection of the 40 degree line and the 30 knot wind velocity arc, then read across to the left side to find the headwind component of 23 knots.

8-12   PLT013
(Refer to figure 37.)

Determine the maximum wind velocity for a 45° crosswind if the maximum crosswind component for the airplane is 25 knots.

A– 25 knots.

B– 29 knots.

C– 35 knots.

8-12. Answer C. GFDPP 8-12, PHB
Start with the crosswind component of 25 knots at the bottom of the chart, and follow the line straight up to where it intersects the 45 degree angle line. This intersection is midway between the 30 and 40 knot wind velocity lines, or 35 knots.

8-13   PLT013
(Refer to figure 37.)

What is the maximum wind velocity for a 30° crosswind if the maximum crosswind component for the airplane is 12 knots?

A– 16 knots.

B– 20 knots.

C– 24 knots.

8-13. Answer C. GFDPP 8-12, PHB
Start with the crosswind component of 12 knots at the bottom of the chart, and follow the line straight up to where it intersects the 30 degree angle line. This intersection is approximately 24 knots on the wind velocity scale.

8-14   PLT013
(Refer to figure 37.)

With a reported wind of north at 20 knots, which runway (6, 29, or 32) is acceptable for use for

an airplane with a 13-knot maximum crosswind component?

A– Runway 6.

B– Runway 29.

C– Runway 32.

8-14. Answer C. GFDPP 8-12, PHB
At first glance, Runway 32 is most closely aligned with north (360°). To verify, find the crosswind component for each runway. Runway 32 is 40 degrees from the wind, and since the windspeed is 20 knots, the crosswind component is slightly less than 13 knots, so Runway 32 is acceptable. Runway 6 is 60 degrees from the wind, and the crosswind component is about 17.5 knots. Runway 29 is 70 degrees from the wind, and the crosswind component is about 19 knots. Both Runways 6 and 29 exceed the 13 knot maximum crosswind component.

8-15   PLT013
(Refer to figure 37.)

With a reported wind of south at 20 knots, which runway (10, 14, or 24) is appropriate for an airplane with a 13-knot maximum crosswind component?

A– Runway 10.

B– Runway 14.

C– Runway 24.

8-15. Answer B. GFDPP 8-12, PHB
Runway 14 is most closely aligned with the wind and would have the least crosswind. The crosswind angle and component for each runway is: Runway 14, 40 degrees, 12.5 knots; Runway 10, 80 degrees, 19.7 knots; Runway 24, 60 degrees, 17.5 knots. Runway 14 is the only appropriate runway because the crosswind component is less than 13 knots.

8-16   PLT013

(Refer to figure 37.)

What is the crosswind component for a landing on Runway 18 if the tower reports the wind as 220° at 30 knots?

A— 19 knots.

B— 23 knots.

C— 30 knots.

8-16. Answer A. GFDPP 8-12, PHB

The crosswind angle is 40 degrees (220° – 180° = 40°). Find the intersection of 40 degrees and 30 knots. Then read down to find the crosswind component of about 19 knots.

8-17   PLT008

(Refer to figure 38.)

Determine the approximate total distance required to land over a 50-foot obstacle.

OAT...90°F

Pressure altitude...4,000 ft

Weight...2,800 lb

Headwind component...10 knots

A— 1,525 feet.

B— 1,950 feet.

C— 1,775 feet.

8-17. Answer C. GFDPP 8-15, PHB

Start at the lower left at 90°F (32°C), and move up to where it intersects the 4,000-foot pressure altitude line. Go right to the weight reference line and then down and to the right to 2,800 lb. Go straight right to the wind component reference line, down and to the right to the 10 knot headwind line, and straight right to the obstacle height reference line. Move up and to the right through the obstacle height and read the landing distance over a 50-foot obstacle on the right-hand scale. It is approximately 1,775 feet.

8-18   PLT008

(Refer to figure 39.)

Determine the approximate landing ground roll distance.

Pressure altitude...Sea level

Headwind...4 knots

Temperature...Std

A— 356 feet.

B— 401 feet.

C— 490 feet.

8-18. Answer B. GFDPP 8-14, 15, PHB

Use the table listed under sea level and 59°F, which is the standard temperature. Since you need to find the landing ground roll distance, do not include obstacle clearance. The ground roll is given as 445, but according to Note 1, you need to correct for headwind by decreasing the distance 10% for each 4 knots of headwind. In this case, subtract 10% of 445 (44.5) from 445. The closest answer is 401 feet.

8-19 PLT008
(Refer to figure 39.)

Determine the total distance required to land over a 50-foot obstacle.

Pressure altitude...7,500 ft

Headwind...8 knots

Temperature...32°F

Runway...Hard surface

A— 1,004 feet.

B— 1,205 feet.

C— 1,506 feet.

8-19. Answer A. GFDPP 8-14, 15, PHB
According to the table, the landing distance over a 50-foot obstacle is 1,255 feet at 7,500 feet and 32°F. Note 1 says to decrease this distance by 10% for each 4 knots of headwind, so with 8 knots headwind, subtract 20 percent. 1,255 ft × 0.80 = 1,004 ft

8-20 PLT008
(Refer to figure 39.)

Determine the total distance required to land over a 50-foot obstacle.

Pressure altitude...5,000 ft

Headwind...8 knots

Temperature...41°F

Runway...Hard surface

A— 837 feet.

B— 956 feet.

C— 1,076 feet.

8-20. Answer B. GFDPP 8-14, 15, PHB
Use the table at 5,000 feet and 41°F. The distance to land over a 50 ft obstacle is 1,195. According to Note 1, decrease the distance by 20% (239 ft) for the 8 knot headwind: (1,195 ft – 239 ft = 956 ft total landing distance).

8-21 PLT008
(Refer to figure 39.)

Determine the approximate landing ground roll distance.

Pressure altitude...5,000 ft

Headwind...Calm

Temperature...101°F

A— 495 feet.

B— 545 feet.

C— 445 feet.

8-21. Answer B. GFDPP 8-14, 15, PHB
At 5,000 feet and 41°F (ISA Standard Temperature), the ground roll distance is 495 feet. According to Note 2, this distance is increased 10% for each 60°F above standard.

8-22   PLT008
(Refer to figure 39.)

Determine the total distance required to land over a 50-foot obstacle.

Pressure altitude...3,750 ft

Headwind...12 knots

Temperature...Std

A– 794 feet.

B– 836 feet.

C– 816 feet.

8-22. Answer C. GFDPP 8-14, 15, PHB

1. At 2,500 feet and Standard ISA temperature, the landing distance over a 50-foot obstacle with zero wind is 1,135 feet. At 5,000 feet this distance is 1,195 feet. At 3,750 feet assume the landing distance is half way between 1,135 and 1,195 feet. (1,135 + 1,195) feet ÷ 2 = 1,165 feet.

2. Note 1 says to decrease the distance 10% for each 4 knots of headwind. The headwind is 12 knots. 12 knots × 10% decrease/4 knots = 30% decrease. 1,165 feet × (100% − 30%) = 816 feet.

8-23   PLT008
(Refer to figure 39.)

Determine the approximate landing ground roll distance.

Pressure altitude...1,250 ft

Headwind...8 knots

Temperature...Std

A– 275 feet.

B– 366 feet.

C– 470 feet.

8-23. Answer B. GFDPP 8-14, 15, PHB
This problem requires that you interpolate between the ground roll distances at sea level and 2,500 feet PA. Since 1,250 feet is midway between the two values, the ground roll would be 457.5 (470 − 445 = 25 ÷ 2 = 13.5 + 445 = 457.5). To correct for headwind, subtract 20% of the distance (10% for each 4 knots). 20% of 457.5 is 91.5. The landing distance is 457.5 − 91.5 or 366 feet.

8-24   PLT208
If an emergency situation requires a downwind landing, pilots should expect a faster

A– airspeed at touchdown, a longer ground roll, and better control throughout the landing roll.

B– groundspeed at touchdown, a longer ground roll, and the likelihood of overshooting the desired touchdown point.

C– groundspeed at touchdown, a shorter ground roll, and the likelihood of undershooting the desired touchdown point.

8-24. Answer B. GFDPP 8-13
Wind should be considered in all landings, whether normal or emergency. When you fly the same indicated airspeed for landing, a headwind lowers the groundspeed at touchdown, resulting in a shorter ground roll. The reverse is true for a tailwind, which is why pilots always try to land into the wind. Additionally, higher ground speed produced by a tailwind results in the aircraft traveling faster in the roundout and flare, which might result in overshooting the desired touchdown point.

8-25   PLT011
(Refer to figure 41.)

Determine the total distance required for takeoff to clear a 50-foot obstacle.

OAT...Std

Pressure altitude...4,000 ft

Takeoff weight...2,800 lb

Headwind component...Calm

A– 1,500 feet.

B– 1,750 feet.

C– 2,000 feet.

8-25. Answer B. GFDPP 8-6, 7, PHB
Since temperature is standard, start at the intersection of the ISA and 4,000 foot pressure altitude line. Move right to the reference line and follow the guide line diagonally downward to the 2,800 pound line. Since winds are calm, move straight across to the obstacle height reference line. Follow the guide line upward to the 50 foot line, which is on the right-hand border. The takeoff distance is approximately 1,700 feet.

8-26   PLT011
(Refer to figure 41.)

Determine the total distance required for takeoff to clear a 50-foot obstacle.

OAT...Std

Pressure altitude...Sea level

Takeoff weight...2,700 lb

Headwind component...Calm

A– 1,000 feet.

B– 1,400 feet.

C– 1,700 feet.

8-26. Answer B. GFDPP 8-6, 7, PHB
Since temperature is standard, start at the intersection of the ISA line and sea level (S.L.). Move right to the reference line and follow the guide line diagonally downward to the 2,700 pound line. Move straight across to the obstacle height reference line, since winds are calm. Follow the guide line upward to the 50 foot line. The takeoff distance is about 1,400 feet.

8-27   PLT011
(Refer to figure 41.)

Determine the approximate ground roll distance required for takeoff.

OAT...100°F

Pressure altitude...2,000 ft

Takeoff weight...2,750 lb

Headwind component...Calm

A– 1,150 feet.

B– 1,300 feet.

C– 1,800 feet.

8-27. Answer A. GFDPP 8-6, 7, PHB
Start at 100°F, move up to the 2,000 foot pressure altitude line, then right to the reference line. Follow the guide line down to 2,750 pounds. Since winds are calm, and there is no obstacle, move straight across to the right-hand border. The ground roll is about 1,150 feet.

8-28   PLT011
(Refer to figure 41.)

Determine the approximate ground roll distance required for takeoff.

OAT...90°F

Pressure altitude...2,000 ft

Takeoff weight...2,500 lb

Headwind component...20 knots

A– 650 feet.

B– 800 feet.

C– 1,000 feet.

8-29   PLT208
If an emergency situation requires a downwind landing, pilots should expect a faster

A– airspeed at touchdown, a longer ground roll, and better control throughout the landing roll.

B– groundspeed at touchdown, a longer ground roll, and the likelihood of overshooting the desired touchdown point.

C– groundspeed at touchdown, a shorter ground roll, and the likelihood of undershooting the desired touchdown point.

8-28. Answer A. GFDPP 8-6, 7, PHB
Start at 90°F, move up to the 2,000 foot pressure altitude line, then right to the reference line. Follow the guide line down to 2,500 pounds. Move across to the next reference line, and follow the headwind guide line down to 20 knots. Since there is no obstacle, move straight across to the right-hand border. The ground roll is about 650 feet.

8-29. Answer B. GFDPP 8-13, AFH
Wind should be considered in all landings, whether normal or emergency. Simply put, when flying the same indicated airspeed for landing, a headwind lowers the groundspeed at touchdown, resulting in a shorter ground roll. The reverse is true for a tailwind, which is why pilots always try to land into the wind. Additionally, higher ground speed produced by a tailwind results in the aircraft traveling farther in the roundout and flare, which might result in overshooting the desired touchdown point.

SECTION B — WEIGHT AND BALANCE

Pilots need to keep weight within specified limits and to balance the load on board the aircraft carefully in order to maintain control of the airplane. This section covers weight and balance charts and tables, how to determine weight and balance, and how to apply the weight shift formula.

WEIGHT AND BALANCE TERMS

- Included in the empty weight of an aircraft are the unusable fuel and undrainable oil.
- The standard weight of gasoline is six pounds per gallon. To determine the amount of fuel to drain, if necessary, divide the excess weight by six.

PRINCIPLES OF WEIGHT AND BALANCE

The CG is the total moment divided by the total weight. Datum is a vertical plane in the aircraft from which weight and balance distances are measured. Arm is the distance from datum of a particular station, or place in the aircraft. To calculate aircraft moment, multiply the weight at a station by the arm. Positive CG values are aft of datum, negative CG values are ahead of datum.

DETERMINING TOTAL WEIGHT AND CENTER OF GRAVITY

There are several formulas which will aid you in calculating your aircraft's center of gravity and total weight, and the change in CG with a shift in weight.

TABLE METHOD

- The best way to determine aircraft weight and balance is to construct a table which lists the stations of the aircraft, the weight at each station, and the arm of each station. From here, you can find the moment at each station, and add up the total weight and moments. The CG is the total moment divided by the total weight.
- (Refer to figures 33 and 34) To find the arm at each station, look for the station, i.e. usable fuel, on the table and read the arm listed at the top. Many charts calculate moments for a specific weight range, so that you can simply read these off the table as well.
- (Refer to figure 35) Other charts provide arm and moment information graphically. To read the moment from the chart, find the line that corresponds to the station, and follow it to the given weight at the station. Move down to the bottom of the graph to find the moment.

WEIGHT SHIFT FORMULA

Use the weight shift formula to determine how far the center of gravity shifts when weight is added to or removed from the aircraft:

- Weight Moved ÷ Weight of Airplane = Distance CG Moves ÷ Distance Between Arms
- Some weight shift questions will require you to construct a table of weights and moments first.

8-30   PLT328
Which items are included in the empty weight of an aircraft?

A– Unusable fuel and undrainable oil

B– Only the airframe, powerplant, and optional equipment.

C– Full fuel tanks and engine oil to capacity.

8-30. Answer A. GFDPP 8-32, PHB
The empty weight of an aircraft includes unusable fuel. The term basic empty weight includes full engine oil. On older airplanes, the term licensed empty weight includes only undrainable oil.

8-31   PLT328
An aircraft is loaded 110 pounds over maximum certificated gross weight. If fuel (gasoline) is drained to bring the aircraft weight within limits, how much fuel should be drained?

A– 15.7 gallons.

B– 16.2 gallons.

C– 18.4 gallons.

8-31. Answer C. GFDPP 8-33, PHB
This problem requires converting the weight of fuel to gallons. Since the standard weight of gasoline is 6 pounds per gallon, divide 110 pounds by 6, to find an answer of 18.33, or 18.4 gallons.

8-32   PLT328
GIVEN:

	WEIGHT (LB)	ARM (IN)	WEIGHT (LB-IN)
Empty weight	1,495.0	101.4	151,593.0
Pilot and Pass	380.0	64.0	-----
Fuel (30 gal usable no reserve)	-----	96.0	-----

The CG is located how far aft of datum?

A– CG 92.44.

B– CG 94.01.

C– CG 119.8.

8-32. Answer B. GFDPP 8-36, PHB
First, fill in the table by entering the fuel weight (30 gal × 6 lb/gal = 180 lb). Then, multiply each weight by the arm to find the moment.

	WEIGHT (LB)	ARM (IN)	WEIGHT (LB-IN)
Empty weight	1,495.0	101.4	151,593.0
Pilot and Pass	380.0	64.0	24,320.0
Fuel 30 gals	180.0	96.0	17,280.0
Totals	2,055.0		193,193.0

CG = 193,193 ÷ 2,055 = 94.01

The CG is the total moment divided by the total weight.

8-33   **PLT328**

(Refer to figures 33 and 34.)

What is the maximum amount of baggage that can be carried when the airplane is loaded as follows?

Front seat occupants...387 lb
Rear seat occupants...293 lb
Fuel...35 gal

A– 45 pounds.

B– 63 pounds.

C– 220 pounds.

8-33. Answer A. GFDPP 8-39, PHB

Add up all the weights and you will find the airplane is 45 lb. underweight. When adding the 45 lb. of baggage, be sure to verify that the resulting center of gravity (CG) is within limits.

8-34   **PLT328**

(Refer to figures 33 and 34.)

Determine if the airplane weight and balance is within limits.

Front seat occupants...415 lb

Rear seat occupants...110 lb

Fuel, main tanks...44 gal

Fuel, aux. tanks...19 gal

Baggage...32 lb

A– 19 pounds overweight, CG within limits.

B– 19 pounds overweight, CG out of limits forward.

C– Weight within limits, CG out of limits.

8-34. Answer C. GFDPP 8-36, 39, PHB

First, construct a weight and moment table.

	WEIGHT (lb)	ARM (in)	MOMENT (lb-in/100)
Empty weight	2,015		1,554.0
Front Seat	415	85	352.8
Rear Seat	110	121	133.1
Fuel 44 gal	264	75	198.0
Aux 19 gal	114	94	107.2
Baggage	32	140	44.8
Totals	2,950		2,389.9

The total weight is at the maximum limit. Divide total moments by total weight to find the CG of 81.0 inches, which is outside the limits.

CG = (2,389 lb-in × 100) ÷ 2,950 lb = 81.0 in

8-35   PLT328
(Refer to figure 35.)

What is the maximum amount of baggage that may be loaded aboard the airplane for the CG to remain within the moment envelope?

	WEIGHT (LB)	MOM/1000
Empty weight	1,350	51.5
Pilot and Front passenger	250	-----
Rear passengers	400	-----
Baggage	-----	-----
Fuel, 30 gal	-----	-----
Oil, 8 qt	-----	-0.2

A– 105 pounds.

B– 110 pounds.

C– 120 pounds.

8-35. Answer A. GFDPP 8-40, PHB
Use figure 35 to convert oil and fuel to pounds. Add up the known weights, for a total of 2,195 pounds. Subtract 2,195 pounds from 2,300 max weight to find the maximum possible baggage weight of 105 pounds. While it appears that choice A is the only correct answer, it is a good idea to check the CG limits. Use the LOADING GRAPH and find the moment for each weight.

	WEIGHT (lb)	MOMENT (lb-in/1000)
Empty Weight	1,350	51.5
Front Seat	250	9.4
Rear Seat	400	29.3
Fuel 30 gal	180	8.7
Oil 8 qt	15	−0.2
Subtotal	2,195	98.7
Baggage	105	10.0
Totals	2,300	108.7

Total the moments and locate the maximum weight on the CENTER OF GRAVITY MOMENT ENVELOPE graph. The intersection of the loaded weight and moment is at the upper right-hand corner of the normal category envelope, and is just barely within limits.

8-36   PLT328
(Refer to figure 35.)

Calculate the moment of the airplane and determine which category is applicable.

	WEIGHT (LB)	MOM/1000
Empty weight	1,350	51.5
Pilot and Front passenger	310	-----
Rear passengers	96	-----
Fuel, 38 gal	-----	-----
Oil, 8 qt	-----	-0.2

A– 79.2, utility category.

B– 80.8, utility category.

C– 81.2, normal category.

8-36. Answer B. GFDPP 8-40, PHB
Complete the table of weights and moments, using the LOADING GRAPH

	WEIGHT (lb.)	MOMENT (lb-in/1000)
Empty Weight	1,350	51.5
Front Seat	310	11.6
Rear Seat	96	7.0
Fuel 38 gal	228	11.0
Oil 8 qt	15	−0.2
Totals	1,999	80.9

The total moment is 80.9. Use the CENTER OF GRAVITY MOMENT ENVELOPE graph to find the total weight and total moment. The intersection falls within the upper right-hand corner of the utility category envelope.

8-37   PLT328

(Refer to figure 35.)

What is the maximum amount of fuel that may be aboard the airplane on takeoff if loaded as follows?

	WEIGHT (LB)	MOM/1000
Empty weight	1,350	51.5
Pilot and Front passenger	340	-----
Rear passengers	310	-----
Baggage	45	-----
Oil, 8 qt	-----	-----

A– 24 gallons.

B– 32 gallons.

C– 40 gallons.

8-37. Answer C. GFDPP 8-40, PHB

Complete the table of weights and moments, using the LOADING GRAPH.

	WEIGHT (lb)	MOMENT (lb-in/1000)
Empty Weight	1,350	51.5
Front Seat	340	12.7
Rear Seat	310	22.6
Baggage	45	4.3
Oil 8 qt	15	–.2
Subtotal	2060	90.9
Fuel 40 gal	240	11.5
Totals	2300	102.4

The total weight without fuel is 2,060 pounds. This is 240 pounds below the maximum of 2,300 pounds.

Dividing by 6 lb/gal, the maximum fuel load is 40 gallons. It is a good idea to check the moments as well. The total moment of 102.4 is within the CG envelope, so 40 gallons is acceptable.

8-38   **PLT328**

(Refer to figure 35.)

Determine the moment with the following data:

	WEIGHT (LB)	MOM/1000
Empty weight	1,350	51.5
Pilot and Front passenger	340	-----
Fuel (std. tanks)	Capacity	-----
Oil, 8 qt	-----	-----

A— 69.9 pound-inches.

B— 74.9 pound-inches.

C— 77.6 pound-inches.

8-39   **PLT328**

(Refer to figure 35.)

Determine the aircraft loaded moment and the aircraft category.

	WEIGHT (LB)	MOM/1000
Empty weight	1,350	51.5
Pilot and Front passenger	380	-----
Fuel, 48 gal	288	-----
Oil, 8 qt	-----	-----

A— 78.2, normal category.

B— 79.2, normal category.

C— 80.4, utility category.

8-38. Answer B. GFDPP 8-40, PHB

Use the LOADING GRAPH to determine the moments. Add these to find the total moment of 74.9.

	WEIGHT (lb.)	MOMENT (lb-in/1000)
Empty Weight	1,350	51.5
Front Seat	340	12.6
Fuel 38 gal	228	11.0
Oil 8 qt.	15	−0.2
Totals	1,933	74.9

8-39. Answer B. GFDPP 8-40, PHB

Use the LOADING GRAPH to determine the moments

	WEIGHT (lb)	MOMENT (lb-in/1000)
Empty Weight	1,350	51.5
Front Seat	380	14.2
Fuel 48 gal	288	13.7
Oil, 8 qt	15	−0.2
Totals	2,033	79.2

The total weight is 2,033 pounds, and the total moment is 79.2. Use the CENTER OF GRAVITY MOMENT ENVELOPE graph with the total weight and total moment. The intersection falls within the normal category, and outside the utility category.

8-40   PLT328

(Refer to figures 33 and 34.)

Upon landing, the front passenger (180 pounds) departs the airplane. A rear passenger (204 pounds) moves to the front passenger position. What effect does this have on the CG if the airplane weighed 2,690 pounds and the MOM/100 was 2,260 just prior to the passenger transfer?

A– The CG moves forward approximately 3 inches.

B– The weight changes, but the CG is not affected.

C– The CG moves forward approximately 0.1 inch.

8-40. Answer A. GFDPP 8-36, 41, PHB

Use the weight shift formula to determine how far the CG shifts.

Weight Moved ÷ Weight of Airplane = Distance CG Moves ÷ Dist. Btwn. Arms

The front passenger that departs reduces the total weight of the aircraft by 180 pounds (2,690 – 180 = 2,510.) The weight that is moved is the rear passenger (204 pounds). The arms for the front and rear passenger seats are found in Figure 33, and the difference is 121 – 85 = 36.

204 ÷ 2,510 = Distance CG Moves ÷ 36

Distance CG Moves = (204 × 36) ÷ 2,510 = 2.93

The change in CG is approximately 2.93, which is closest to answer (A).

8-41   **PLT328**

(Refer to figures 33 and 34.)

Which action can adjust the airplane's weight to maximum gross weight and the CG within limits for take-off?

Front seat occupants...425 lb

Rear seat occupants...300 lb

Fuel, main tanks...44 gal

A– Drain 12 gallons of fuel.

B– Drain 9 gallons of fuel.

C– Transfer 12 gallons of fuel from the main tanks to the auxiliary tanks.

8-41. Answer B. GFDPP 8-39, PHB

Complete the weight and moment table as shown below.

	WEIGHT (lb)	ARM (in)	MOMENT (lb-in/100)
Empty Weight	2,015		1,554.0
Front Seat	425	85	361.3
Rear Seat	300	121	363.0
Fuel 44 gal	264	75	198.0
Total	3,004		2,476.3
Max Weight	−2,950		
	54		

The total weight of 3,004 is 54 pounds over maximum weight. If we drain 54 pounds of fuel to attain the maximum weight, this is equal to 9 gallons (54 pounds ÷ 6 = 9 gallons). Now adjust the moments by entering a new fuel moment for the 35 gallons that remain, and find a total moment of 2,436.

	WEIGHT (lb)	ARM (in)	MOMENT (lb-in/100)
Empty Weight	2,015		1,554.0
Front Seat	425	85	361.3
Rear Seat	300	121	363.0
Fuel 35 gal	210	75	157.5
Total	2,950		2,435.8

Using the table in Figure 8-7, you'll find the total weight and total moment are within the limits.

8-42   PLT328

(Refer to figures 33 and 34.)

What effect does a 35-gallon fuel burn (main tanks) have on the weight and balance if the airplane weighed 2,890 pounds and the MOM/100 was 2,452 at takeoff?

A– Weight is reduced by 210 pounds and the CG is aft of limits.

B– Weight is reduced by 210 pounds and the CG is unaffected.

C– Weight is reduced to 2,680 pounds and the CG moves forward.

8-42. Answer A. GFDPP 8-39, PHB

Use the chart in Figure 33 to find the weight and moment for 35 gallons of fuel (main tanks), and subtract these values from the total weight and moment. The result is the total weight and moment after the fuel burn.

	WEIGHT (lb)	MOMENT (lb-in/100)
Total	2,890	2,452
Fuel 35 gal	−210	−158
Adjusted	2,680	2,294

Refer to the chart in Figure 34 for the weight of 2,680 lb. The moment of 2,294 lb-in exceeds the maximum (aft) limit.

8-43   **PLT328**

(Refer to figures 33 and 34.)

With the airplane loaded as follows, what action can be taken to balance the airplane?

Front seat occupants..411 lb

Rear seat occupants...100 lb

Main wing tanks...44 gal

A— Fill the auxiliary wing tanks.

B— Add a 100-pound weight to the baggage compart-ment.

C— Transfer 10 gallons of fuel from the main tanks to the auxiliary tanks.

8-43. Answer B. GFDPP 8-36, 39, 41, PHB

Construct the table as shown below, find the subtotal weight and moment, and use the chart in Figure 34. The subtotal moment (2,222.4) at the original weight is less than the minimum (forward) limit.

	WEIGHT (lb)	ARM (in)	MOMENT (lb-in/100)
Empty Weight	2,015		1,554.0
Front Seat	411	85	349.4
Rear Seat	100	121	121.0
Fuel 44 gal	264	75	198.0
Subtotal	2,790		2,222.4
Baggage	100		140.0
Total	2,890		2,362.4

Since the baggage compartment is in an aft location, adding weight to this part of the airplane will shift the CG aft. Add the baggage weight and moment to the subtotals to find adjusted totals. Check the chart in Figure 34 to ensure that the moment is within limits. Answer (A) is wrong because if the auxiliary wing tanks are filled and the total weight and moment are adjusted, the moment will be less than the minimum. To check answer (C), find the original CG using the subtotals:

CG = Total Moments ÷ Total Weight
     = 2,222.4 lb-in ÷ 2,790 lb

     = 79.7 in

Then use the weight shift formula:

Weight Moved ÷ Weight of Airplane
= Distance CG Moves ÷ Distance Between Arms

The weight of fuel is 10 gal × 6 lb/gal = 60 lb. The dis-tance between arms is 94 inches − 75 inches = 19 inches. Since the fuel is transferred from an arm of 75 inches to an arm of 94 inches, the CG moves aft 0.4 inches.

Distance CG Moves = 60 lb × 19 in ÷ 2,790 lb = 0.4 in

The new CG is 80.1 (79.7 + 0.4). Then, find the new moment on the chart in Figure 34. The new moment is less than the minimum.

8-44   **PLT328**
(Refer to figure 62.)

If 50 pounds of weight is located at point X and 100 pounds at point Z, how much weight must be located at point Y to balance the plank?

A– 30 pounds.

B– 50 pounds.

C– 300 pounds.

8-44. Answer C. GFDPP 8-35
To solve this problem, you must calculate the moments generated by the weights on each side of the fulcrum, then solve for the unknown weight as shown below.

$(50 \times 50) + (Y \times 25) = (100 \times 100)$

8-45   **PLT328**
(Refer to figure 61.)

How should the 500-pound weight be shifted to balance the plank on the fulcrum?

A– 1 inch to the left.

B– 1 inch to the right.

C– 4.5 inches to the right.

8-45. Answer A. GFDPP 8-41, 42
To solve this problem, the moment of the 500 pound weight on the left side of the fulcrum must equal the sum of the moments of the 250 pound weight and the unequal weight of the plank on the right side.

$500X = (250 \times 20) + (200 \times 15)$

$500X = 5,000$ lb-in $+ 3,000$ lb-in

$500X = 8,000$ lb-in $X = 16$ in.

Since the 500 pound weight is now sitting at 15 inches from the fulcrum, it must be moved 1 inch to the left.

SECTION C — FLIGHT COMPUTERS

Flight computers help the pilot manage a variety of calculations. Whether flight computers are mechanical or electronic, they are essential for flight planning. This section looks at the basic principles of flight computers, as well as covering detailed procedures for problem solving.

MECHANICAL FLIGHT COMPUTERS

In some questions, you will need to calculate the groundspeed and then the estimated time of arrival.

1. Determine the groundspeed of the aircraft: measure the distance between the departure point and the destination. Determine the elapsed time. Divide the distance by the time to derive the groundspeed.

2. Determine the estimated time of arrival (ETA) at the destination by adding the elapsed time to the departure time.

Some questions require you to calculate groundspeed and then complete a time-speed-distance problem.

1. Measure the distance between the departure point and the destination.

2. Determine the true course (TC).

3. Determine the groundspeed, using your flight computer: Enter the wind direction and speed. Enter the TC. Enter the true airspeed (TAS) and find the groundspeed.

4. Determine the time enroute- distance divided by time equals speed.

5. Add departure and climbout time (if any is given). Round as needed to arrive at one of the answer selections.

8-46   PLT005

(Refer to figure 8.)

What is the effect of a temperature increase from 25 to 50°F on the density altitude if the pressure altitude remains at 5,000 feet?

A– 1,200-foot increase.

B– 1,400-foot increase.

C– 1,650-foot increase.

8-46. Answer C. GFDPP 8-9, 56, PHB

Follow the line above 25°F up to where it intersects 5,000 feet pressure altitude, and read 3,750 feet density altitude on the left scale. Do the same with 50°F, up to 5,000 feet, and then left to read 5,400 feet. The difference is an increase of 1,650 feet.

8-47   PLT005

(Refer to figure 8.)

Determine the pressure altitude with an indicated altitude of 1,380 feet MSL with an altimeter setting of 28.22 at standard temperature.

A– 3,010 feet MSL.

B– 2,991 feet MSL.

C– 2,913 feet MSL.

8-47. Answer B. GFDPP 8-9, 56, PHB

Using the table on the right side of the chart, interpolate between 28.2 and 28.3 to get a conversion factor of 1,611 (a value 20% of the way between 1,630 and 1,533). Add this to the indicated altitude of 1,380 for a pressure altitude of 2,991 feet.

8-48   PLT005
(Refer to figure 8.)

Determine the density altitude for these conditions:

Altimeter setting...29.25

Runway temperature...+81°F

Airport elevation...5,250 ft MSL

A– 4,600 feet MSL.

B– 5,877 feet MSL.

C– 8,500 feet MSL.

8-48. Answer C. GFDPP 8-9, 56, PHB
First find the pressure altitude by using the pressure altitude conversion factor scale and interpolate for 29.25. The conversion factor is 626 (673 – 579 = 94 ÷ 2 = 47 + 579 = 626). This is added to 5,250 feet to find a pressure altitude of 5,876 feet. Now, find 81°F on the OAT scale at the bottom of the graph and follow its line vertically to where it intersects with the 5,876-foot pressure altitude line. From this point, follow the horizontal density altitude line to the left scale to find an approximate density altitude of 8,500 feet.

8-49   PLT019
(Refer to figure 8.)

Determine the pressure altitude at an airport that is 3,563 feet MSL with an altimeter setting of 29.96.

A– 3,527 feet MSL.

B– 3,556 feet MSL.

C– 3,639 feet MSL.

8-49. Answer A. GFDPP 8-9, 56, PHB
Find the conversion factors for 30.00 and 29.92, and interpolate to find the factor for 29.96 (–73 – 0 = –73 ÷ 2 = –36.5). Subtract 36.5 from the elevation of 3,563 feet, to find a pressure altitude of 3,526.5 feet. This is rounded to 3,527 feet.

8-50   PLT124
(Refer to figure 8.) What is the effect of a temperature increase from 35 to 50 °F on the density altitude if the pressure altitude remains at 3,000 feet MSL?

A– 1,000-foot increase.

B– 1,100-foot decrease.

C– 1,300-foot increase.

8-50. Answer A. GFDPP 8-9,56, PHB
An increase in temperature increases density altitude (DA). Find the DA for 35°F—about 1,900 feet. At 50°F, the DA is about 2,900 feet, for an increase of 1,000 feet.

8-51   PLT005
(Refer to figure 8.)

Determine the pressure altitude at an airport that is 1,386 feet MSL with an altimeter setting of 29.97.

A– 1,341 feet MSL.

B– 1,451 feet MSL.

C– 1,562 feet MSL.

8-51. Answer A. GFDPP 8-9, 56, PHB
First you must interpolate to find the conversion factor for 29.97 (–73 – 0 = –73 ÷ 8 increments = –9 × 5 increments = –45). Subtract 45 from 1,386 to find the pressure altitude of 1,341 feet.

8-52   **PLT005**

(Refer to figure 8.)

What is the effect of a temperature decrease and a pressure altitude increase on the density altitude from 90°F and 1,250 feet pressure altitude to 55°F and 1,750 feet pressure altitude?

A– 1,750-foot increase.

B– 1,350-foot decrease.

C– 1,750-foot decrease.

8-53   **PLT012**

(Refer to figure 21.)

Enroute to First Flight Airport (area 5), your flight passes over Hampton Roads Airport (area 2) at 1456 and then over Chesapeake Municipal at 1501. At what time should your flight arrive at First Flight?

A– 1516.

B– 1521.

C– 1526.

8-52. Answer C. GFDPP 8-9, 56, PHB

1. Enter the graph at 90°F on the bottom scale. Draw a line straight up to meet the upsloping 1,250 ft. pressure altitude line (visualize this line or draw it in between the 1,000 and 2,000 ft. lines), then go left to 3,600 feet on the density altitude scale.

2. Repeat for 55°F and 1,750 ft. pressure altitude to get a density altitude of 1,850 feet.

3. The difference is (1,850 – 3,600) feet = –1,750 ft.

8-53. Answer C. GFDPP 8-54, PHB

NOTE: Use scale at top of chart for distance.

This question requires you to calculate groundspeed and then estimated time of arrival.

1. Determine the actual groundspeed (GS) of the aircraft.

    a. Measure the distance between Hampton Roads Airport and Chesapeake Municipal (CPK)—10 NM.

    b. Determine the elapsed time (15:01 – 14:56 = 5 min).

    c. Determine the GS (10 NM in 5 min = 2 NM/min × 60 min = 120 knots groundspeed).

2. Determine the estimated time of arrival (ETA) at First Flight Airport.

    a. Measure the distance between Chesapeake Municipal and First Flight Airport (50 NM).

    b. Determine the time enroute between the two points (50 NM at 120 knots = approximately 25 minutes).

    c. If the aircraft was over Chesapeake Municipal at 15:01, the ETA at First Flight Airport is about 15:26. (15:01 + 25 min = 15:26).

8-54   PLT012
(Refer to figure 22.)

What is the estimated time enroute from Mercer County Regional Airport (area 3) to Minot International (area 1)? The wind is from 330° at 25 knots and the true airspeed is 100 knots. Add 3-1/2 minutes for departure and climbout.

A– 44 minutes.

B– 48 minutes.

C– 52 minutes.

8-54. Answer B. GFDPP 8-54, PHB
This question requires you to calculate groundspeed and then complete a time-speed-distance problem.

1. Measure the distance between Mercer County Regional Airport and Minot International (59 NM).

2. Determine the True Course (TC) (012°).

3. Determine the groundspeed using your flight computer.

    a. Enter the wind direction and speed (330° True at 25 knots)

    b. Enter the TC (012°)

    c. Enter the True Air Speed (TAS) (100 knots)

    d. GS = 80 knots

4. Determine the time enroute using your flight computer (59 NM at 80 NM/hr = 44 min 15 sec)

5. Add departure and climbout time (3 min 30 sec + 44 min 15 sec = 47 min 45 sec) This is rounded to 48 minutes.

8-55   PLT012
(Refer to figure 23.)

What is the estimated time enroute from Sandpoint Airport (area 1) to St. Maries Airport (area 4)? The wind is from 215° at 25 knots and the true airspeed is 125 knots.

A– 38 minutes.

B– 34 minutes.

C– 30 minutes.

8-55. Answer B. GFDPP 08-54, PHB
This question requires you to calculate groundspeed and then complete a time-speed-distance problem.

1. Measure the distance from Sandpoint Airport Maries Airport (approximately 58 NM).

2. Determine the true course (TC = 181°).

3. Determine groundspeed using the flight computer.

    a. Enter the wind direction and speed (215° True at 25 knots).

    b. Enter the TC (181°).

    c. Enter the True Airspeed (125 knots).

    d. GS=103 knots

4. Determine the time enroute using the flight computer (58 NM at 103 NM/hr = 34 min).

8-56 **PLT012**

(Refer to figure 23.)

Determine the estimated time enroute for a flight from Priest River Airport (area 1) to Shoshone County Airport (area 3). The wind is from 030 at 12 knots and the true airspeed is 95 knots. Add 2 minutes for climbout.

A– 27 minutes.

B– 29 minutes.

C– 31 minutes.

8-56. Answer C. GFDPP 8-54, PHB

This question requires you to calculate groundspeed and then complete a time-speed-distance problem.

1. Measure the distance from Priest River Airport to Shoshone County Airport (48 NM).

2. Determine the true course (TC = 143°).

3. Determine groundspeed using the flight computer.

   a. Enter the wind direction and speed (030° True at 12 knots).

   b. Enter the TC (143°).

   c. Enter the True Airspeed (95 knots).

   d. GS=99 knots

4. Determine the time enroute using the flight computer (48 NM at 99 NM/hr = 29 min).

5. Add 2 min for departure and climbout (2 min+ 29 min = 31 min).

8-57 **PLT012**

(Refer to figure 23.)

What is the estimated time enroute for a flight from St. Maries Airport (area 4) to Priest River Airport (area 1)? The wind is from 300° at 14 knots and the true airspeed is 90 knots. Add 3 minutes for climbout.

A– 38 minutes.

B– 43 minutes.

C– 48 minutes.

8-57. Answer B. GFDPP 8-54, PHB

This question requires you to calculate groundspeed and then complete a time-speed-distance problem.

1. Measure the distance from St. Maries Airport to Priest River Airport (53 NM).

2. Determine the True Course (345°).

3. Determine groundspeed using your flight computer.

   a. Enter the wind direction and speed (300° at 14 knots).

   b. Enter the True Course (345°).

   c. Enter the TAS (90 knots).

   d. GS = 80 knots

4. Determine the time enroute using your flight computer (53 NM at 80 NM/hr = 39 min 45 sec).

5. Add 3 min for departure and climbout (3 min + 39 min 45 sec = 42 min 45 sec). This is rounded to 43 minutes.

8-58   PLT012
(Refer to figure 24.)

What is the estimated time enroute for a flight from Allendale County Airport (area 1) to Claxton-Evans County Airport (area 2)? The wind is from 100° at 18 knots and the true airspeed is 115 knots. Add 2 minutes for climbout.

A– 33 minutes.

B– 27 minutes.

C– 30 minutes.

8-58. Answer C. GFDPP 8-54, PHB
This question requires you to calculate groundspeed and then complete a time-speed-distance problem.

1. Measure the distance from Allendale County to Claxton-Evans County Airport (57 NM).

2. Determine the true course (TC = 212°).

3. Determine groundspeed using the flight computer.

    a. Enter the wind direction and speed (100° True at 18 knots).

    b. Enter the TC (212°).

    c. Enter the True Airspeed (115 knots).

    d. GS = 121 knots

4. Determine the time enroute using the flight computer (57 NM ÷ a121 NM/hr = 28 min 15 sec).

5. Add 2 min for departure and climbout (2 min + 28 min 15 sec = 30 min 15 sec). This is rounded to 30 minutes.

8-59   PLT012
(Refer to figure 24.)

What is the estimated time enroute for a flight from Claxton-Evans County Airport (area 2) to Hampton Varnville Airport (area 1)? The wind is from 290° at 18 knots and the true airspeed is 85 knots. Add 2 minutes for climbout.

A– 35 minutes.

B– 39 minutes.

C– 44 minutes.

8-59. Answer B. GFDPP 8-54, PHB
This question requires you to calculate groundspeed and then complete a Time-Speed-Distance problem.

1. Measure the distance from Claxton-Evans County Airport to Hampton Varnville Airport (57 NM).

2. Determine the True Course (045°).

3. Determine the groundspeed using your flight computer.

    a. Enter the wind direction and speed (290° at 18 knots).

    b. Enter the True Course (045°).

    c. Enter the TAS (85 knots).

    d. GS = 91 knots

4. Determine the time enroute using your flight computer (57 NM ÷ 91 NM/hr = 37 min 30 sec).

5. Add 2 minutes for departure and climbout (2 min + 37 min 30 sec = 39 min 30 sec) The closest answer is 39 minutes.

8-60   **PLT012**
(Refer to figure 24.)

While enroute on Victor 185, a flight crosses the 248° radial of Allendale VOR at 0953 and then crosses the 216° radial of Allendale VOR at 1000. What is the estimated time of arrival at Savannah VORTAC?

A– 1023.

B– 1036.

C– 1028.

8-60. Answer C. GFDPP 8-54, PHB
This question requires you to calculate groundspeed and then estimated time of arrival.

1.   Determine actual groundspeed of the aircraft.

   a. Measure the distance along Victor 185 where it crosses the 248° radial and the 216° radial of Allendale VOR (10 NM).

   b. Determine the elapsed time. (10:00 – 09:53 = 7 min).

   c. Determine the groundspeed (10 NM in 7 min = 86 knots).

2.   Determine the Estimated Time of Arrival (ETA) over the Savannah VORTAC.

   a. Measure the Distance along Victor 185 from the 216° radial of Allendale VORTAC to the Savannah VORTAC (40 NM).

   b. Determine time enroute (GS is 86 knots) (40 NM ÷ 86 NM/hr = 28 min)

   c. Determine estimated time of arrival (10:00 + 28 mins. = 10:28).

8-61   **PLT012**
(Refer to figure 26.)

What is the estimated time enroute for a flight from Denton Muni (area 1) to Addison (area 2)? The wind is from 200° at 20 knots, the true airspeed is 110 knots, and the magnetic variation is 7° east.

A– 13 minutes.

B– 16 minutes.

C– 19 minutes.

8-61. Answer A. GFDPP 8-54, PHB
This question requires you to calculate groundspeed, then complete a time-speed-distance problem.

1.   Measure the distance from Denton Muni to Addison Airport (23 NM).

2.   Determine True Course (128°).

3.   Determine the groundspeed using your flight computer.

   a. Enter the wind direction and speed (200° at 20 knots).

   b. Enter the True Course (128°).

   c. Enter the TAS (110 knots).

   d. GS = 102 knots

4.   Determine time enroute (23 NM ÷ 102 NM/hr = 13 min 30 sec). The closest answer is 13 minutes.

8-62   PLT012
(Refer to figure 26.)

Estimate the time enroute from Addison (area 2) to Redbird (area 3). The wind is from 300° at 15 knots, the true airspeed is 120 knots, and the magnetic variation is 7° east.

A– 8 minutes.

B– 11 minutes.

C– 14 minutes.

8-62. Answer A. GFDPP 8-54, PHB
This question requires you to calculate groundspeed, then complete a time-speed-distance problem.

1. Measure the distance from Addison Airport to Redbird Airport (17 NM).

2. Determine the true course (186°).

3. Determine the groundspeed using your flight computer.

    a. Enter the wind direction and speed (300° at 15 knots).

    b. Enter the TC (186°).

    c. Enter the TAS (120 knots).

    d. GS = 125 knots

4. Determine time enroute:
    17 NM ÷ 125 NM/hr × 60 min/hr = 8 min

8-63   PLT012
If a true heading of 135° results in a ground track of 130° and a true airspeed of 135 knots results in a groundspeed of 140 knots, the wind would be from

A– 019° and 12 knots

B– 200° and 13 knots

C– 246° and 13 knots

8-63. Answer C. GFDPP 8-61
Use a flight computer to solve for wind direction and velocity. This calculation is essentially the reverse of predicting groundspeed from forecast winds aloft.

8-64   PLT012
(Refer to figure 63.)

In flying the rectangular course, when would the aircraft be turned less than 90°?

A– Corners 1 and 4

B– Corners 1 and 2

C– Corners 2 and 4

8-64. Answer A. GFDPP 8-58, AFH
To maintain the rectangular ground track at turn 1, the aircraft is turned less than 90 degrees to establish a right crab into the wind. Approaching turn 4, the aircraft is crabbed left into the wind and is therefore turned less than 90 degrees into the direct headwind.

8-65 PLT219
(Refer to figure 67.)

While practicing S-turns, a consistently smaller half-circle is made on one side of the road than on the other, and this turn is not completed before crossing the road or reference line. This would most likely occur in turn

A— 1-2-3 because the bank is decreased too rapidly during the latter part of the turn.

B— 4-5-6 because the bank is increased too rapidly during the early part of the turn.

C— 4-5-6 because the bank is increased too slowly during the latter part of the turn.

8-65. Answer B. AFH
Turn 4-5-6 begins with an upwind leg (i.e., traveling into a headwind), resulting in a slower ground speed. The slower ground speed requires the pilot to add bank more slowly than on the downwind leg, so the aircraft has more time to travel equidistant from the "road" as it did on the other side, helping to create a semicircles with the same radii.

8-66 PLT012
How far will an aircraft travel in 2-1/2 minutes with a groundspeed of 98 knots?

A— 2.45 NM.

B— 3.35 NM.

C— 4.08 NM.

8-66. Answer C. GFDPP 8-54
You can solve this problem using a flight computer or mathematically. The basic formula for time, speed, distance calculations is:

Distance = Groundspeed × Time

Distance = 98 NM/hr × 2.5 min ÷ 60 min/hr

8-67 PLT012
How far will an aircraft travel in 7.5 minutes with a ground speed of 114 knots?

A— 14.25 NM.

B— 15.00 NM.

C— 14.50 NM.

8-67. Answer A. GFDPP 8C, PHB
You can calculate this on a flight computer or do the basic math:

114 NM/hr × 7.5 min ÷ 60 min/hr = 14.25 NM

8-68   PLT012

On a cross-country flight, point A is crossed at 1500 hours and the plan is to reach point B at 1530 hours. Use the following information to determine the indicated airspeed required to reach point B on schedule.

Distance between A and B: 70 NM

Forecast wind: 310° at 15 knots

Pressure altitude: 8,000 ft

Ambient temperature: -10°C

True course: 270°

The required indicated airspeed would be approximately

A– 126 knots.

B– 137 knots.

C– 152 knots.

8-68. Answer B. GFDPP 8-56, 8-60, PHB

1. Determine the groundspeed required to reach point B by 1530. Use a flight computer or calculate mathematically:
    70 NM ÷ 30 min × 60 min/hr = 140 knots

2. Use the Winds function of your flight computer to determine the required TAS with the given right quartering headwind: 152 knots

3. Use the airspeed function of your flight computer to determine the indicated airspeed (or calibrated airspeed): 137 knots

CHAPTER 9

NAVIGATION

SECTION A — PILOTAGE AND DEAD RECKONING

Pilotage and dead reckoning allow pilots to navigate over unfamiliar terrain. The two systems are used to cross-check each other, and together they let pilots to create a course and stay on that course. This section covers pilotage, which is navigating through the use of checkpoints, and dead reckoning, which allows you to predict your course along an intended route. Using a navigation log and filling out a flight plan form are also covered.

DEAD RECKONING

Dead reckoning involves calculating distance, speed, time, and direction as a means of navigating from your departure to your destination.

COURSE

- In order to determine a magnetic course, you must first find the true course, using a plotter. Then, find the nearest isogonic line to the course. Next, add or subtract the variation. When the variation listed is west, add it to the true course to derive the magnetic course. If the variation is east, you must subtract it.
- To determine the magnetic heading, you must first determine the true heading by correcting the true course for winds. For this, you'll use the wind side of your flight computer. Then, correct true heading for magnetic variation.

VFR CRUISING ALTITUDES

- On an easterly course (0° to 179°) above 3,000 feet AGL, VFR cruising altitudes are odd thousands plus 500 feet.
- On a westerly course (180° to 359°), VFR cruising altitudes are even thousands plus 500 feet.

FUEL REQUIREMENTS

- For a VFR night flight in an airplane, there must be enough fuel, considering wind and forecast weather conditions, to fly to the first point of intended landing, and, assuming normal cruising speed, 45 minutes beyond that point.
- For VFR day flight in an airplane, there must be enough fuel to fly to the first point of intended landing, and to fly for 30 minutes after that, assuming normal cruising speed.

9-1   PLT467
Which cruising altitude is appropriate for a VFR flight on a magnetic course of 135°?

A— Even thousands.

B— Even thousands plus 500 feet.

C— Odd thousands plus 500 feet.

9-1. Answer C. GFDPP 9-12, FAR 91.159
On an easterly magnetic course (0° to 179°) above 3,000 feet AGL, VFR cruising altitudes are odd thousands plus 500 feet.

9-2   PLT467
Which VFR cruising altitude is acceptable for a flight on a Victor Airway with a magnetic course of 175°? The terrain is less than 1,000 feet.

A– 4,500 feet.

B– 5,000 feet.

C– 5,500 feet.

9-2. Answer C. GFDPP 9-12, FAR 91.159
On an westerly magnetic course (180° to 359°) above 3,000 feet AGL, VFR cruising altitudes are even thousands plus 500 feet.

9-3   PLT467
Which VFR cruising altitude is appropriate when flying above 3,000 feet AGL on a magnetic course of 185°?

A– 4,000 feet.

B– 4,500 feet.

C– 5,000 feet.

9-3. Answer B. GFDPP 9-12, FAR 91.159
On a westerly magnetic course (180° to 359°) above 3,000 feet AGL, VFR cruising altitudes are even thousands plus 500 feet.

9-4   PLT467
Each person operating an aircraft at a VFR cruising altitude shall maintain an odd-thousand plus 500-foot altitude while on a

A– magnetic heading of 0° through 179°.

B– magnetic course of 0° through 179°.

C– true course of 0° through 179°.

9-4. Answer B. GFDPP 9-12, FAR 91.159
On an easterly magnetic course (0° to 179°) above 3,000 feet AGL, VFR cruising altitudes are even thousands plus 500 feet.

9-5   PLT012
(Refer to figure 21.) Determine the magnetic course from First Flight Airport (area 5) to Hampton Roads Airport (area 2).

A– 141°.

B– 321°.

C– 331°.

9-5. Answer C. GFDPP 9-11, PHB
This question requires finding the magnetic course by determining true course, then correcting for magnetic variation.

1. Determine the True Course with a plotter (321°).

2. Locate the nearest isogonic line (10° West).

3. Convert TC to MC by adding west variation (321° + 10° = 331°).

9-6   PLT012
(Refer to figure 22.) Determine the magnetic heading for a flight from Mercer County Regional Airport (area 3) to Minot International (area 1). The wind is from 330° at 25 knots, the true airspeed is 100 knots, and the magnetic variation is 10° east.

A– 002°.

B– 012°.

C– 352°.

9-6. Answer C. GFDPP 9-11, PHB
This question requires you to find magnetic heading. This is done by first determining true heading by correcting true course for winds. Then, correct true heading for magnetic variation.

1. Use your plotter to determine true course (012°).
2. Use your flight computer to determine true heading.
   a. Enter wind direction and speed (330° at 25 kts.).
   b. Enter the true course (012°).
   c. Enter the TAS (100 kts.).
   d. TH = 002°.
3. Convert TH to MH by correcting for magnetic variation (10°E). (Since this is an east variation, you must subtract it from the true heading.) TH ± Variation = MH (002° − 10° = 352°)

9-7   PLT012
(Refer to figure 23.) Determine the magnetic heading for a flight from Sandpoint Airport (area 1) to St. Maries Airport (area 4). The wind is from 215° at 25 knots, and the true airspeed is 125 knots.

A– 169°.

B– 349°.

C– 187°.

9-7. Answer A. GFDPP 9-11, PHB
This question requires you to find magnetic heading. This is done by first determining true heading by correcting true course for winds. Then, correct true heading for magnetic variation.

1. The plotter is used to measure true course (181°).
2. The flight computer is used to determine true heading.
   a. Enter the wind direction and speed (215° at 25 kts.).
   b. Enter the true course (181°).
   c. Enter the TAS (125 kts.).
   d. Determine true heading (TH = 187°).
3. Convert TH to MH by correcting for magnetic variation (18°E). Since this is an east variation, you must subtract it from the true heading.) TH ± Variation = MH (187° − 18° = 169°).

9-8   PLT012
(Refer to figure 23.) What is the magnetic heading for a flight from Priest River Airport (area 1) to Shoshone County Airport (area 3)? The wind is from 030° at 12 knots and the true airspeed is 95 knots.

A– 143°.

B– 118°.

C– 136°.

9-8. Answer B. GFDPP 9-11, PHB
This question requires you to find magnetic heading. This is done by first determining true heading by correcting true course for winds. Then, correct true heading for magnetic variation.

1. The plotter is used to measure true course (143°).
2. The flight computer is used to determine true heading.
   a. Enter the wind direction and speed (030° at 12 kts.).
   b. Enter the true course (143°).
   c. Enter the TAS (95 kts.).
   d. TH = 136°
3. Convert TH to MH by correcting for magnetic variation (18°E). Since this is an east variation, you must subtract it from the true heading.) TH ± Variation = MH (136° − 18° = 118°).

9-9   PLT012
(Refer to figure 23.) Determine the magnetic heading for a flight from St. Maries Airport (area 4) to Priest River Airport (area 1). The wind is from 340° at 10 knots and the true airspeed is 90 knots.

A– 345°.

B– 320°.

C– 327°.

9-9. Answer C. GFDPP 9-11, PHB
This question requires you to find magnetic heading. This is done by first determining true heading by correcting true course for winds. Then, correct true heading for magnetic variation.

1. The plotter is used to measure true course (345°).
2. The flight computer is used to determine true heading.
   a. Enter the wind direction and speed (340° at 10 kts.).
   b. Enter the true course (345°).
   c. Enter the TAS (90 kts.).
   d. TH = 345°
3. Convert TH to MH by correcting for magnetic variation (18°E). Since this is an east variation, you must subtract it from the true heading.) TH± Variation = MH (345° − 18° = 327°).

9-10   PLT012
(Refer to figure 24.) Determine the magnetic heading for a flight from Allendale County Airport (area 1) to Claxton-Evans County Airport (area 2). The wind is from 090° at 16 knots and the true airspeed is 90 knots.

A– 208°.

B– 230°.

C– 212°.

9-10. Answer A. GFDPP 9-11, PHB
This question requires you to find magnetic heading. This is done by first determining true heading by correcting true course for winds. Then, correct true heading for magnetic variation.

1. The plotter is used to measure true course (212°).
2. The flight computer is used to determine true heading.
   a. Enter the wind direction and speed (090° at 16 kts.).
   b. Enter the true course (212°).
   c. Enter the TAS (90 kts.).
   d. TH = 203°
3. Convert TH to MH by correcting for magnetic variation (5°W). Since this is a west variation, you must add it from the true heading.) TH ± Variation = MH (203° + 5° = 208°).

9-11   PLT012
(Refer to figure 24 and 59.) Determine the compass heading for a flight from Claxton-Evans County Airport (area 2) to Hampton Varnville Airport (area 1). The wind is from 280° at 08 knots, and the true airspeed is 85 knots.

A– 033°.

B– 042°.

C– 038°.

9-11. Answer B. GFDPP 9-11, PHB
This question requires you to find the heading, then correct for variation and deviation to achieve compass heading.

1. Use plotter to determine true course (044°).
2. Use flight computer to calculate true heading (040°).
3. Add variation (5°W) to TH to get magnetic heading (045°).
4. Adjust per compass card (-3°) to determine compass heading (042°).

9-12   PLT012
(Refer to figure 25.)

Determine the magnetic course from Airpark East Airport (area 1) to Winnsboro Airport (area 2).

Magnetic variation is 6°30'E.

A– 075°.

B– 082°.

C– 091°

9-12. Answer A. GFDPP 9-11, PHB
This question requires you find the magnetic course by determining true course, then correcting it for magnetic variation.

1. Use your plotter to determine True Course (082°).
2. Locate the nearest isogonic line to the course (6°30'E). (Add West, Subtract East variation)
3. Convert TC to MC by correcting for variation. (Since this is an east variation, you must subtract it from true course.) TC ± Variation = MC (082° – 6°30 = 075°30')

The closest answer is 075°.

9-13   PLT012
(Refer to figure 26.) Determine the magnetic heading for a flight from Fort Worth Meacham (area 4) to Denton Muni (area 1). The wind is from 330° at 25 knots, the true airspeed is 110 knots, and the magnetic variation is 7° east.

A– 003°.

B– 017°.

C– 023°.

9-13. Answer A. GFDPP 9-11, PHB
This question requires you to find magnetic heading. This is done by first determining true heading by correcting true course for winds. Then, correct true heading for magnetic variation.

1. Use your plotter to determine true course (021°).
2. Use your flight computer to determine true heading.
   a. Enter the wind direction and speed (330° at 25 kts.).
   b. Enter the true course (021°).
   c. Enter the TAS (110 kts.).
   d. TH = 011°
3. Convert TH to MH by correcting for magnetic variation (7°E). (Since this is an east variation, you must subtract it from the true heading.) TH ± Variation = MH (011° − 7° = 004°)

The closest answer is 003°.

9-14   PLT012
(Refer to figure 27.) Determine the magnetic course from Breckheimer (Pvt) Airport (area 1) to Jamestown Airport (area 4).

A– 180°.

B– 188°.

C– 360°.

9-14. Answer A. GFDPP 9-11, PHB
The true course, as measured with a plotter, is 190°. The isogonic line down the right side of the figure indicates a 7° east magnetic variation. Subtract easterly variation to get magnetic course (190° − 7° = 183°). 180° is the nearest answer.

9-15   PLT455
(Refer to figure 52.) If more than one cruising altitude is intended, which should be entered in block 7 of the flight plan?

A– Initial cruising altitude.

B– Highest cruising altitude.

C– Lowest cruising altitude.

9-15. Answer A. GFDPP 9-15, PHB
The initial cruising altitude should be entered on the flight plan. Any subsequent altitude changes should be requested from the enroute controller.

9-16   PLT455
(Refer to figure 52.) What information should be entered in block 9 for a VFR day flight?

A– The name of the airport of first intended landing.

B– The name of destination airport if no stopover for more than 1 hour is anticipated.

C– The name of the airport where the aircraft is based.

9-16. Answer B. GFDPP 9-16, PHB
FAR 91.153 states that the flight plan shall include the point of first intended landing. However, the AIM says to enter the destination airport. It also recommends that for a stopover of more than 1 hour, a separate flight plan should be filed.

9-17   PLT455
(Refer to figure 52.) What information should be entered in block 12 for a VFR day flight?

A– The estimated time en route plus 30 minutes.

B– The estimated time en route plus 45 minutes.

C– The amount of usable fuel on board expressed in time.

9-17. Answer C. GFDPP 9-15, 16, PHB
The fuel on board is the total amount of fuel in hours and minutes (usable fuel is assumed).

9-18   PLT455
How should a VFR flight plan be closed at the completion of the flight at a controlled airport?

A– The tower will automatically close the flight plan when the aircraft turns off the runway.

B– The pilot must close the flight plan with the nearest FSS or other FAA facility upon landing.

C– The tower will relay the instructions to the nearest FSS when the aircraft contacts the tower for landing.

9-18. Answer B. GFDPP 9-16, PHB
To close a VFR flight plan, you must notify an FSS or other FAA facility.

SECTION B — VOR NAVIGATION

VOR navigation is the most commonly used system in the country, with over 1,000 installations. VOR navigation is projected to remain central to navigation through the foreseeable future. This section covers the components of the VOR system, including distance measuring equipment (DME), and how to use this equipment in the airplane.

NAVIGATION PROCEDURES

- To find your position relative to a VOR on the sectional chart, draw a line along a radial until it intersects your position, or the position of the object you wish to locate. Determine the radial using the compass rose depicted on the chart. Measure the distance from the VOR using a plotter.

- To determine your course to a VOR, find your position along a radial, and find the reciprocal by adding or subtracting 180° from the radial.

- The magnetic course can be determined by plotting a line from your position or departure point to the VOR. Remember that the radial you read off of the compass rose is the reciprocal of what you would select on the OBS to fly TO the station.

- You can find your position by triangulation, using two or more VORs. Determine the radial you are on from one VOR, and draw a line from the VOR through the compass rose on that radial. Repeat the procedure with another VOR facility. The intersection point will be your location.

- Your position is reflected on the VOR receiver by the position of the CDI needle. If the needle is vertical, you are on the radial selected on the OBS. If the needle shows a left or right deflection, you are left or right of course. If the needle is centered with a FROM indication, the heading tuned in on the OBS reflects the radial you are on. Make sure you have the correct radial selected on the OBS; if you have tuned in the reciprocal, the CDI will reverse-sense.

- If the TO/FROM indicator is blank, you are over the cone of confusion, and the aircraft is either over the station, or on a radial offset 90° from the radial selected on the OBS.

- When the CDI needle is centered during an omnireceiver check using a VOR test signal (VOT), the OBS and the TO/FROM indicator should read 0° FROM or 180° TO, regardless of the aircraft's position in relation to the VOT.

9-19   **PLT014**

(Refer to figure 21.) What is your approximate position on low altitude airway Victor 1, southwest of Norfolk (area 1), if the VOR receiver indicates you are on the 340° radial of Elizabeth City VOR (area 3)?

A– 15 nautical miles from Norfolk VORTAC.

B– 18 nautical miles from Norfolk VORTAC.

C– 23 nautical miles from Norfolk VORTAC.

9-19. Answer B. GFDPP 9-27, PHB

Using the compass rose of the Elizabeth City VOR, draw a line along the 340° radial until it intersects Victor 1. Measure the distance from this point to the Norfolk VORTAC. The distance is 18 nautical miles. 15 NM from Norfolk is the intersection of Victor 1 and the 345° radial. 23 NM from Norfolk VORTAC is the intersection of Victor 1 and the 330° radial. Don't be misled by the number 340 which appears near the 33 on the compass rose. This is the elevation of an obstacle.

9-20   **PLT090**

(Refer to figure 21, Area 3 and figure 29.) The VOR is tuned to Elizabeth City VOR, and the aircraft is positioned over Shawboro, a small town 3 NM west of Currituck County Regional (ONX). Which VOR indication is correct?

A– 2.

B– 5.

C– 9.

9-20. Answer A. GFDPP 9-23, PHB

Shawboro is on the 030° radial of Elizabeth City VOR. A VOR needle would be centered on 030° with a FROM indication or 210° with a TO indication.

9-21   PLT014
(Refer to figure 22.) What course should be selected on the omnibearing selector (OBS) to make a direct flight from Mercer County Regional Airport (area 3) to the Minot VORTAC (area 1) with a TO indication

A– 359°.

B– 179°.

C– 001°.

9-21. Answer A. GFDPP 9-23, PHB
The magnetic course can be determined by plotting a line from Mercer County Regional Airport to the Minot VORTAC. The line intersects the Minot VORTAC compass rose at 179°. The reciprocal of 179° is 359°. This is what you would set in the OBS.

9-22   PLT012
(Refer to figure 24.) What is the approximate position of the aircraft if the VOR receivers indicate the 320° radial of Savannah VORTAC (area 3) and the 184° radial of Allendale VOR (area 1)?

A– Town of Guyton.

B– Town of Springfield.

C– 3 miles east of Marlow.

9-22. Answer B. GFDPP 9-24, PHB
The intersection of these two radials places the aircraft near the town of Springfield. The town of Guyton is southwest of Springfield. Three miles east of Marlow is derived from the intersection of the 185° radial of Allendale VOR and the 300° radial of Savannah VOR.

9-23   PLT014
(Refer to figure 24.) On what course should the VOR receiver (OBS) be set to navigate direct from Hampton Varnville Airport (area 1) to Savannah VORTAC (area 3)?

A– 200°.

B– 183°.

C– 003°.

9-23. Answer B. GFDPP 9-23, PHB
If you draw a line between Hampton Varnville Airport and Savannah VORTAC, it crosses the Savannah compass rose at 003°. To navigate inbound with a "TO" indication, would require the reciprocal of 003°, or 183°, to be set in the OBS.

9-24   PLT014
(Refer to figure 25.) What is the approximate position of the aircraft if the VOR receivers indicate the 245° radial of Sulphur Springs VOR-DME (area 5) and the 140° radial of Bonham VORTAC (area 3)?

A– Meadowview Airport.

B– Glenmar Airport.

C– Majors Airport.

9-24. Answer B. GFDPP 9-23, PHB
Draw the radials from these VORs. The intersection of these two radials puts the aircraft near the Glenmar Airport. Meadowview and Majors Airports are incorrect because they are both west of the Bonham 140° radial.

9-25   PLT014
(Refer to figure 25.) On what course should the VOR receiver (OBS) be set in order to navigate direct from Majors Airport (area 1) to Quitman VORTAC (area 2)?

A– 101°.

B– 108°.

C– 281°.

9-25. Answer A. GFDPP 9-27, PHB
A direct course from Majors Airport to Quitman VORTAC crosses the compass rose at 283°. The inbound course to be set in the OBS is the reciprocal of 283°, or 103°.

9-26   PLT014
(Refer to figure 25 and 29.) The VOR is tuned to Bonham VORTAC (area 3), and the aircraft is positioned over the town of Sulphur Springs (area 5). Which VOR indication is correct?

A– 1

B– 7

C– 8

9-26. Answer B. GFDPP 9-28, PHB
Sulfur Springs lies near the 120° radial of the Bonham VORTAC. Because all of the VOR indicators in the figure have either 030° or 210° set in the OBS, you must determine the position of the aircraft in relation to these settings and the VOR station. Since the 120° radial is perpendicular to the 030°/210° radials, the TO-FROM indicator will indicate "OFF". With the OBS set to 210°, the CDI will be deflected to the right, which is the display on VOR indicator #7. VOR indicators #1 and #8 are incorrect because the TO/FROM indicators indicate "TO" instead of "OFF".

9-27   PLT014
(Refer to figure 26, Area 5.) The VOR is tuned to the Dallas/Fort Worth VORTAC. The omnibearing selector (OBS) is set on 253°, with a TO indication, and a right course deviation indicator (CDI) deflection. What is the aircraft's position from the VORTAC?

A– East-northeast.

B– North-northeast.

C– West-southwest.

9-27. Answer A. GFDPP 9-28, PHB
A course of 253° will take the aircraft to the station. This means the aircraft is currently on the east side of the station near the 073° radial. A CDI deflection to the right places the aircraft to the left of the 073° radial.

9-28   PLT014
(Refer to figure 27, areas 4 and 3, and figure 29.)

The VOR is tuned to Jamestown VOR, and the aircraft is positioned over Cooperstown Airport. Which VOR indication is correct?

A– 1

B– 4

C– 6

9-28. Answer C. GFDPP 9-28, PHB
The FAA question is unclear and should reference areas 4 and 2. Jamestown VOR is in area 4 and the aircraft is positioned over Cooperstown Airport in area 2. The aircraft is on the 027° radial. With the OBS set to 030º, the to-from indicator will read "FROM", and the CDI will show the aircraft left of course as in OBS number 6.

9-29 PLT014
(Refer to figure 29, illustration 1.) The VOR receiver has the indications shown. What is the aircraft's position relative to the station?

A– North.

B– East.

C– South.

9-29. Answer C. GFDPP 9-28, PHB
With the 030° course selected, a "TO" indication, and a left CDI deflection, the aircraft is right of course, between the 120° and 210° radials. Therefore, south is the correct answer.

9-30 PLT014
(Refer to figure 29, illustration 3.) The VOR receiver has the indications shown. What is the aircraft's position relative to the station?

A– East.

B– Southeast.

C– West.

9-30. Answer B. GFDPP 9-28, PHB
Since the TO-FROM indicator is blank, the aircraft is either over the station or on either the 120° or 300° radial. These radials are 90° from the 030° setting. The left CDI deflection puts the aircraft right of the selected radial. Therefore, the correct answer is southeast of the station.

9-31 PLT014
(Refer to figure 29, illustration 8.) The VOR receiver has the indications shown. What radial is the aircraft crossing?

A– 030°.

B– 210°.

C– 300°.

9-31. Answer A. GFDPP 9-28, PHB
The selected course of 210° would take the aircraft to the station, as indicated by a "TO" in the TO-FROM window. This places the aircraft northeast of the station on the reciprocal radial of 210°, which is the 030° radial.

9-32 PLT014
When the course deviation indicator (CDI) needle is centered using a VOR test signal (VOT), the omnibearing selector (OBS) and the TO/FROM indicator should read

A– 180° FROM, only if the pilot is due north of the VOT.

B– 0° TO or 180° FROM, regardless of the pilot's position from the VOT.

C– 0° FROM or 180° TO, regardless of the pilot's position from the VOT.

9-32. Answer C. GFDPP 9-29, AIM
No matter where the aircraft is located in relation to the VOT, the VOR should always read 180° with a "TO" indication or 0° with a "FROM"

SECTION C — ADF NAVIGATION

Another radio navigation system is the Automatic Direction Finder (ADF). ADFs are useful in remote or mountainous locations, where the line of sight nature of the VOR would limit its usefulness. This section covers ADF components, navigation procedures and limitations. The associated ground facilities, called nondirectional radio beacons (NDBs), are also included.

- When using an ADF receiver, remember that the needle simply points to the station.

- To find the magnetic bearing to the station, use the following formula: Magnetic Heading + Relative Bearing = Magnetic Bearing.

The FAA has removed questions relating to ADF Navigation from the Private Pilot Airman Knowledge Test.

SECTION D — ADVANCED NAVIGATION

The pace of technological advances has made it possible for astonishingly accurate and versatile navigation radios to be available at a relatively low cost. Nearly all new aircraft are equipped with global positioning system (GPS) receivers that provide and area navigation (RNAV) capability. The GPS constellation consists of a minimum of 24 satellites, plus a number of spares. It takes 4 satellites to trilaterate your position in three dimensions.

9-33   PLT354
How many satellites make up the Global Positioning System (GPS)?

A– 25.

B– 24.

C– 22.

9-33. Answer B. GFDPPT 9-51
The GPS constellation of 24 satellites is arrayed in orbit so that a minimum of 5 are always observable by a user anywhere on earth.

9-34   PLT354
How many Global Positioning System (GPS) satellites are required to yield a three dimensional position (latitude, longitude, and altitude) and time solution?

A– 5.

B– 4.

C– 6.

9-34. Answer B. GFDPPT 9-51, AIM
The GPS receiver needs access to at least 4 satellites to yield a three-dimensional position (latitude, longitude, and altitude) and time solution.

9-35   PLT354
If Receiver Autonomous Integrity Monitoring (RAIM) capability is lost in-flight,

A– the pilot may still rely on GPS derived altitude for vertical information.

B– the pilot has no assurance of the accuracy of the GPS position.

C– GPS position is reliable provided at least 3 GPS satellites are available.

9-35. Answer B. GFDPPT 9-51, PHB
Receiver Autonomous Integrity Monitoring (RAIM) verifies that enough satellites are in view by your aircraft that if a satellite goes out of view or if the information from a satellite is corrupt, the information from the remaining satellites still provides an accurate position. RAIM provides the degree of reliability necessary for IFR operations. Without RAIM, the accuracy of the GPS position solution is questionable.

APPLYING HUMAN FACTORS PRINCIPLES

SECTION A — AVIATION PHYSIOLOGY

Humans are designed to be earthbound creatures, but we possess a remarkable ability to adapt to our surroundings. Our bodies can adjust to the demands of aviation to a certain extent, but you should be aware of the limitations to what humans can cope with in the air. This section covers the role that vision plays in flight, and the dangers of spatial disorientation, carbon monoxide poisoning, hypoxia and hyperventilation.

VISION IN FLIGHT

Understanding how your eyes work under different conditions is crucial to safe flying. Night flying brings on specific issues of which you should be aware.

NIGHT VISION

- The most effective way to look for traffic during night flight is to scan slowly, to permit off-center viewing. Look to the side of an object for the clearest focus.
- During a night flight, you observe a steady red light and a flashing red light ahead and at the same altitude. The other aircraft is crossing to the left.
- During a night flight, you observe a steady white light and a flashing red light ahead and at the same altitude. The other aircraft is flying away from you.
- During a night flight, you observe steady red and green lights ahead and at the same altitude. The other aircraft is approaching head-on.
- VFR approaches to land at night should be accomplished the same as during the daytime.
- To adapt the eyes for night flying, the pilot should avoid bright white lights for at least 30 minutes before the flight.

DISORIENTATION

- A lack of orientation with regard to the position, attitude, or movement of the aircraft in space is defined as spatial disorientation.
- You can reduce the danger of spatial disorientation during flight in poor visual conditions by trusting in the instruments rather than taking a chance on your kinesthetic senses. Pilots are more subject to spatial disorientation if using body signals to interpret flight attitude.
- If experiencing spatial disorientation during flight in restricted visibility, the best way to overcome the effect is to rely on the aircraft instrument indications.

RESPIRATION AND ALTITUDE

As humans, we depend on oxygen for our survival. During flight, you can climb to altitudes where oxygen is scarce, and you need to be familiar with the effects that decreased oxygen can have on your body's ability to perform.

HYPOXIA

Hypoxia is a state of oxygen deficiency in the body.

CARBON MONOXIDE POISONING

- Large accumulations of carbon monoxide in the body result in the loss of muscular power.
- Susceptibility to carbon monoxide poisoning increases as altitude increases.

HYPERVENTILATION

- Rapid or extra deep breathing while using oxygen can cause a condition known as hyperventilation.
- Emotional tension, anxiety or fear can cause hyperventilation.
- A pilot should be able to overcome the symptoms, or avoid future occurrences of hyperventilation, by slowing the breathing rate, breathing into a bag or talking aloud.

10-1   PLT099
What is the most effective way to use the eyes during night flight?

A— Look only at far away, dim lights.

B— Scan slowly to permit offcenter viewing.

C— Concentrate directly on each object for a few seconds.

10-1. Answer B. GFDPP 10-4, AFH
The rods in the retina are used for night vision. Because they are not located directly behind the pupil, you must use offcenter viewing. Also, in dim light, you might need to move your eyes more slowly to prevent blurring of images than during the day.

10-2   PLT099
The best method to use when looking for other traffic at night is to

A— look to the side of the object and scan slowly.

B— scan the visual field very rapidly.

C— look to the side of the object and scan rapidly.

10-2. Answer A. GFDPP 10-4, AFH
The most effective method of night scanning is to use off center vision, which means looking to the side of an object, and to scan slowly to prevent blurring.

10-3   PLT099
The most effective method of scanning for other aircraft for collision avoidance during nighttime hours is to use

A— regularly spaced concentration on the 3-, 9-, and 12-o'clock positions.

B— a series of short, regularly spaced eye movements to search each 30-degree sector.

C— peripheral vision by scanning small sectors and utilizing offcenter viewing.

10-3. Answer C. GFDPP 10-4, FTH
As with the previous questions, scanning should be done slowly, in small sectors, using offcenter (peripheral) vision.

10-4   PLT333
During a night flight, you observe a steady red light and a flashing red light ahead and at the same altitude. What is the general direction of movement of the other aircraft?

A– The other aircraft is crossing to the left.

B– The other aircraft is crossing to the right.

C– The other aircraft is approaching head-on.

10-4. Answer A. GFDPP 10-5, AFH
The steady red light is a position light on the left wing and the flashing red light is an anticollision beacon. If you are looking at the left wingtip, the other aircraft would be crossing to the left.

10-5   PLT119
During a night flight, you observe a steady white light and a flashing red light ahead and at the same altitude. What is the general direction of movement of the other aircraft?

A– The other aircraft is flying away from you.

B– The other aircraft is crossing to the left.

C– The other aircraft is crossing to the right.

10-5. Answer A. GFDPP 10-5, AFH
The white position light is on the tail and the flashing red light is the anticollision light. Therefore, you would be looking at the rear of the aircraft, which indicates it is flying away from you.

10-6   PLT119
During a night flight, you observe steady red and green lights ahead and at the same altitude. What is the general direction of movement of the other aircraft?

A– The other aircraft is crossing to the left.

B– The other aircraft is flying away from you.

C– The other aircraft is approaching head-on.

10-6. Answer C. GFDPP 10-5, AFH
In this case, you are seeing both wingtip lights. If there was no white tail light in between them, you would most likely be looking head-on at the aircraft.

10-7   PLT333
VFR approaches to land at night should be accomplished

A– at a higher airspeed.

B– with a steeper descent.

C– the same as during daytime.

10-7. Answer C. GFDPP 10-8, AFH
You should try to make night VFR approaches the same as day approaches.

10-8   PLT330
Large accumulations of carbon monoxide in the human body result in

A– tightness across the forehead.

B– loss of muscular power.

C– an increased sense of well-being.

10-8. Answer B. GFDPP 10-15, AC 20-32
The key word in this question is "large" accumulations. This condition can produce a loss of muscle power.

10-9   PLt330
Which statement best defines hypoxia?

A– A state of oxygen deficiency in the body.

B– An abnormal increase in the volume of air breathed.

C– A condition of gas bubble formation around the joints or muscles.

10-9. Answer A. GFDPP 10-13, AIM
Hypoxia occurs when the body tissues do not receive enough oxygen.

10-10   PLT332
When a stressful situation is encountered in flight, an abnormal increase in the volume of air breathed in and out can cause a condition known as

A– hyperventilation.

B– aerosinusitis.

C– aerotitis.

10-10. Answer A. GFDPP 10-18, AIM
Hyperventilation occurs when the breathing rate is too rapid or too deep. It usually occurs with stress and can occur with or without the use of supplemental oxygen. Aerosinusitis is an inflammation of the sinuses and aerotitis is an inflammation of the middle ear. Both are caused by changes in air pressure.

10-11   PLT332
Which would most likely result in hyperventilation?

A– Emotional tension, anxiety, or fear.

B– The excessive consumption of alcohol.

C– An extremely slow rate of breathing and insufficient oxygen.

10-11. Answer A. GFDPP 10-18, AIM
Emotional tension, anxiety, and fear can cause the rapid, deep breathing associated with hyperventilation.

10-12   PLT332
A pilot experiencing the effects of hyperventilation should be able to restore the proper carbon dioxide level in the body by

A– slowing the breathing rate, breathing into a paper bag, or talking aloud.

B– breathing spontaneously and deeply or gaining mental control of the situation.

C– increasing the breathing rate in order to increase lung ventilation.

10-12. Answer A. GFDPP 10-18, AIM
Slowing the breathing rate is one of the best ways to stop hyperventilation. Breathing into a bag and talking aloud are also helpful.

10-13   PLT097
Susceptibility to carbon monoxide poisoning increases as

A– altitude increases.

B– altitude decreases.

C– air pressure increases.

10-13. Answer A. GFDPP 10-14, 15, AC 20-32
Since carbon monoxide poisoning is a form of hypoxia, its effects are increased with altitude, where there is less oxygen available.

10-14   PLT333
What preparation should a pilot make to adapt the eyes for night flying?

A– Wear sunglasses after sunset until ready for flight.

B– Avoid red lights at least 30 minutes before the flight.

C– Avoid bright white lights at least 30 minutes before the flight.

10-14. Answer C. GFDPP 10-5, AIM
The rods in the human eye can take up to 30 minutes to fully adapt to the dark. Bright lights must be avoided for this amount of time.

10-15   PLT334
The danger of spatial disorientation during flight in poor visual conditions may be reduced by

A– shifting the eyes quickly between the exterior visual field and the instrument panel.

B– having faith in the instruments rather than taking a chance on the sensory organs.

C– leaning the body in the opposite direction of the motion of the aircraft.

10-15. Answer B. GFDPP 10-9, AIM
To avoid spatial disorientation, a pilot must rely on the instruments in the cockpit and not the feelings from the sensory organs.

10-16   PLT334
A lack of orientation with regard to the position, attitude, or movement of the aircraft in space is defined as

A– spatial disorientation.

B– hyperventilation.

C– hypoxia.

10-16. Answer A. GFDPP 10-8, PHB
Spatial disorientation occurs when visual cues are removed and the vestibular system in the inner ear and the somatosensory system (nerves and hearing) provide conflicting information to the brain.

10-17   PLT334
Pilots are more subject to spatial disorientation if

A– they ignore the sensations of muscles and inner ear.

B– visual cues are taken away, as they are in instrument meteorological conditions (IMC).

C– eyes are moved often in the process of cross-checking the flight instruments.

10-17. Answer B. GFDPP 10-9, PHB
During flight in visual meteorological conditions (VMC), the eyes are the major orientation source and usually prevail over false sensations from other sensory systems. When these visual cues are taken away, as they are in instrument meteorological conditions (IMC), false sensations can cause a pilot to quickly become disoriented. Pilots can overcome spatial disorientation if they ignore the sensations of muscles and innerear and focus on the flight instruments. Moving the eyes often to cross-check the flight instruments is a proper scanning technique that helps prevent spatial disorientation.

10-18   PLT334

If a pilot experiences spatial disorientation during flight in a restricted visibility condition, the best way to overcome the effect is to

A– rely upon the aircraft instrument indications.

B– concentrate on yaw, pitch, and roll sensations.

C– consciously slow the breathing rate until symptoms clear and then resume normal breathing rate.

10-18. Answer A. GFDPP 10-9, AIM

Since the brain receives confusing messages from the body's senses, the pilot must rely on the aircraft's instruments.

SECTION B — AERONAUTICAL DECISION MAKING

As pilot in command, you are presented with a continuous stream of decisions to make during each flight. Although you can't prepare specifically for every situation you'll encounter, you can be prepared to make effective decisions when these situations arise. Good aeronautical decision making is central to flying safely.

10-19   PLT103
What is it often called when a pilot pushes his or her capabilities and the aircraft's limits by trying to maintain visual contact with the terrain in low visibility and ceiling?

A– Scud running.

B– Mind set.

C– Peer pressure.

10-19. Answer A. AC 60-22
Scud running is one of the operational pitfalls, describing a pilot that tries to maintain visual contact with the surface in low visibility and ceiling. Mind set is another operational pitfall that describes the inability to recognize and cope with changes in the situation different from those anticipated or planned. Peer pressure is an operational pitfall that describes poor decision making based upon emotional response to peers, rather than evaluating a situation objectively.

10-20   PLT103
What is the antidote when a pilot has a hazardous attitude, such as "Antiauthority"?

A– Rules do not apply in this situation.

B– I know what I am doing.

C– Follow the rules.

10-20. Answer C. GFDPP 10B, AC 60-22
The antidote for the hazardous attitude, "Antiauthority" is: Follow the rules, they are usually right. "Rules do not apply in this situation" and "I know what I am doing" are not antidotes to any of the hazardous attitudes.

10-21   PLT103
What antidotal phrase can help reverse the hazardous attitude of impulsivity?

A– It could happen to me.

B– Do it quickly to get it over with.

C– Not so fast, think first.

10-21. Answer C. GFDPP 10B, AC 60-22
The antidote for the hazardous attitude, "Impulsivity" is: Not so fast, think first. "It could happen to me" and "Do it quickly to get it over with" are not antidotes to any of the hazardous attitudes.

10-22   PLT103
What is the antidote when a pilot has a hazardous attitude, such as "Invulnerability"?

A– It will not happen to me.

B– It cannot be that bad.

C– It could happen to me.

10-22. Answer C. GFDPP 10B, AC 60-22
The antidote for the hazardous attitude, "Invulnerability" is: It could happen to me. "It will not happen to me" and "It can not be that bad" are not antidotes to any of the hazardous attitudes.

10-23   PLT104
What is the antidote when a pilot has a hazardous attitude, such as "Macho"?

A– I can do it.

B– Taking chances is foolish.

C– Nothing will happen.

10-23. Answer B. GFDPP 10B, AC 60-22
The antidote for the hazardous attitude, "Macho" is: Taking chances is foolish. "I can do it" and "Nothing will happen" are not antidotes to any of the hazardous attitudes.

10-24   PLT104
What is the antidote when a pilot has a hazardous attitude, such as "Resignation"?

A– What is the use.

B– Someone else is responsible.

C– I am not helpless.

10-24. Answer C. GFDPP 10B, AC 60-22
The antidote for the hazardous attitude, "Resignation" is: I am not helpless. "What is the use" and "Someone else is responsible" are not antidotes to any of the hazardous attitudes.

10-25   PLT104
Who is responsible for determining whether a pilot is fit to fly for a particular flight, even though he or she holds a current medical certificate?

A– The FAA.

B– The medical examiner.

C– The pilot.

10-25. Answer C. GFDPP 10B, AC 60-22
You, the pilot, are always responsible for determining if you are fit to fly for a particular flight. The FAA and medical examiners determine if you are fit to hold a medical certificate.

10-26   PLT104
What is the one common factor which affects most preventable accidents?

A– Structural failure.

B– Mechanical malfunction.

C– Human error.

10-26. Answer C. GFDPP 10B, AC 60-22
Most preventable accidents have one common factor: human error rather than a mechanical malfunction or structural failure. According to NTSB statistics gathered from 1992 to 1996, the pilot was the general cause or a contributing factor in 49% of the accidents. Whereas the aircraft only accounted for 19% of the accidents.

10-27   PLT103
What often leads to spatial disorientation or collision with ground/obstacles when flying under Visual Flight Rules (VFR)?

A– Continual flight into instrument conditions.

B– Getting behind the aircraft.

C– Duck-under syndrome.

10-27. Answer A. GFDPP 10B, AC 60-22
Continuing flight under VFR into instrument conditions often leads to spatial disorientation or collision with ground/obstacles. Getting behind the aircraft does not normally result in spatial disorientation or collision with the ground. Although duck-under syndrome often leads to impact with the ground, it normally does not result in spatial disorientation.

10-28　　　PLT104
What is one of the neglected items when a pilot relies on short and long term memory for repetitive tasks?

A– Checklists.

B– Situation awareness.

C– Flying outside the envelope.

10-28. Answer A. AC 60-22
Pilots that rely on their memory for repetitive tasks, do not normally use checklists.

10-29　　　PLT103
Hazardous attitudes occur to every pilot to some degree at some time. What are some of these hazardous attitudes?

A– Poor risk management and lack of stress management.

B– Antiauthority, impulsivity, macho, resignation, and invulnerability.

C– Poor situational awareness, snap judgments, and lack of a decision making process.

10-29. Answer B. GFDPP 10B, PHB
The commonly listed hazardous attitudes are antiauthority, impulsivity, macho, resignation, and invulnerability. Each has its own "antidote" indicated below:

Anti-authority—Follow the rules, they are usually right.

Impulsivity—Not so fast. Think first.

Macho—taking chances is foolish.

Resignation—I'm not helpless, I can make a difference.

Invulnerability—It could happen to me.

10-30　　　PLT103
In the aeronautical decision making (ADM) process, what is the first step in neutralizing a hazardous attitude?

A– Making a rational judgment.

B– Recognizing hazardous thoughts.

C– Recognizing the invulnerability of the situation.

10-30. Answer B. GFDPP 10B, PHB
To prevent hazardous attitudes from endangering a flight, pilots must recognize a hazardous attitude, correctly label the thought, and recall its antidote.

10-31　　　PLT104
Risk management, as part of the aeronautical decision making (ADM) process, relies on which features to reduce the risks associated with each flight?

A– Application of stress management and risk element procedures.

B– Situational awareness, problem recognition, and good judgment.

C– The mental process of analyzing all information in a particular situation and making a timely decision on what action to take.

10-31. Answer B. GFDPP 10B, PHB
As defined by the FAA, Risk Management is the part of the decision making process which relies on situational awareness, problem recognition, and good judgment to reduce risks associated with each flight.

10-32   PLT011

A pilot and two passengers landed on a 2,100-foot east-west gravel strip with an elevation of 1,800 feet. The temperature is warmer than expected and after computing the density altitude it is determined the takeoff distance over a 50 foot obstacle is 1,980 feet. The airplane is 75 pounds under gross weight. What would be the best choice?

A— Take off to the west because the headwind will give the extra climb-out time needed.

B— Try a takeoff without the passengers to make sure the climb is adequate.

C— Wait until the temperature decreases, and recalculate the takeoff performance.

10B. Answer C. AOPA ASI SA18

ADM and risk management questions often don't have a clear-cut answer. Technically, the airplane could take off under the conditions given if no obstacles were present, but the safety margin is not as much as planned (which you can infer from the warmer-than-expected temperature in the scenario). The AOPA Air Safety Institute 50/50 solution, a widely accepted safety recommendation, is to add 50 percent to the takeoff distance over a 50-foot obstacle. In this case, the required runway length would be $1,980 \times 1.50 = 2,970$ feet. Therefore, waiting for the temperature to decrease is the most prudent option.

Nothing in the scenario suggests that taking off to the west would provide a more favorable headwind. Taking off without passengers to "test" the performance might seem like a good option, but it does not provide conclusive performance data by which to risk subsequently taking off with the passengers.

CHAPTER 11

FLYING CROSS-COUNTRY

SECTION A — THE FLIGHT PLANNING PROCESS

Thorough preflight planning has made cross-country flight much safer since the early days. Preflight planning utilizes the knowledge and skills that you have acquired during the course of your training. This section covers aspects of preflight protocol, including airworthiness, preflight inspection, route selection, weather considerations, completing a navigation log and cockpit management.

PREFLIGHT INSPECTION

- Each pilot in command shall, before beginning a flight, become familiar with all available information concerning that flight.
- Preflight action, as required for all flights away from the vicinity of an airport, shall include an alternate course of action if the flight cannot be completed as planned.
- In addition to the other preflight actions for a VFR flight away from the vicinity of the departure airport, regulations specifically require the pilot in command to determine runway lengths at airports of intended use and the aircraft's takeoff and landing distance data.

AIRWORTHINESS

- The Airworthiness Certificate of an airplane remains valid as long as the aircraft is maintained and operated as required by Federal Aviation Regulations.
- The owner or operator of an aircraft is responsible for ensuring that an aircraft is maintained in an airworthy condition.

WALK-AROUND INSPECTION

- The pilot in command is responsible for determining if an aircraft is in condition for safe flight.
- In regard to preflighting an aircraft, the minimum expected of a pilot prior to every flight is to perform a walk-around inspection.
- The use of a written checklist is recommended for preflight inspection and engine start to ensure that all necessary items are checked in a logical sequence.
- After an aircraft has been stored for an extended period of time, the pilot should make a special check for damage or obstructions caused by animals, birds, or insects.

11-1   PLT377
How long does the Airworthiness Certificate of an aircraft remain valid?

A– As long as the aircraft has a current Registration Certificate.

B– Indefinitely, unless the aircraft suffers major damage.

C– As long as the aircraft is maintained and operated as required by Federal Aviation Regulations.

11-1. Answer C. GFDPP 11-11, PHB
The Airworthiness Certificate remains valid only as long as the aircraft is maintained and operated in accordance with the FARs.

11-2   PLT444
During the preflight inspection who is responsible for determining the aircraft is safe for flight?

A– The owner or operator.

B– The certificated mechanic who performed the annual inspection.

C– The pilot in command.

11-2. Answer C. GFDPP 11-11, PHB
The owner or operator is generally responsible to make sure that the required maintenance and inspections are performed. These tasks may be assigned to a certificated maintenance technician, but the responsibility for compliance remains with the owner or operator. Preflight inspection is the responsibility of the pilot in command (PIC). Prior to every flight, the PIC is required to accomplish a thorough and systematic preflight to ensure that the aircraft is safe for flight. The preflight inspection should be completed according to procedures recommended by the manufacturer. Normally, this means the PIC should use a checklist for the preflight inspection.

11-3   PLT444
How should an aircraft preflight inspection be accomplished for the first flight of the day?

A– Thorough and systematic means recommended by the manufacturer.

B– Quick walk around with a check of gas and oil.

C– Any sequence as determined by the pilot-in-command.

11-3. Answer A. GFDPP 11-11, 12, PHB
The owner or operator is generally responsible to make sure that the required maintenance and inspections are performed. These tasks may be assigned to a certificated maintenance technician, but the responsibility for compliance remains with the owner or operator. Preflight inspection is the responsibility of the pilot in command (PIC). Prior to every flight, the PIC is required to accomplish a thorough and systematic preflight to ensure that the aircraft is safe for flight. The preflight inspection should be completed according to procedures recommended by the manufacturer. Normally, this means the PIC should use a checklist for the preflight inspection.

11-4   PLT377
Who is primarily responsible for maintaining an aircraft in airworthy condition?

A– Pilot-in-command.

B– Owner or operator.

C– Mechanic.

11-4. Answer B. GFDPP 11-11, PHB
The owner or operator is generally responsible to make sure that the required maintenance and inspections are performed. These tasks may be assigned to a certificated maintenance technician, but the responsibility for compliance remains with the owner or operator. Preflight inspection is the responsibility of the pilot in command (PIC). Prior to every flight, the PIC is required to accomplish a thorough and systematic preflight to ensure that the aircraft is safe for flight. The preflight inspection should be completed according to procedures recommended by the manufacturer. Normally, this means the PIC should use a checklist for the preflight inspection.

SECTION B — THE FLIGHT

Not every flight follows the carefully laid plans you've set during the flight planning process. However, this preparation allows you to better deal with any contingency that might arise. Although no FAA test questions specifically relate to this section, Chapter 11 of the *Private Pilot* textbook contains a valuable, detailed walkthrough of a typical cross-country flight.

FEDERAL AVIATION REGULATIONS

SECTION A — 14 CFR PART 1— DEFINITIONS AND ABBREVIATIONS

As a private pilot, you should have a working understanding of Parts 1, 61, 91, and NTSB 830 of the Federal Aviation Regulations (FARs). Although some information regarding FARs is included in the Private Pilot Manual, you should include a current publication of the FARs in your test preparation, to ensure that you learn all appropriate flight regulations. A FAR/AIM book and CD-ROM, published by Jeppesen Sanderson, are available along with other private pilot training materials. These books include a recommended study list, along with exercises to assist you in preparing for the computer test. This section covers pertinent definitions and abbreviations from Part 1.

NIGHT
The definition of nighttime is the time between the end of evening civil twilight and the beginning of morning civil twilight.

V-SPEEDS
* V_{FE} represents the maximum flap operating speed.
* V_{LE} represents the maximum landing gear extended speed.
* V_{NO} is defined as the maximum structural cruising speed.
* V_{SO} is defined as the stalling speed or minimum steady flight speed in the landing configuration.

PREVENTIVE MAINTENANCE
Preventive maintenance includes such items as servicing landing gear wheel bearings and replenishing hydraulic fluid.

12-1   PLT383
The definition of nighttime is

A– sunset to sunrise.

B– 1 hour after sunset to 1 hour before sunrise.

C– the time between the end of evening civil twilight and the beginning of morning civil twilight.

12-1. Answer C. FAR 1.1
Night is the time between the end of evening civil twilight and the beginning of morning civil twilight. One hour after sunset to one hour before sunrise is used for night currency, because it approximately corresponds to nighttime.

12-2   PLT506
Which V-speed represents maximum flap extended speed?

A – V_{FE}.

B – V_{LOF}.

C – V_{FC}.

12-2. Answer A. FAR 1.2
V_{FE} is defined as maximum flap extended speed.

12-3   PLT506
Which V-speed represents maximum landing gear extended speed?

A– V_{LE}.

B– V_{LO}.

C – V_{FE}.

12-3. Answer A. FAR 1.2
V_{LE} is defined as maximum landing gear extended speed.

12-4   PLT506
V_{NO} is defined as the

A– normal operating range.

B – never-exceed speed.

C – maximum structural cruising speed.

12-4. Answer C. FAR 1.2
V_{NO} is defined as maximum structural cruising speed.

12-5   PLT506
V_{SO} is defined as the

A– stalling speed or minimum steady flight speed in the landing configuration.

B – stalling speed or minimum steady flight speed in a specified configuration.

C – stalling speed or minimum takeoff safety speed.

12-5. Answer A. FAR 1.2
V_{SO} is stalling speed or minimum steady flight speed in a landing configuration.

12-6   PLT446
Which operation would be described as preventive maintenance?

A– Repair of landing gear brace struts.

B– Replenishing hydraulic fluid.

C– Repair of portions of skin sheets by making additional seams.

12-6. Answer B. FAR 1.1, FAR 43 App A
Replenishing hydraulic fluid is listed as preventive maintenance in FAR Part 43, Appendix A. Structural repairs, such as those to landing gear brace struts, or adding seams to skin, are *not* preventive maintenance and require an appropriate aircraft mechanic certificate.

SECTION B — 14 CFR PART 61 — CERTIFICATION: PILOTS, FLIGHT INSTRUCTORS, AND GROUND INSTRUCTORS

As a pilot, you'll need to know the Part 61 requirements for obtaining certificates and ratings, and the privileges and limitations associated with your license.

PILOT DOCUMENTS

- While operating an aircraft as pilot in command, you must have both your medical certificate and your pilot certificate in your personal possession.

- Each person who holds a pilot certificate or a medical certificate shall present it for inspection upon the request of the Administrator, the National Transportation Safety Board, or any federal, state, or local law enforcement officer.

MEDICAL CERTIFICATES

- A third-class medical certificate is good until the end of the 24th calendar month after the date of examination, if the pilot is age 40 or over.

- A third-class medical is good until the end of the 60th calendar month after the date of examination, if the pilot is under age 40.

- To exercise the privileges of a commercial pilot, a second-class medical is good until the end of the 12th calendar month after the date of examination. For private pilot operations, a second-class medical is good until the end of the 24th calendar month after the date of examination, if over age 40, and until the end of the 60th month after the date of examination, if under age 40.

- For pilots 40 or over, a first-class medical is valid to exercise the privileges of an ATP, until the end of the 6th calendar month after the date of examination. At that point, the medical allows for second-class privileges, such as those requiring a commercial certificate, until the end of the 12th calendar month following the date of examination. After that, the certificate is good for third class privileges, such as those allowed by a private pilot certificate, until the end of the 24th calendar month after the date of examination. If the pilot is under age 40, the first-class medical certificate is valid until the end of the 12th month for first and second class privileges, with third-class privileges available until the end of the 60th calendar month after the date of examination.

TYPE RATINGS

The pilot in command is required to hold a type rating for the operation of aircraft having a gross weight of more than 12,500 pounds.

HIGH-PERFORMANCE AND COMPLEX AIRPLANES

- The definition of a high-performance airplane is an airplane that has an engine with more than 200 horsepower.

- Before a person holding a private pilot certificate may act as pilot in command of a high-performance airplane, that person must have received flight instruction from an authorized flight instructor, who then endorses that person's logbook. The instruction must be given in a high-performance airplane.

- The definition of a complex airplane is an airplane with retractable landing gear, flaps, and a controllable propeller or full autority digital engine control (FADEC).

- Before a person holding a private pilot certificate may act as pilot in command of a complex airplane, that person must have received flight instruction from an authorized flight instructor, who then endorses that person's logbook. The instruction must be given in a complex airplane.

FLIGHT REVIEW

To act as pilot in command of an aircraft carrying passengers, a pilot must show by logbook endorsement the satisfactory completion of a flight review or completion of a pilot proficiency check within the preceding 24 calendar months.

RECENCY OF FLIGHT EXPERIENCE

- If recency of experience requirements for night flight are not met, the latest time passengers may be carried is 1 hour after official sunset. The three takeoffs and landings required to act as pilot in command at night must be done during the time period from 1 hour after sunset to 1 hour before sunrise.

- To act as pilot in command of an aircraft carrying passengers, the pilot must have made at least three takeoffs and three landings in an aircraft of the same category and class, and if a type rating is required, of the same type, within the preceding 90 days.

- The takeoffs and landings required to meet the recency of flight experience requirements for carrying passengers in a tailwheel airplane must be to a full stop.

- To meet the recency of experience requirements to act as pilot in command carrying passengers at night, a pilot must have made at least three takeoffs and three landings to a full stop within the preceding 90 days in the same category and class of aircraft to be used.

CHANGE OF ADDRESS

If a certificated pilot changes permanent mailing address and fails to notify the FAA Airmen Certification Branch of the new address, the pilot is entitled to exercise the privileges of the pilot certificate for a period of only 30 days after the date of the move.

GLIDER TOWING

- A certificated pilot may not act as pilot in command of an aircraft towing a glider unless there is entered in the pilot's logbook a minimum of 100 hours of pilot flight time in powered aircraft.

- To act as pilot in command of an aircraft towing a glider, a person is required to have made within the preceding 12 months at least three actual or simulated glider tows while accompanied by a qualified pilot.

PRIVATE PILOT LIMITATIONS

- A private pilot may share the pro rata share of the operating expenses of the flight with a passenger.

- A private pilot may act as pilot in command of an aircraft used in a passenger-carrying airlift sponsored by a charitable organization, and for which the passengers make a donation to the organization.

12-7   PLT399

What document(s) must be in your personal possession or readily accessible in the aircraft while operating as pilot in command of an aircraft?

A– A pilot certificate with an endorsement showing accomplishment of an annual flight review and a pilot logbook showing recency of experience.

B– Certificates showing accomplishment of a checkout in the aircraft and a current biennial flight review.

C– An appropriate pilot certificate and an appropriate current medical certificate if required.

12-7. Answer C. FAR 61.3
Both an appropriate pilot certificate and an appropriate medical certificate if required, must be in your personal possession or readily accessible in the aircraft in order to act as pilot in command of an aircraft.

12-8   PLT399

When must a current pilot certificate be in the pilot's personal possession or readily accessible in the aircraft?

A– When acting as a crew chief during launch and recovery.

B– Only when passengers are carried.

C– Anytime when acting as pilot in command or as a required crewmember.

12-8. Answer C. FAR 61.3
You must have a current pilot certificate in your personal possession or readily accessible in the aircraft whenever you are pilot in command or acting as a required pilot flight crewmember.

12-9   PLT399

A private pilot acting as pilot in command, or in any other capacity as a required pilot flight crewmember, must have in his or her personal possession or readily accessible in the aircraft a current

A– endorsement on the pilot certificate to show that a flight review has been satisfactorily accomplished.

B– medical certificate if required and an appropriate pilot certificate.

C– logbook endorsement to show that a flight review has been satisfactorily accomplished.

12-9. Answer B. FAR 61.3
To act as PIC or as a required crewmember, you must have an appropriate medical certificate, if required, and an appropriate pilot certificate. Although you must have a logbook (not pilot certificate) endorsement of completing a flight review within the preceding 24 calendar months, you are not required to carry the logbook that contains this endorsement.

12-10   PLT399

Each person who holds a pilot certificate or a medical certificate shall present it for inspection upon the request of the Administrator, the National Transportation Safety Board, or any

A— authorized representative of the Department of Transportation.

B— person in a position of authority.

C— Federal, state, or local law enforcement officer.

12-10. Answer C. FAR 61.3

By regulation you, as the pilot, are required to present your pilot certificate upon request of the administrator, an authorized representative of the National Transportation Safety Board (NTSB) or any Federal, State, or local law enforcement officer.

12-11   PLT427

A Third-Class Medical Certificate is issued to a

36-year-old pilot on August 10, this year. To exercise the privileges of a Private Pilot Certificate, the medical certificate will be valid until midnight on

A— August 10, 3 years later.

B— August 31, 3 years later.

C— August 31, 5 years later.

12-11. Answer C. FAR 61.23

A recent change in the regulations extended the duration of this certificate from three to five years for pilots under 40 years of age. Their Third-Class Medical Certificate expires at the end of the 60th month after the examination.

12-12   PLT427

A Third-Class Medical Certificate is issued to a 51-year-old pilot on May 3, this year. To exercise the privileges of a Private Pilot Certificate, the medical certificate will be valid until midnight on

A— May 3, 1 year later.

B— May 31, 1 year later.

C— May 31, 2 years later.

12-12. Answer C. FAR 61.23

A third-class medical is good until the end of the 24th calendar month after the date of examination, if age 40 and over.

12-13   PLT427

For private pilot operations, a Second-Class Medical Certificate issued to a 42-year-old pilot on July 15, this year, will expire at midnight on

A— July 15, 2 years later.

B— July 31, 1 year later.

C— July 31, 2 years later.

12-13. Answer C. FAR 61.23

To exercise the privileges of a commercial pilot, a second-class medical is good until the end of the 12th calendar month after the date of examination. For private pilot operations, a second-class medical is good until the end of the 24th calendar month after the date of examination, if age 40 and over.

12-14   PLT447
For private pilot operations, a First-Class Medical Certificate issued to a 23-year-old pilot on October 21, this year, will expire at midnight on

A— October 21, 2 years later.

B— October 31, next year.

C— October 31, 5 years later.

12-14. Answer C. FAR 61.23
For pilots under 40 years of age, to exercise the privileges of an ATP, a first-class medical is good until the end of the 12th calendar month after the date of examination. From the beginning of the 13th month to the end of the 60th calendar month, a first-class medical is good only for operations requiring a third-class medical.

12-15   PLT399
The pilot in command is required to hold a type rating in which aircraft?

A— Aircraft involved in ferry flights, training flights, or test flights.

B— Aircraft having a gross weight of more than 12,500 pounds.

C— Aircraft operated under an authorization issued by the Administrator.

12-15. Answer B. FAR 1.1, FAR 61.5, FAR 61.31
FAR 61.31 indicates that a type rating is required for a large aircraft. FAR 1.1 defines large aircraft as having a gross weight greater than 12,500 pounds.

12-16   PLT399
What is the definition of a high-performance airplane?

A— An airplane with 180 horsepower, or retractable landing gear, flaps, and a fixed-pitch propeller.

B— An airplane with a normal cruise speed in excess of 200 knots.

C— An airplane with an engine of more than 200 horsepower.

12-16. Answer C. FAR 61.31
A high-performance airplane has an engine with more than 200 horsepower. A complex airplane has retractable landing gear, flaps, and a controllable propeller. Cruise speed is not used to determine whether an airplane is high performance.

12-17   PLT399
Before a person holding a private pilot certificate may act as pilot in command of a high-performance airplane, that person must have

A— passed a flight test in that airplane from an FAA inspector.

B— an endorsement in that person's logbook that he or she is competent to act as pilot in command.

C— received ground and flight instruction from an authorized flight instructor who then endorses that person's logbook.

12-17. Answer C. FAR 61.31
In order to act as pilot in command of a high-performance airplane, you must have received ground and flight instruction from an authorized flight instructor who then endorses that person's logbook.

12-18   PLT448

In order to act as pilot in command of a high-performance airplane, a pilot must have

A— received and logged ground and flight instruction in an airplane that has more than 200 horsepower.

B— made and logged three solo takeoffs and landings in a high-performance airplane.

C— passed a flight test in a high-performance airplane.

12-18. Answer A. FAR 61.31

No person may act as pilot in command of a high-performance airplane (an airplane with an engine of more than 200 horsepower) unless that person has received ground and flight instruction from an authorized flight instructor in a high-performance airplane and received a one-time endorsement in that person's logbook showing proficiency.

12-19   PLT444

To act as pilot in command of an aircraft carrying passengers, a pilot must show by logbook endorsement the satisfactory completion of a flight review or completion of a pilot proficiency check within the preceding

A— 6 calendar months.

B— 12 calendar months.

C— 24 calendar months.

12-19. Answer C. FAR 61.56

To act as pilot in command of any aircraft, whether you are carrying passengers or not, you must have, within the preceding 24 calendar months, complied with the flight review requirements.

12-20   PLT444

If recency of experience requirements for night flight are not met and official sunset is 1830, the latest time passengers may be carried is

A— 1829.

B— 1859.

C— 1929.

12-20. Answer C. FAR 61.57

No person may act as pilot in command of an aircraft carrying passengers during the period beginning 1 hour after sunset and ending 1 hour before sunrise, unless that person meets night experience requirements.

12-21   PLT444

To act as pilot in command of an aircraft carrying passengers, the pilot must have made at least three takeoffs and three landings in an aircraft of the same category, class, and if a type rating is required, of the same type, within the preceding

A— 90 days.

B— 12 calendar months.

C— 24 calendar months.

12-21. Answer A. FAR 61.57

To meet recent flight experience requirements for carrying passengers, the pilot in command must have, within the preceding 90 days, made three takeoffs and landings (to a full stop for night currency requirements).

12-22   PLT444
To act as pilot in command of an aircraft carrying passengers, the pilot must have made three takeoffs and three landings within the preceding 90 days in an aircraft of the same

A– make and model.

B– category and class, but not type.

C– category, class, and type, if a type rating is required.

12-22. Answer C. FAR 61.57
To meet the recency of experience requirements for carrying passengers, FAR 61.57(c) states that you must have made three takeoffs and landings within the preceding 90 days in an aircraft of the same category and class, and if a type rating is required, of the same type.

12-23   PLT451
The takeoffs and landings required to meet the recency of experience requirements for carrying passengers in a tailwheel airplane

A– may be touch and go or full stop.

B– must be touch and go.

C– must be to a full stop.

12-23. Answer C. FAR 61.57
On a tailwheel airplane, skillful handling is required to avoid ground looping the airplane, especially in adverse wind conditions. Touch and go landings, especially wheel landings, would be inadequate for obtaining this difficult practice. That is why the FAA requires full-stop landings for currency in a tail dragger.

12-24   PLT451
The three takeoffs and landings that are required to act as pilot in command at night must be done during the time period from

A– sunset to sunrise.

B– 1 hour after sunset to 1 hour before sunrise.

C– the end of evening civil twilight to the beginning of morning civil twilight.

12-24. Answer B. FAR 61.57
To act as pilot in command of an aircraft carrying passengers between one-hour after sunset and one-hour before sunrise, the pilot must have, within the preceding 90 days, made three takeoffs and landings to a full stop.

12-25   PLT444
To meet the recency of experience requirements to act as pilot in command carrying passengers at night, a pilot must have made at least three takeoffs and three landings to a full stop within the preceding 90 days in

A– the same category and class of aircraft to be used.

B– the same type of aircraft to be used.

C– any aircraft.

12-25. Answer A. FAR 61.57
No person may act as pilot in command of an aircraft carrying passengers at night unless that person has made three takeoffs and three landings to a full stop within the preceding 90 days. The takeoffs and landings must be at night and in the same category and class of aircraft that is to be used for the carriage of passengers.

12-26   PLT387
If a certificated pilot changes permanent mailing address and fails to notify the FAA Airmen Certification Branch of the new address, the pilot is entitled to exercise the privileges of the pilot certificate for a period of only

A– 30 days after the date of the move.

B– 60 days after the date of the move.

C– 90 days after the date of the move.

12-26. Answer A. FAR 61.60
As a pilot, you may not exercise the privileges of your certificate after 30 days from the date of your permanent mailing address change unless you notify the FAA's Airman Certificate Branch in writing of the new address.

12-27   PLT444
A certificated private pilot may not act as pilot in command of an aircraft towing a glider unless there is entered in the pilot's logbook a minimum of

A– 100 hours of pilot-in-command time in the aircraft category, class, and type, if required, that the pilot is using to tow a glider.

B– 200 hours of pilot-in-command time in the aircraft category, class, and type, if required, that the pilot is using to tow a glider.

C– 100 hours of pilot flight time in any aircraft, that the pilot is using to tow a glider.

12-27. Answer A. FAR 61.69
No person may act as pilot in command for towing a glider unless that person has logged at least 100 hours of pilot-in-command time in the aircraft category, class, and type, if required, that the pilot is using to tow a glider.

12-28   PLT444
To act as pilot in command of an aircraft towing a glider, a pilot is required to have made within the preceding 12 months

A– at least three flights in a powered glider.

B– at least three flights as observer in a glider being towed by an aircraft.

C– at least three actual or simulated glider tows while accompanied by a qualified pilot.

12-28. Answer C. FAR 61.69
The pilot in command of an aircraft towing a glider must have, within the preceding 12 months, made at least three actual or simulated glider tows while accompanied by a qualified pilot, or made at least three flights as PIC of a glider towed by an aircraft.

12-29   **PLT427**

A third-class medical certificate was issued to a 19-year-old pilot on August 10, this year. To exercise the privileges of a private pilot certificate, the medical certificate will expire at midnight on

A– August 31, 5 years later.

B– August 31, 2 years later.

C– August 10, 2 years later.

12-29. Answer A. FAR 61.23

A third-class medical, which is appropriate to exercise the privileges of a private pilot, expires at the end of the 60th calendar month after the date of examination, if under the age of 40.

12-30   **PLT407**

If a private pilot had a flight review on August 8, this year, when is the next flight review required?

A– August 31, next year.

B– August 8, 2 years later.

C– August 31, 2 years later.

12-30. Answer C. FAR 61.56

To act as pilot in command of an aircraft, a private pilot must have, within the preceding 24 calendar months, complied with the biennial flight review (BFR) requirement. (Calendar month means the review is good until the end of the month in which it expires.)

12-31   **PLT407**

Each private pilot is required to have

A– an annual flight review.

B– a biennial flight review.

C– a semiannual flight review.

12-31. Answer B. FAR 61.56

In order for any pilot to act as pilot in command of an aircraft, that person must have, within the preceding 24 calendar months, complied with the biennial flight review (BFR) requirements.

12-32   **PLT 407**

If a private pilot had a flight review on August 8, this year, when is the next flight review required?

A– August 31, 2 years later.

B– August 31, 1 year later.

C– August 8, next year.

12-32. Answer A. FAR 61.56

To act as pilot in command of an aircraft, a private pilot must have, within the preceding 24 calendar months, complied with the biennial flight review (BFR) requirement. (Calendar month means the review is good until the end of the month in which it expires.)

12-33   PLT448
In regard to privileges and limitations, a private pilot may

A– not be paid in any manner for the operating expenses of a flight.

B– not pay less than the pro rata share of the operating expenses of a flight with passengers provided the expenses involve only fuel, oil, airport expenditures, or rental fees.

C– act as pilot in command of an aircraft carrying a passenger for compensation if the flight is in connection with a business or employment.

12-33. Answer B. FAR 61.113
A private pilot may not pay less than the pro rata share of the operating expenses of a flight with passengers, provided the expenses involve only fuel, oil, airport expenditures, or rental fees.

12-34   PLT448
According to regulations pertaining to privileges and limitations, a private pilot may

A– not pay less than the pro rata share of the operating expenses of a flight with passengers provided the expenses involve only fuel, oil, airport expenditures, or rental fees.

B– not be paid in any manner for the operating expenses of a flight.

C– be paid for the operating expenses of a flight if at least three takeoffs and three landings were made by the pilot within the preceding 90 days.

12-34. Answer A. FAR 61.113
A private pilot may not pay less than the pro rata share of the operating expenses of a flight with passengers, provided the expenses involve only fuel, oil, airport expenditures, or rental fees.

12-35   PLT448
What exception, if any, permits a private pilot to act as pilot in command of an aircraft carrying passengers who pay for the flight?

A– If the passengers pay all the operating expenses.

B– If a donation is made to a charitable organization for the flight.

C– There is no exception.

12-35. Answer B. FAR 61.113
Paragraph 61.113 of the FARs indicates a private pilot may act as pilot in command of an aircraft used in a passenger-carrying airlift sponsored by a charitable organization, and for which the passengers make a donation to the organization.

SECTION C — 14 CFR PART 91 — GENERAL OPERATING AND FLIGHT RULES

As a pilot, you must be familiar with the "rules of the sky" in order to operate safely in the National Airspace System. The regulations covered in this section are an important part of your aeronautical knowledge.

PREVENTIVE MAINTENANCE

When preventive maintenance has been performed on an aircraft, the signature, certificate number, and kind of certificate held by the person approving the work must be entered in the aircraft maintenance records.

PILOT IN COMMAND

- The pilot in command is the final authority as to the operation of an aircraft.

- The pilot in command is directly responsible for the pre-launch briefing of the passengers for a flight.

- If an in-flight emergency requires immediate action, the pilot in command may deviate from the FARs to the extent required to meet that emergency. A written report is not required unless requested by the FAA.

DROPPING OBJECTS

Objects may be dropped from an aircraft if precautions are taken to avoid injury or damage to persons or property on the surface.

DRUGS AND ALCOHOL

- A pilot may allow a person who is obviously under the influence of drugs to be carried aboard the aircraft in an emergency, or if the person is a medical patient under proper care.

- A person may not act as a crewmember of a civil aircraft if alcoholic beverages have been consumed within the preceding 8 hours.

- No person may act as a crewmember of a civil aircraft with .04 percent by weight or more alcohol in the blood.

SAFETY BELTS

- Flight crewmembers are required to keep their safety belts and shoulder harnesses fastened during takeoffs and landings. Safety belts must stay fastened while en route.

- The pilot in command must brief the passengers on the use of safety belts and notify them to fasten their safety belts during taxi, takeoff and landing. Passengers must have their safety belts fastened during taxi, takeoffs and landings.

FORMATION FLIGHT

No person may operate an aircraft in formation flight except by prior arrangement with the pilot in command of each aircraft.

SEAPLANES

When an aircraft, or an aircraft and a vessel, are on crossing courses, the aircraft or vessel to the other's right has the right-of-way.

AIRSPEED

- Unless otherwise authorized, the maximum indicated airspeed at which a person may operate an aircraft below 10,000 feet MSL is 250 knots. This is also the maximum indicated airspeed within Class B airspace.

- Under Class B airspace, or in a VFR corridor through a Class B area, no person shall operate at an indicated airspeed of more than 200 knots.

ATC CLEARANCES

- When an ATC clearance has been obtained, no pilot may deviate from that clearance, unless that pilot obtains an amended clearance. The exception to this regulation is in an emergency.

- A pilot who deviates from a clearance, and is given priority by ATC because of that emergency, shall submit a detailed report of that emergency within 48 hours to the manager of that facility, if requested by ATC.

TRAFFIC PATTERNS

The correct traffic pattern procedure to use at a noncontrolled airport is to comply with any FAA traffic pattern established for the airport.

AIRCRAFT DOCUMENTS

In addition to a valid Airworthiness Certificate, operating limitations and the registration certificate must also be on board an aircraft during flight.

ELT

When the ELT has been in use for more than 1 cumulative hour, or if 50 percent of the useful life the batteries expires, the batteries must be replaced or recharged.

POSITION LIGHTS

During sunset to sunrise, except in Alaska, lighted position lights must be displayed on an aircraft.

SUPPLEMENTAL OXYGEN

- When operating an aircraft at cabin pressure altitudes above 12,500 feet MSL up to and including 14,000 feet MSL, supplemental oxygen shall be used, by required crewmembers, during that flight time in excess of 30 minutes at those altitudes.

- Unless each person is provided with supplemental oxygen, no person may operate a civil aircraft of US registry above a maximum cabin pressure altitude of 15,000 feet MSL.

AEROBATIC FLIGHT

- No person may operate an aircraft in aerobatic flight when over any congested area of a city, town or settlement.

- Aerobatic flight is prohibited in Class D airspace, and Class E airspace designated for Federal Airways.

- The lowest altitude permitted for aerobatic flight is 1500 feet AGL. In-flight visibility must be at least 3 miles.

PARACHUTES

- A parachute with natural canopy, shroud, and harness components must have been packed by a certificated and appropriately-rated parachute rigger within the preceding 60 days.

- A parachute with synthetic canopy, shroud, and harness components must have been packed by a certificated and appropriately-rated parachute rigger within the preceding 180 days.

RESTRICTED/EXPERIMENTAL AIRCRAFT

- Flight over densely populated areas is prohibited in restricted category aircraft.

- Unless specifically authorized, no person may operate an aircraft that has an experimental certificate over a densely populated area or in a congested airway.

MAINTENANCE

- The responsibility for ensuring that maintenance personnel make the appropriate entries in the aircraft maintenance records, indicating the aircraft has been approved for return to service, lies with the owner or operator.

- Completion of an annual inspection and the return of the aircraft to service should always be indicated by an appropriate notation in the aircraft maintenance records.

- If an alteration or repair substantially affects an aircraft's operation in flight, that aircraft must be flown by an appropriately rated private pilot and approved for return to service before being operated with passengers aboard.

- No person may operate an aircraft unless, within the preceding 12 calendar months, it has had an annual inspection.

- To determine the expiration date of the last annual inspection, a person should refer to the aircraft maintenance records.

- The required inspections for rental aircraft that are used for flight instruction are annual and 100-hour inspections.

- No person may operate an aircraft carrying any person for hire, or give flight instruction for hire in an aircraft, which that person provides, unless within the preceding 100 hours of time in service, the aircraft has received an annual or 100-hour inspection. The aircraft may be flown beyond the 100 hours if it is being transported to a place where service can be completed. However, the next 100 hour inspection must be completed within 100 hours of the original expiration time.

- The owner or operator of an aircraft shall keep a record of current status of applicable airworthiness directives in the aircraft maintenance records.

TRANSPONDERS

- An ATC transponder must be inspected, tested, and found to comply with standards every 24 calendar months.

- All operations within Class C airspace must be in an aircraft equipped with a 4096-code transponder with Mode C encoding capability.

12-36   PLT378
What should an owner or operator know about Airworthiness Directives (ADs)?

A– For Informational purposes only.

B– They are mandatory.

C– They are voluntary.

12-36. Answer B. FAR 39
ADs are published as part of the FARs. You may not operate an aircraft to which an airworthiness directive applies, except in accordance with that airworthiness directive.

12-37   PLT377
May a pilot operate an aircraft that is not in compliance with an Airworthiness Directive (AD)?

A– Yes, under VFR conditions only.

B– Yes, ADs are only voluntary.

C– Yes, if allowed by the AD.

12-37. Answer C. FAR 39
ADs are published as part of the FARs. You may not operate an aircraft to which an airworthiness directive applies, except in accordance with that airworthiness directive.

12-38   PLT446

Preventive maintenance has been performed on an aircraft. What paperwork is required?

A– A full, detailed description of the work done must be entered in the airframe logbook.

B– The date the work was completed, and the name of the person who did the work must be entered in the airframe and engine logbook.

C– The signature, certificate number, and kind of certificate held by the person approving the work and a description of the work must be entered in the aircraft maintenance records.

12-38. Answer C. FAR 43.9, FAR 91.417

FAR 91.417 states that records of preventive maintenance must include a description of the work performed, the date of completion, and the signature and certificate number of the person approving the aircraft for return to service. In addition, FAR 43.9 also indicates that the kind of certificate held by the person approving the work must be included in the record.

12-39   PLT446

What regulation allows a private pilot to perform preventive maintenance?

A– 14 CFR Part 43.7.

B– 14 CFR Part 91.403.

C– 14 CFR Part 61.113.

12-39. Answer A. FAR 43.7

14 CFR Part 43 covers preventive maintenance. If you hold at least a private pilot certificate, you may perform preventive maintenance such as replacing and servicing batteries, replacing spark plugs, servicing wheel bearings, etc.

12-40   PLT446

Who may perform preventive maintenance on an aircraft and approve it for return to service?

A– Student or Recreational pilot.

B– Private or Commercial pilot.

C– None of the above.

12-40. Answer B. FAR 43.7

14 CFR Part 43 covers preventive maintenance. If you hold at least a private pilot certificate, you may perform preventive maintenance such as replacing and servicing batteries, replacing spark plugs, servicing wheel bearings, etc.

12-41   PLT444

The final authority as to the operation of an aircraft is the

A– Federal Aviation Administration.

B– pilot in command.

C– aircraft manufacturer.

12-41. Answer B. FAR 91.3

As clearly indicated in the regulation, the pilot in command of an aircraft is directly responsible for, and is the final authority as to, the operation of that aircraft.

12-42   PLT444

Pre-takeoff briefing of passengers for a flight is the responsibility of

A– all passengers.

B– the pilot.

C– a crewmember.

12-42. Answer B. FAR 91.107, 91.519

Even if nonpilot crewmembers deliver the passenger briefings, the pilot in command is responsible for ensuring that these briefings are completed.

12-43   PLT444
If an in-flight emergency requires immediate action, the pilot in command may

A– deviate from the FAR's to the extent required to meet the emergency, but must submit a written report to the Administrator within 24 hours.

B– deviate from the FAR's to the extent required to meet that emergency.

C– not deviate from the FAR's unless prior to the deviation approval is granted by the Administrator.

12-43. Answer B. FAR 91.3
In an in-flight emergency requiring immediate action, the pilot in command may deviate from any rule to the extent required to meet that emergency.

12-44   PLT444
When must a pilot who deviates from a regulation during an emergency send a written report of that deviation to the Administrator?

A– Within 7 days.

B– Within 10 days.

C– Upon request.

12-44. Answer C. FAR 91.3
The regulations clearly indicate that a written report is not required, unless a report is requested from the FAA.

12-45   PLT444
Who is responsible for determining if an aircraft is in condition for safe flight?

A– A certificated aircraft mechanic.

B– The pilot in command.

C– The owner or operator.

12-45. Answer B. FAR 91.7
The pilot in command of a civil aircraft is responsible, and has final authority, for determining whether that aircraft is in condition for safe flight.

12-46   PLT401
Under what conditions may objects be dropped from an aircraft?

A– Only in an emergency.

B– If precautions are taken to avoid injury or damage to persons or property on the surface.

C– If prior permission is received from the Federal Aviation Administration.

12-46. Answer B. FAR 91.15
Objects can be dropped from an aircraft in flight, if reasonable precautions are taken to avoid injury or damage to persons or property.

12-47   PLT463

A person may not act as a crewmember of a civil aircraft if alcoholic beverages have been consumed by that person within the preceding

A– 8 hours.

B– 12 hours.

C– 24 hours.

12-47. Answer A. FAR 91.17

A common saying used in aviation for this regulation is "eight hours from bottle to throttle." In other words, no person may act or attempt to act as a crewmember of a civil aircraft within eight hours after the consumption of any alcoholic beverage.

12-48   PLT463

Under what condition, if any, may a pilot allow a person who is obviously under the influence of drugs to be carried aboard an aircraft?

A– In an emergency or if the person is a medical patient under proper care.

B– Only if the person does not have access to the cockpit or pilot's compartment.

C– Under no condition.

12-48. Answer A. FAR 91.17

Except in an emergency, no pilot of a civil aircraft may allow a person who appears to be intoxicated or who demonstrates by manner or physical indications that the individual is under the influence of drugs (except a patient under proper care) to be carried in that aircraft.

12-49   PLT463

No person may attempt to act as a crewmember of a civil aircraft with

A– .008 percent by weight or more alcohol in the blood.

B– .004 percent by weight or more alcohol in the blood.

C– .04 percent by weight or more alcohol in the blood.

12-49. Answer C. FAR 91.17

No person may act or attempt to act as a crewmember of a civil aircraft while having .04 percent by weight or more alcohol in the blood.

12-50   PLT440

Which preflight action is specifically required of the pilot prior to each flight?

A– Check the aircraft logbooks for appropriate entries.

B– Become familiar with all available information concerning the flight.

C– Review wake turbulence avoidance procedures.

12-50. Answer B. FAR 91.103

Each pilot in command shall, before beginning a flight, become familiar with all available information concerning that flight.

12-51   PLT440
Preflight action, as required for all flights away from the vicinity of an airport, shall include

A– the designation of an alternate airport.

B– a study of arrival procedures at airports/heliports of intended use.

C– an alternate course of action if the flight cannot be completed as planned.

12-51. Answer C. FAR 91.103
The preflight action for flights away from the vicinity of an airport include checking weather reports and forecasts, fuel requirements, alternatives available if the flight cannot be completed as planned, and any known traffic delays.

12-52   PLT440
In addition to other preflight actions for a VFR flight away from the vicinity of the departure airport, regulations specifically require the pilot in command to

A– review traffic control light signal procedures.

B– check the accuracy of the navigation equipment and the emergency locator transmitter (ELT).

C– determine runway lengths at airports of intended use and the aircraft's takeoff and landing distance data.

12-52. Answer C. FAR 91.103
For any flight, a pilot must determine runway lengths at airports of use and the airplane's takeoff and landing distance data.

12-53   PLT465
Flight crewmembers are required to keep their safety belts and shoulder harnesses fastened during

A– takeoffs and landings.

B– all flight conditions.

C– flight in turbulent air.

12-53. Answer A. FAR 91.105
According to the regulation, safety belts are required during takeoff and landing and while enroute. In addition, shoulder harnesses are required during takeoff and landing, unless the seat of the crewmembers' stations are not equipped with shoulder harnesses, or the crewmembers are not able to perform their duties with the shoulder harness fastened.

12-54   PLT465
Which best describes the flight conditions under which flight crewmembers are specifically required to keep their safety belts and shoulder harnesses fastened?

A– Safety belts during takeoff and landing; shoulder harnesses during takeoff and landing.

B– Safety belts during takeoff and landing; shoulder harnesses during takeoff and landing and while en route.

C– Safety belts during takeoff and landing and while en route; shoulder harnesses during takeoff and landing.

12-54. Answer C. FAR 91.105
During takeoff and landing, and while enroute, each required flight crewmember shall keep the safety belt fastened while at the crewmember station. In addition, each required flight crewmember shall, during takeoff and landing, keep the shoulder harness fastened while at the crewmember station.

12-55   PLT465

With respect to passengers, what obligation, if any, does a pilot in command have concerning the use of safety belts?

A– The pilot in command must instruct the passengers to keep safety belts fastened for the entire flight.

B– The pilot in command must brief the passengers on the use of safety belts and notify them to fasten their safety belts during taxi, takeoff, and landing.

C– The pilot in command has no obligation in regard to passengers' use of safety belts.

12-55. Answer B. FAR 91.107

The pilot in command must ensure that each person on board is briefed on how to fasten and unfasten the safety belt and shoulder harness, as well as ensure all persons on board are notified to fasten their safety belt (and shoulder harness, if installed) during taxi, takeoff, or landing.

12-56   PLT465

With certain exceptions, safety belts are required to be secured about passengers during

A– taxi, takeoffs, and landings.

B– all flight conditions.

C– flight in turbulent air.

12-56. Answer A. FAR 91.107

Passengers are only required to have safety belts (and shoulder harnesses, if installed) fastened during taxi, takeoff, and landing.

12-57   PLT465

Safety belts are required to be properly secured about which persons in an aircraft and when?

A– Pilots only, during takeoffs and landings.

B– Passengers, during taxi, takeoffs, and landings only.

C– Each person on board the aircraft during the entire flight.

12-57. Answer B. FAR 91.107

Passengers are required to have safety belts (and shoulder harnesses, if installed) fastened during taxi, takeoff, and landing.

12-58   PLT444

No person may operate an aircraft in formation flight

A– over a densely populated area.

B– in Class D Airspace under special VFR.

C– except by prior arrangement with the pilot in command of each aircraft.

12-58. Answer C. FAR 91.111

No person may operate an aircraft in formation flight except by arrangement with the pilot in command of each aircraft in the formation.

12-59   PLT414
A seaplane and a motorboat are on crossing courses. If the motorboat is to the left of the seaplane, which has the right-of-way?

A– The motorboat.

B– The seaplane.

C– Both should alter course to the right.

12-59. Answer B. FAR 91.115
When an aircraft, or an aircraft and a vessel, are on crossing courses, the aircraft or vessel to the other's right has the right-of-way.

12-60   PLT383
Unless otherwise authorized, what is the maximum indicated airspeed at which a person may operate an aircraft below 10,000 feet MSL?

A– 200 knots.

B– 250 knots.

C– 288 knots.

12-60. Answer B. FAR 91.117
Unless otherwise authorized by the Administrator, no person may operate an aircraft below 10,000 feet MSL at an indicated airspeed of more than 250 knots.

12-61   PLT161
Unless otherwise authorized, the maximum indicated airspeed at which aircraft may be flown when at or below 2,500 feet AGL and within 4 nautical miles of the primary airport of Class C airspace is

A– 200 knots.

B– 230 knots.

C– 250 knots.

12-61. Answer A. FAR 91.117
The maximum indicated airspeed inside or within 4 NM of the primary airport in Class C airspace is 200 knots.

12-62   PLT161
When flying in the airspace underlying Class B airspace, the maximum speed authorized is

A– 200 knots.

B– 230 knots.

C– 250 knots.

12-62. Answer A. FAR 91.117
No person may operate an aircraft in the airspace underlying a Class B airspace area, or in a VFR corridor designated through a Class B airspace area, at an indicated airspeed of more than 200 knots.

12-63   PLT161
When flying in a VFR corridor designated through Class B airspace the maximum speed authorized is

A– 180 knots.

B– 200 knots.

C– 250 knots.

12-63. Answer B. FAR 91.117
No person may operate an aircraft in a VFR corridor designated through a Class B airspace area, or in the airspace underlying a Class B airspace area, at an indicated airspeed of more than 200 knots.

12-64   PLT370

When an ATC clearance has been obtained, no pilot in command may deviate from that clearance, unless that pilot obtains an amended clearance. The one exception to this regulation is

A– when the clearance states "at pilot's discretion."

B– an emergency.

C– if the clearance contains a restriction.

12-64. Answer B. FAR 91.123

According the FAR 91.23(a), when an ATC clearance has been obtained, no pilot in command may deviate from that clearance, except in an emergency, unless an amended clearance is obtained.

12-65   PLT370

When would a pilot be required to submit a detailed report of an emergency which caused the pilot to deviate from an ATC clearance?

A– When requested by ATC.

B– Immediately.

C– Within 7 days.

12-65. Answer A. FAR 91.3, FAR 91.123

According to FAR 91.123(d), a pilot in command who deviates from a clearance and then is given priority by ATC because of that emergency, shall submit a detailed report of that emergency within 48 hours to the manager of that ATC facility, if requested by ATC.

12-66   PLT403

What action, if any, is appropriate if the pilot deviates from an ATC instruction during an emergency and is given priority?

A– Take no special action since you are pilot in command.

B– File a detailed report within 48 hours to the chief of the appropriate ATC facility, if requested.

C– File a report to the FAA Administrator, as soon as possible.

12-66. Answer B. FAR 91.123

A pilot in command who is given priority by ATC because of an emergency, shall submit a detailed report of that emergency within 48 hours to the manager of that ATC facility, if requested by ATC.

12-67   PLT435

Which is the correct traffic pattern departure procedure to use at a noncontrolled airport?

A– Depart in any direction consistent with safety, after crossing the airport boundary.

B– Make all turns to the left.

C– Comply with any FAA traffic pattern established for the airport.

12-67. Answer C. FAR 91.127

Each person operating an aircraft to or from an airport without an operating control tower shall, in the case of an aircraft departing the airport, comply with any traffic patterns established for that airport in Part 93.

12-68   PLT413
What is the specific fuel requirement for flight under VFR during daylight hours in an airplane?

A— Enough to complete the flight at normal cruising speed with adverse wind conditions.

B— Enough to fly to the first point of intended landing and to fly after that for 30 minutes at normal cruising speed.

C— Enough to fly to the first point of intended landing and to fly after that for 45 minutes at normal cruising speed.

12-68. Answer B. FAR 91.151
For day VFR flight in an airplane, there must be enough fuel (considering wind and forecast weather conditions) to fly to the first point of intended landing, and, assuming normal cruising speed, 30 minutes thereafter.

12-69   PLT413
What is the specific fuel requirement for flight under VFR at night in an airplane?

A— Enough to complete the flight at normal cruising speed with adverse wind conditions.

B— Enough to fly to the first point of intended landing and to fly after that for 30 minutes at normal cruising speed.

C— Enough to fly to the first point of intended landing and to fly after that for 45 minutes at normal cruising speed.

12-69. Answer C. FAR 91.151
For night VFR flight in an airplane, there must be enough fuel (considering wind and forecast weather conditions) to fly to the first point of intended landing, and assuming normal cruising speed, 45 minutes thereafter.

12-70   PLT400
In addition to a valid Airworthiness Certificate, what documents or records must be aboard an aircraft during flight?

A— Aircraft engine and airframe logbooks, and owner's manual.

B— Radio operator's permit, and repair and alteration forms.

C— Operating limitations and Registration Certificate.

12-70. Answer C. FAR 91.203, FAR 91.9
An acronym commonly used by pilots for remembering the required certificates and documents is ARROW. The ARROW acronym means AIRWORTHINESS certificate; aircraft REGISTRATION; RADIO station permit; OPERATING limitations; and WEIGHT and balance.

12-71   PLT402

When must batteries in an emergency locator transmitter (ELT) be replaced or recharged, if rechargeable?

A– After any inadvertent activation of the ELT.

B– When the ELT has been in use for more than 1 cumulative hour.

C– When the ELT can no longer be heard over the airplane's communication radio receiver.

12-71. Answer B. FAR 91.207

Batteries used in the emergency locator transmitters must be replaced (or recharged, if the battery is rechargeable) when the transmitter has been in use for more than one cumulative hour.

12-72   PLT402

When are non-rechargeable batteries of an emergency locator transmitter (ELT) required to be replaced?

A– Every 24 months.

B– When 50 percent of their useful life expires.

C– At the time of each 100-hour or annual inspection.

12-72. Answer B. FAR 91.207

Non-rechargeable batteries used in the ELT must be replaced when 50 percent of their useful life, as established by the manufacturer, has expired.

12-73   PLT461

Except in Alaska, during what time period should lighted position lights be displayed on an aircraft?

A– End of evening civil twilight to the beginning of morning civil twilight.

B– 1 hour after sunset to 1 hour before sunrise.

C– Sunset to sunrise.

12-73. Answer C. FAR 91.209

No person may, during the period from sunset to sunrise, operate an aircraft unless it has lighted position lights.

12-74   PLT438

When operating an aircraft at cabin pressure altitudes above 12,500 feet MSL up to and including 14,000 feet MSL, supplemental oxygen shall be used during

A– the entire flight time at those altitudes.

B– that flight time in excess of 10 minutes at those altitudes.

C– that flight time in excess of 30 minutes at those altitudes.

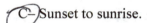

12-74. Answer C. FAR 91.211

Between cabin pressure altitudes of 12,500 feet MSL and 14,000 feet MSL, the required minimum flight crew is required to use supplemental oxygen for any duration of the flight past 30 minutes.

12-75   PLT438
Unless each occupant is provided with supplemental oxygen, no person may operate a civil aircraft of U.S. registry above a maximum cabin pressure altitude of

A– 12,500 feet MSL.

B– 14,000 feet MSL.

C– 15,000 feet MSL.

12-75. Answer C. FAR 91.211
At cabin pressure altitudes above 15,000 feet MSL, each occupant of the aircraft must be provided with supplemental oxygen.

12-76   PLT369
No person may operate an aircraft in aerobatic flight when

A– flight visibility is less than 5 miles.

B– over any congested area of a city, town, or settlement.

C– less than 2,500 feet AGL.

12-76. Answer B. FAR 91.303
No person may operate an aircraft in aerobatic flight over any congested area of a city, town, or settlement.

12-77   PLT369
In which class of airspace is aerobatic flight prohibited?

A– Class E airspace not designated for Federal Airways above 1,500 feet AGL.

B– Class E airspace below 1,500 feet AGL.

C– Class G airspace above 1,500 feet AGL.

12-77. Answer B. FAR 91.303
No person may operate an aircraft in aerobatic flight within class B, C, or D airspace, class E airspace designated for an airport, or within 4 NM of the centerline of any Federal airway. Aerobatic flight is also prohibited below 1,500 feet AGL and when the flight visibility is less than 3 statute miles.

12-78   PLT369
What is the lowest altitude permitted for aerobatic flight?

A– 1,000 feet AGL.

B– 1,500 feet AGL.

C– 2,000 feet AGL.

12-78. Answer B. FAR 91.303
No person may operate an aircraft in aerobatic flight below an altitude of 1,500 feet above the surface.

12-79   PLT369
No person may operate an aircraft in aerobatic flight when the flight visibility is less than

A– 3 miles.

B– 5 miles.

C– 7 miles.

12-79. Answer A. FAR 91.303
No person may operate an aircraft in aerobatic flight when flight visibility is less than three statute miles.

12-80   PLT405
An approved parachute constructed of natural materials must have been packed by a certificated and appropriately rated parachute rigger within the preceding

A– 60 days.

B– 90 days.

C– 120 days.

12-80. Answer A. FAR 91.307
Parachutes must be repacked periodically to satisfy regulations. The materials used determine the interval. No pilot of a civil aircraft may allow an emergency parachute to be carried in that aircraft unless it is an approved type and has been packed by a certificated and appropriately rated parachute rigger within the preceding 60 days if its canopy, shrouds, and harness are composed exclusively of natural fiber or materials.

12-81   PLT405
An approved synthetic parachute may be carried in an aircraft for emergency use if it has been packed by an appropriately rated parachute rigger within the preceding

A– 120 days.

B– 180 days.

C– 365 days.

12-81. Answer B. FAR 91.307
Parachutes must be repacked periodically to satisfy regulations. The materials used determine the interval. No pilot of a civil aircraft may allow an emergency parachute to be carried in that aircraft unless it is an approved type and has been packed by a certificated and appropriately rated parachute rigger within the preceding 180 days if its canopy, shrouds, and harness are composed exclusively of nylon, rayon, or other similar synthetic fiber or materials.

12-82   PLT405
With certain exceptions, when must each occupant of an aircraft wear an approved parachute?

A– When a door is removed from the aircraft to facilitate parachute jumpers.

B– When intentionally pitching the nose of the aircraft up or down 30° or more.

C– When intentionally banking in excess of 30°.

12-82. Answer B. FAR 91.307
Unless each occupant of the aircraft is wearing an approved parachute, no pilot of a civil aircraft, carrying any person (other than a crewmember) may execute any intentional maneuver that exceeds a nose-up or nose-down attitude of 30 degrees relative to the horizon.

12-83   PLT373
Which is normally prohibited when operating a restricted category civil aircraft?

A– Flight under instrument flight rules.

B– Flight over a densely populated area.

C– Flight within Class D airspace.

12-83. Answer B. FAR 91.313
No person may operate a restricted category civil aircraft within the United States over a densely populated area.

12-84   PLT373
Unless otherwise specifically authorized, no person may operate an aircraft that has an experimental certificate

A– beneath the floor of Class B airspace.

B– over a densely populated area or in a congested airway.

C– from the primary airport within Class D airspace.

12-84. Answer B. FAR 91.319
Unless otherwise authorized by the Administrator in special operating limitations, no person may operate an aircraft that has an experimental certificate over a densely populated area or in a congested airway.

12-85   PLT374
The responsibility for ensuring that an aircraft is maintained in an airworthy condition is primarily that of the

A– pilot in command.

B– owner or operator.

C– mechanic who performs the work.

12-85. Answer B. FAR 91.403
The owner or operator of an aircraft is primarily responsible for maintaining that aircraft in an airworthy condition.

12-86   PLT377
The airworthiness of an aircraft can be determined by a preflight inspection and a

A– statement from the owner or operator that the aircraft is airworthy.

B– log book endorsement from a flight instructor.

C– review of the maintenance records.

12-86. Answer C. FAR 91.403
The maintenance records document whether all of the required inspections have been completed, and whether all of the airworthiness directives (ADs) have been complied with.

12-87   PLT426
The responsibility for ensuring that maintenance personnel make the appropriate entries in the aircraft maintenance records indicating the aircraft has been approved for return to service lies with the

A– owner or operator.

B– pilot in command.

C– mechanic who performed the work.

12-87. Answer A. FAR 91.405
Each owner or operator of an aircraft shall ensure that maintenance personnel make appropriate entries in the aircraft maintenance record.

12-88   PLT374
Who is responsible for ensuring appropriate entries are made in maintenance records indicating the aircraft has been approved for return to service?

A– Repair station.

B– Certified mechanic.

C– Owner or operator.

12-88. Answer C. FAR 91.405
Each owner or operator of an aircraft shall ensure that maintenance personnel make appropriate entries in the aircraft maintenance records indicating the aircraft has been approved for return to service.

12-89   PLT374
Who is responsible for ensuring Airworthiness Directives (ADs) are complied with?

A– Mechanic with inspection authorization (IA).

B– Owner or operator.

C– Repair station.

12-89. Answer B. FAR 91.403
The owner or operator of an aircraft is primarily responsible for maintaining that aircraft in an airworthy condition, including compliance with 14 CFR Part 39 (ADs).

12-90   PLT375

Completion of an annual inspection and the return of the aircraft to service should always be indicated by

A– the relicensing date on the Registration Certificate.

B– an appropriate notation in the aircraft maintenance records.

C– an inspection sticker placed on the instrument panel that lists the annual inspection completion date.

12-90. Answer B. FAR 91.409

No person may operate an aircraft unless, within the preceding 12 calendar months it has had an annual inspection by a person authorized to do that type of inspection and is entered as an annual inspection in the required maintenance records.

12-91   PLT375

If an alteration or repair substantially affects an aircraft's operation in flight, that aircraft must be test flown by an appropriately-rated pilot and approved for return to service prior to being operated

A– by any private pilot.

B– with passengers aboard.

C– for compensation or hire.

12-91. Answer B. FAR 91.407

Before any person (other than a crewmember) can fly in an aircraft that has been maintained, rebuilt, or altered in a manner that may have appreciably changed its flight characteristics or substantially affected the operation in flight, an appropriately rated pilot with at least a private pilot certificate must first conduct a test flight and log the flight in aircraft records.

12-92   PLT375

Before passengers can be carried in an aircraft that has been altered in a manner that may have appreciably changed its flight characteristics, it must be flight tested by an appropriately rated pilot who holds at least a

A– Commercial Pilot Certificate with an instrument rating.

B– Private Pilot Certificate.

C– Commercial Pilot Certificate and a mechanic's certificate.

12-92. Answer B. FAR 91.407

An appropriately rated pilot with at least a private pilot certificate is authorized to flight test the aircraft.

12-93   PLT372

An aircraft's annual inspection was performed on July 12, this year. The next annual inspection will be due no later than

A– July 1, next year.

B– July 13, next year.

C– July 31, next year.

12-93. Answer C. FAR 91.409

No person may operate an aircraft unless, within the preceding 12 calendar months, it has had an annual inspection. The term "calendar month" is defined as to the end of the month.

12-94   PLT372
To determine the expiration date of the last annual aircraft inspection, a person should refer to the

A– Airworthiness Certificate.

B– Registration Certificate.

C– aircraft maintenance records.

12-94. Answer C. FAR 91.417
The registered owner or operator shall keep records of the maintenance, preventive maintenance, alterations, records of the 100-hour, annual, progressive, and other required or approved inspections, as appropriate, for each aircraft. This information is found in the aircraft's maintenance records.

12-95   PLT372
What aircraft inspections are required for rental aircraft that are also used for flight instruction?

A– Annual and 100-hour inspections.

B– Biannual and 100-hour inspections.

C– Annual and 50-hour inspections.

12-95. Answer A. FAR 91.409
No person may operate an aircraft carrying any person (other than a crewmember) for hire, or give flight instruction for hire in an aircraft, which that person provides, unless within the preceding 100-hours of time in service, the aircraft has received an annual or 100-hour inspection.

12-96   PLT372
An aircraft had a 100-hour inspection when the tachometer read 1259.6. When is the next 100-hour inspection due?

A– 1349.6 hours.

B– 1359.6 hours.

C– 1369.6 hours.

12-96. Answer B. FAR 91.409
No person may operate an aircraft carrying any person (other than a crewmember) for hire, or give flight instruction for hire in an aircraft, which that person provides, unless within the preceding 100-hours of time in service, the aircraft has received an annual or 100-hour inspection.

12-97   PLT372
A 100-hour inspection was due at 3302.5 hours on the tachometer. The 100-hour inspection was actually done at 3309.5 hours. When is the next 100-hour inspection due?

A– 3312.5 hours.

B– 3402.5 hours.

C– 3409.5 hours.

12-97. Answer B. FAR 91.409
The 100-hour limitation may be exceeded by not more than 10 hours while enroute to reach a place where the inspection can be done. However, the excess time used to reach a place must be included in computing the next 100 hours of time in service.

12-98   PLT372
Maintenance records show the last transponder inspection was performed on September 1, 2014. The next inspection will be due no later than

A– September 1, 2016.

2 years

B– September 30, 2015.

C– September 30, 2016.

12-98. Answer C. FAR 91.413
No person may use an ATC transponder unless, within the preceding 24 calendar months, that transponder has been tested and found to comply with the appropriate standards listed in Appendix F of 14 CFR Part 43. The term "calendar month" refers to the end of the month when an inspection is due.

12-99   PLT374

Which records or documents shall the owner or operator of an aircraft keep to show compliance with an applicable airworthiness directive?

A– Aircraft maintenance records.

B– Airworthiness Certificate and Pilot's Operating Handbook.

C– Airworthiness and Registration Certificates.

12-99. Answer A. FAR 91.417

The owner or operator of an aircraft shall keep a record of current status of applicable airworthiness directives (ADs) in the appropriate aircraft maintenance records.

12-100   PLT161

All operations within Class C airspace must be in

A– accordance with instrument flight rules.

B– compliance with ATC clearances and instructions.

C– an aircraft equipped with a Mode A or Mode S transponder with Mode C altitude encoding capability.

12-100. Answer C. FAR 91.215, FAR 91.130

All aircraft must have an altitude encoding transponder in order to operate within or above Class C airspace.

SECTION D — NTSB 830 — AIRCRAFT ACCIDENT AND INCIDENT REPORTING

Pilots need to be familiar with the procedures and requirements for reporting aircraft accidents, incidents and overdue aircraft to the National Transportation Safety Board (NTSB).

ACCIDENTS

- If an aircraft is involved in an accident which results in substantial damage to the aircraft, the nearest NTSB field office should be notified immediately.

- Aircraft wreckage may be moved prior to the time the NTSB takes custody, but only to protect the wreckage from further damage.

- The owner of an aircraft that has been involved in an accident is required to file an accident report within 10 days.

INCIDENTS

- A flight control system malfunction or failure, and an in flight fire are two incidents that require immediate notification to the nearest NTSB field office.

- An overdue aircraft that is believed to be involved in an accident must be immediately reported to the nearest NTSB field office.

- The operator of an aircraft that has been involved in an incident is required to submit a report to the nearest NTSB field office when requested.

12-101   PLT366
If an aircraft is involved in an accident which results in substantial damage to the aircraft, the nearest NTSB field office should be notified

A— immediately.

B— within 48 hours.

C— within 7 days.

12-101. Answer A. NTSB 830.5
The operator of an aircraft shall immediately, and by the most expeditious means available, notify the nearest National Transportation Safety Board field office when an aircraft accident occurs.

12-102   PLT366
Which incident requires an immediate notification to the nearest NTSB field office?

A— A forced landing due to engine failure.

B— Landing gear damage, due to a hard landing.

C— Flight control system malfunction or failure.

12-102. Answer C. NTSB 830.5
The operator of an aircraft shall immediately, and by the most expeditious means available, notify the nearest National Transportation Safety Board field office when a flight control system malfunction or failure occurs.

12-103   PLT366
Which incident would necessitate an immediate notification to the nearest NTSB field office?

A— An in-flight generator/alternator failure.

B— An in-flight fire.

C— An in-flight loss of VOR receiver capability.

12-103. Answer B. NTSB 830.5
The operator of an aircraft shall immediately, and by the most expeditious means available, notify the nearest National Transportation Safety Board field office when a fire in flight occurs.

12-104   PLT366
Which incident requires an immediate notification be made to the nearest NTSB field office?

A– An overdue aircraft that is believed to be involved in an accident.

B– An in-flight radio communications failure.

C– An in-flight generator or alternator failure.

12-104. Answer A. NTSB 830.5
The operator of an aircraft shall immediately, and by the most expeditious means available, notify the nearest National Transportation Safety Board field office when an overdue aircraft is believed to be involved in an accident.

12-105   PLT366
May aircraft wreckage be moved prior to the time the NTSB takes custody?

A– Yes, but only if moved by a federal, state, or local law enforcement officer.

B– Yes, but only to protect the wreckage from further damage.

C– No, it may not be moved under any circumstances.

12-105. Answer B. NTSB 830.10
Prior to the time the Board or its authorized representative takes custody of aircraft wreckage, mail, or cargo, such wreckage may not be disturbed or moved except to the extent necessary to protect the wreckage from further damage.

12-106   PLT366
The operator of an aircraft that has been involved in an accident is required to file an accident report within how many days?

A– 5.

B– 7.

C– 10.

12-106. Answer C. NTSB 830.15
The operator of an aircraft shall file a report within 10 days after an accident, or after 7 days if an overdue aircraft is still missing.

12-107   PLT366
The operator of an aircraft that has been involved in an incident is required to submit a report to the nearest field office of the NTSB

A– within 7 days.

B– within 10 days.

C– when requested.

12-107. Answer C. NTSB 830.15
A report on an incident for which notification is required by 830.5(a) shall be filed only when requested by an authorized representative of t

APPENDIX
1

FAA LEGENDS

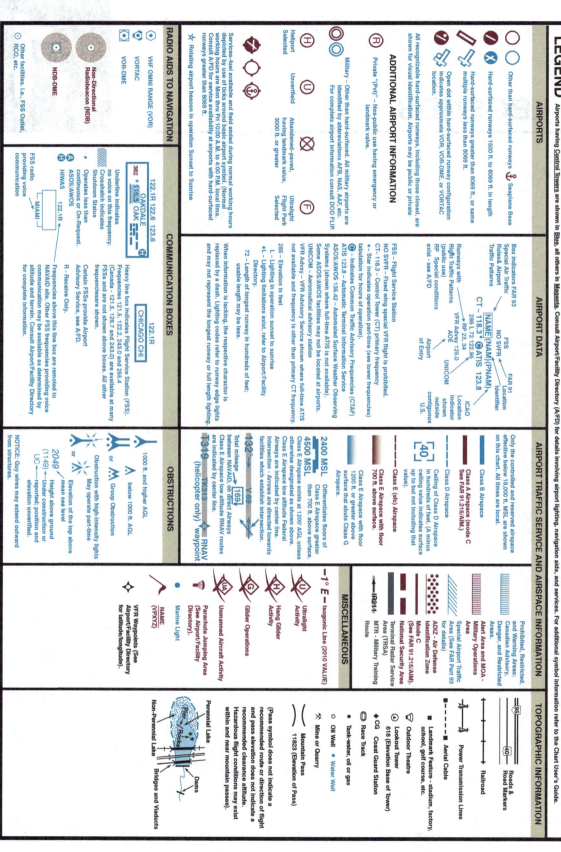

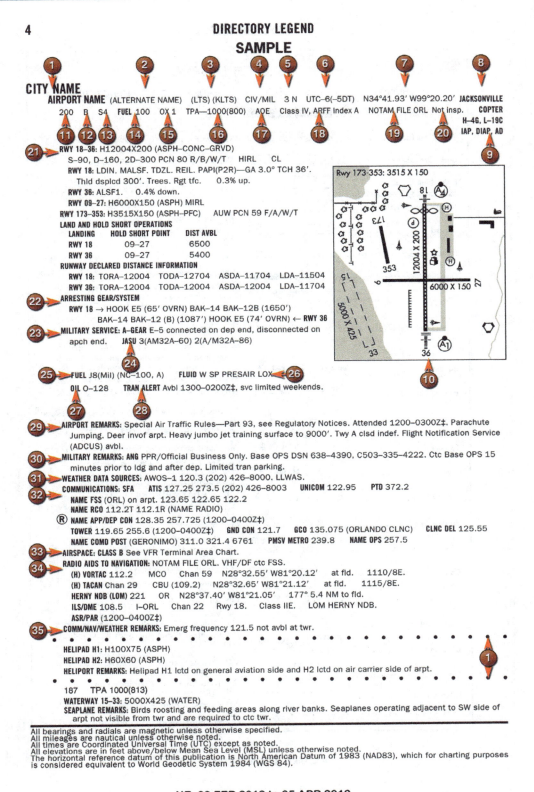

4

DIRECTORY LEGEND
SAMPLE

CITY NAME
AIRPORT NAME (ALTERNATE NAME) (LTS) (KLTS) CIV/MIL 3 N UTC–6(–5DT) N34°41.93′ W99°20.20′ JACKSONVILLE
200 B S4 FUEL 100 OX 1 TPA—1000(800) AOE Class IV, ARFF Index A NOTAM FILE ORL Not insp. COPTER
H–4G, L–19C
IAP, DIAP, AD

RWY 18–36: H12004X200 (ASPH–CONC–GRVD)
S–90, D–160, 2D–300 PCN 80 R/B/W/T   HIRL   CL
RWY 18: LDIN. MALSF. TDZL. REIL. PAPI(P2R)—GA 3.0° TCH 36′.
Thld dsplcd 300′. Trees. Rgt tfc.   0.3% up.
RWY 36: ALSF1.   0.4% down.
RWY 09–27: H6000X150 (ASPH) MIRL
RWY 173–353: H3515X150 (ASPH–PFC)   AUW PCN 59 F/A/W/T
LAND AND HOLD SHORT OPERATIONS
LANDING   HOLD SHORT POINT   DIST AVBL
RWY 18   09–27   6500
RWY 36   09–27   5400
RUNWAY DECLARED DISTANCE INFORMATION
RWY 18: TORA–12004   TODA–12704   ASDA–11704   LDA–11504
RWY 36: TORA–12004   TODA–12004   ASDA–12004   LDA–11704
ARRESTING GEAR/SYSTEM
RWY 18 → HOOK E5 (65′ OVRN) BAK–14 BAK–12B (1650′)
BAK–14 BAK–12 (B) (1087′) HOOK E5 (74′ OVRN) ← RWY 36
MILITARY SERVICE: A–GEAR E–5 connected on dep end, disconnected on
apch end.   JASU 3(AM32A–60) 2(A/M32A–86)

FUEL J8(Mil) (NC–100, A)   FLUID W SP PRESAIR LOX
OIL O–128   TRAN ALERT Avbl 1300–0200Z‡, svc limited weekends.

AIRPORT REMARKS: Special Air Traffic Rules—Part 93, see Regulatory Notices. Attended 1200–0300Z‡. Parachute
Jumping. Deer invof arpt. Heavy jumbo jet training surface to 9000′. Twy A clsd indef. Flight Notification Service
(ADCUS) avbl.
MILITARY REMARKS: ANG PPR/Official Business Only. Base OPS DSN 638–4390, C503–335–4222. Ctc Base OPS 15
minutes prior to ldg and after dep. Limited tran parking.
WEATHER DATA SOURCES: AWOS–1 120.3 (202) 426–8000. LLWAS.
COMMUNICATIONS: SFA   ATIS 127.25 273.5 (202) 426–8003   UNICOM 122.95   PTD 372.2
NAME FSS (ORL) on arpt. 123.65 122.65 122.2
NAME RCO 112.2T 112.1R (NAME RADIO)
Ⓡ NAME APP/DEP CON 128.35 257.725 (1200–0400Z‡)
TOWER 119.65 255.6 (1200–0400Z‡)   GND CON 121.7   GCO 135.075 (ORLANDO CLNC)   CLNC DEL 125.55
NAME COMD POST (GERONIMO) 311.0 321.4 6761   PMSV METRO 239.8   NAME OPS 257.5
AIRSPACE: CLASS B See VFR Terminal Area Chart.
RADIO AIDS TO NAVIGATION: NOTAM FILE ORL. VHF/DF ctc FSS.
(H) VORTAC 112.2   MCO   Chan 59   N28°32.55′ W81°20.12′   at fld.   1110/8E.
(H) TACAN Chan 29   CBU (109.2)   N28°32.65′ W81°21.12′   at fld.   1115/8E.
HERNY NDB (LOM) 221   OR   N28°37.40′ W81°21.05′   177° 5.4 NM to fld.
ILS/DME 108.5   I–ORL   Chan 22   Rwy 18.   Class IIE.   LOM HERNY NDB.
ASR/PAR (1200–0400Z‡)
COMM/NAV/WEATHER REMARKS: Emerg frequency 121.5 not avbl at twr.

. . . .

HELIPAD H1: H100X75 (ASPH)
HELIPAD H2: H60X60 (ASPH)
HELIPORT REMARKS: Helipad H1 lctd on general aviation side and H2 lctd on air carrier side of arpt.

. . . .

187   TPA 1000(813)
WATERWAY 15–33: 5000X425 (WATER)
SEAPLANE REMARKS: Birds roosting and feeding areas along river banks. Seaplanes operating adjacent to SW side of
arpt not visible from twr and are required to ctc twr.

All bearings and radials are magnetic unless otherwise specified.
All mileages are nautical unless otherwise noted.
All times are Coordinated Universal Time (UTC) except as noted.
All elevations are in feet above/below Mean Sea Level (MSL) unless otherwise noted.
The horizontal reference datum of this publication is North American Datum of 1983 (NAD83), which for charting purposes
is considered equivalent to World Geodetic System 1984 (WGS 84).

NE, 09 FEB 2012 to 05 APR 2012

Legend 2. *Airport/facility directory.*

DIRECTORY LEGEND   5

SKETCH LEGEND

RUNWAYS/LANDING AREAS

Hard Surfaced . . . .

Metal Surface . . . .

Sod, Gravel, etc. . . . .

Light Plane, ...
Ski Landing Area or Water
Under Construction . . . . .

Closed . . . .

Helicopter Landings Area . . . . (H)

Displaced Threshold . . . .

Taxiway, Apron and Stopways . .

RADIO AIDS TO NAVIGATION

VORTAC . . .   VOR . . . .

VOR/DME . .   NDB . . . .

TACAN . . . .   NDB/DME . . . .

MISCELLANEOUS AERONAUTICAL FEATURES

Airport Beacon . . . .

Wind Cone . . . .

Landing Tee . . . .

Tetrahedron . . . .

Control Tower . . . .   or TWR

When control tower and rotating beacon
are co-located beacon symbol will be
used and further identified as TWR.

MISCELLANEOUS BASE AND CULTURAL FEATURES

Buildings . . . .

Power Lines . . . .

Fence . . . .

Towers . . . .

Tanks . . . .

Oil Well . . . .

Smoke Stack . . . .

Obstruction   5812

Controlling Obstruction . . . .   +5812

Trees . . . .

Populated Places . . . .

Cuts and Fills . . . . . .   Cut   Fill

Cliffs and Depressions . .

Ditch . . . .

Hill . . . .

APPROACH LIGHTING SYSTEMS

A dot "•" portrayed with approach lighting
letter identifier indicates sequenced flashing
lights (F) installed with the approach lighting
system e.g. (A1) Negative symbology, e.g., (A1)
(V) indicates Pilot Controlled Lighting (PCL).

Runway Centerline Lighting . . . . .

(A) Approach Lighting System ALSF-2 . .

(A1) Approach Lighting System ALSF-1 . .

(A2) Short Approach Lighting System
SALS/SALSF . . . .

(A3) Simplified Short Approach Lighting
System (SSALR) with RAIL . . . . .

(A4) Medium Intensity Approach Lighting System
(MALS and MALSF)/(SSALS
(A4) and SSALF) . . . .

(A5) Medium Intensity Approach Lighting
System (MALSR) and RAIL . . . . . .

Omnidirectional Approach
Lighting System (ODALS) . . . .

(D) Navy Parallel Row and Cross Bar . . .

(‡) Air Force Overrun . . . .

(V) Visual Approach Slope Indicator with
Standard Threshold Clearance provided

(V2) Pulsating Visual Approach Slope Indicator
(PVASI)

(V3) Visual Approach Slope Indicator with a
threshold crossing height to accomodate
long bodied or jumbo aircraft

(V4) Tri-color Visual Approach Slope Indicator
(TRCV)

(V5) Approach Path Alignment Panel (APAP)

(P) Precision Approach Path Indicator (PAPI)

NE, 09 FEB 2012 to 05 APR 2012

Legend 3. *Airport/facility directory.*

6   **DIRECTORY LEGEND**

LEGEND

This directory is a listing of data on record with the FAA on all open to the public airports, military facilities and selected private use facilities specifically requested by the Department of Defense (DoD) for which a DoD Instrument Approach Procedure has been published in the U.S. Terminal Procedures Publication. Additionally this listing contains data for associated terminal control facilities, air route traffic control centers, and radio aids to navigation within the conterminous United States, Puerto Rico and the Virgin Islands. Joint civil/military and civil airports are listed alphabetically by state, associated city and airport name and cross-referenced by airport name. Military facilities are listed alphabetically by state and official airport name and cross-referenced by associated city name. Navaids, flight service stations and remote communication outlets that are associated with an airport, but with a different name, are listed alphabetically under their own name, as well as under the airport with which they are associated.

The listing of an open to the public airport in this directory merely indicates the airport operator's willingness to accommodate transient aircraft, and does not represent that the facility conforms with any Federal or local standards, or that it has been approved for use on the part of the general public. Military and private use facilities published in this directory are open to civil pilots only in an emergency or with prior permission. See Special Notice Section, Civil Use of Military Fields.

The information on obstructions is taken from reports submitted to the FAA. Obstruction data has not been verified in all cases. Pilots are cautioned that objects not indicated in this tabulation (or on the airports sketches and/or charts) may exist which can create a hazard to flight operation. Detailed specifics concerning services and facilities tabulated within this directory are contained in the Aeronautical Information Manual, Basic Flight Information and ATC Procedures.

The legend items that follow explain in detail the contents of this Directory and are keyed to the circled numbers on the sample on the preceding pages.

① CITY/AIRPORT NAME

Civil and joint civil/military airports and facilities in this directory are listed alphabetically by state and associated city. Where the city name is different from the airport name the city name will appear on the line above the airport name. Airports with the same associated city name will be listed alphabetically by airport name and will be separated by a dashed rule line. A solid rule line will separate all others. FAA approved helipads and seaplane landing areas associated with a land airport will be separated by a dotted line. Military airports are listed alphabetically by state and official airport name.

② ALTERNATE NAME

Alternate names, if any, will be shown in parentheses.

③ LOCATION IDENTIFIER

The location identifier is a three or four character FAA code followed by a four-character ICAO code assigned to airports. ICAO codes will only be published at joint civil/military, and military facilities. If two different military codes are assigned, both codes will be shown with the primary operating agency's code listed first. These identifiers are used by ATC in lieu of the airport name in flight plans, flight strips and other written records and computer operations. Zeros will appear with a slash to differentiate them from the letter "O".

④ OPERATING AGENCY

Airports within this directory are classified into two categories, Military/Federal Government and Civil airports open to the general public, plus selected private use airports. The operating agency is shown for military, private use and joint civil/military airports. The operating agency is shown by an abbreviation as listed below. When an organization is a tenant, the abbreviation is enclosed in parenthesis. No classification indicates the airport is open to the general public with no military tenant.

A	US Army	MC	Marine Corps
AFRC	Air Force Reserve Command	N	Navy
AF	US Air Force	NAF	Naval Air Facility
ANG	Air National Guard	NAS	Naval Air Station
AR	US Army Reserve	NASA	National Air and Space Administration
ARNG	US Army National Guard	P	US Civil Airport Wherein Permit Covers
CG	US Coast Guard		Use by Transient Military Aircraft
CIV/MIL	Joint Use Civil/Military	PVT	Private Use Only (Closed to the Public)
DND	Department of National Defense Canada		

⑤ AIRPORT LOCATION

Airport location is expressed as distance and direction from the center of the associated city in nautical miles and cardinal points, e.g., 4 NE.

⑥ TIME CONVERSION

Hours of operation of all facilities are expressed in Coordinated Universal Time (UTC) and shown as "Z" time. The directory indicates the number of hours to be subtracted from UTC to obtain local standard time and local daylight saving time UTC–5(–4DT). The symbol ‡ indicates that during periods of Daylight Saving Time effective hours will be one hour earlier than shown. In those areas where daylight saving time is not observed the (–4DT) and ‡ will not be shown. Daylight saving time is in effect from 0200 local time the second Sunday in March to 0200 local time the first Sunday in November. Canada and all U.S. Conterminous States observe daylight saving time except Arizona and Puerto Rico, and the Virgin Islands. If the state observes daylight saving time and the operating times are other than daylight saving times, the operating hours will include the dates, times and no ‡ symbol will be shown, i.e., April 15–Aug 31 0630–1700Z, Sep 1–Apr 14 0600–1700Z.

NE, 09 FEB 2012 to 05 APR 2012

Legend 4. *Airport/facility directory.*

DIRECTORY LEGEND   7

7 GEOGRAPHIC POSITION OF AIRPORT—AIRPORT REFERENCE POINT (ARP)

Positions are shown as hemisphere, degrees, minutes and hundredths of a minute and represent the approximate geometric center of all usable runway surfaces.

8 CHARTS

Charts refer to the Sectional Chart and Low and High Altitude Enroute Chart and panel on which the airport or facility is located. Helicopter Chart locations will be indicated as COPTER. IFR Gulf of Mexico West and IFR Gulf of Mexico Central will be depicted as GOMW and GOMC.

9 INSTRUMENT APPROACH PROCEDURES, AIRPORT DIAGRAMS

IAP indicates an airport for which a prescribed (Public Use) FAA Instrument Approach Procedure has been published. DIAP indicates an airport for which a prescribed DoD Instrument Approach Procedure has been published in the U.S. Terminal Procedures. See the Special Notice Section of this directory, Civil Use of Military Fields and the Aeronautical Information Manual 5–4–5 Instrument Approach Procedure Charts for additional information. AD indicates an airport for which an airport diagram has been published. Airport diagrams are located in the back of each A/FD volume alphabetically by associated city and airport name.

10 AIRPORT SKETCH

The airport sketch, when provided, depicts the airport and related topographical information as seen from the air and should be used in conjunction with the text. It is intended as a guide for pilots in VFR conditions. Symbology that is not self-explanatory will be reflected in the sketch legend. The airport sketch will be oriented with True North at the top. Airport sketches will be added incrementally.

11 ELEVATION

The highest point of an airport's usable runways measured in feet from mean sea level. When elevation is sea level it will be indicated as "00". When elevation is below sea level a minus "−" sign will precede the figure.

12 ROTATING LIGHT BEACON

B indicates rotating beacon is available. Rotating beacons operate sunset to sunrise unless otherwise indicated in the AIRPORT REMARKS or MILITARY REMARKS segment of the airport entry.

13 SERVICING—CIVIL

S1: Minor airframe repairs.	S5: Major airframe repairs.
S2: Minor airframe and minor powerplant repairs.	S6: Minor airframe and major powerplant repairs.
S3: Major airframe and minor powerplant repairs.	S7: Major powerplant repairs.
S4: Major airframe and major powerplant repairs.	S8: Minor powerplant repairs.

14 FUEL

CODE	FUEL	CODE	FUEL
80	Grade 80 gasoline (Red)	B+	Jet B, Wide-cut, turbine fuel with FS–II*, FP** minus 50° C.
100	Grade 100 gasoline (Green)		
100LL	100LL gasoline (low lead) (Blue)	J4 (JP4)	(JP–4 military specification) FP** minus 58° C.
115	Grade 115 gasoline (115/145 military specification) (Purple)	J5 (JP5)	(JP–5 military specification) Kerosene with FS–11, FP** minus 46°C.
A	Jet A, Kerosene, without FS–II*, FP** minus 40° C.	J8 (JP8)	(JP–8 military specification) Jet A–1, Kerosene with FS–II*, FP** minus 47°C.
A+	Jet A, Kerosene, with FS–II*, FP** minus 40°C.	J8+100	(JP–8 military specification) Jet A–1, Kerosene with FS–II*, FP** minus 47°C, with-fuel additive package that improves thermo stability characteristics of JP–8.
A1	Jet A–1, Kerosene, without FS–II*, FP** minus 47°C.		
A1+	Jet A–1, Kerosene with FS–II*, FP** minus 47° C.	J	(Jet Fuel Type Unknown)
B	Jet B, Wide-cut, turbine fuel without FS–II*, FP** minus 50° C.	MOGAS	Automobile gasoline which is to be used as aircraft fuel.

*(Fuel System Icing Inhibitor)
**(Freeze Point)

NOTE: Certain automobile gasoline may be used in specific aircraft engines if a FAA supplemental type certificate has been obtained. Automobile gasoline, which is to be used in aircraft engines, will be identified as "MOGAS", however, the grade/type and other octane rating will not be published.

Data shown on fuel availability represents the most recent information the publisher has been able to acquire. Because of a variety of factors, the fuel listed may not always be obtainable by transient civil pilots. Confirmation of availability of fuel should be made directly with fuel suppliers at locations where refueling is planned.

15 OXYGEN—CIVIL

OX 1 High Pressure	OX 3 High Pressure—Replacement Bottles
OX 2 Low Pressure	OX 4 Low Pressure—Replacement Bottles

16 TRAFFIC PATTERN ALTITUDE

Traffic Pattern Altitude (TPA)—The first figure shown is TPA above mean sea level. The second figure in parentheses is TPA above airport elevation. Multiple TPA shall be shown as "TPA—See Remarks" and detailed information shall be shown in the Airport or Military Remarks Section. Traffic pattern data for USAF bases, USN facilities, and U.S. Army airports (including those on which ACC or U.S. Army is a tenant) that deviate from standard pattern altitudes shall be shown in Military Remarks.

Legend 5. *Airport/facility directory.*

8   **DIRECTORY LEGEND**

 AIRPORT OF ENTRY, LANDING RIGHTS, AND CUSTOMS USER FEE AIRPORTS

U.S. CUSTOMS USER FEE AIRPORT—Private Aircraft operators are frequently required to pay the costs associated with customs processing.

AOE—Airport of Entry. A customs Airport of Entry where permission from U.S. Customs is not required to land. However, at least one hour advance notice of arrival is required.

LRA—Landing Rights Airport. Application for permission to land must be submitted in advance to U.S. Customs. At least one hour advance notice of arrival is required.

NOTE: Advance notice of arrival at both an AOE and LRA airport may be included in the flight plan when filed in Canada or Mexico. Where Flight Notification Service (ADCUS) is available the airport remark will indicate this service. This notice will also be treated as an application for permission to land in the case of an LRA. Although advance notice of arrival may be relayed to Customs through Mexico, Canada, and U.S. Communications facilities by flight plan, the aircraft operator is solely responsible for ensuring that Customs receives the notification. (See Customs, Immigration and Naturalization, Public Health and Agriculture Department requirements in the International Flight Information Manual for further details.)

US Customs Air and Sea Ports, Inspectors and Agents

Northeast Sector (New England and Atlantic States—ME to MD)	407-975-1740
Southeast Sector (Atlantic States—DC, WV, VA to FL)	407-975-1780
Central Sector (Interior of the US, including Gulf states—MS, AL, LA)	407-975-1760
Southwest East Sector (OK and eastern TX)	407-975-1840
Southwest West Sector (Western TX, NM and AZ)	407-975-1820
Pacific Sector (WA, OR, CA, HI and AK)	407-975-1800

18 **CERTIFICATED AIRPORT (14 CFR PART 139)**

Airports serving Department of Transportation certified carriers and certified under 14 CFR part 139 are indicated by the Class and the ARFF Index; e.g. Class I, ARFF Index A, which relates to the availability of crash, fire, rescue equipment. Class I airports can have an ARFF Index A through E, depending on the aircraft length and scheduled departures. Class II, III, and IV will always carry an Index A.

14 CFR PART 139 CERTIFICATED AIRPORTS
AIRPORT CLASSIFICATIONS

Type of Air Carrier Operation	Class I	Class II	Class III	Class IV
Scheduled Air Carrier Aircraft with 31 or more passenger seats	X			
Unscheduled Air Carrier Aircraft with 31 or more passengers seats	X	X		X
Scheduled Air Carrier Aircraft with 10 to 30 passenger seats	X	X	X	

14 CFR—PART 139 CERTIFICATED AIRPORTS
INDICES AND AIRCRAFT RESCUE AND FIRE FIGHTING EQUIPMENT REQUIREMENTS

Airport Index	Required No. Vehicles	Aircraft Length	Scheduled Departures	Agent + Water for Foam
A	1	<90'	≥1	500#DC or HALON 1211 or 450#DC + 100 gal H_2O
B	1 or 2	≥90', <126'	≥5	Index A + 1500 gal H_2O
		≥126', <159'	<5	
C	2 or 3	≥126', <159'	≥5	Index A + 3000 gal H_2O
		≥159', <200'	<5	
D	3	≥159', <200'		Index A + 4000 gal H_2O
		>200'	<5	
E	3	≥200'	≥5	Index A + 6000 gal H_2O

> Greater Than; < Less Than; ≥ Equal or Greater Than; ≤ Equal or Less Than; H_2O—Water; DC–Dry Chemical.

NOTE: The listing of ARFF index does not necessarily assure coverage for non-air carrier operations or at other than prescribed times for air carrier. ARFF Index Ltd.—indicates ARFF coverage may or may not be available, for information contact airport manager prior to flight.

 NOTAM SERVICE

All public use landing areas are provided NOTAM service. A NOTAM FILE identifier is shown for individual langing areas, e.g., "NOTAM FILE BNA". See the AIM, Basic Flight Information and ATC Procedures for a detailed description of NOTAMs.

NE, 09 FEB 2012 to 05 APR 2012

Legend 6. *Airport/facility directory.*

DIRECTORY LEGEND   9

Current NOTAMs are available from flight service stations at 1–800–WX–BRIEF (992–7433) or online through the FAA PilotWeb at https://pilotweb.nas.faa.gov. Military NOTAMs are available using the Defense Internet NOTAM Service (DINS) at https://www.notams.jcs.mil.

Pilots flying to or from airports not available through the FAA PilotWeb or DINS can obtain assistance from Flight Service.

20 FAA INSPECTION

All airports not inspected by FAA will be identified by the note: Not insp. This indicates that the airport information has been provided by the owner or operator of the field.

21 RUNWAY DATA

Runway information is shown on two lines. That information common to the entire runway is shown on the first line while information concerning the runway ends is shown on the second or following line. Runway direction, surface, length, width, weight bearing capacity, lighting, and slope, when available are shown for each runway. Multiple runways are shown with the longest runway first. Direction, length, width, and lighting are shown for sea-lanes. The full dimensions of helipads are shown, e.g., 50X150. Runway data that requires clarification will be placed in the remarks section.

RUNWAY DESIGNATION

Runways are normally numbered in relation to their magnetic orientation rounded off to the nearest 10 degrees. Parallel runways can be designated L (left)/R (right)/C (center). Runways may be designated as Ultralight or assault strips. Assault strips are shown by magnetic bearing.

RUNWAY DIMENSIONS

Runway length and width are shown in feet. Length shown is runway end to end including displaced thresholds, but excluding those areas designed as overruns.

RUNWAY SURFACE AND LENGTH

Runway lengths prefixed by the letter "H" indicate that the runways are hard surfaced (concrete, asphalt, or part asphalt–concrete). If the runway length is not prefixed, the surface is sod, clay, etc. The runway surface composition is indicated in parentheses after runway length as follows:

(AFSC)—Aggregate friction seal coat	(GRVD)—Grooved	(PSP)—Pierced steel plank
(AMS)—Temporary metal planks coated with nonskid material	(GRVL)—Gravel, or cinders	(RFSC)—Rubberized friction seal coat
(ASPH)—Asphalt	(MATS)—Pierced steel planking, landing mats, membranes	(TURF)—Turf
(CONC)—Concrete	(PEM)—Part concrete, part asphalt	(TRTD)—Treated
(DIRT)—Dirt	(PFC)—Porous friction courses	(WC)—Wire combed

RUNWAY WEIGHT BEARING CAPACITY

Runway strength data shown in this publication is derived from available information and is a realistic estimate of capability at an average level of activity. It is not intended as a maximum allowable weight or as an operating limitation. Many airport pavements are capable of supporting limited operations with gross weights in excess of the published figures. Permissible operating weights, insofar as runway strengths are concerned, are a matter of agreement between the owner and user. When desiring to operate into any airport at weights in excess of those published in the publication, users should contact the airport management for permission. Runway strength figures are shown in thousand of pounds, with the last three figures being omitted. Add 000 to figure following S, D, 2S, 2T, AUW, SWL, etc., for gross weight capacity. A blank space following the letter designator is used to indicate the runway can sustain aircraft with this type landing gear, although definite runway weight bearing capacity figures are not available, e.g., S, D. Applicable codes for typical gear configurations with S=Single, D=Dual, T=Triple and Q=Quadruple:

CURRENT	NEW	NEW DESCRIPTION
S	S	Single wheel type landing gear (DC3), (C47), (F15), etc.
D	D	Dual wheel type landing gear (BE1900), (B737), (A319), etc.
T	D	Dual wheel type landing gear (P3, C9).
ST	2S	Two single wheels in tandem type landing gear (C130).
TRT	2T	Two triple wheels in tandem type landing gear (C17), etc.
DT	2D	Two dual wheels in tandem type landing gear (B707), etc.
TT	2D	Two dual wheels in tandem type landing gear (B757, KC135).
SBTT	2D/D1	Two dual wheels in tandem/dual wheel body gear type landing gear (KC10).
None	2D/2D1	Two dual wheels in tandem/two dual wheels in tandem body gear type landing gear (A340–600).
DDT	2D/2D2	Two dual wheels in tandem/two dual wheels in double tandem body gear type landing gear (B747, E4).
TTT	3D	Three dual wheels in tandem type landing gear (B777), etc.
TT	D2	Dual wheel gear two struts per side main gear type landing gear (B52).
TDT	C5	Complex dual wheel and quadruple wheel combination landing gear (C5).

NE, 09 FEB 2012 to 05 APR 2012

Legend 7. *Airport/facility directory.*

10　　　　　　　　　　　　DIRECTORY LEGEND

　　AUW—All up weight. Maximum weight bearing capacity for any aircraft irrespective of landing gear configuration.
　　SWL—Single Wheel Loading. (This includes information submitted in terms of Equivalent Single Wheel Loading (ESWL) and Single Isolated Wheel Loading).
　　PSI—Pounds per square inch. PSI is the actual figure expressing maximum pounds per square inch runway will support, e.g., (SWL 000/PSI 535).

Omission of weight bearing capacity indicates information unknown.

The ACN/PCN System is the ICAO standard method of reporting pavement strength for pavements with bearing strengths greater than 12,500 pounds. The Pavement Classification Number (PCN) is established by an engineering assessment of the runway. The PCN is for use in conjunction with an Aircraft Classification Number (ACN). Consult the Aircraft Flight Manual, Flight Information Handbook, or other appropriate source for ACN tables or charts. Currently, ACN data may not be available for all aircraft. If an ACN table or chart is available, the ACN can be calculated by taking into account the aircraft weight, the pavement type, and the subgrade category. For runways that have been evaluated under the ACN/PCN system, the PCN will be shown as a five-part code (e.g. PCN 80 R/B/W/T). Details of the coded format are as follows:

(1) The PCN NUMBER—The reported PCN indicates that an aircraft with an ACN equal or less than the reported PCN can operate on the pavement subject to any limitation on the tire pressure.

(2) The type of pavement:
　R — Rigid
　F — Flexible

(3) The pavement subgrade category:
　A — High
　B — Medium
　C — Low
　D — Ultra-low

(4) The maximum tire pressure authorized for the pavement:
　W — High, no limit
　X — Medium, limited to 217 psi
　Y — Low, limited to 145 psi
　Z — Very low, limited to 73 psi

(5) Pavement evaluation method:
　T — Technical evaluation
　U — By experience of aircraft using the pavement

NOTE: Prior permission from the airport controlling authority is required when the ACN of the aircraft exceeds the published PCN or aircraft tire pressure exceeds the published limits.

RUNWAY LIGHTING

Lights are in operation sunset to sunrise. Lighting available by prior arrangement only or operating part of the night and/or pilot controlled lighting with specific operating hours are indicated under airport or military remarks. At USN/USMC facilities lights are available only during airport hours of operation. Since obstructions are usually lighted, obstruction lighting is not included in this code. Unlighted obstructions on or surrounding an airport will be noted in airport or military remarks. Runway lights nonstandard (NSTD) are systems for which the light fixtures are not FAA approved L-800 series: color, intensity, or spacing does not meet FAA standards. Nonstandard runway lights, VASI, or any other system not listed below will be shown in airport remarks or military service. Temporary, emergency or limited runway edge lighting such as flares, smudge pots, lanterns or portable runway lights will also be shown in airport remarks or military service. Types of lighting are shown with the runway or runway end they serve.

NSTD—Light system fails to meet FAA standards.
LIRL—Low Intensity Runway Lights.
MIRL—Medium Intensity Runway Lights.
HIRL—High Intensity Runway Lights.
RAIL—Runway Alignment Indicator Lights.
REIL—Runway End Identifier Lights.
CL—Centerline Lights.
TDZL—Touchdown Zone Lights.
ODALS—Omni Directional Approach Lighting System.
AF OVRN—Air Force Overrun 1000′ Standard Approach Lighting System.
LDIN—Lead-In Lighting System.
MALS—Medium Intensity Approach Lighting System.
MALSF—Medium Intensity Approach Lighting System with Sequenced Flashing Lights.
MALSR—Medium Intensity Approach Lighting System with Runway Alignment Indicator Lights.

SALS—Short Approach Lighting System.
SALSF—Short Approach Lighting System with Sequenced Flashing Lights.
SSALS—Simplified Short Approach Lighting System.
SSALF—Simplified Short Approach Lighting System with Sequenced Flashing Lights.
SSALR—Simplified Short Approach Lighting System with Runway Alignment Indicator Lights.
ALSAF—High Intensity Approach Lighting System with Sequenced Flashing Lights.
ALSF1—High Intensity Approach Lighting System with Sequenced Flashing Lights, Category I, Configuration.
ALSF2—High Intensity Approach Lighting System with Sequenced Flashing Lights, Category II, Configuration.
SF—Sequenced Flashing Lights.
OLS—Optical Landing System.
WAVE–OFF.

NOTE: Civil ALSF2 may be operated as SSALR during favorable weather conditions. When runway edge lights are positioned more than 10 feet from the edge of the usable runway surface a remark will be added in the "Remarks" portion of the airport entry. This is applicable to Air Force, Air National Guard and Air Force Reserve Bases, and those joint civil/military airfields on which they are tenants.

Legend 8. *Airport/facility directory.*

DIRECTORY LEGEND   11

VISUAL GLIDESLOPE INDICATORS

APAP—A system of panels, which may or may not be lighted, used for alignment of approach path.

PNIL	APAP on left side of runway	PNIR	APAP on right side of runway

PAPI—Precision Approach Path Indicator

P2L	2-identical light units placed on left side of runway	P4L	4-identical light units placed on left side of runway
P2R	2-identical light units placed on right side of runway	P4R	4-identical light units placed on right side of runway

PVASI—Pulsating/steady burning visual approach slope indicator, normally a single light unit projecting two colors.

PSIL	PVASI on left side of runway	PSIR	PVASI on right side of runway

SAVASI—Simplified Abbreviated Visual Approach Slope Indicator

S2L	2-box SAVASI on left side of runway	S2R	2-box SAVASI on right side of runway

TRCV—Tri-color visual approach slope indicator, normally a single light unit projecting three colors.

TRIL	TRCV on left side of runway	TRIR	TRCV on right side of runway

VASI—Visual Approach Slope Indicator

V2L	2-box VASI on left side of runway	V6L	6-box VASI on left side of runway
V2R	2-box VASI on right side of runway	V6R	6-box VASI on right side of runway
V4L	4-box VASI on left side of runway	V12	12-box VASI on both sides of runway
V4R	4-box VASI on right side of runway	V16	16-box VASI on both sides of runway

NOTE: Approach slope angle and threshold crossing height will be shown when available; i.e., –GA 3.5° TCH 37'.

PILOT CONTROL OF AIRPORT LIGHTING

Key Mike	Function
7 times within 5 seconds	Highest intensity available
5 times within 5 seconds	Medium or lower intensity (Lower REIL or REIL-Off)
3 times within 5 seconds	Lowest intensity available (Lower REIL or REIL-Off)

Available systems will be indicated in the airport or military remarks, e.g., ACTIVATE HIRL Rwy 07–25, MALSR Rwy 07, and VASI Rwy 07—122.8.

Where the airport is not served by an instrument approach procedure and/or has an independent type system of different specification installed by the airport sponsor, descriptions of the type lights, method of control, and operating frequency will be explained in clear text. See AIM, "Basic Flight Information and ATC Procedures," for detailed description of pilot control of airport lighting.

RUNWAY SLOPE

When available, runway slope data will only be provided for those airports with an approved FAA instrument approach procedure. Runway slope will be shown only when it is 0.3 percent or greater. On runways less than 8000 feet, the direction of the slope up will be indicated, e.g., 0.3% up NW. On runways 8000 feet or greater, the slope will be shown (up or down) on the runway end line, e.g., RWY 13: 0.3% up., RWY 21: Pole. Rgt tfc. 0.4% down.

RUNWAY END DATA

Information pertaining to the runway approach end such as approach lights, touchdown zone lights, runway end identification lights, visual glideslope indicators, displaced thresholds, controlling obstruction, and right hand traffic pattern, will be shown on the specific runway end. "Rgt tfc"—Right traffic indicates right turns should be made on landing and takeoff for specified runway end.

LAND AND HOLD SHORT OPERATIONS (LAHSO)

LAHSO is an acronym for "Land and Hold Short Operations." These operations include landing and holding short of an intersection runway, an intersecting taxiway, or other predetermined points on the runway other than a runway or taxiway. Measured distance represents the available landing distance on the landing runway, in feet.

Specific questions regarding these distances should be referred to the air traffic manager of the facility concerned. The Aeronautical Information Manual contains specific details on hold–short operations and markings.

RUNWAY DECLARED DISTANCE INFORMATION

TORA—Take-off Run Available. The length of runway declared available and suitable for the ground run of an aeroplane take–off.

TODA—Take-off Distance Available. The length of the take–off run available plus the length of the clearway, if provided.

ASDA—Accelerate-Stop Distance Available. The length of the take–off run available plus the length of the stopway, if provided.

LDA—Landing Distance Available. The length of runway which is declared available and suitable for the ground run of an aeroplane landing.

22 ARRESTING GEAR/SYSTEMS

Arresting gear is shown as it is located on the runway. The a–gear distance from the end of the appropriate runway (or into the overrun) is indicated in parentheses. A–Gear which has a bi–direction capability and can be utilized for emergency approach end engagement is indicated by a (B). The direction of engaging device is indicated by an arrow. Up to 15 minutes advance notice may be required for rigging A–Gear for approach and engagement. Airport listing may show availability of other than US Systems. This information is provided for emergency requirements only. Refer to current aircraft operating manuals for specific engagement weight and speed criteria based on aircraft structural restrictions and arresting system limitations.

Following is a list of current systems referenced in this publication identified by both Air Force and Navy terminology:

NE, 09 FEB 2012 to 05 APR 2012

Legend 9. *Airport/facility directory.*

12   **DIRECTORY LEGEND**

BI–DIRECTIONAL CABLE (B)

TYPE	DESCRIPTION
BAK–9	Rotary friction brake.
BAK–12A	Standard BAK–12 with 950 foot run out, 1–inch cable and 40,000 pound weight setting. Rotary friction brake.
BAK–12B	Extended BAK–12 with 1200 foot run, 1¼ inch Cable and 50,000 pounds weight setting. Rotary friction brake.
E28	Rotary Hydraulic (Water Brake).
M21	Rotary Hydraulic (Water Brake) Mobile.

The following device is used in conjunction with some aircraft arresting systems:

BAK–14	A device that raises a hook cable out of a slot in the runway surface and is remotely positioned for engagement by the tower on request. (In addition to personnel reaction time, the system requires up to five seconds to fully raise the cable.)
H	A device that raises a hook cable out of a slot in the runway surface and is remotely positioned for engagement by the tower on request. (In addition to personnel reaction time, the system requires up to one and one–half seconds to fully raise the cable.)

UNI–DIRECTIONAL CABLE

TYPE	DESCRIPTION
MB60	Textile brake—an emergency one–time use, modular braking system employing the tearing of specially woven textile straps to absorb the kinetic energy.
E5/E5–1/E5–3	Chain Type. At USN/USMC stations E–5 A–GEAR systems are rated, e.g., E–5 RATING–13R–1100 HW (DRY), 31L/R–1200 STD (WET). This rating is a function of the A–GEAR chain weight and length and is used to determine the maximum aircraft engaging speed. A dry rating applies to a stabilized surface (dry or wet) while a wet rating takes into account the amount (if any) of wet overrun that is not capable of withstanding the aircraft weight. These ratings are published under Military Service.

FOREIGN CABLE

TYPE	DESCRIPTION	US EQUIVALENT
44B–3H	Rotary Hydraulic) (Water Brake)	
CHAG	Chain	E–5

UNI–DIRECTIONAL BARRIER

TYPE	DESCRIPTION
MA–1A	Web barrier between stanchions attached to a chain energy absorber.
BAK–15	Web barrier between stanchions attached to an energy absorber (water squeezer, rotary friction, chain). Designed for wing engagement.

NOTE: Landing short of the runway threshold on a runway with a BAK–15 in the underrun is a significant hazard. The barrier in the down position still protrudes several inches above the underrun. Aircraft contact with the barrier short of the runway threshold can cause damage to the barrier and substantial damage to the aircraft.

OTHER

TYPE	DESCRIPTION
EMAS	Engineered Material Arresting System, located beyond the departure end of the runway, consisting of high energy absorbing materials which will crush under the weight of an aircraft.

㉓ MILITARY SERVICE

Specific military services available at the airport are listed under this general heading. Remarks applicable to any military service are shown in the individual service listing.

㉔ JET AIRCRAFT STARTING UNITS (JASU)

The numeral preceding the type of unit indicates the number of units available. The absence of the numeral indicates ten or more units available. If the number of units is unknown, the number one will be shown. Absence of JASU designation indicates non–availability.

The following is a list of current JASU systems referenced in this publication:

USAF JASU (For variations in technical data, refer to T.O. 35–1–7.)

ELECTRICAL STARTING UNITS:

A/M32A–86	AC: 115/200v, 3 phase, 90 kva, 0.8 pf, 4 wire
	DC: 28v, 1500 amp, 72 kw (with TR pack)
MC–1A	AC: 115/208v, 400 cycle, 3 phase, 37.5 kva, 0.8 pf, 108 amp, 4 wire
	DC: 28v, 500 amp, 14 kw
MD–3	AC: 115/208v, 400 cycle, 3 phase, 60 kva, 0.75 pf, 4 wire
	DC: 28v, 1500 amp, 45 kw, split bus
MD–3A	AC: 115/208v, 400 cycle, 3 phase, 60 kva, 0.75 pf, 4 wire
	DC: 28v, 1500 amp, 45 kw, split bus
MD–3M	AC: 115/208v, 400 cycle, 3 phase, 60 kva, 0.75 pf, 4 wire
	DC: 28v, 500 amp, 15 kw

NE, 09 FEB 2012 to 05 APR 2012

Legend 10. *Airport/facility directory.*

DIRECTORY LEGEND   13

MD–4	AC: 120/208v, 400 cycle, 3 phase, 62.5 kva, 0.8 pf, 175 amp, "WYE" neutral ground, 4 wire, 120v, 400 cycle, 3 phase, 62.5 kva, 0.8 pf, 303 amp, "DELTA" 3 wire, 120v, 400 cycle, 1 phase, 62.5 kva, 0.8 pf, 520 amp, 2 wire

AIR STARTING UNITS

AM32–95	150 +/− 5 lb/min (2055 +/− 68 cfm) at 51 +/− 2 psia
AM32A–95	150 +/− 5 lb/min @ 49 +/− 2 psia (35 +/− 2 psig)
LASS	150 +/− 5 lb/min @ 49 +/− 2 psia
MA–1A	82 lb/min (1123 cfm) at 130° air inlet temp, 45 psia (min) air outlet press
MC–1	15 cfm, 3500 psia
MC–1A	15 cfm, 3500 psia
MC–2A	15 cfm, 200 psia
MC–11	8,000 cu in cap, 4000 psig, 15 cfm

COMBINED AIR AND ELECTRICAL STARTING UNITS:

AGPU	AC: 115/200v, 400 cycle, 3 phase, 30 kw gen
	DC: 28v, 700 amp
	AIR: 60 lb/min @ 40 psig @ sea level
AM32A–60*	AIR: 120 +/− 4 lb/min (1644 +/− 55 cfm) at 49 +/− 2 psia
	AC: 120/208v, 400 cycle, 3 phase, 75 kva, 0.75 pf, 4 wire, 120v, 1 phase, 25 kva
	DC: 28v, 500 amp, 15 kw
AM32A–60A	AIR: 150 +/− 5 lb/min (2055 +/− 68 cfm at 51 +/− psia
	AC: 120/208v, 400 cycle, 3 phase, 75 kva, 0.75 pf, 4 wire
	DC: 28v, 200 amp, 5.6 kw
AM32A–60B*	AIR: 130 lb/min, 50 psia
	AC: 120/208v, 400 cycle, 3 phase, 75 kva, 0.75 pf, 4 wire
	DC: 28v, 200 amp, 5.6 kw

*NOTE: During combined air and electrical loads, the pneumatic circuitry takes preference and will limit the amount of electrical power available.

USN JASU

ELECTRICAL STARTING UNITS:

NC–8A/A1	DC: 500 amp constant, 750 amp intermittent, 28v; AC: 60 kva @ .8 pf, 115/200v, 3 phase, 400 Hz.
NC–10A/A1/B/C	DC: 750 amp constant, 1000 amp intermittent, 28v; AC: 90 kva, 115/200v, 3 phase, 400 Hz.

AIR STARTING UNITS:

GTC–85/GTE–85	120 lbs/min @ 45 psi.
MSU–200NAV/A/U47A–5	204 lbs/min @ 56 psia.
WELLS AIR START SYSTEM	180 lbs/min @ 75 psi or 120 lbs/min @ 45 psi. Simultaneous multiple start capability.

COMBINED AIR AND ELECTRICAL STARTING UNITS:

NCPP–105/RCPT	180 lbs/min @ 75 psi or 120 lbs/min @ 45 psi. 700 amp, 28v DC. 120/208v, 400 Hz AC, 30 kva.

JASU (ARMY)

59B2–1B	28v, 7.5 kw, 280 amp.

OTHER JASU

ELECTRICAL STARTING UNITS (DND):

CE12	AC 115/200v, 140 kva, 400 Hz, 3 phase
CE13	AC 115/200v, 60 kva, 400 Hz, 3 phase
CE14	AC/DC 115/200v, 140 kva, 400 Hz, 3 phase, 28vDC, 1500 amp
CE15	DC 22–35v, 500 amp continuous 1100 amp intermittent
CE16	DC 22–35v, 500 amp continuous 1100 amp intermittent soft start

AIR STARTING UNITS (DND):

CA2	ASA 45.5 psig, 116.4 lb/min

COMBINED AIR AND ELECTRICAL STARTING UNITS (DND)

CEA1	AC 120/208v, 60 kva, 400 Hz, 3 phase DC 28v, 75 amp
	AIR 112.5 lb/min, 47 psig

ELECTRICAL STARTING UNITS (OTHER)

C–26	28v 45kw 115–200v 15kw 380–800 Hz 1 phase 2 wire
C–26–B, C–26–C	28v 45kw: Split Bus: 115–200v 15kw 380–800 Hz 1 phase 2 wire
E3	DC 28v/10kw

AIR STARTING UNITS (OTHER):

A4	40 psi/2 lb/sec (LPAS Mk12, Mk12L, Mk12A, Mk1, Mk2B)
MA–1	150 Air HP, 115 lb/min 50 psia
MA–2	250 Air HP, 150 lb/min 75 psia

CARTRIDGE:

MXU–4A	USAF

NE, 09 FEB 2012 to 05 APR 2012

Legend 11. *Airport/facility directory.*

14 DIRECTORY LEGEND

 FUEL—MILITARY

Fuel available through US Military Base supply, DESC Into–Plane Contracts and/or reciprocal agreement is listed first and is followed by (Mil). At commercial airports where Into–Plane contracts are in place, the name of the refueling agent is shown. Military fuel should be used first if it is available. When military fuel cannot be obtained but Into–Plane contract fuel is available, Government aircraft must refuel with the contract fuel and applicable refueling agent to avoid any breach in contract terms and conditions. Fuel not available through the above is shown preceded by NC (no contract). When fuel is obtained from NC sources, local purchase procedures must be followed. The US Military Aircraft Identaplates DD Form 1896 (Jet Fuel), DD Form 1897 (Avgas) and AF Form 1245 (Avgas) are used at military installations only. The US Government Aviation Into–Plane Reimbursement (AIR) Card (currently issued by AVCARD) is the instrument to be used to obtain fuel under a DESC Into–Plane Contract and for NC purchases if the refueling agent at the commercial airport accepts the AVCARD. A current list of contract fuel locations is available online at www.desc.dla.mil/Static/ProductsAndServices.asp; click on the Commercial Airports button.

See legend item 14 for fuel code and description.

 SUPPORTING FLUIDS AND SYSTEMS—MILITARY

CODE

ADI	Anti–Detonation Injection Fluid—Reciprocating Engine Aircraft.
W	Water Thrust Augmentation—Jet Aircraft.
WAI	Water–Alcohol Injection Type, Thrust Augmentation—Jet Aircraft.
SP	Single Point Refueling.
PRESAIR	Air Compressors rated 3,000 PSI or more.
De–Ice	Anti–icing/De–icing/Defrosting Fluid (MIL–A–8243).

OXYGEN:

LPOX	Low pressure oxygen servicing.
HPOX	High pressure oxygen servicing.
LHOX	Low and high pressure oxygen servicing.
LOX	Liquid oxygen servicing.
OXRB	Oxygen replacement bottles. (Maintained primarily at Naval stations for use in acft where oxygen can be replenished only by replacement of cylinders.)
OX	Indicates oxygen servicing when type of servicing is unknown.

NOTE: Combinations of above items is used to indicate complete oxygen servicing available;

LHOXRB	Low and high pressure oxygen servicing and replacement bottles;
LPOXRB	Low pressure oxygen replacement bottles only, etc.

NOTE: Aircraft will be serviced with oxygen procured under military specifications only. Aircraft will not be serviced with medical oxygen.

NITROGEN:

LPNIT — Low pressure nitrogen servicing.
HPNIT — High pressure nitrogen servicing.
LHNIT — Low and high pressure nitrogen servicing.

 OIL—MILITARY

US AVIATION OILS (MIL SPECS):

CODE	GRADE, TYPE
O–113	1065, Reciprocating Engine Oil (MIL–L–6082)
O–117	1100, Reciprocating Engine Oil (MIL–L–6082)
O–117+	1100, O–117 plus cyclohexanone (MIL–L–6082)
O–123	1065, (Dispersant), Reciprocating Engine Oil (MIL–L–22851 Type III)
O–128	1100, (Dispersant), Reciprocating Engine Oil (MIL–L–22851 Type II)
O–132	1005, Jet Engine Oil (MIL–L–6081)
O–133	1010, Jet Engine Oil (MIL–L–6081)
O–147	None, MIL–L–6085A Lubricating Oil, Instrument, Synthetic
O–148	None, MIL–L–7808 (Synthetic Base) Turbine Engine Oil
O–149	None, Aircraft Turbine Engine Synthetic, 7.5c St
O–155	None, MIL–L–6086C, Aircraft, Medium Grade
O–156	None, MIL–L–23699 (Synthetic Base), Turboprop and Turboshaft Engines
JOAP/SOAP	Joint Oil Analysis Program. JOAP support is furnished during normal duty hours, other times on request. (JOAP and SOAP programs provide essentially the same service, JOAP is now the standard joint service supported program.)

28 TRANSIENT ALERT (TRAN ALERT)—MILITARY

Tran Alert service is considered to include all services required for normal aircraft turn–around, e.g., servicing (fuel, oil, oxygen, etc.), debriefing to determine requirements for maintenance, minor maintenance, inspection and parking assistance of transient aircraft. Drag chute repack, specialized maintenance, or extensive repairs will be provided within the capabilities and priorities of the base. Delays can be anticipated after normal duty hours/holidays/weekends regardless of the hours of transient maintenance operation. Pilots should not expect aircraft to be serviced for TURN–AROUNDS during time periods when servicing or maintenance manpower is not available. In the case of airports not operated exclusively by US military, the servicing indicated by the remarks will not always be available for US military

NE, 09 FEB 2012 to 05 APR 2012

Legend 12. *Airport/facility directory.*

DIRECTORY LEGEND   15

aircraft. When transient alert services are not shown, facilities are unknown. NO PRIORITY BASIS—means that transient alert services will be provided only after all the requirements for mission/tactical assigned aircraft have been accomplished.

AIRPORT REMARKS

The Attendance Schedule is the months, days and hours the airport is actually attended. Airport attendance does not mean watchman duties or telephone accessibility, but rather an attendant or operator on duty to provide at least minimum services (e.g., repairs, fuel, transportation).

Airport Remarks have been grouped in order of applicability. Airport remarks are limited to those items of information that are determined essential for operational use, i.e., conditions of a permanent or indefinite nature and conditions that will remain in effect for more than 30 days concerning aeronautical facilities, services, maintenance available, procedures or hazards, knowledge of which is essential for safe and efficient operation of aircraft. Information concerning permanent closing of a runway or taxiway will not be shown. A note "See Special Notices" shall be applied within this remarks section when a special notice applicable to the entry is contained in the Special Notices section of this publication.

Parachute Jumping indicates parachute jumping areas associated with the airport. See Parachute Jumping Area section of this publication for additional information.

Landing Fee indicates landing charges for private or non-revenue producing aircraft. In addition, fees may be charged for planes that remain over a couple of hours and buy no services, or at major airline terminals for all aircraft.

Note: Unless otherwise stated, remarks including runway ends refer to the runway's approach end.

 MILITARY REMARKS

Military Remarks published at a joint Civil/Military facility are remarks that are applicable to the Military. At Military Facilities all remarks will be published under the heading Military Remarks. Remarks contained in this section may not be applicable to civil users. The first group of remarks is applicable to the primary operator of the airport. Remarks applicable to a tenant on the airport are shown preceded by the tenant organization, i.e., (A) (AF) (N) (ANG), etc. Military airports operate 24 hours unless otherwise specified. Airport operating hours are listed first (airport operating hours will only be listed if they are different than the airport attended hours or if the attended hours are unavailable) followed by pertinent remarks in order of applicability. Remarks will include information on restrictions, hazards, traffic pattern, noise abatement, customs/agriculture/immigration, and miscellaneous information applicable to the Military.

Type of restrictions:

CLOSED: When designated closed, the airport is restricted from use by all aircraft unless stated otherwise. Any closure applying to specific type of aircraft or operation will be so stated. USN/USMC/USAF airports are considered closed during non–operating hours. Closed airports may be utilized during an emergency provided there is a safe landing area.

OFFICIAL BUSINESS ONLY: The airfield is closed to all transient military aircraft for obtaining routine services such as fueling, passenger drop off or pickup, practice approaches, parking, etc. The airfield may be used by aircrews and aircraft if official government business (including civilian) must be conducted on or near the airfield and prior permission is received from the airfield manager.

AF OFFICIAL BUSINESS ONLY OR NAVY OFFICIAL BUSINESS ONLY: Indicates that the restriction applies only to service indicated.

PRIOR PERMISSION REQUIRED (PPR): Airport is closed to transient aircraft unless approval for operation is obtained from the appropriate commander through Chief, Airfield Management or Airfield Operations Officer. Official Business or PPR does not preclude the use of US Military airports as an alternate for IFR flights. If a non–US military airport is used as a weather alternate and requires a PPR, the PPR must be requested and confirmed before the flight departs. The purpose of PPR is to control volume and flow of traffic rather than to prohibit it. Prior permission is required for all aircraft requiring transient alert service outside the published transient alert duty hours. All aircraft carrying hazardous materials must obtain prior permission as outlined in AFJI 11–204, AR 95–27, OPNAVINST 3710.7.

Note: OFFICIAL BUSINESS ONLY AND PPR restrictions are not applicable to Special Air Mission (SAM) or Special Air Resource (SPAR) aircraft providing person or persons on aboard are designated Code 6 or higher as explained in AFJMAN 11–213, AR 95–11, OPNAVINST 3722–8J. Official Business Only or PPR do not preclude the use of the airport as an alternate for IFR flights.

WEATHER DATA SOURCES

Weather data sources will be listed alphabetically followed by their assigned frequencies and/or telephone number and hours of operation.

ASOS—Automated Surface Observing System. Reports the same as an AWOS–3 plus precipitation identification and intensity, and freezing rain occurrence;

AWOS—Automated Weather Observing System

  AWOS–A—reports altimeter setting (all other information is advisory only).

  AWOS–AV—reports altimeter and visibility.

  AWOS–1—reports altimeter setting, wind data and usually temperature, dew point and density altitude.

  AWOS–2—reports the same as AWOS–1 plus visibility.

  AWOS–3—reports the same as AWOS–1 plus visibility and cloud/ceiling data.

  AWOS–3P reports the same as the AWOS–3 system, plus a precipitation identification sensor.

  AWOS–3PT reports the same as the AWOS–3 system, plus precipitation identification sensor and a thunderstorm/lightning reporting capability.

  AWOS–3T reports the same as AWOS–3 system and includes a thunderstorm/lightning reporting capability.

NE, 09 FEB 2012 to 05 APR 2012

Legend 13. *Airport/facility directory.*

16   DIRECTORY LEGEND

See AIM, Basic Flight Information and ATC Procedures for detailed description of Weather Data Sources.

AWOS–4—reports same as AWOS–3 system, plus precipitation occurence, type and accumulation, freezing rain, thunderstorm, and runway surface sensors.

HIWAS—See RADIO AIDS TO NAVIGATION

LAWRS—Limited Aviation Weather Reporting Station where observers report cloud height, weather, obstructions to vision, temperature and dewpoint (in most cases), surface wind, altimeter and pertinent remarks.

LLWAS—Indicates a Low Level Wind Shear Alert System consisting of a center field and several field perimeter anemometers.

SAWRS—identifies airports that have a Supplemental Aviation Weather Reporting Station available to pilots for current weather information.

SWSL—Supplemental Weather Service Location providing current local weather information via radio and telephone.

TDWR—indicates airports that have Terminal Doppler Weather Radar.

WSP—indicates airports that have Weather System Processor.

When the automated weather source is broadcast over an associated airport NAVAID frequency (see NAVAID line), it shall be indicated by a bold ASOS, AWOS, or HIWAS followed by the frequency, identifier and phone number, if available.

32 COMMUNICATIONS

Airport terminal control facilities and radio communications associated with the airport shall be shown. When the call sign is not the same as the airport name the call sign will be shown. Frequencies shall normally be shown in descending order with the primary frequency listed first. Frequencies will be listed, together with sectorization indicated by outbound radials, and hours of operation. Communications will be listed in sequence as follows:

Single Frequency Approach (SFA), Common Traffic Advisory Frequency (CTAF), Automatic Terminal Information Service (ATIS) and Aeronautical Advisory Stations (UNICOM) or (AUNICOM) along with their frequency is shown, where available, on the line following the heading "COMMUNICATIONS." When the CTAF and UNICOM frequencies are the same, the frequency will be shown as CTAF/UNICOM 122.8.

The FSS telephone nationwide is toll free 1–800–WX–BRIEF (1–800–992–7433). When the FSS is located on the field it will be indicated as "on arpt". Frequencies available at the FSS will follow in descending order. Remote Communications Outlet (RCO) providing service to the airport followed by the frequency and FSS RADIO name will be shown when available.

FSS's provide information on airport conditions, radio aids and other facilities, and process flight plans. Airport Advisory Service (AAS) is provided on the CTAF by FSS's for select non-tower airports or airports where the tower is not in operation.

(See AIM, Para 4–1–9 Traffic Advisory Practices at Airports Without Operating Control Towers or AC 90–42C.)

Aviation weather briefing service is provided by FSS specialists. Flight and weather briefing services are also available by calling the telephone numbers listed.

Remote Communications Outlet (RCO)—An unmanned air/ground communications facility that is remotely controlled and provides UHF or VHF communications capability to extend the service range of an FSS.

Civil Communications Frequencies-Civil communications frequencies used in the FSS air/ground system are operated on 122.0, 122.2, 123.6; emergency 121.5; plus receive-only on 122.1.

     a.   122.0 is assigned as the Enroute Flight Advisory Service frequency at selected FSS RADIO outlets.

     b.   122.2 is assigned as a common enroute frequency.

     c.   123.6 is assigned as the airport advisory frequency at select non-tower locations. At airports with a tower, FSS may provide airport advisories on the tower frequency when tower is closed.

     d.   122.1 is the primary receive-only frequency at VOR's.

     e.   Some FSS's are assigned 50 kHz frequencies in the 122–126 MHz band (eg. 122.45). Pilots using the FSS A/G system should refer to this directory or appropriate charts to determine frequencies available at the FSS or remoted facility through which they wish to communicate.

Emergency frequency 121.5 and 243.0 are available at all Flight Service Stations, most Towers, Approach Control and RADAR facilities.

Frequencies published followed by the letter "T" or "R", indicate that the facility will only transmit or receive respectively on that frequency. All radio aids to navigation (NAVAID) frequencies are transmit only.

TERMINAL SERVICES

SFA—Single Frequency Approach.

CTAF—A program designed to get all vehicles and aircraft at airports without an operating control tower on a common frequency.

ATIS—A continuous broadcast of recorded non-control information in selected terminal areas.

D–ATIS—Digital ATIS provides ATIS information in text form outside the standard reception range of conventional ATIS via landline & data link communications and voice message within range of existing transmitters.

AUNICOM—Automated UNICOM is a computerized, command response system that provides automated weather, radio check capability and airport advisory information selected from an automated menu by microphone clicks.

UNICOM—A non-government air/ground radio communications facility which may provide airport information.

PTD—Pilot to Dispatcher.

APP CON—Approach Control. The symbol ⓡ indicates radar approach control.

TOWER—Control tower.

GCA—Ground Control Approach System.

GND CON—Ground Control.

GCO—Ground Communication Outlet—An unstaffed, remotely controlled, ground/ground communications facility. Pilots at

NE, 09 FEB 2012 to 05 APR 2012

Legend 14. *Airport/facility directory.*

DIRECTORY LEGEND   17

uncontrolled airports may contact ATC and FSS via VHF to a telephone connection to obtain an instrument clearance or close a VFR or IFR flight plan. They may also get an updated weather briefing prior to takeoff. Pilots will use four "key clicks" on the VHF radio to contact the appropriate ATC facility or six "key clicks" to contact the FSS. The GCO system is intended to be used only on the ground.

DEP CON—Departure Control. The symbol ® indicates radar departure control.

CLNC DEL—Clearance Delivery.

PRE TAXI CLNC—Pre taxi clearance.

VFR ADVSY SVC—VFR Advisory Service. Service provided by Non-Radar Approach Control.

    Advisory Service for VFR aircraft (upon a workload basis) ctc APP CON.

COMD POST—Command Post followed by the operator call sign in parenthesis.

PMSV—Pilot-to-Metro Service call sign, frequency and hours of operation, when full service is other than continuous. PMSV installations at which weather observation service is available shall be indicated, following the frequency and/or hours of operation as "Wx obsn svc 1900–0000Z‡" or "other times" may be used when no specific time is given. PMSV facilities manned by forecasters are considered "Full Service". PMSV facilities manned by weather observers are listed as "Limited Service".

OPS—Operations followed by the operator call sign in parenthesis.

CON

RANGE

FLT FLW—Flight Following

MEDIVAC

NOTE: Communication frequencies followed by the letter "X" indicate frequency available on request.

㉝ AIRSPACE

Information concerning Class B, C, and part-time D and E surface area airspace shall be published with effective times. Class D and E surface area airspace that is continuous as established by Rulemaking Docket will not be shown.

CLASS B—Radar Sequencing and Separation Service for all aircraft in CLASS B airspace.

CLASS C—Separation between IFR and VFR aircraft and sequencing of VFR arrivals to the primary airport.

TRSA—Radar Sequencing and Separation Service for participating VFR Aircraft within a Terminal Radar Service Area.

Class C, D, and E airspace described in this publication is that airspace usually consisting of a 5 NM radius core surface area that begins at the surface and extends upward to an altitude above the airport elevation (charted in MSL for Class C and Class D). Class E surface airspace normally extends from the surface up to but not including the overlying controlled airspace.

When part-time Class C or Class D airspace defaults to Class E, the core surface area becomes Class E. This will be formatted as:

AIRSPACE: CLASS C svc "times" ctc APP CON other times CLASS E:

or

AIRSPACE: CLASS D svc "times" other times CLASS E.

When a part-time Class C, Class D or Class E surface area defaults to Class G, the core surface area becomes Class G up to, but not including, the overlying controlled airspace. Normally, the overlying controlled airspace is Class E airspace beginning at either 700' or 1200' AGL and may be determined by consulting the relevant VFR Sectional or Terminal Area Charts. This will be formatted as:

AIRSPACE: CLASS C svc "times" ctc APP CON other times CLASS G, with CLASS E 700' (or 1200') AGL & abv:

or

AIRSPACE: CLASS D svc "times" other times CLASS G with CLASS E 700' (or 1200') AGL & abv:

or

AIRSPACE: CLASS E svc "times" other times CLASS G with CLASS E 700' (or 1200') AGL & abv.

NOTE: AIRSPACE SVC "TIMES" INCLUDE ALL ASSOCIATED ARRIVAL EXTENSIONS. Surface area arrival extensions for instrument approach procedures become part of the primary core surface area. These extensions may be either Class D or Class E airspace and are effective concurrent with the times of the primary core surface area. For example, when a part-time Class C, Class D or Class E surface area defaults to Class G, the associated arrival extensions will default to Class G at the same time. When a part-time Class C or Class D surface area defaults to Class E, the arrival extensions will remain in effect as Class E airspace.

NOTE: CLASS E AIRSPACE EXTENDING UPWARD FROM 700 FEET OR MORE ABOVE THE SURFACE, DESIGNATED IN CONJUNCTION WITH AN AIRPORT WITH AN APPROVED INSTRUMENT PROCEDURE.

Class E 700' AGL (shown as magenta vignette on sectional charts) and 1200' AGL (blue vignette) areas are designated when necessary to provide controlled airspace for transitioning to/from the terminal and enroute environments. Unless otherwise specified, these 700'/1200' AGL Class E airspace areas remain in effect continuously, regardless of airport operating hours or surface area status. These transition areas should not be confused with surface areas or arrival extensions.

(See Chapter 3, AIRSPACE, in the Aeronautical Information Manual for further details)

NE, 09 FEB 2012 to 05 APR 2012

Legend 15. *Airport/facility directory.*

18   **DIRECTORY LEGEND**

34 **RADIO AIDS TO NAVIGATION**

The Airport/Facility Directory lists, by facility name, all Radio Aids to Navigation that appear on FAA, AeroNav Products Visual or IFR Aeronautical Charts and those upon which the FAA has approved an Instrument Approach Procedure, with exception of selected TACANs. Military TACAN information will be published for Military facilities contained in this publication. All VOR, VORTAC, TACAN, ILS and MLS equipment in the National Airspace System has an automatic monitoring and shutdown feature in the event of malfunction. Unmonitored, as used in this publication, for any navigational aid, means that monitoring personnel cannot observe the malfunction or shutdown signal. The NAVAID NOTAM file identifier will be shown as "NOTAM FILE IAD" and will be listed on the Radio Aids to Navigation line. When two or more NAVAIDS are listed and the NOTAM file identifier is different from that shown on the Radio Aids to Navigation line, it will be shown with the NAVAID listing. NOTAM file identifiers for ILSs and its components (e.g., NDB (LOM) are the same as the associated airports and are not repeated. Automated Surface Observing System (ASOS), Automated Weather Observing System (AWOS), and Hazardous Inflight Weather Advisory Service (HIWAS) will be shown when this service is broadcast over selected NAVAIDs.

NAVAID information is tabulated as indicated in the following sample:

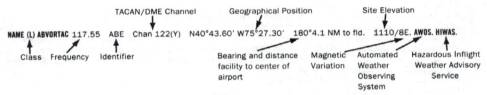

VOR unusable 020°–060° byd 26 NM blo 3,500'

Restriction within the normal altitude/range of the navigational aid (See primary alphabetical listing for restrictions on VORTAC and VOR/DME).

Note: Those DME channel numbers with a (Y) suffix require TACAN to be placed in the "Y" mode to receive distance information.

HIWAS—Hazardous Inflight Weather Advisory Service is a continuous broadcast of inflight weather advisories including summarized SIGMETs, convective SIGMETs, AIRMETs and urgent PIREPs. HIWAS is presently broadcast over selected VOR's throughout the U.S.

ASR/PAR—Indicates that Surveillance (ASR) or Precision (PAR) radar instrument approach minimums are published in the U.S. Terminal Procedures. Only part-time hours of operation will be shown.

RADIO CLASS DESIGNATIONS

VOR/DME/TACAN Standard Service Volume (SSV) Classifications

SSV Class	Altitudes	Distance (NM)
(T) Terminal	1000' to 12,000'	25
(L) Low Altitude	1000' to 18,000'	40
(H) High Altitude	1000' to 14,500'	40
	14,500' to 18,000'	100
	18,000' to 45,000'	130
	45,000' to 60,000'	100

NOTE: Additionally, (H) facilities provide (L) and (T) service volume and (L) facilities provide (T) service. Altitudes are with respect to the station's site elevation. Coverage is not available in a cone of airspace directly above the facility.

CONTINUED ON NEXT PAGE

NE, 09 FEB 2012 to 05 APR 2012

Legend 16. *Airport/facility directory.*

DIRECTORY LEGEND   19
CONTINUED FROM PRECEDING PAGE

The term VOR is, operationally, a general term covering the VHF omnidirectional bearing type of facility without regard to the fact that the power, the frequency protected service volume, the equipment configuration, and operational requirements may vary between facilities at different locations.

AB	Automatic Weather Broadcast.
DF	Direction Finding Service.
DME	UHF standard (TACAN compatible) distance measuring equipment.
DME(Y)	UHF standard (TACAN compatible) distance measuring equipment that require TACAN to be placed in the "Y" mode to receive DME.
GS	Glide slope.
H	Non-directional radio beacon (homing), power 50 watts to less than 2,000 watts (50 NM at all altitudes).
HH	Non-directional radio beacon (homing), power 2,000 watts or more (75 NM at all altitudes).
H-SAB	Non-directional radio beacons providing automatic transcribed weather service.
ILS	Instrument Landing System (voice, where available, on localizer channel).
IM	Inner marker.
ISMLS	Interim Standard Microwave Landing System.
LDA	Localizer Directional Aid.
LMM	Compass locator station when installed at middle marker site (15 NM at all altitudes).
LOM	Compass locator station when installed at outer marker site (15 NM at all altitudes).
MH	Non-directional radio beacon (homing) power less than 50 watts (25 NM at all altitudes).
MLS	Microwave Landing System.
MM	Middle marker.
OM	Outer marker.
S	Simultaneous range homing signal and/or voice.
SABH	Non-directional radio beacon not authorized for IFR or ATC. Provides automatic weather broadcasts.
SDF	Simplified Direction Facility.
TACAN	UHF navigational facility-omnidirectional course and distance information.
VOR	VHF navigational facility-omnidirectional course only.
VOR/DME	Collocated VOR navigational facility and UHF standard distance measuring equipment.
VORTAC	Collocated VOR and TACAN navigational facilities.
W	Without voice on radio facility frequency.
Z	VHF station location marker at a LF radio facility.

Legend 17. *Airport/facility directory.*

20

DIRECTORY LEGEND
ILS FACILITY PEFORMANCE CLASSIFICATION CODES

Codes define the ability of an ILS to support autoland operations. The two portions of the code represent Official Category and farthest point along a Category I, II, or III approach that the Localizer meets Category III structure tolerances.

Official Category: I, II, or III; the lowest minima on published or unpublished procedures supported by the ILS.

Farthest point of satisfactory Category III Localizer performance for Category I, II, or III approaches: A – 4 NM prior to runway threshold, B – 3500 ft prior to runway threshold, C – glide angle dependent but generally 750–1000 ft prior to threshold, T – runway threshold, D – 3000 ft after runway threshold, and E – 2000 ft prior to stop end of runway.

ILS information is tabulated as indicated in the following sample:

ILS/DME   108.5   I–ORL   Chan 22   Rwy 18.   Class IIE.   LOM HERNY NDB.

ILS Facility Performance
Classification Code

FREQUENCY PAIRING PLAN AND MLS CHANNELING

MLS CHANNEL	VHF FREQUENCY	TACAN CHANNEL	MLS CHANNEL	VHF FREQUENCY	TACAN CHANNEL	MLS CHANNEL	VHF FREQUENCY	TACAN CHANNEL
500	108.10	18X	568	109.45	31Y	636	114.15	88Y
502	108.30	20X	570	109.55	32Y	638	114.25	89Y
504	108.50	22X	572	109.65	33Y	640	114.35	90Y
506	108.70	24X	574	109.75	34Y	642	114.45	91Y
508	108.90	26X	576	109.85	35Y	644	114.55	92Y
510	109.10	28X	578	109.95	36Y	646	114.65	93Y
512	109.30	30X	580	110.05	37Y	648	114.75	94Y
514	109.50	32X	582	110.15	38Y	650	114.85	95Y
516	109.70	34X	584	110.25	39Y	652	114.95	96Y
518	109.90	36X	586	110.35	40Y	654	115.05	97Y
520	110.10	38X	588	110.45	41Y	656	115.15	98Y
522	110.30	40X	590	110.55	42Y	658	115.25	99Y
524	110.50	42X	592	110.65	43Y	660	115.35	100Y
526	110.70	44X	594	110.75	44Y	662	115.45	101Y
528	110.90	46X	596	110.85	45Y	664	115.55	102Y
530	111.10	48X	598	110.95	46Y	666	115.65	103Y
532	111.30	50X	600	111.05	47Y	668	115.75	104Y
534	111.50	52X	602	111.15	48Y	670	115.85	105Y
536	111.70	54X	604	111.25	49Y	672	115.95	106Y
538	111.90	56X	606	111.35	50Y	674	116.05	107Y
540	108.05	17Y	608	111.45	51Y	676	116.15	108Y
542	108.15	18Y	610	111.55	52Y	678	116.25	109Y
544	108.25	19Y	612	111.65	53Y	680	116.35	110Y
546	108.35	20Y	614	111.75	54Y	682	116.45	111Y
548	108.45	21Y	616	111.85	55Y	684	116.55	112Y
550	108.55	22Y	618	111.95	56Y	686	116.65	113Y
552	108.65	23Y	620	113.35	80Y	688	116.75	114Y
554	108.75	24Y	622	113.45	81Y	690	116.85	115Y
556	108.85	25Y	624	113.55	82Y	692	116.95	116Y
558	108.95	26Y	626	113.65	83Y	694	117.05	117Y
560	109.05	27Y	628	113.75	84Y	696	117.15	118Y
562	109.15	28Y	630	113.85	85Y	698	117.25	119Y
564	109.25	29Y	632	113.95	86Y			
566	109.35	30Y	634	114.05	87Y			

FREQUENCY PAIRING PLAN AND MLS CHANNELING

The following is a list of paired VOR/ILS VHF frequencies with TACAN channels and MLS channels.

TACAN CHANNEL	VHF FREQUENCY	MLS CHANNEL	TACAN CHANNEL	VHF FREQUENCY	MLS CHANNEL	TACAN CHANNEL	VHF FREQUENCY	MLS CHANNEL
2X	134.5	-	19Y	108.25	544	25X	108.80	-
2Y	134.55	-	20X	108.30	502	25Y	108.85	556
11X	135.4	-	20Y	108.35	546	26X	108.90	508
11Y	135.45	-	21X	108.40	-	26Y	108.95	558
12X	135.5	-	21Y	108.45	548	27X	109.00	-
12Y	135.55	-	22X	108.50	504	27Y	109.05	560
17X	108.00	-	22Y	108.55	550	28X	109.10	510
17Y	108.05	540	23X	108.60	-	28Y	109.15	562
18X	108.10	500	23Y	108.65	552	29X	109.20	-
18Y	108.15	542	24X	108.70	506	29Y	109.25	564
19X	108.20	-	24Y	108.75	554	30X	109.30	512

NE, 09 FEB 2012 to 05 APR 2012

Legend 18. *Airport/facility directory.*

APPENDIX
2

FAA FIGURES

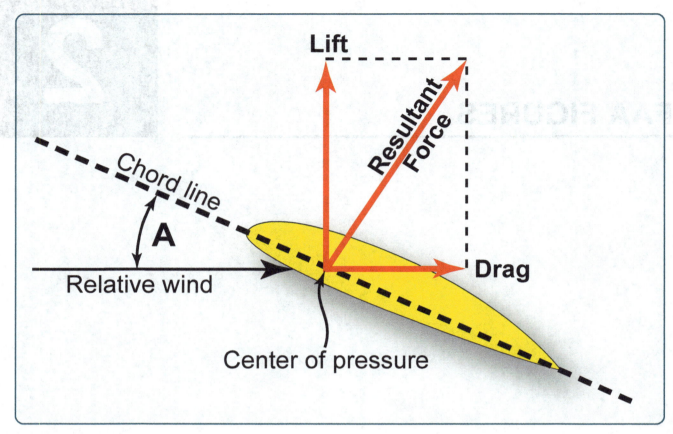

Figure 1. *Lift vector.*

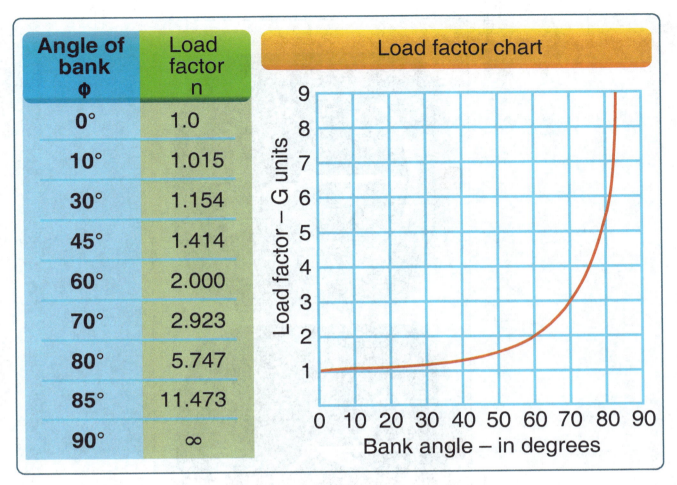

Angle of bank ϕ	Load factor n
0°	1.0
10°	1.015
30°	1.154
45°	1.414
60°	2.000
70°	2.923
80°	5.747
85°	11.473
90°	∞

Figure 2. *Load factor chart.*

Figure 3. *Altimeter.*

Figure 4. *Airspeed indicator.*

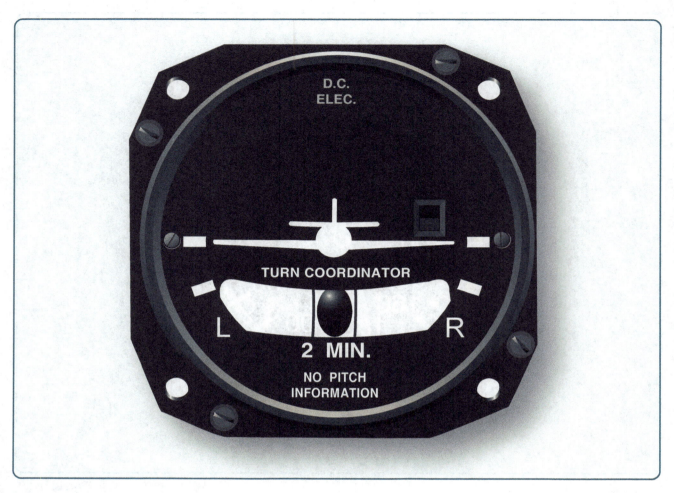

Figure 5. *Turn coordinator.*

Figure 6. *Heading indicator.*

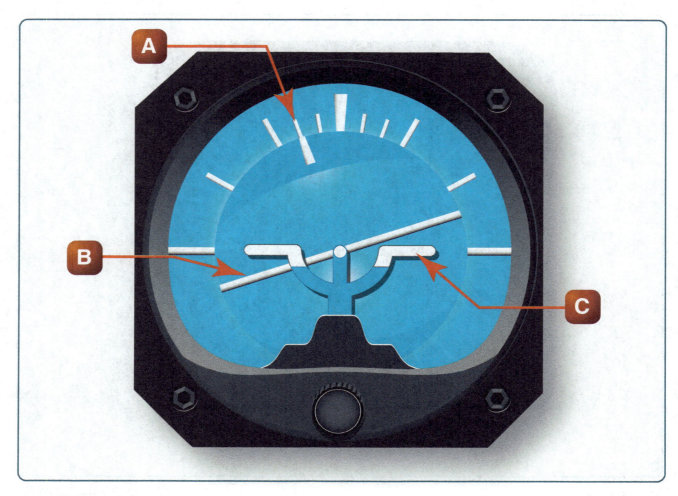

Figure 7. *Attitude indicator.*

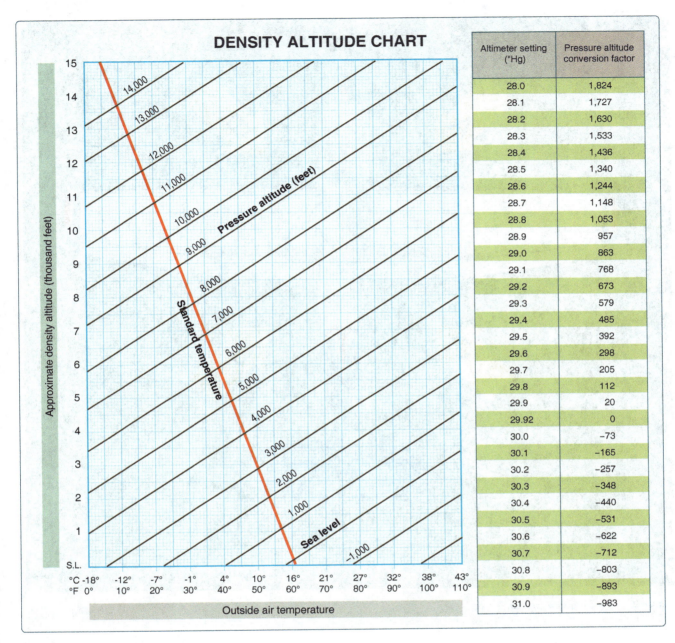

Figure 8. *Density altitude chart.*

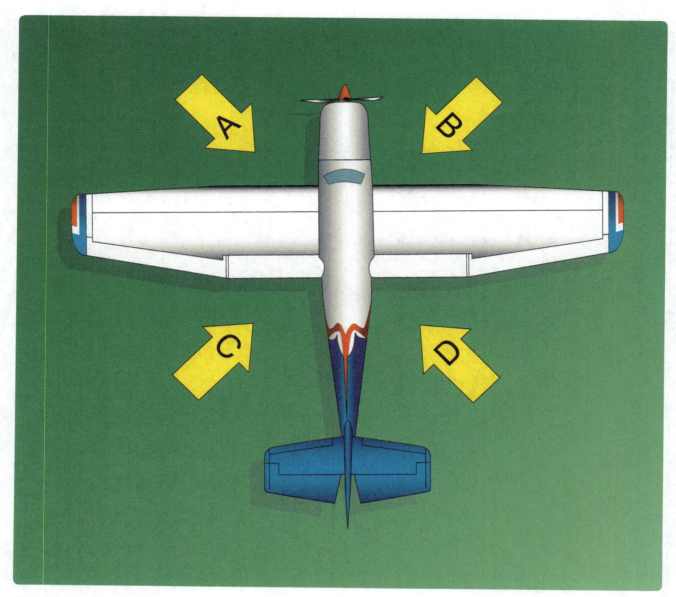

Figure 9. *Control position for taxi.*

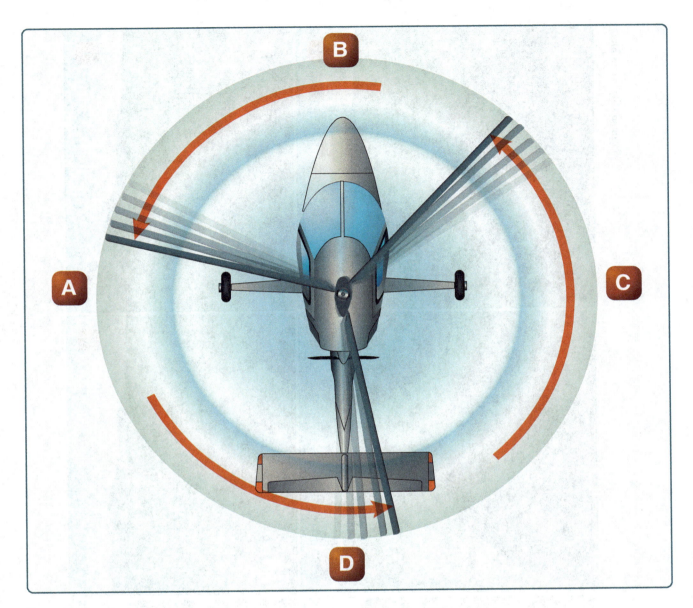

Figure 10. *Gyroplane rotor blade position.*

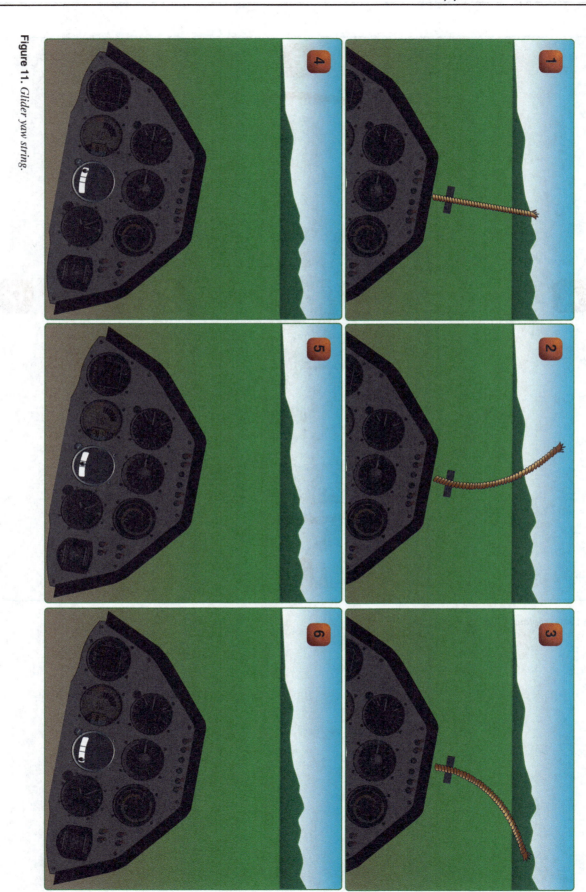

Figure 11. *Glider yaw string.*

METAR KINK 121845Z 11012G18KT 15SM SKC 25/17 A3000

METAR KBOI 121854Z 13004KT 30SM SCT150 17/6 A3015

METAR KLAX 121852Z 25004KT 6SM BR SCT007 SCT007 SCT250 16/15 A2991

SPECI KMDW 121856Z 32005KT 1 1/2SM RA OVC007 17/16 A2980 RMK RAB35

SPECI KJFK 121853Z 18004KT 1/2SM FG R04/2200 OVC005 20/18 A3006

Figure 12. *Aviation routine weather reports (METAR).*

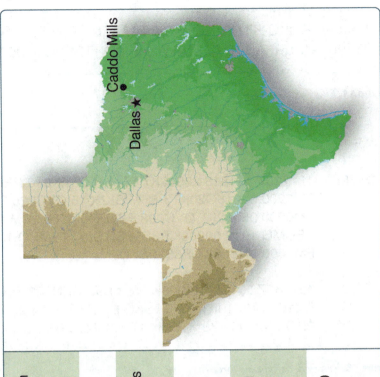

This is a telephone weather briefing from the Dallas FSS for local operation of gliders and lighter-than-air at Caddo Mills, Texas (about 30 miles east of Dallas). The briefing is at 13Z.

"There are no adverse conditions reported or forecast for today."

"A weak low pressure over the Texas Panhandle and eastern New Mexico is causing a weak southerly flow over the area."

"Current weather here at Dallas is wind south 5 knots, visibility 12 miles, clear, temperature 21, dewpoint 9, altimeter 29 point 78."

"By 15Z, we should have a few scattered cumuliform clouds at 5 thousand AGL, with higher scattered cirrus at 25 thousand MSL. After 20Z, the wind should pick up to about 15 knots from the south."

"The winds aloft are: 3 thousand 170 at 7, temperature 20; 6 thousand 200 at 18, temperature 14; 9 thousand 210 at 22, temperature 8; 12 thousand 225 at 27, temperature 0; 18 thousand 240 at 30, temperature −7."

Figure 13. *Telephone weather briefing.*

UA/OV KOKC-KTUL/TM 1800/FL 120/TP BE90//SK BKN018-TOP055/OVC072-TOP089/CLR ABV/TA M7/WV 08021/TB LGT 055-072/IC LGT-MOD RIME 072-089

Figure 14. *Pilot weather report.*

TAF	
KMEM	121720Z 121818 20012KT 5SM HZ BKN030 PROB40 2022 1SM TSRA OVC008CB
	FM2200 33015G20KT P6SM BKN015 OVC025 PROB40 2202 3SM SHRA
	FM0200 35012KT OVC008 PROB40 0205 2SM-RASN BECMG 0608 02008KT BKN012
	BECMG 1012 00000KT 3SM BR SKC TEMPO 1214 1/2SM FG
	FM1600 VRB06KT P6SM SKC=
KOKC	051130Z 051212 14008KT 5SM BR BKN030 TEMPO 1316 1 1/2SM BR
	FM1600 18010KT P6SM SKC BECMG 2224 20013G20KT 4SM SHRA OVC020
	PROB40 0006 2SM TSRA OVC008CB BECMG 0608 21015KT P6SM SCT040=

Figure 15. *Terminal aerodrome forecasts (TAF).*

```
BOSC FA 241845
SYNOPSIS AND VFR CLDS/WX
SYNOPSIS VALID UNTIL 251300
CLDS/WX VALID UNTIL 250700...OTLK VALID 250700-251300
ME NH VT MA RI CT NY LO NJ PA OH LE WV MD DC DE VA AND CSTL WTRS
.
SEE AIRMET SIERRA FOR IFR CONDS AND MTN OBSCN.
TS IMPLY SEV OR GTR TURB SEV ICE LLWS AND IFR CONDS.
NON MSL HGTS DENOTED BY AGL OR CIG.
.
SYNOPSIS...19Z CDFNT ALG A 16NE ACK-ENE LN...CONTG AS A QSTNRY
FNT ALG AN END-50SW MSS LN. BY 13Z...CDFNT ALG A 140ESE ACK-HTO
LN...CONTG AS A QSTNRY FNT ALG A HTO-SYR-YYZ LN. TROF ACRS CNTRL
PA INTO NRN VA. ...REYNOLDS...
.
OH LE
NRN HLF OH LE...SCT-BKN025 OVC045. CLDS LYRD 150. SCT SHRA. WDLY
     SCT TSRA. CB TOPS FL350. 23-01Z OVC020-030. VIS 3SM BR. OCNL-
     RA. OTLK...IFR CIG BR FG.
SWRN QTR OH...BKN050-060 TOPS 100. OTLK...MVFR BR.
SERN QTR OH...SCT-BKN040 BKN070 TOPS 120. WDLY SCT-TSRA. 00Z
     SCT-BKN030 OVC050. WDLY SCT-TSRA. CB TOPS FL350. OTLK...VFR
     SHRA.
.
CHIC FA 241945
SYNOPSIS AND VFR CLDS/WX
SYNOPSIS VALID UNTIL 251400
CLDS/WX VALID UNTIL 250800...OTLK VALID 250800-251400
ND SD NE KS MN IA MO WI LM LS MI LH IL IN KY
.
SEE AIRMET SIERRA FOR IFR CONDS AND MTN OBSCN.
TS IMPLY SEV OR GTR TURB SEV ICE LLWS AND IFR CONDS.
NON MSL HGTS DENOTED BY AGL OR CIG.
.
SYNOPSIS...LOW PRES AREA 20Z CNTRD OVR SERN WI FCST MOV NEWD INTO
LH BY 12Z AND WKN. LOW PRES FCST DEEPEN OVR ERN CO DURG PD AND
MOV NR WRN KS BORDER BY 14Z. DVLPG CDFNT WL MOV EWD INTO S CNTRL
NE-CNTRL KS BY 14Z. ...SMITH..
.
UPR MI LS
WRN PTNS...AGL SCT030 SCT 030 SCT-BKN050. TOPS 080. 02-05Z BECMG CIG
     OVC010 VIS 3-5SM BR. OTLK...IFR CIG BR.
ERN PTNS...CIG BKN020 OVC040. OCNL VIS 3-5SM -RA BR. TOPS FL200.
     23Z CIG OVC010 VIS 3-5SM -RA BR. OTLK...IFR CIG BR.
.
LWR MI LM LH
CNTRL/NRN PTNS...CIG OVC010 VIS 3-5SM -RA BR. TOPS FL200
     OTLK...IFR CIG BR.
.
SRN THIRD...CIG OVC015-025. SCT -SHRA. TOPS 150. 00-02Z BECMG CIG
     OVC010 VIS 3-5SM BR. TOPS 060. OTLK...IFR CIG BR.
.
IN
NRN HALF...CIG BKN035 BKN080. TOPS FL200. SCT -SHRA. 00Z CIG
     BKN-SCT040 BKN-SCT080. TOPS 120. 06Z AGL SCT-BKN030. TOPS 080.
     OCNL VIS 3-5SM BR. OTLK...MVFR CIG BR.
SRN HALF...AGL SCT050 SCT-BKN100. TOPS 120. 07Z AGL SCT 030
     SCT100. OTLK...VFR.
```

Figure 16. *Area forecast.*

FT	3000	6000	9000	12000	18000	24000	30000	34000	39000
ALS			2420	2635-08	2535-18	2444-30	245945	246755	246862
AMA		2714	2725+00	2625-04	2531-15	2542-27	265842	256352	256762
DEN			2321-04	2532-08	2434-19	2441-31	235347	236056	236262
HLC		1707-01	2113-03	2219-07	2330-17	2435-30	244145	244854	245561
MKC	0507	2006+03	2215-01	2322-06	2338-17	2348-29	236143	237252	238160
STL	2113	2325+07	2332+02	2339-04	2356-16	2373-27	239440	730649	731960

FD WBC 151745
DATA BASED ON 151200Z
VALID 1600Z FOR USE 1800-0300Z. TEMPS NEG ABV 24000

Figure 17. *Winds and temperatures aloft forecast.*

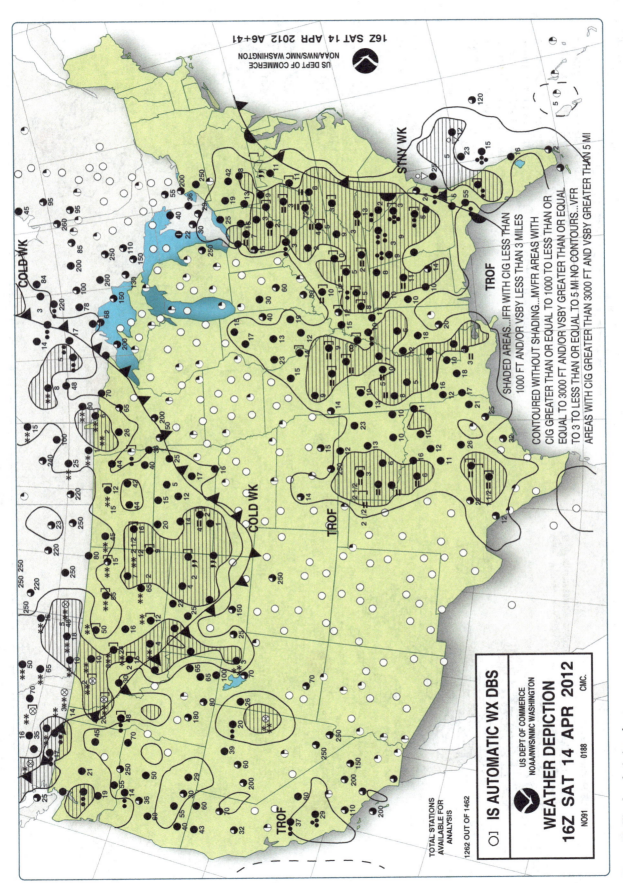

Figure 18. *Weather depiction chart.*

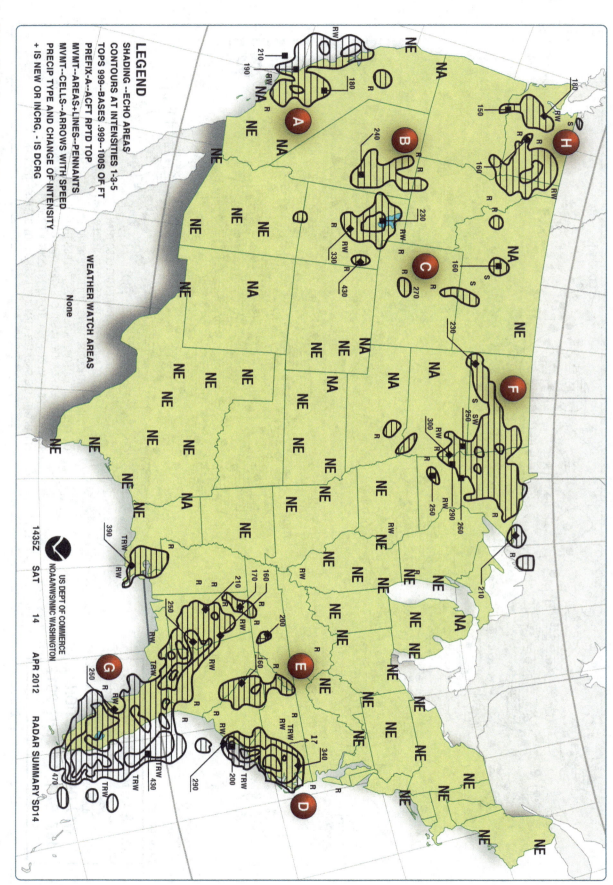

Figure 19. *Radar summary chart.*

Figure 20. *Low-level significant weather (SIGWX) prognostic charts.*

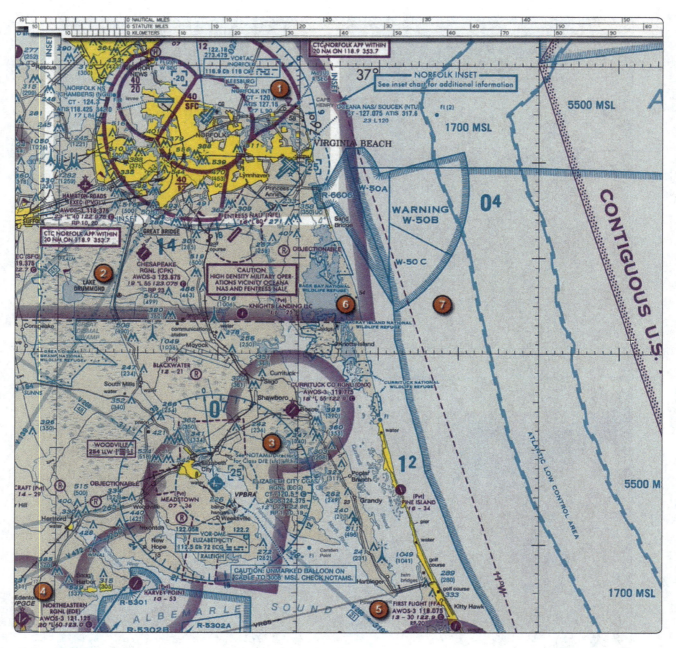

Figure 21. *Sectional chart excerpt.*

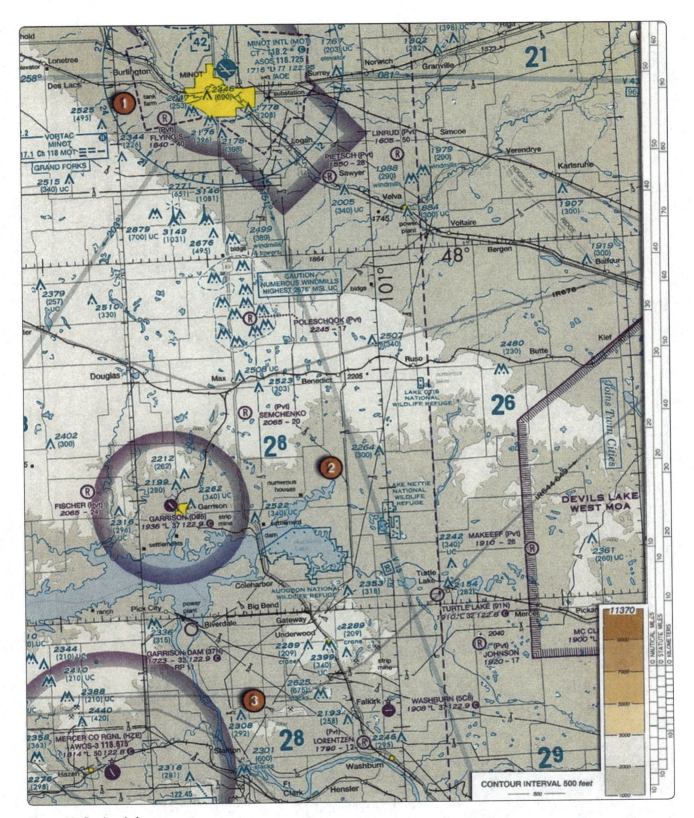

Figure 22. *Sectional chart excerpt.*

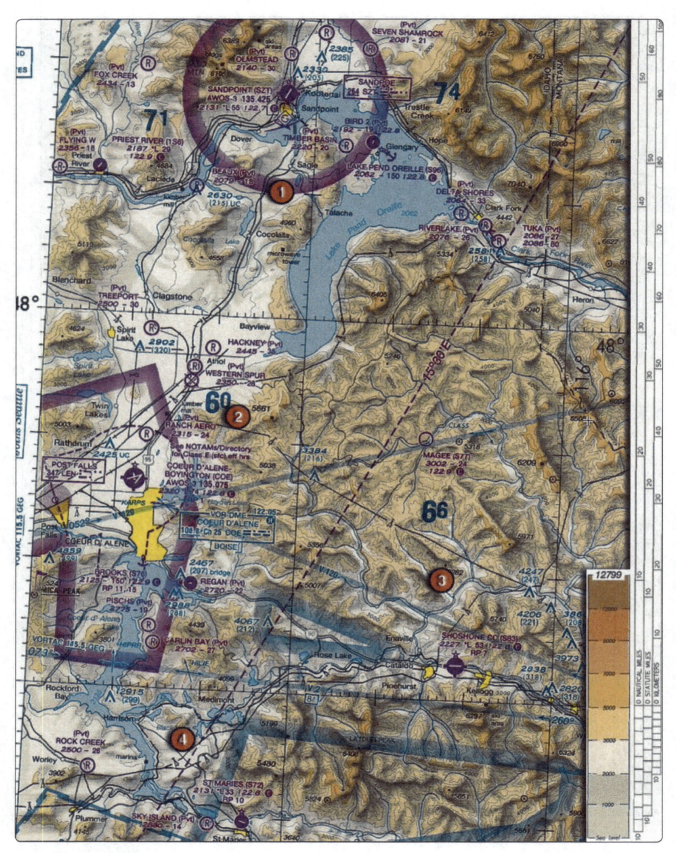

Figure 23. *Sectional chart excerpt.*

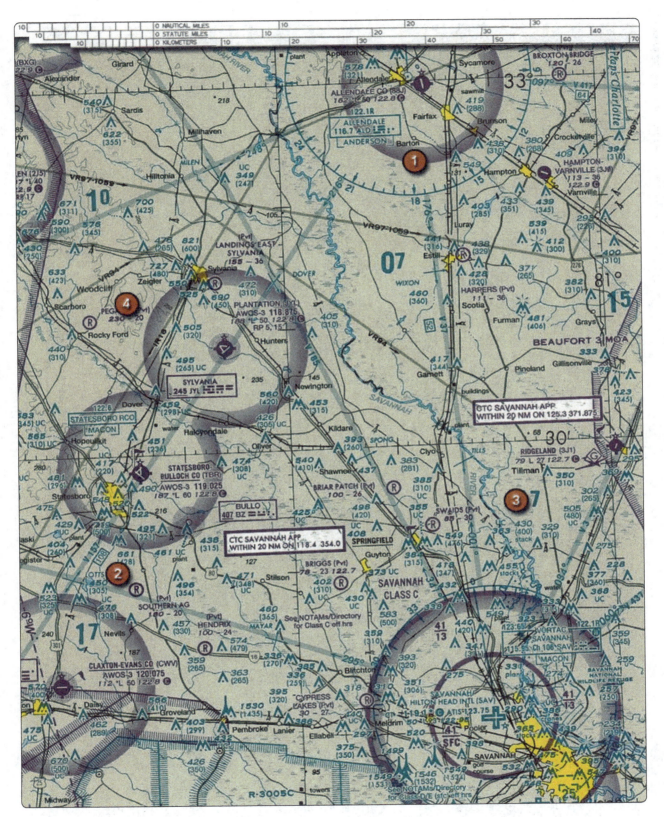

Figure 24. *Sectional chart excerpt.*

Flag is a visual checkpoint

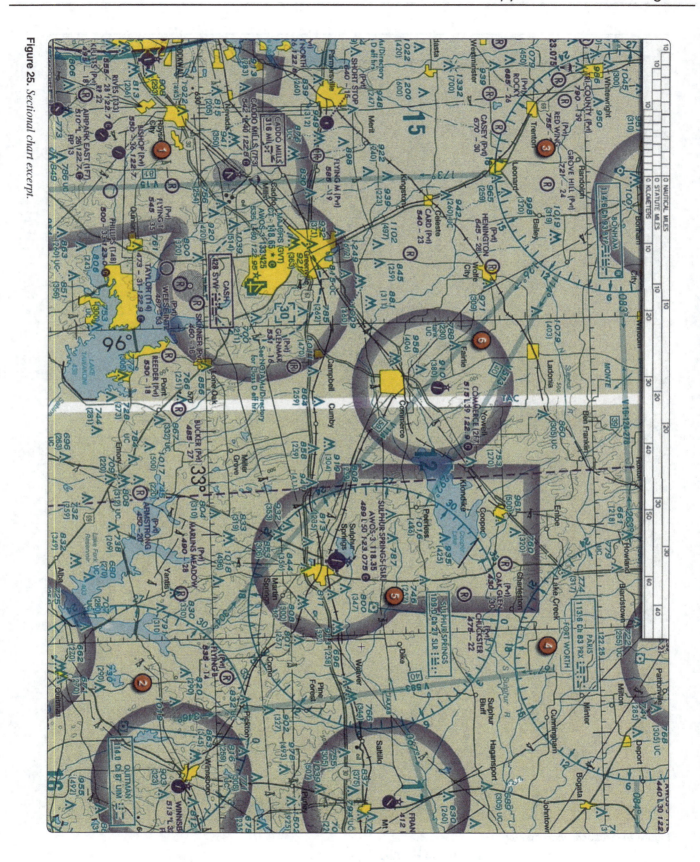

Figure 25. *Sectional chart excerpt.*

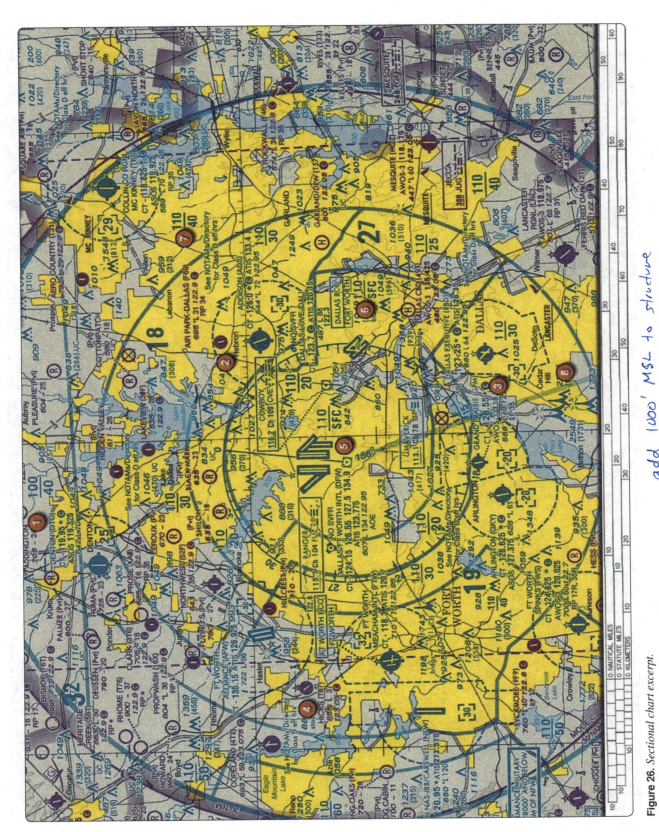

Figure 26. Sectional chart excerpt.

add 1000' MSL to structure

Figure 27. *Sectional chart excerpt.*

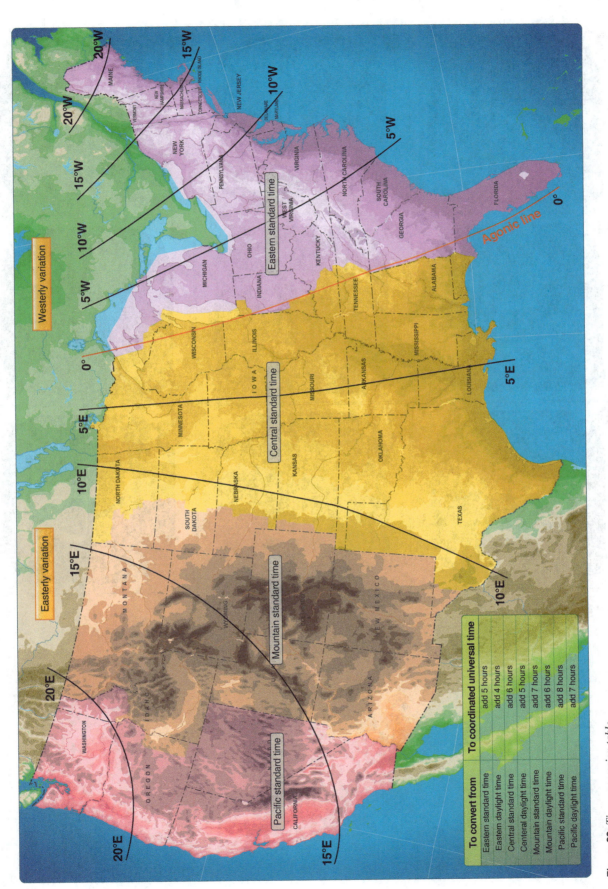

To convert from	To coordinated universal time
Eastern standard time	add 5 hours
Eastern daylight time	add 4 hours
Central standard time	add 6 hours
Centeral daylight time	add 5 hours
Mountain standard time	add 7 hours
Mountain daylight time	add 6 hours
Pacific standard time	add 8 hours
Pacific daylight time	add 7 hours

Figure 28. *Time conversion table.*

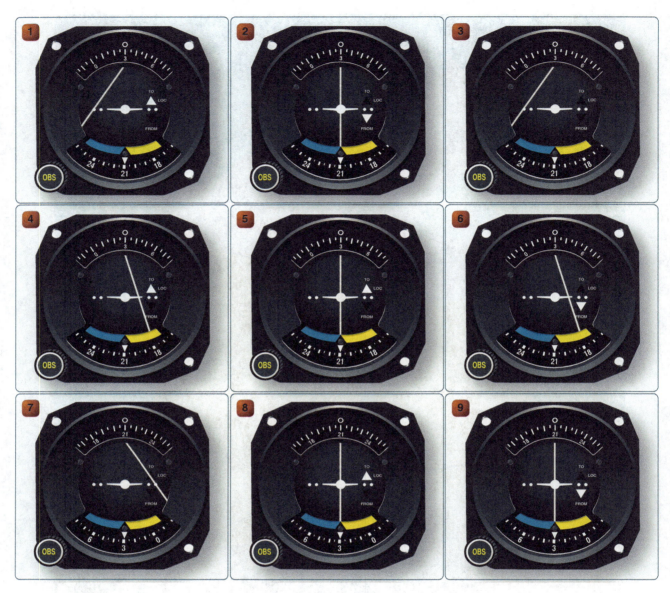

Figure 29. *VOR.*

Figure 30. ADF (movable card).

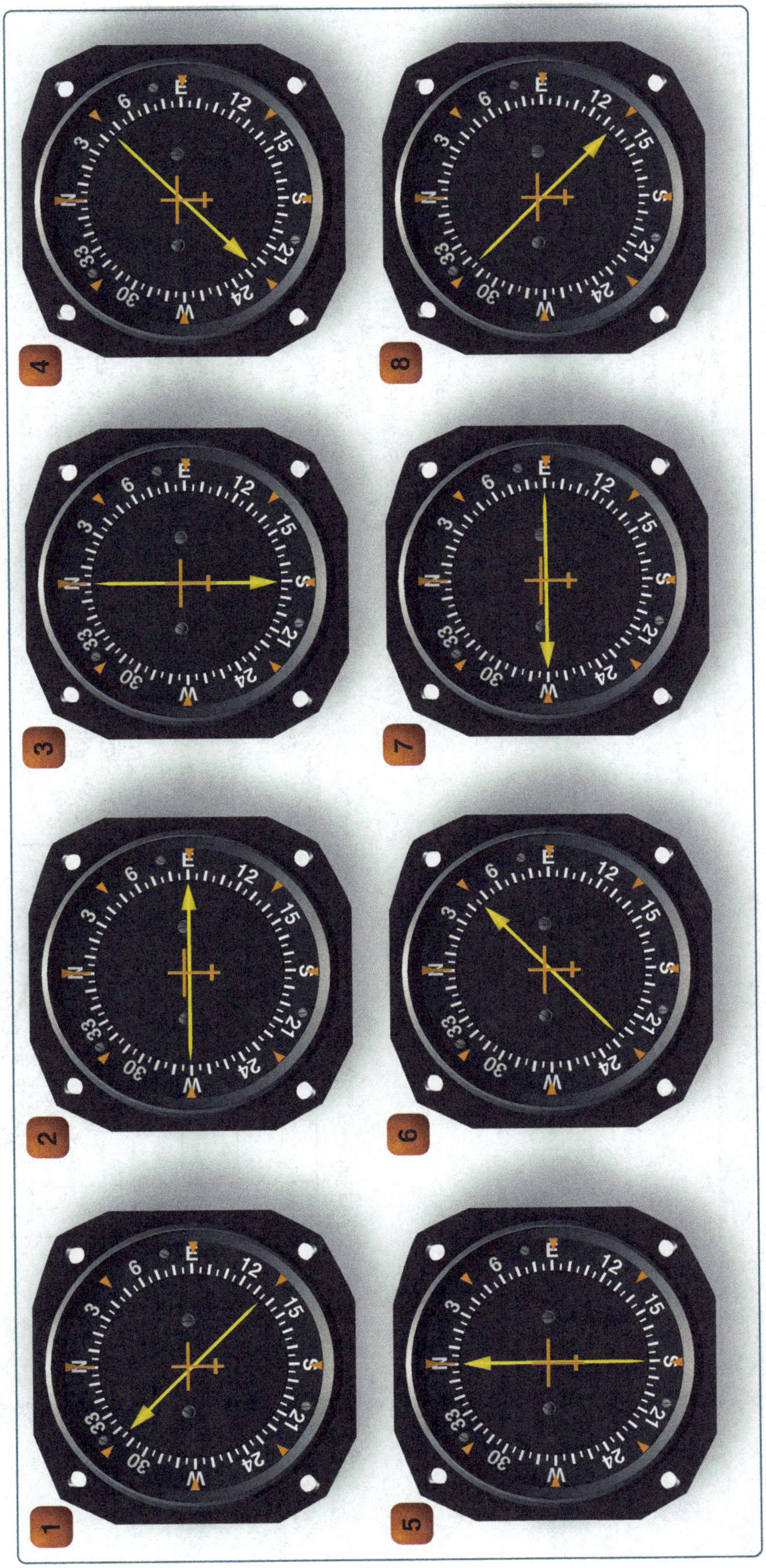

Figure 31. ADF (fixed card).

Figure 32. *Airport/facility directory excerpt.*

IDAHO
      31

COEUR D'ALENE—PAPPY BOYINGTON FLD   (COE)   9 NW   UTC−8(−7DT)
                                                       GREAT FALLS

N47°46.46′ W116°49.18′   **H−1C, L−13B**

2320   B   S4   **FUEL** 100, JET A   OX 1, 2, 3, 4   Class IV, ARFF Index A   NOTAM FILE COE   **IAP**

RWY 05−23: H7400X100 (ASPH−GRVD)   S−57, D−95, 2S−121, 2D−165   HIRL   0.6% up NE

RWY 05: MALSR (NSTD). PAPI(P4R)—GA 3.0° TCH 56′.

RWY 23: REIL. PAPI(P4R)—GA 3.0° TCH 50′.

RWY 01−19: H5400X75 (ASPH)   S−50, D−83, 2S−105, 2D−150

MIRL   0.3% up N

RWY 01: REIL. PAPI(P2L)—GA 3.0° TCH 39′. Rgt tfc.

RWY 19: PAPI(P2L)—GA 3.0° TCH 41′.

RUNWAY DECLARED DISTANCE INFORMATION

RWY 01:	TORA−5400	TODA−5400	ASDA−5400	LDA−5400
RWY 05:	TORA−7400	TODA−7400	ASDA−7400	LDA−7400
RWY 19:	TORA−5400	TODA−5400	ASDA−5400	LDA−5400
RWY 23:	TORA−7400	TODA−7400	ASDA−7400	LDA−7400

AIRPORT REMARKS: Attended Mon−Fri 1500−0100‡. For after hrs
fuel-self svc avbl or call 208−772−6404, 208−661−4174,
208−661−7449, 208−699−5433. Self svc fuel avbl with credit
card. 48 hr PPR for unscheduled ops with more than 30
passenger seats call arpt manager 208−446−1860. Migratory
birds on and invof arpt Oct−Nov. Remote cntl airstrip is 2.3 miles
west AER 05. Arpt conditions avbl on AWOS. Rwy 05 NSTD
MALSR, thld bar extends 5′ byd rwy edge lgts each side. ACTIVATE
MIRL Rwy 01−19, HIRL Rwy 05−23, REIL Rwy 01 and Rwy 23, MALSR Rwy 05—CTAF. PAPI Rwy 01, Rwy 19, Rwy
05, and Rwy 23 opr continuously.

WEATHER DATA SOURCES: AWOS−3 135.075 (208) 772−8215.

HIWAS 108.8 COE.

COMMUNICATIONS: CTAF/UNICOM 122.8

RCO 122.05 (BOISE RADIO)

Ⓡ **SPOKANE APP/DEP CON** 132.1

AIRSPACE: CLASS E svc continuous.

RADIO AIDS TO NAVIGATION: NOTAM FILE COE.

(T) **VORW/DME** 108.8   COE   Chan 25   N47°46.42′ W116°49.24′   at fld. 2320/19E.   **HIWAS.**
    DME portion unusable:
    220°−240° byd 15 NM
POST FALLS NDB (MHW) 347   LEN   N47°44.57′ W116°57.66′   280°−315° byd 15 NM blo 11,000′.
ILS 110.7   I−COE   Rwy 05   Class ID.   Localizer unusable 25° left and right of course.

Useful load weights and moments

Baggage or 5th seat occupant

ARM 140	
Weight	Moment/100
10	14
20	28
30	42
40	56
50	70
60	84
70	98
80	112
90	126
100	140
110	154
120	168
130	182
140	196
150	210
160	224
170	238
180	252
190	266
200	280
210	294
220	308
230	322
240	336
250	350
260	364
270	378

Occupants

Front seats ARM 85		Rear seats ARM 121	
Weight	Moment/100	Weight	Moment/100
120	102	120	145
130	110	130	157
140	119	140	169
150	128	150	182
160	136	160	194
170	144	170	206
180	153	180	218
190	162	190	230
200	170	200	242

Usable fuel

Main wing tanks ARM 75		
Gallons	Weight	Moment/100
5	30	22
10	60	45
15	90	68
20	120	90
25	150	112
30	180	135
35	210	158
40	240	180
44	264	198

Auxiliary wing tanks ARM 94		
Gallons	Weight	Moment/100
5	30	28
10	60	56
15	90	85
19	114	107

*Oil		
Quarts	Weight	Moment/100
10	19	5

*Included in basic empty weight.

Empty weight~2,015
MOM/100~1,554
Moment limits vs weight
Moment limits are based on the following weight and center of gravity limit data (landing gear down).

Weight condition	Forward CG limit	AFT CG limit
2,950 lb (takeoff or landing)	82.1	84.7
2,525 lb	77.5	85.7
2,475 lb or less	77.0	85.7

Figure 33. *Airplane weight and balance tables.*

Moment limits vs weight (continued)

Weight	Minimum Moment 100	Maximum Moment 100	Weight	Minimum Moment 100	Maximum Moment 100
2,100	1,617	1,800	2,500	1,932	2,143
2,110	1,625	1,808	2,510	1,942	2,151
2,120	1,632	1,817	2,520	1,953	2,160
2,130	1,640	1,825	2,530	1,963	2,168
2,140	1,648	1,834	2,540	1,974	2,176
2,150	1,656	1,843	2,550	1,984	2,184
2,160	1,663	1,851	2,560	1,995	2,192
2,170	1,671	1,860	2,570	2,005	2,200
2,180	1,679	1,868	2,580	2,016	2,208
2,190	1,686	1,877	2,590	2,026	2,216
2,200	1,694	1,885	2,600	2,037	2,224
2,210	1,702	1,894	2,610	2,048	2,232
2,220	1,709	1,903	2,620	2,058	2,239
2,230	1,717	1,911	2,630	2,069	2,247
2,240	1,725	1,920	2,640	2,080	2,255
2,250	1,733	1,928	2,650	2,090	2,263
2,260	1,740	1,937	2,660	2,101	2,271
2,270	1,748	1,945	2,670	2,112	2,279
2,280	1,756	1,954	2,680	2,123	2,287
2,290	1,763	1,963	2,690	2,133	2,295
2,300	1,771	1,971	2,700	2,144	2,303
2,310	1,779	1,980	2,710	2,155	2,311
2,320	1,786	1,988	2,720	2,166	2,319
2,330	1,794	1,997	2,730	2,177	2,326
2,340	1,802	2,005	2,740	2,188	2,334
2,350	1,810	2,014	2,750	2,199	2,342
2,360	1,817	2,023	2,760	2,210	2,350
2,370	1,825	2,031	2,770	2,221	2,358
2,380	1,833	2,040	2,780	2,232	2,366
2,390	1,840	2,048	2,790	2,243	2,374
2,400	1,848	2,057	2,800	2,254	2,381
2,410	1,856	2,065	2,810	2,265	2,389
2,420	1,863	2,074	2,820	2,276	2,397
2,430	1,871	2,083	2,830	2,287	2,405
2,440	1,879	2,091	2,840	2,298	2,413
2,450	1,887	2,100	2,850	2,309	2,421
2,460	1,894	2,108	2,860	2,320	2,428
2,470	1,902	2,117	2,870	2,332	2,436
2,480	1,911	2,125	2,880	2,343	2,444
2,490	1,921	2,134	2,890	2,354	2,452
			2,900	2,365	2,460
			2,910	2,377	2,468
			2,920	2,388	2,475
			2,930	2,399	2,483
			2,940	2,411	2,491
			2,950	2,422	2,499

Figure 34. *Airplane weight and balance tables.*

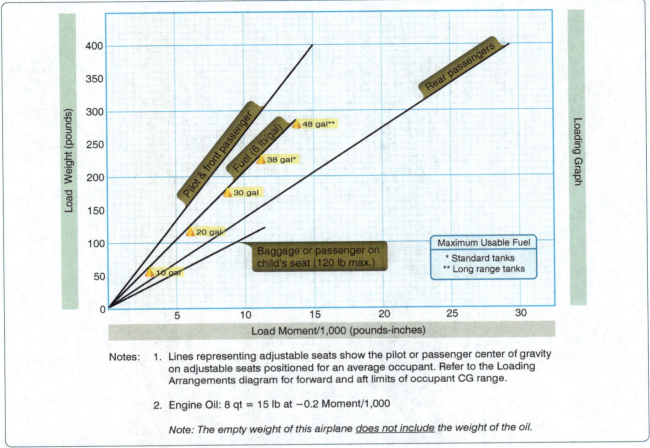

Notes: 1. Lines representing adjustable seats show the pilot or passenger center of gravity on adjustable seats positioned for an average occupant. Refer to the Loading Arrangements diagram for forward and aft limits of occupant CG range.

2. Engine Oil: 8 qt = 15 lb at −0.2 Moment/1,000

Note: The empty weight of this airplane does not include the weight of the oil.

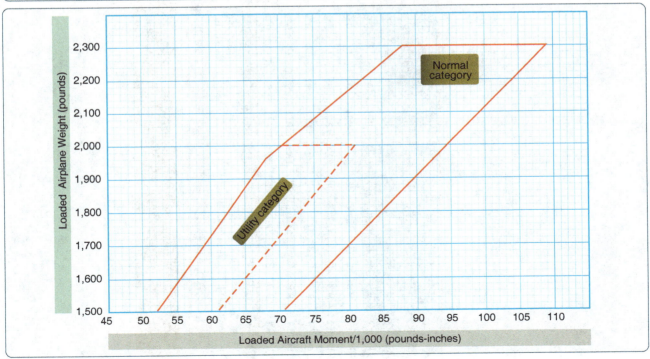

Figure 35. *Airplane weight and balance graphs.*

Cruise power settings

65% Maximum continuous power (or full throttle 2,800 pounds)

Press ALT.	IOAT		ISA –20 °C (–36 °F) Engine speed	MAN. press	Fuel flow per engine		TAS		IOAT		Standard day (ISA) Engine speed	MAN. press	Fuel flow per engine		TAS		IOAT		ISA +20 °C (+36 °F) Engine speed	MAN. press	Fuel flow per engine		TAS	
Feet	°F	°C	RMP	IN HG	PSI	GPH	KTS	MPH	°F	°C	RMP	IN HG	PSI	GPH	KTS	MPH	°F	°C	RMP	IN HG	PSI	GPH	KTS	MPH
SL	27	–3	2,450	20.7	6.6	11.5	147	169	63	17	2,450	21.2	6.6	11.5	150	173	99	37	2,450	21.8	6.6	11.5	153	176
2,000	19	–7	2,450	20.4	6.6	11.5	149	171	55	13	2,450	21.0	6.6	11.5	153	176	91	33	2,450	21.5	6.6	11.5	156	180
4,000	12	–11	2,450	20.1	6.6	11.5	152	175	48	9	2,450	20.7	6.6	11.5	156	180	84	29	2,450	21.3	6.6	11.5	159	183
6,000	5	–15	2,450	19.8	6.6	11.5	155	178	41	5	2,450	20.4	6.6	11.5	158	182	79	26	2,450	21.0	6.6	11.5	161	185
8,000	–2	–19	2,450	19.5	6.6	11.5	157	181	36	2	2,450	20.2	6.6	11.5	161	185	72	22	2,450	20.8	6.6	11.5	164	189
10,000	–8	–22	2,450	19.2	6.6	11.5	160	184	28	–2	2,450	19.9	6.6	11.5	163	188	64	18	2,450	20.3	6.5	11.4	166	191
12,000	–15	–26	2,450	18.8	6.4	11.5	162	186	21	–6	2,450	18.8	6.1	10.9	163	188	57	14	2,450	18.8	5.9	10.6	163	188
14,000	–22	–30	2,450	17.4	5.8	10.5	159	183	14	–10	2,450	17.4	5.6	10.1	160	184	50	10	2,450	17.4	5.4	9.8	160	184
16,000	–29	–34	2,450	16.1	5.3	9.7	156	180	7	–14	2,450	16.1	5.1	9.4	156	180	43	6	2,450	16.1	4.9	9.1	155	178

Note: 1. Full throttle manifold pressure settings are approximate.
2. Shaded area represents operation with full throttle.

Figure 36. *Airplane power setting table.*

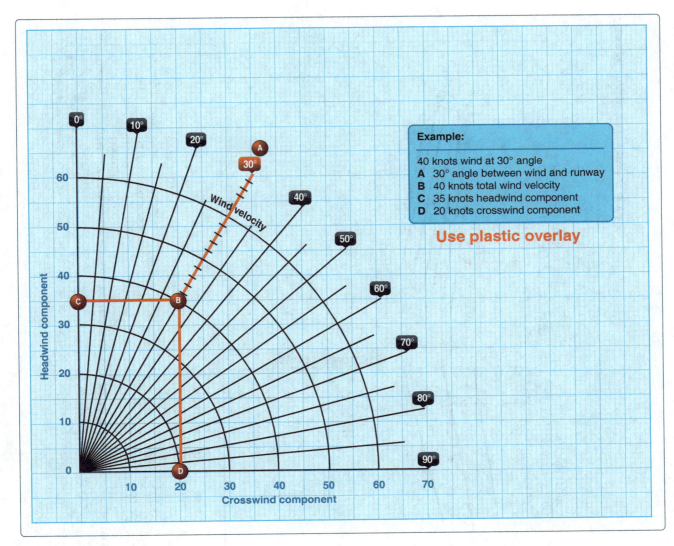

Example:

40 knots wind at 30° angle
A 30° angle between wind and runway
B 40 knots total wind velocity
C 35 knots headwind component
D 20 knots crosswind component

Use plastic overlay

Figure 37. *Crosswind component graph.*

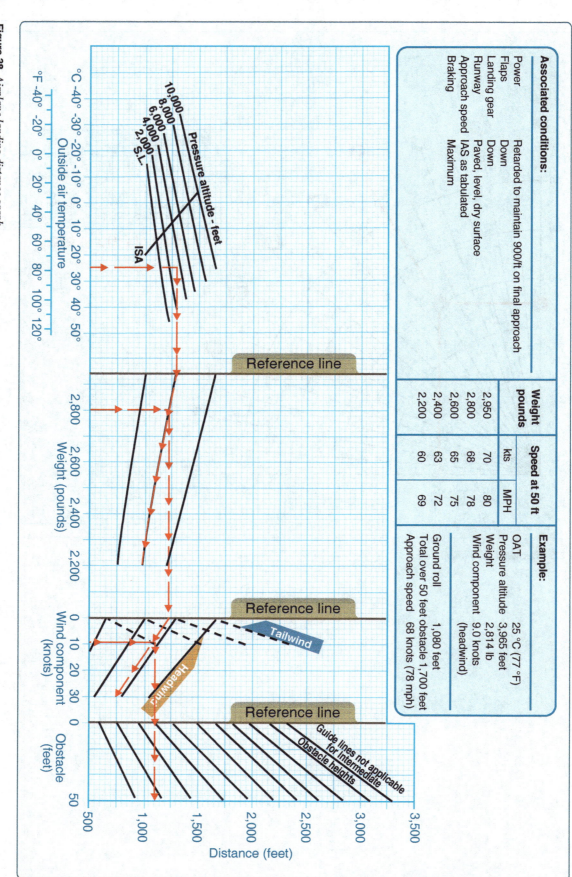

Figure 38. *Airplane landing distance graph.*

Landing distance

Flaps lowered to 40° – Power off – Hard surface runway – Zero wind

Gross weight lb	Approach speed, IAS, MPH	At sea level & 59 °F		At 2,500 feet & 50 °F		At 5,000 feet & 41 °F		At 7,500 feet & 32 °F	
		Ground roll	Total to clear 50 feet OBS	Ground roll	Total to clear 50 feet OBS	Ground roll	Total to clear 50 feet OBS	Ground roll	Total to clear 50 feet OBS
1,600	60	445	1,075	470	1,135	495	1,195	520	1,255

NOTE:
1. Decrease the distances shown by 10% for each 4 knots of headwind.
2. Increase the distance by 10% for each 60 °F temperature increase above standard.
3. For operation on a dry, grass runway, increase distance (both "ground roll" and "total to clear 50 feet obstacle") by 20% of the "total to clear 50 feet obstacle" figure.

Figure 39. Airplane landing distance table.

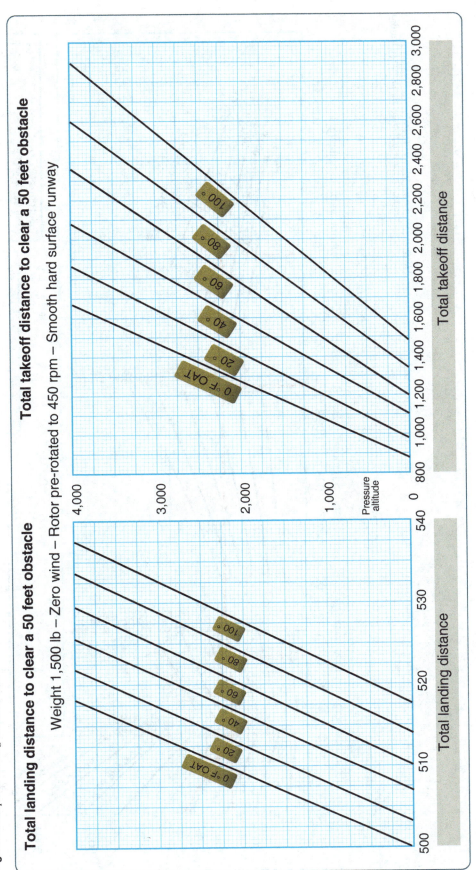

Total takeoff distance to clear a 50 feet obstacle

Weight 1,500 lb – Zero wind – Rotor pre-rotated to 450 rpm – Smooth hard surface runway

Total landing distance to clear a 50 feet obstacle

Figure 40. Gyroplane takeoff and landing graphs.

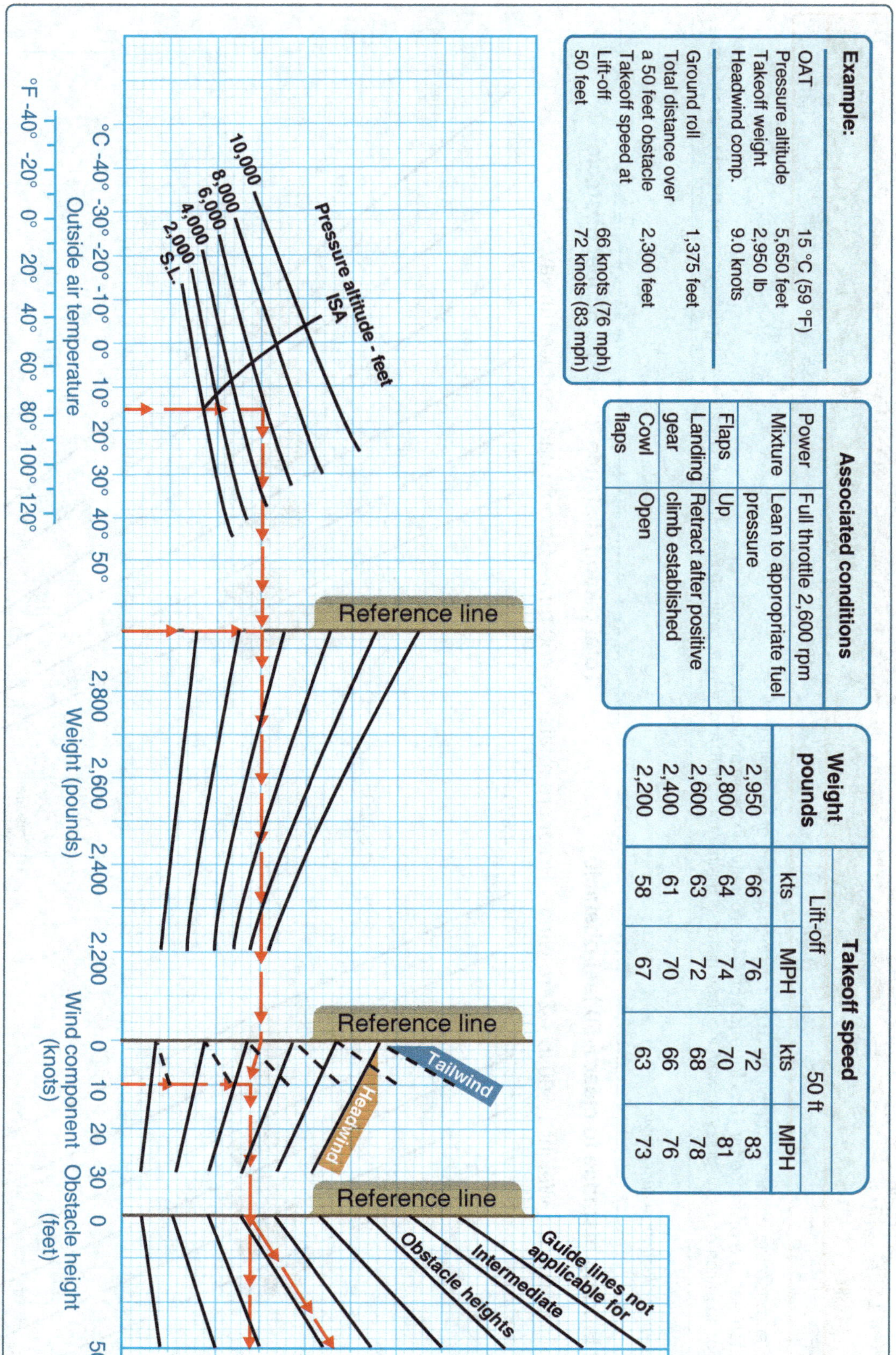
Example:
OAT 15 °C (59 °F)
Pressure altitude 5,650 feet
Takeoff weight 2,950 lb
Headwind comp. 9.0 knots
Ground roll 1,375 feet
Total distance over a 50 feet obstacle 2,300 feet
Takeoff speed at
Lift-off 66 knots (76 mph)
50 feet 72 knots (83 mph)
Associated conditions
Power Full throttle 2,600 rpm
Mixture Lean to appropriate fuel pressure
Flaps Up
Landing gear Retract after positive climb established
Cowl flaps Open
Weight pounds
Takeoff speed
Lift-off
50 ft
kts
MPH
kts
MPH
2,950 66 76 72 83
2,800 64 74 70 81
2,600 63 72 68 78
2,400 61 70 66 76
2,200 58 67 63 73
Pressure altitude - feet
ISA
10,000
8,000
6,000
4,000
2,000
S.L.
°C -40° -30° -20° -10° 0° 10° 20° 30° 40° 50°
°F -40° -20° 0° 20° 40° 60° 80° 100° 120°
Outside air temperature
Reference line
2,800 2,600 2,400 2,200
Weight (pounds)
Reference line
Tailwind
Headwind
0 10 20 30
Wind component (knots)
Reference line
Guide lines not applicable for
Intermediate
Obstacle heights
0 50
Obstacle height (feet)
0 1,000 2,000 3,000 4,000 5,000 6,000

Figure 41. *Airplane takeoff distance graph.*

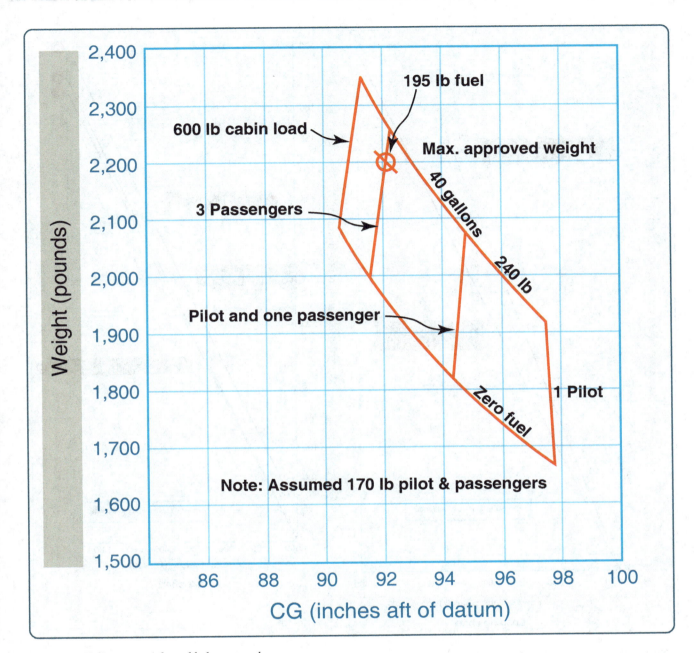

Figure 42. *Helicopter weight and balance graph.*

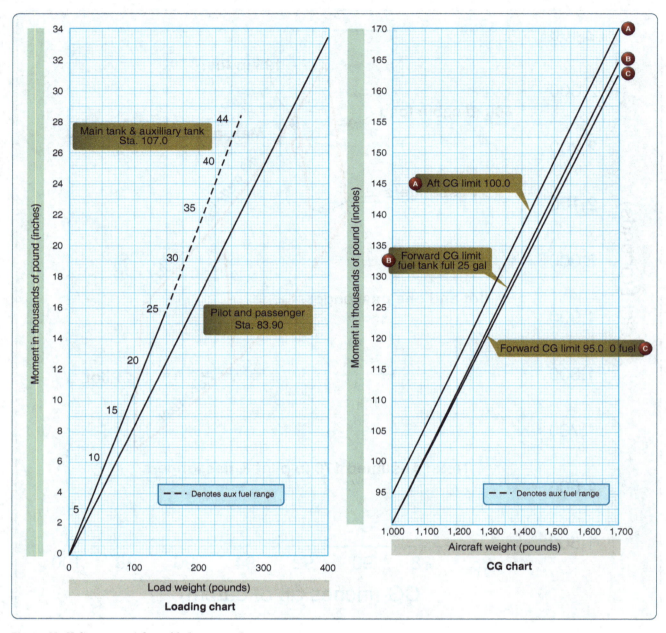

Figure 43. *Helicopter weight and balance graphs.*

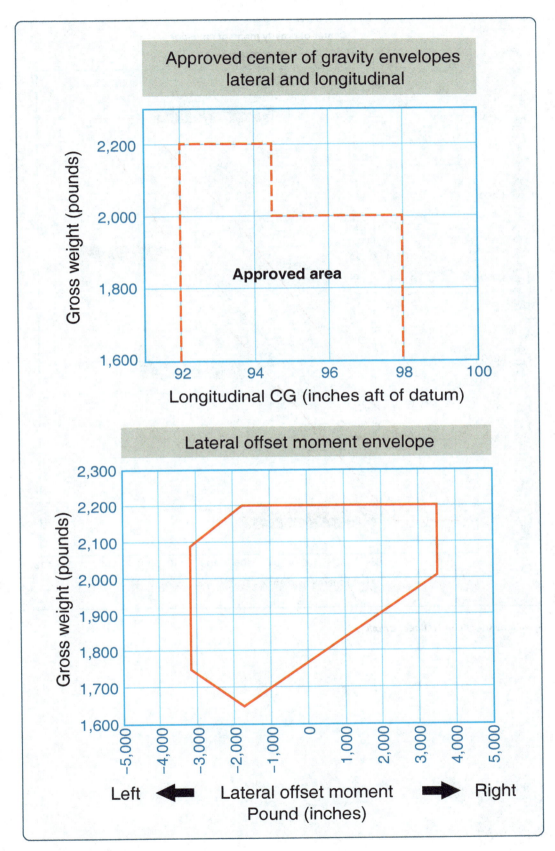

Figure 44. *Helicopter CG envelopes.*

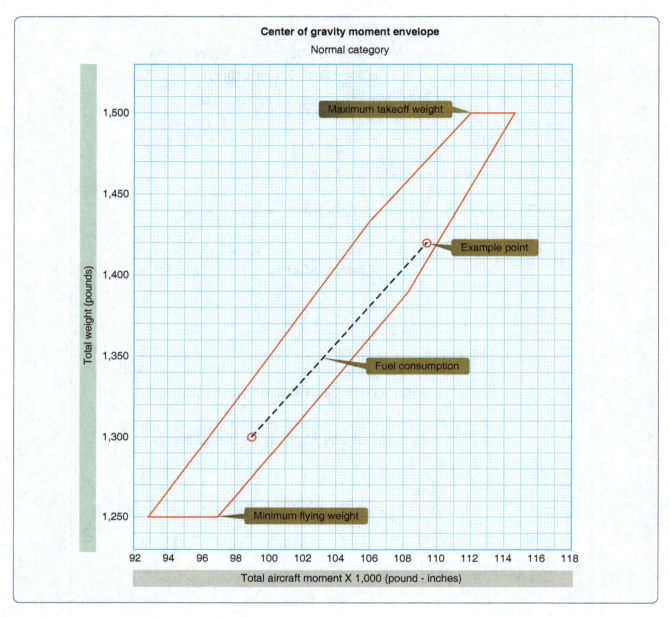

Figure 45. *Gyroplane weight and balance graph.*

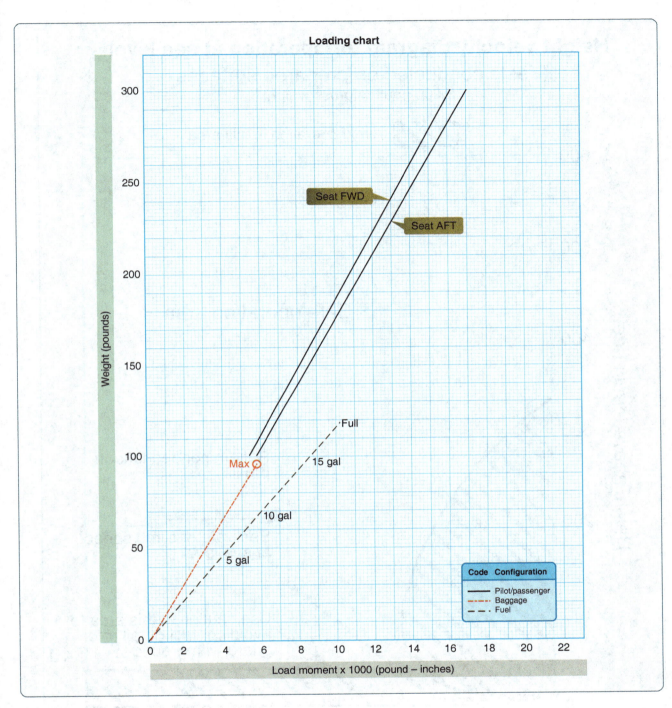

Figure 46. *Gyroplane weight and balance graph.*

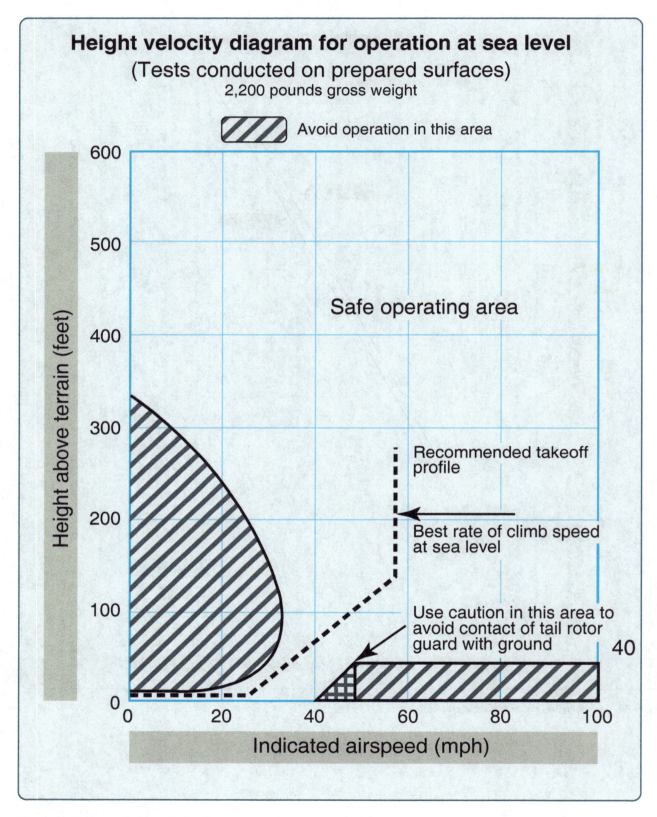

Figure 47. *Helicopter height velocity diagram.*

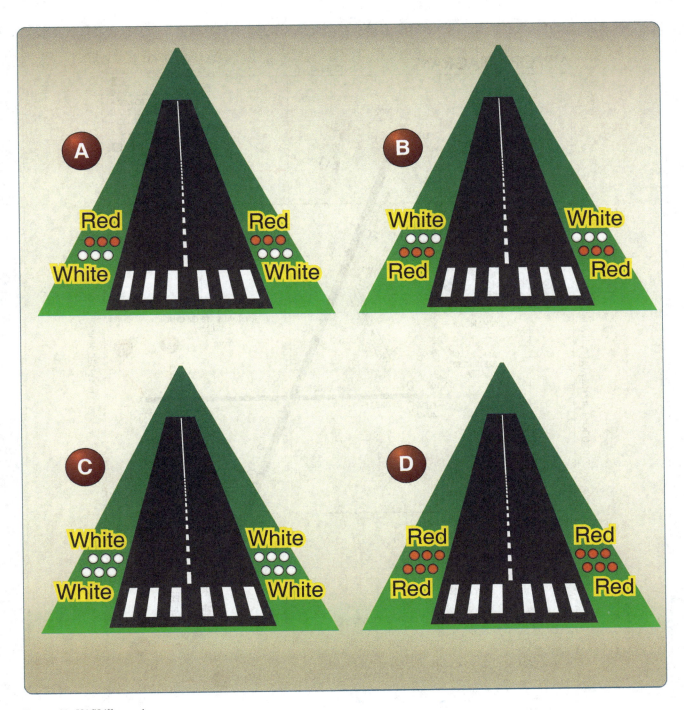

Figure 48. *VASI illustrations.*

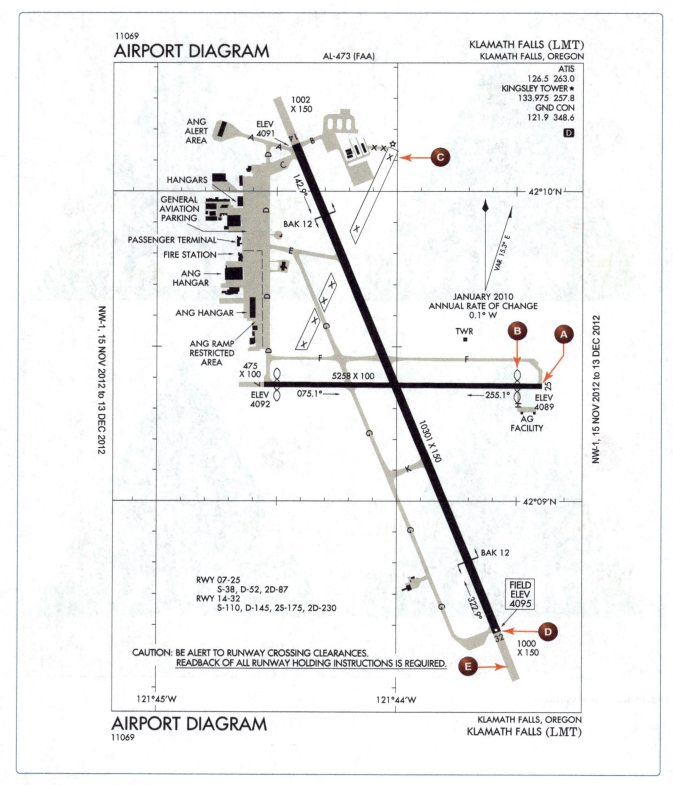

Figure 49. *Airport diagram.*

Figure 50. *Airport diagram.*

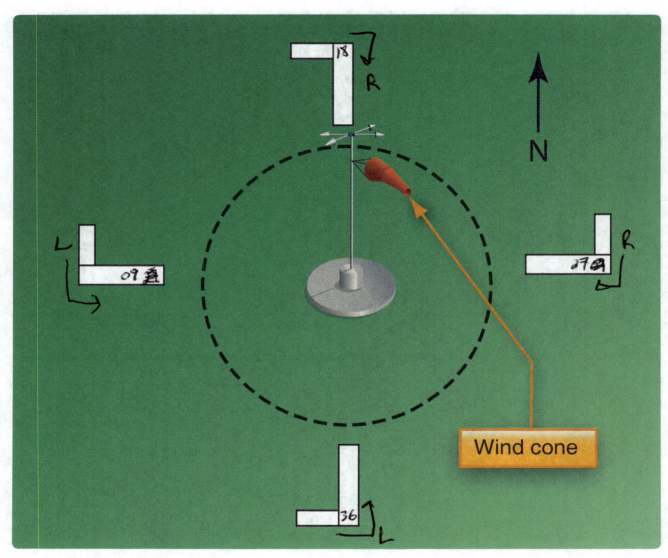

Figure 51. *Wind cone airport landing indicator.*

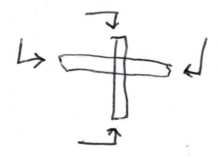

Form Approved OMB No. 2120-0026

U.S. DEPARTMENT OF TRANSPORTATION FEDERAL AVIATION ADMINISTRATION	(FAA USE ONLY) ☐ PILOT BRIEFING ☐ VNR ☐ STOPOVER		TIME STARTED	SPECIALIST INITIALS
FLIGHT PLAN				

1. TYPE	2. AIRCRAFT IDENTIFICATION	3. AIRCRAFT TYPE/ SPECIAL EQUIPMENT	4. TRUE AIRSPEED	5. DEPARTURE POINT	6. DEPARTURE TIME		7. CRUISING ALTITUDE
VFR					PROPOSED (Z)	ACTUAL (Z)	
IFR							
DVFR			KTS				

8. ROUTE OF FLIGHT

9. DESTINATION (Name of airport and city)	10. EST. TIME ENROUTE		11. REMARKS
	HOURS	MINUTES	

12. FUEL ON BOARD		13. ALTERNATE AIRPORT(S)	14. PILOT'S NAME, ADDRESS & TELEPHONE NUMBER & AIRCRAFT HOME BASE	15. NUMBER ABOARD
HOURS	MINUTES			
			17. DESTINATION CONTACT/TELEPHONE (OPTIONAL)	

16. COLOR OF AIRCRAFT	CIVIL AIRCRAFT PILOTS. 14 CFR Part 91 requires you file an IFR flight plan to operate under instrument flight rules in controlled airspace. Failure to file could result in a civil penalty not to exceed $1,000 for each violation (Section 901 of the Federal Aviation Act of 1958, as amended). Filing of a VFR flight plan is recommended as a good operating practice. See also Part 99 for requirements concerning DVFR flight plans.

FAA Form 7233-1 (8-82)   CLOSE VFR FLIGHT PLAN WITH _____ FSS ON ARRIVAL

Figure 52. *Flight plan form.*

NEBRASKA 271

LINCOLN (LNK)   4 NW   UTC–6(–5DT)   N40°51.05′ W96°45.55′   OMAHA
  1219 B S4 **FUEL** 100LL, JET A   TPA—See Remarks   ARFF Index—See Remarks   H–5C, L–10I
    NOTAM FILE LNK   IAP, AD
  RWY 18–36: H12901X200 (ASPH–CONC–GRVD)   S–100, D–200,
    2S–175, 2D–400   HIRL
    RWY 18: MALSR. PAPI(P4L)—GA 3.0° TCH 55′. Rgt tfc.   0.4%
      down.
    RWY 36: MALSR. PAPI(P4L)—GA 3.0° TCH 57′.
  RWY 14–32: H8649X150 (ASPH–CONC–GRVD)   S–80, D–170,
    2S–175, 2D–280   MIRL
    RWY 14: REIL. VASI(V4L)—GA 3.0° TCH 48′. Thld dsplcd 363′.
    RWY 32: VASI(V4L)—GA 3.0° TCH 50′. Thld dsplcd 470′.
      Pole.   0.3% up.
  RWY 17–35: H5800X100 (ASPH–CONC–AFSC)   S–49, D–60
    HIRL   0.8% up S
    RWY 17: REIL. PAPI(P4L)—GA 3.0° TCH 44′.
    RWY 35: ODALS. PAPI(P4L)—GA 3.0° TCH 30′. Rgt tfc.
  RUNWAY DECLARED DISTANCE INFORMATION

RWY 14: TORA–8649	TODA–8649	ASDA–8649	LDA–8286
RWY 17: TORA–5800	TODA–5800	ASDA–5400	LDA–5400
RWY 18: TORA–12901	TODA–12901	ASDA–12901	LDA–12901
RWY 32: TORA–8649	TODA–8649	ASDA–8286	LDA–7816
RWY 35: TORA–5800	TODA–5800	ASDA–5800	LDA–5800
RWY 36: TORA–12901	TODA–12901	ASDA–12901	LDA–12901

  AIRPORT REMARKS: Attended continuously. Birds invof arpt. Rwy 18 designated calm wind rwy. Rwy 32 apch holdline
    on South A twy. TPA–2219 (1000), heavy military jet 3000 (1781). Class I, ARFF Index B. ARFF Index C level
    equipment provided. Rwy 18–36 touchdown and rollout rwy visual range avbl. When twr clsd MIRL Rwy 14–32
    preset on low ints, HIRL Rwy 18–36 and Rwy 17–35 preset on med ints, ODALS Rwy 35 operate continuously on
    med ints, MALSR Rwy 18 and Rwy 36 operate continuously and REIL Rwy 14 and Rwy 17 operate continuously
    on low ints. VASI Rwy 14 and Rwy 32, PAPI Rwy 17, Rwy 35, Rwy 18 and Rwy 36 on continuously.
  WEATHER DATA SOURCES: ASOS (402) 474–9214. LLWAS
  COMMUNICATIONS: CTAF 118.5   **ATIS** 118.05   **UNICOM** 122.95
    RCO 122.65 (COLUMBUS RADIO)
  ® **APP/DEP CON** 124.0 (180°–359°) 124.8 (360°–179°)
    TOWER 118.5 125.7 (1130–0600Z‡)   **GND CON** 121.9   **CLNC DEL** 120.7
  AIRSPACE: CLASS C svc 1130–0600Z‡ ctc **APP CON** other times CLASS E.
  RADIO AIDS TO NAVIGATION: NOTAM FILE LNK.
    (H) VORTACW 116.1   LNK   Chan 108   N40°55.43′ W96°44.52′   181° 4.4 NM to fld. 1370/9E
    POTTS NDB (MHW/LOM) 385   LN   N40°44.83′ W96°45.75′   355° 6.2 NM to fld. Unmonitored when twr clsd.
    ILS 111.1   I–OCZ   Rwy 18.   Class IB   OM unmonitored.
    ILS 109.9   I–LNK   Rwy 36   Class IA   LOM POTTS NDB. MM unmonitored. LOM unmonitored when twr
      clsd.
  COMM/NAV/WEATHER REMARKS: Emerg frequency 121.5 not available at twr.

LOUP CITY MUNI   (0F4)   1 NW   UTC–6(–5DT)   N41°17.20′ W98°59.41′   OMAHA
  2071 B **FUEL** 100LL   NOTAM FILE OLU   L–10H, 12H
  RWY 16–34: H3200X60 (CONC)   S–12.5   MIRL
    RWY 34: Trees.
  RWY 04–22: 2040X100 (TURF)
    RWY 04: Tree.   **RWY 22:** Road.
  AIRPORT REMARKS: Unattended. For svc call 308–745–1344/1244/0664.
  COMMUNICATIONS: CTAF 122.9
  RADIO AIDS TO NAVIGATION: NOTAM FILE OLU.
    WOLBACH (H) VORTAC 114.8   OBH   Chan 95   N41°22.54′ W98°21.22′   253° 29.3 NM to fld. 2010/7E.

MARTIN FLD   (See SO SIOUX CITY)

Figure 53. *Airport/facility directory excerpt.*

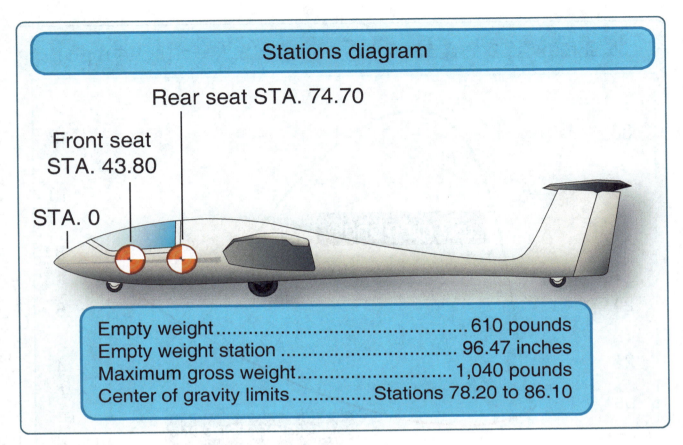

Stations diagram

Rear seat STA. 74.70

Front seat STA. 43.80

STA. 0

Empty weight .... 610 pounds
Empty weight station .... 96.47 inches
Maximum gross weight............................. 1,040 pounds
Center of gravity limits .... Stations 78.20 to 86.10

Figure 54. *Glider weight and balance diagram.*

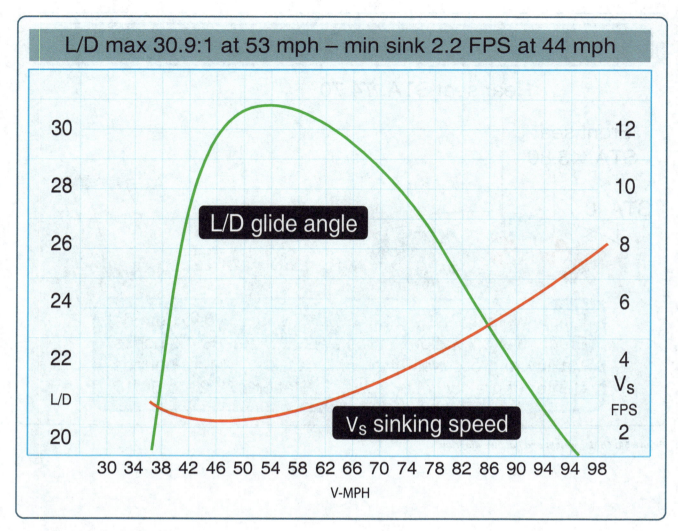

Figure 55. *Glider performance graph.*

Figure 56. *Standard soaring signals.*

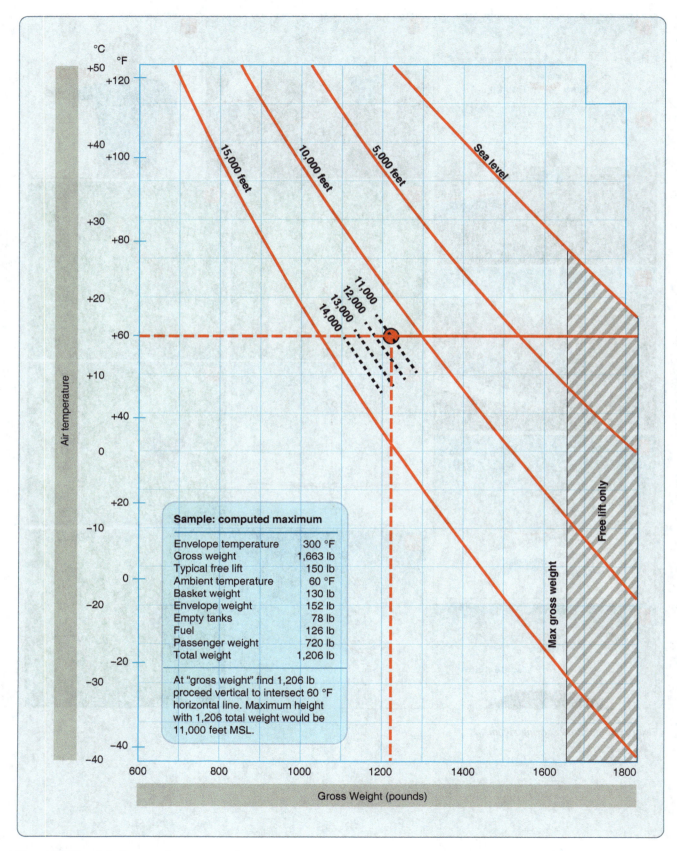

Sample: computed maximum

Envelope temperature	300 °F
Gross weight	1,663 lb
Typical free lift	150 lb
Ambient temperature	60 °F
Basket weight	130 lb
Envelope weight	152 lb
Empty tanks	78 lb
Fuel	126 lb
Passenger weight	720 lb
Total weight	1,206 lb

At "gross weight" find 1,206 lb proceed vertical to intersect 60 °F horizontal line. Maximum height with 1,206 total weight would be 11,000 feet MSL.

Figure 57. *Hot air balloon performance graph.*

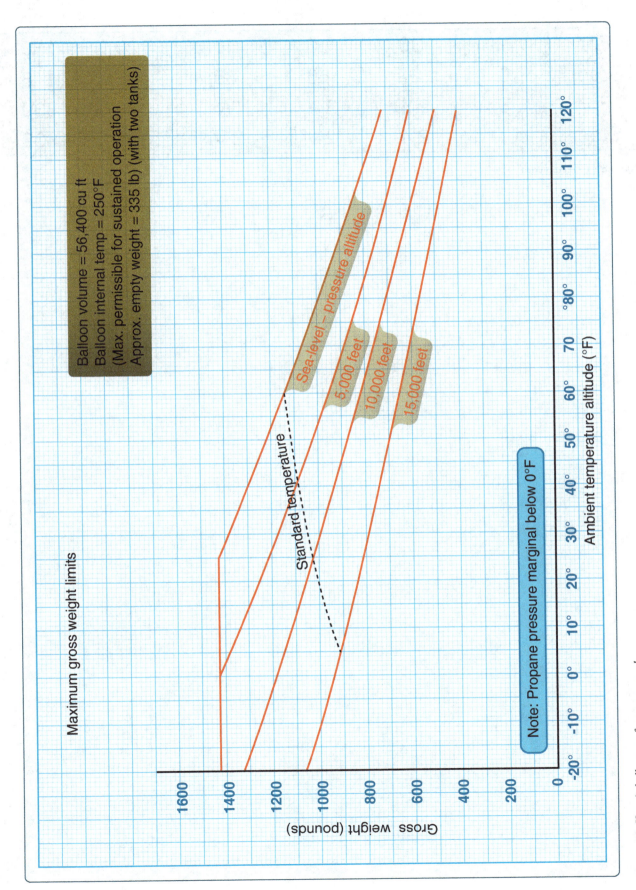

Figure 58. *Hot air balloon performance graph.*

For	N	30	60	E	120	150
Steer	0	27	56	85	116	148
For	S	210	240	W	300	330
Steer	181	214	244	274	303	332

Figure 59. *Compass card.*

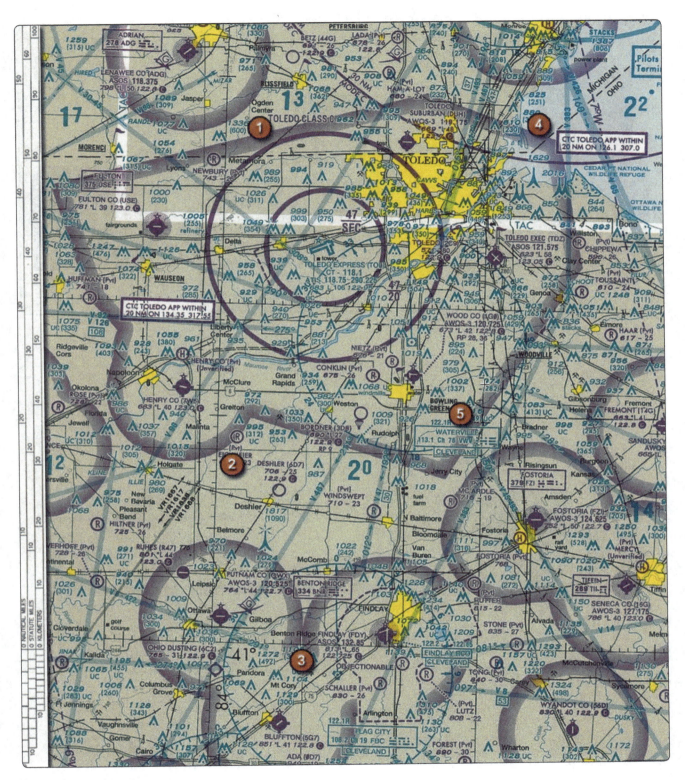

Figure 60. *Sectional chart excerpt.*

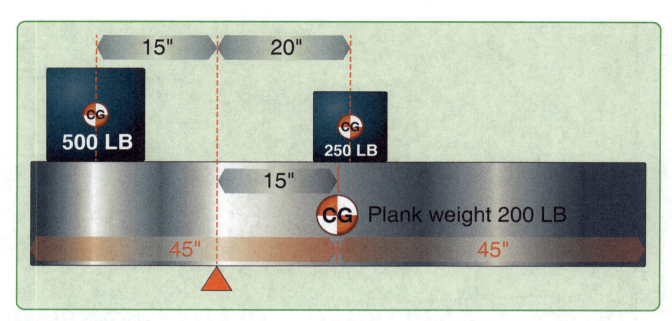

Figure 61. *Weight and balance diagram.*

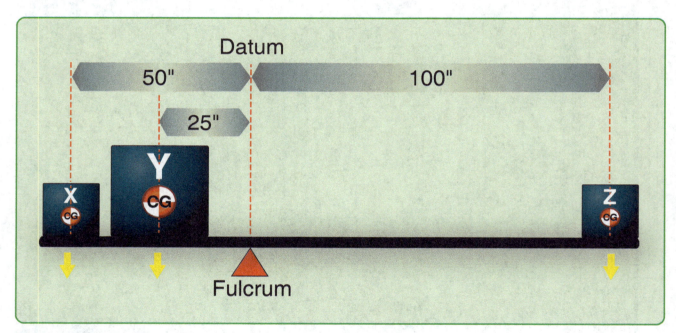

Figure 62. *Weight and balance diagram.*

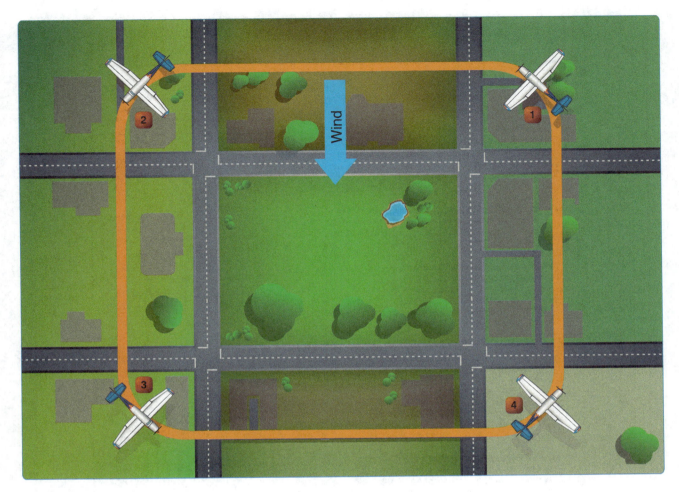

Figure 63. *Rectangular course.*

OHIO

263

TOLEDO

TOLEDO EXECUTIVE (TDZ) 6 SE UTC−5(−4DT) N41°33.90' W83°28.93' DETROIT
  623 B S4 FUEL 100LL, JET A OX 1, 3 NOTAM FILE TDZ H−10G, L−28J
  RWY 14−32: H5829X100 (ASPH−GRVD) S−63, D−85, 2S−107 MIRL IAP
    RWY 14: REIL. PAPI(P4L)—GA 3.0° TCH 34'. Thld dsplcd 225'.
    Tower.
    RWY 32: VASI(V4L)—GA 3.0° TCH 43'. Thld dsplcd 351'. Road.
  RWY 04−22: H3799X75 (ASPH) S−63, D−85, 2S−107 MIRL
    RWY 04: REIL. PAPI(P4L)—GA 3.5° TCH 35'. Thld dsplcd 100'.
    Road.
    RWY 22: REIL. PAPI(P4L)—GA 3.0° TCH 25'. Thld dsplcd 380'.
    Railroad.
  AIRPORT REMARKS: Attended Mon−Fri continuously, Sat−Sun
    1300−0100Z‡. Parallel twy Rwy 04−22 and Rwy 14−32 35' wide.
    Seagulls on and invof arpt. Ldg fee. ACTIVATE MIRL Rwy 04−22
    and Rwy 14−32, REIL and PAPI Rwy 04, Rwy 22, Rwy 14 and VASI
    Rwy 32—CTAF.
  WEATHER DATA SOURCES: ASOS 121.575 (419) 838−5034.
  COMMUNICATIONS: CTAF/UNICOM 123.05
  Ⓡ APP/DEP CON 126.1 CLNC DEL 125.6
  RADIO AIDS TO NAVIGATION: NOTAM FILE CLE.
    WATERVILLE (L) VOR/DME 113.1 VWV Chan 78 N41°27.09'
    W83°38.32' 048° 9.8 NM to fld. 664/2W.

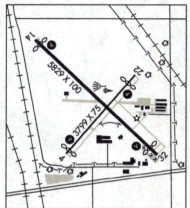

TOLEDO EXPRESS (TOL) 10 W UTC−5(−4DT) N41°35.21' W83°48.47' DETROIT
  683 B S4 FUEL 100LL, JET A OX 3 LRA Class I, ARFF Index B NOTAM FILE TOL H−10G, L−28J
  RWY 07−25: H10599X150 (ASPH−GRVD) S−100, D−174, 2S−175, 2D−300, 2D/2D2−550 IAP, AD
    HIRL CL
    RWY 07: ALSF2. TDZL. Trees.
    RWY 25: MALSR. VASI(V4L)—GA 3.0° TCH 51'. Trees. 0.3% up.
  RWY 16−34: H5599X150 (ASPH−GRVD) S−100, D−174, 2S−175,
    2D−300 MIRL
    RWY 16: REIL. PAPI(P4L)—GA 3.0° TCH 48'. Trees.
    RWY 34: REIL.
  RUNWAY DECLARED DISTANCE INFORMATION

	TORA	TODA	ASDA	LDA
RWY 07:	TORA 10599	TODA 10599	ASDA 10599	LDA 10599
RWY 16:	TORA 5599	TODA 5599	ASDA 5599	LDA 5599
RWY 25:	TORA 10599	TODA 10599	ASDA 10599	LDA 10599
RWY 34:	TORA 5599	TODA 5599	ASDA 5599	LDA 5599

  ARRESTING GEAR/SYSTEM
    RWY 07 ←BAK−12 BAK−12 →RWY 25
  AIRPORT REMARKS: Attended continuously. Fuel and svc avbl
    1300−0500Z‡. Birds on and invof arpt. Twy A west of Rwy 16 and
    the ramp between Twy B9 and B13 not visible from twr. Twy D
    intersection of Twy D1, heavy acft use minimal power to reduce
    foreign object damage on Air National Guard ramp. Customs:
    Sat−Sun req must be made prior to 2200Z‡ on Fri, phone 419−259−6424.
  WEATHER DATA SOURCES: ASOS (419) 865−8351.
  COMMUNICATIONS: ATIS 118.75 UNICOM 122.95
  Ⓡ APP/DEP CON 126.1 (360°−179°) 134.35 (180°−359°) 123.975
    TOWER 118.1 GND CON 121.9 CLNC DEL 121.75
  AIRSPACE: CLASS C svc continuous ctc APP CON
  RADIO AIDS TO NAVIGATION: NOTAM FILE CLE.
    WATERVILLE (L) VOR/DME 113.1 VWV Chan 78 N41°27.09' W83°38.32' 319° 11.1 NM to fld. 664/2W.
    TOPHR NDB (LOM) 219 TO N41°33.21' W83°55.27' 074° 5.5 NM to fld. Unmonitored. NOTAM FILE TOL.
    ILS 109.7 I−TOL Rwy 07. Class IE. LOM TOPHR NDB.
    ILS 108.7 I−BQE Rwy 25. Class IA. LOC unusable 0.4 NM inbound. ILS unmonitored when twr clsd.
    ASR

SEAGATE HELISTOP (6T2) 00 N UTC−5(−4DT) N41°39.25' W83°31.88' DETROIT
  650 NOTAM FILE CLE
  HELIPAD H1: H50X50 (CONC)
  HELIPORT REMARKS: Unattended. ACTIVATE orange perimeter lgts—CTAF. Helipad H1 NSTD 1−box (2 VASIS). Helipad
    H1 not marked with ''H.'' Helipad H1 perimeter lgts.
  COMMUNICATIONS: CTAF/UNICOM 123.05

Figure 64. *Airport/facility excerpt.*

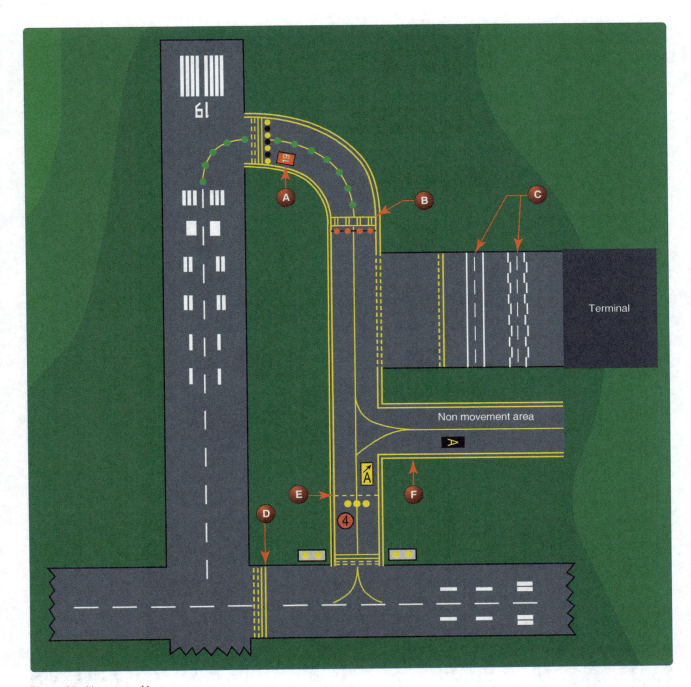

Figure 65. *Airport markings.*

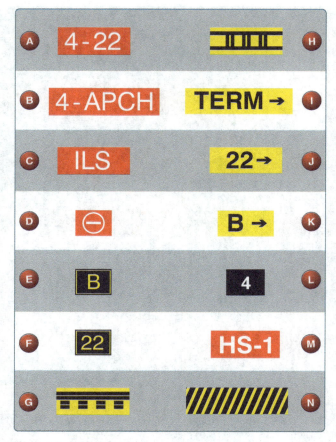

Figure 66. *U.S. airport signs.*

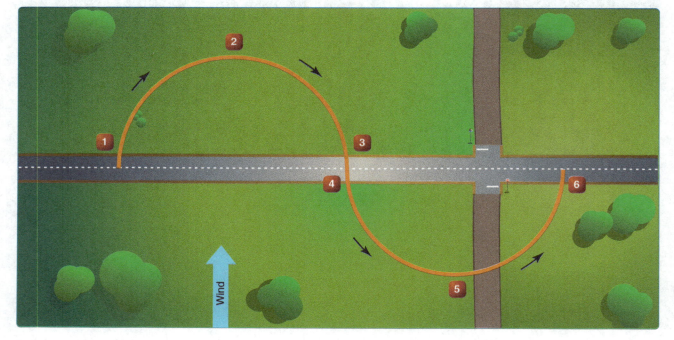

Figure 67. *S-turn diagram.*

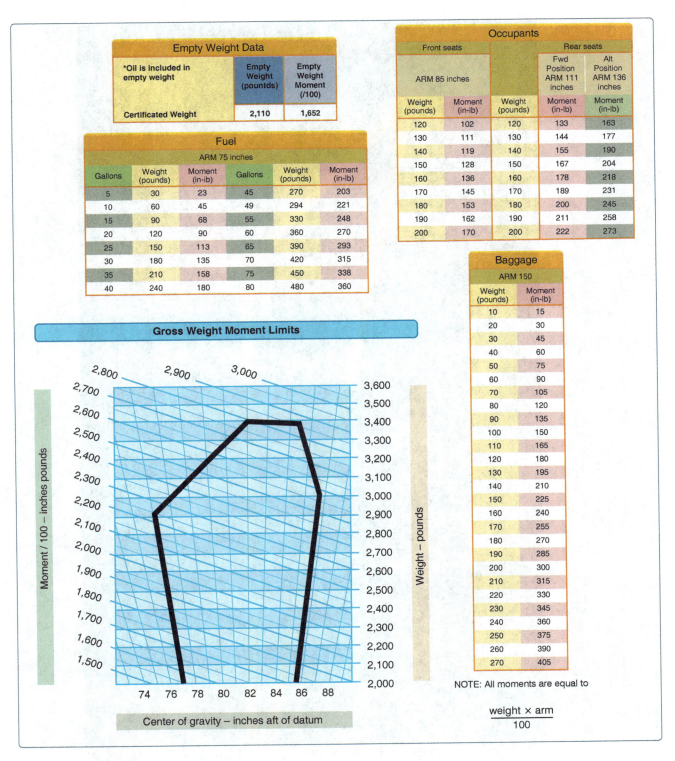

Empty Weight Data

*Oil is included in empty weight	Empty Weight (pountds)	Empty Weight Moment (/100)
Certificated Weight	2,110	1,652

Fuel

ARM 75 inches

Gallons	Weight (pounds)	Moment (in-ib)	Gallons	Weight (pounds)	Moment (in-lb)
5	30	23	45	270	203
10	60	45	49	294	221
15	90	68	55	330	248
20	120	90	60	360	270
25	150	113	65	390	293
30	180	135	70	420	315
35	210	158	75	450	338
40	240	180	80	480	360

Occupants

Front seats			Rear seats	
ARM 85 inches			Fwd Position ARM 111 inches	Alt Position ARM 136 inches
Weight (pounds)	Moment (in-lb)	Weight (pounds)	Moment (in-lb)	Moment (in-lb)
120	102	120	133	163
130	111	130	144	177
140	119	140	155	190
150	128	150	167	204
160	136	160	178	218
170	145	170	189	231
180	153	180	200	245
190	162	190	211	258
200	170	200	222	273

Baggage

ARM 150

Weight (pounds)	Moment (in-lb)
10	15
20	30
30	45
40	60
50	75
60	90
70	105
80	120
90	135
100	150
110	165
120	180
130	195
140	210
150	225
160	240
170	255
180	270
190	285
200	300
210	315
220	330
230	345
240	360
250	375
260	390
270	405

NOTE: All moments are equal to

$$\frac{weight \times arm}{100}$$

Gross Weight Moment Limits

Moment / 100 – inches pounds

Weight – pounds

Center of gravity – inches aft of datum

Figure 68. *Weight and balance chart.*

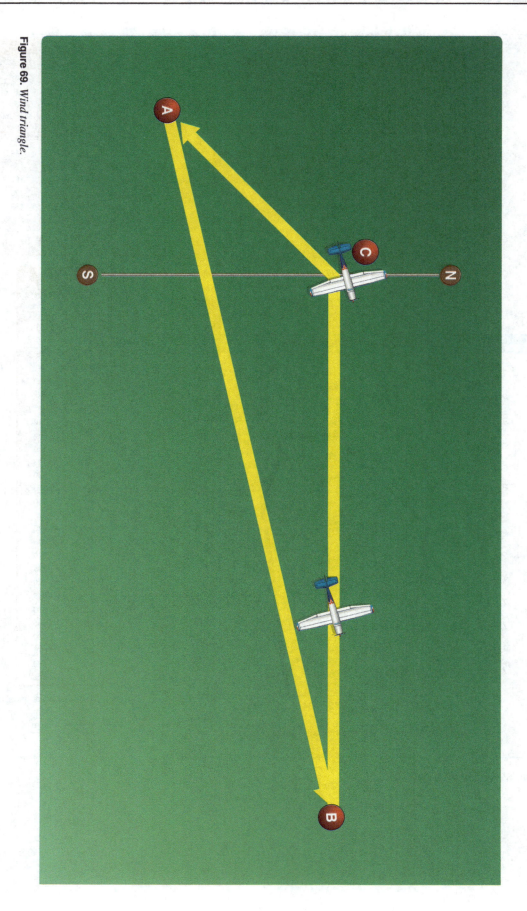

Figure 69. *Wind triangle.*

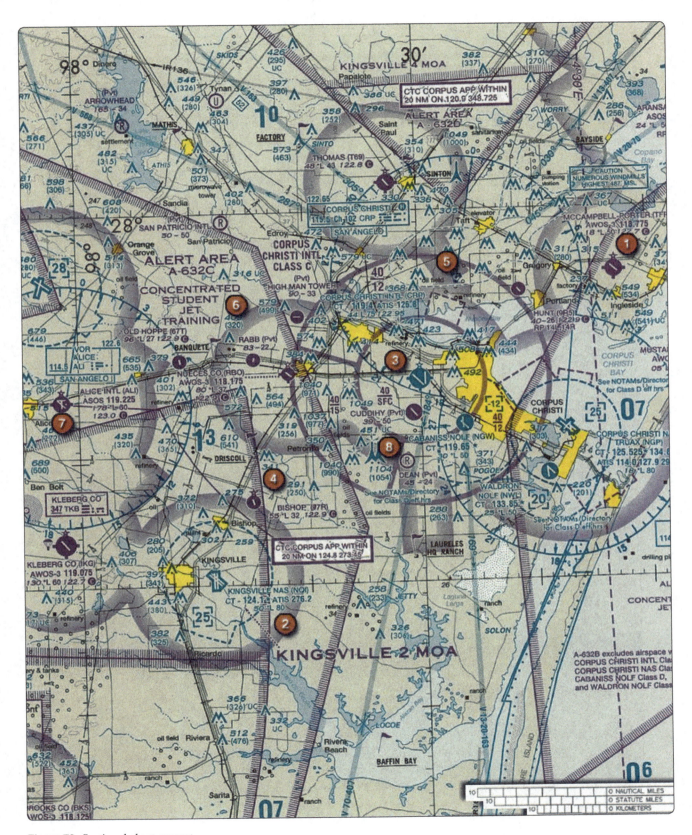

Figure 70. *Sectional chart excerpt.*

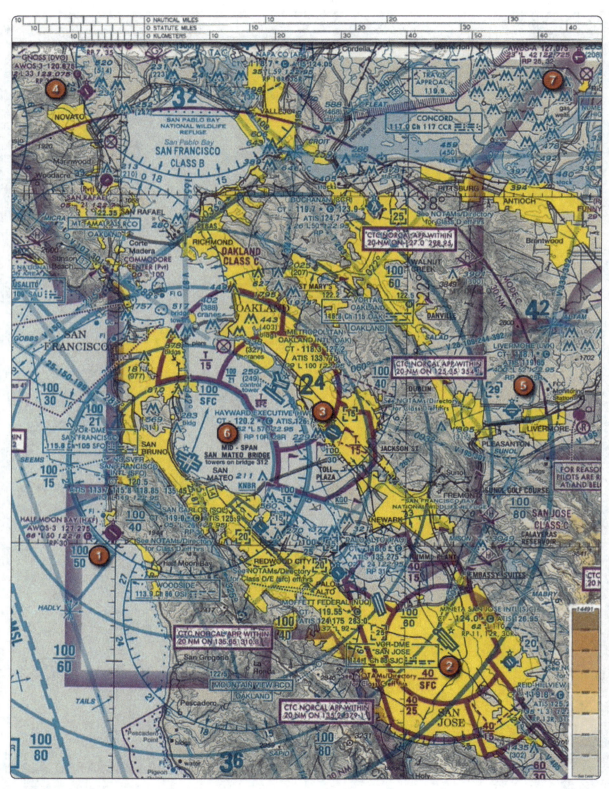

Figure 71. *Sectional chart excerpt.*

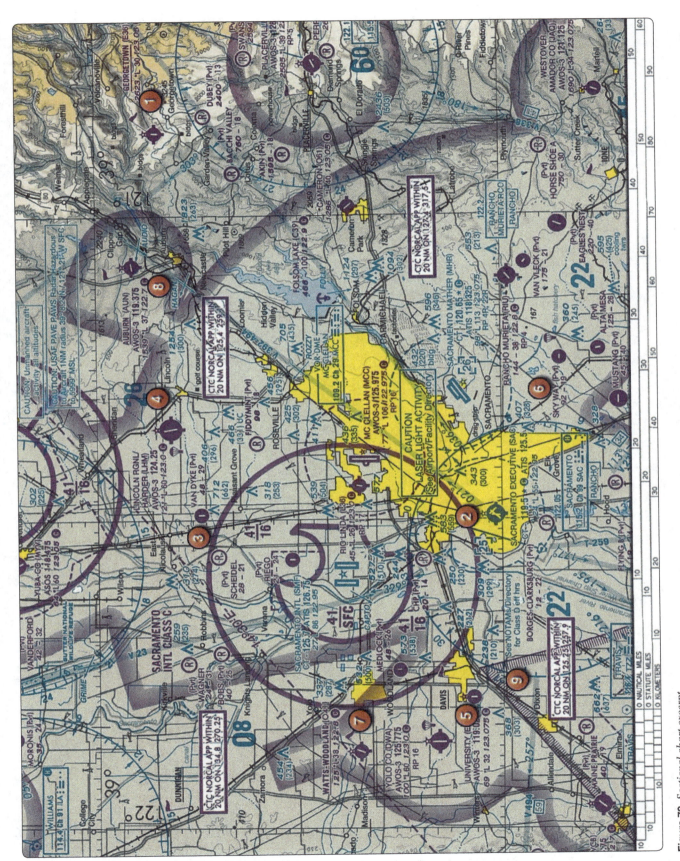

Figure 72. Sectional chart excerpt.

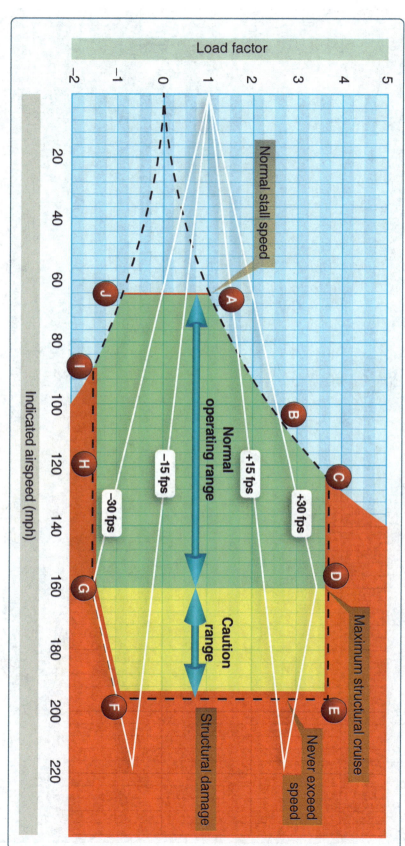

Figure 73. *Velocity vs. G-loads.*

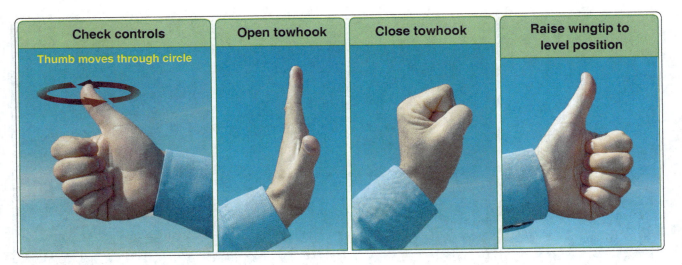

Figure 74. *Glider hand signals.*

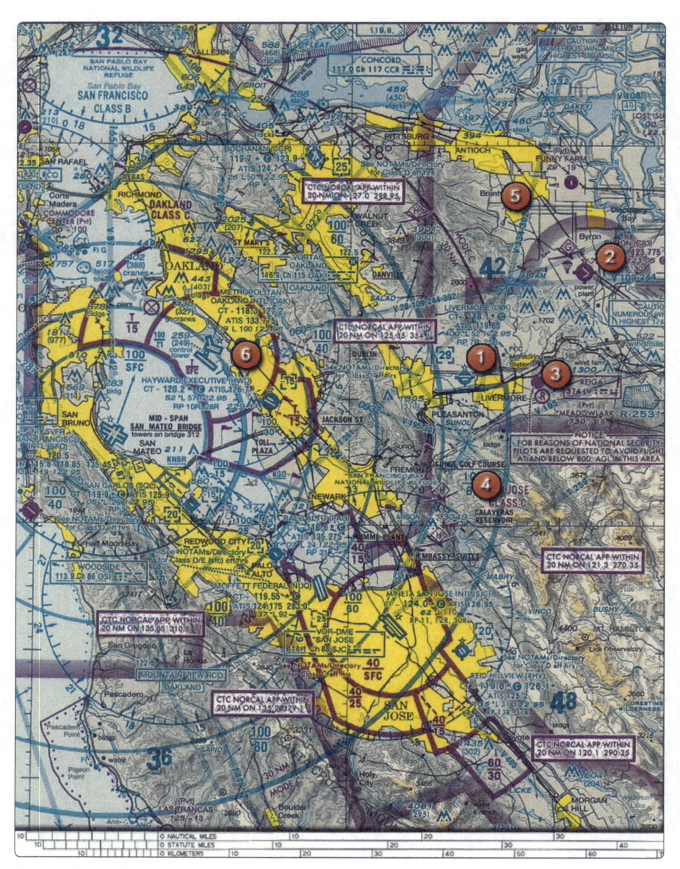

Figure 75. *Sectional chart excerpt.*

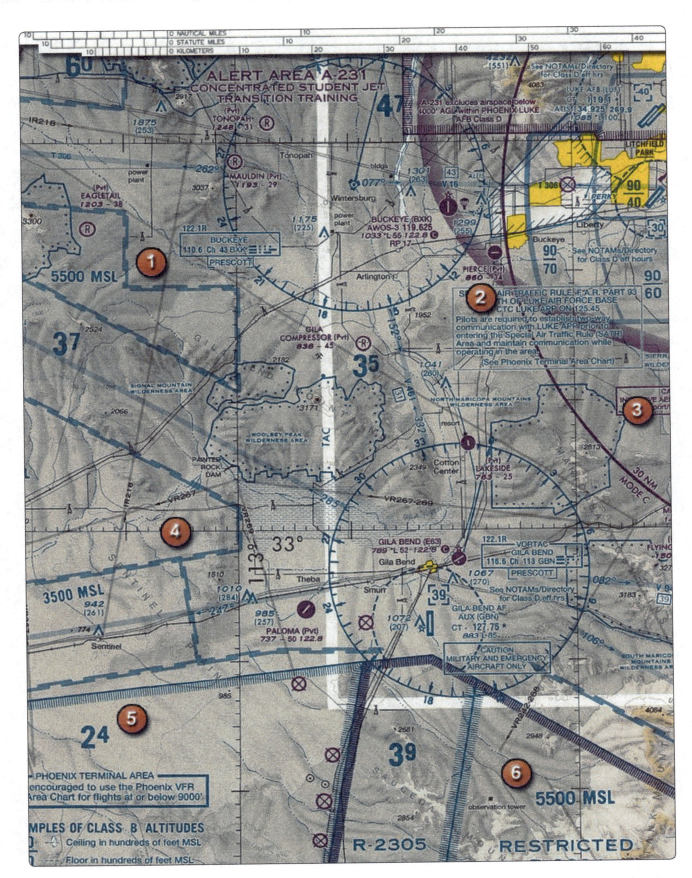

Figure 76. *Sectional chart excerpt.*

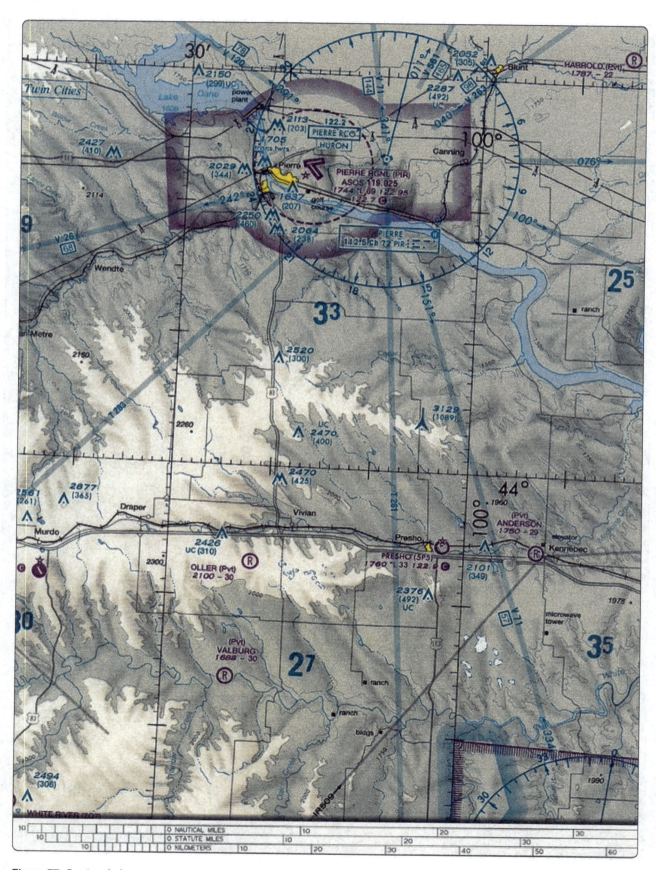

Figure 77. *Sectional chart excerpt.*

340   **SOUTH DAKOTA**

PIERRE RGNL   (PIR)   3 E   UTC −6(−5DT)   N44°22.96′ W100°17.16′   **OMAHA**
  1744   B   S4   **FUEL** 100LL, JET A   OX 1, 2, 3, 4   Class I, ARFF Index A   NOTAM FILE PIR   **H−2I, L−12H**
  RWY 13−31: H6900X100 (ASPH−GRVD)   S−91, D−108, 2S−137, 2D−168   HIRL   **IAP**

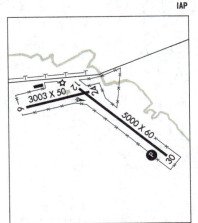

    RWY 13: REIL. PAPI(P4L)—GA 3.0 ° TCH 52′.
    RWY 31: MALSR. PAPI(P4L)—GA 3.0 ° TCH 52′.
  RWY 07−25: H6881X150 (ASPH−GRVD)   S−91, D−114, 2S−145,
    2D−180   HIRL   0.6% up W
    RWY 07: REIL. PAPI(P4L)—GA 3.0 ° TCH 47′. Tank.
    RWY 25: REIL. PAPI(P4L)—GA 3.0 ° TCH 54′.
  RUNWAY DECLARED DISTANCE INFORMATION

RWY	TORA	TODA	ASDA	LDA
RWY 07:	TORA−6881	TODA−6881	ASDA−6830	LDA−6830
RWY 13:	TORA−6900	TODA−6900	ASDA−6900	LDA−6900
RWY 25:	TORA−6881	TODA−6881	ASDA−6881	LDA−6881
RWY 31:	TORA−6900	TODA−6900	ASDA−6900	LDA−6900

  AIRPORT REMARKS: Attended Mon−Fri 1100−0600Z‡, Sat−Sun
    1100−0400Z‡. For attendant other times call
    605−224−9000/8621. Arpt conditions unmonitored during
    0530−1000Z‡. Numerous non−radio acft operating in area. Birds
    on and invof arpt and within a 25 NM radius. No line of sight
    between rwy ends of Rwy 07−25. ARFF provided for part 121 air
    carrier ops only. 48 hr PPR for unscheduled acr ops involving acft
    designed for 31 or more passenger seats call 605−773−7447 or
    605−773−7405. Taxiway C is 50′ wide and restricted to acft 75,000 pounds or less. ACTIVATE HIRL Rwy 13−31
    and Rwy 07−25, MALSR Rwy 31, REIL Rwy 07, Rwy 13 and Rwy 25, PAPI Rwy 07, Rwy 25, Rwy 13 and Rwy
    31−CTAF 122.7. NOTE: See Special Notices Section—
    Aerobatic Practice Areas.
  WEATHER DATA SOURCES: ASOS 119.025 (605) 224−6087.   **HIWAS** 112.5 PIR.
  COMMUNICATIONS: CTAF 122.7   **UNICOM** 122.95
    RCO 122.2 (HURON RADIO)
  Ⓡ **MINNEAPOLIS CENTER APP/DEP CON** 125.1
  RADIO AIDS TO NAVIGATION: NOTAM FILE PIR.
    (L) VORTACW 112.5   PIR   Chan 72   N44°23.67′ W100°09.77′   251° 5.3 NM to fld. 1789/11E.   **HIWAS.**
    ILS/DME 111.9   I−PIR   Chan 56   Rwy 31.   Class IA   ILS GS unusable for coupled apch blo 2,255′. GS
    unusable blo 2135′.

PINE RIDGE   (IEN)   2 E   UTC −7(−6DT)   N43°01.35′ W102°30.66′   **CHEYENNE**
  3333   B   NOTAM FILE IEN   **H−5B, L−12G**
  RWY 12−30: H5000X60 (ASPH)   S−12   MIRL   0.7% up SE   **IAP**
    RWY 12: P−line.
    RWY 30: PAPI(P2L)—GA 3.0 ° TCH 26′. Fence.
  RWY 06−24: H3003X50 (ASPH)   S−12   0.7% up NE
    RWY 24: Fence.
  AIRPORT REMARKS: Unattended. Rwy 06−24 CLOSED indef. MIRL Rwy
    12−30 and PAPI Rwy 30 opr dusk−0530Z‡, after 0530Z‡
    ACTIVATE—CTAF.
  WEATHER DATA SOURCES: ASOS 126.775 (605) 867−1584.
  COMMUNICATIONS: CTAF 122.9
    DENVER CENTER APP/DEP CON 127.95
  RADIO AIDS TO NAVIGATION: NOTAM FILE RAP.
    RAPID CITY (H) VORTAC 112.3   RAP   Chan 70   N43°58.56′
    W103°00.74′   146° 61.3 NM to fld. 3160/13E.

Figure 78. *Airport/facility directory excerpt.*

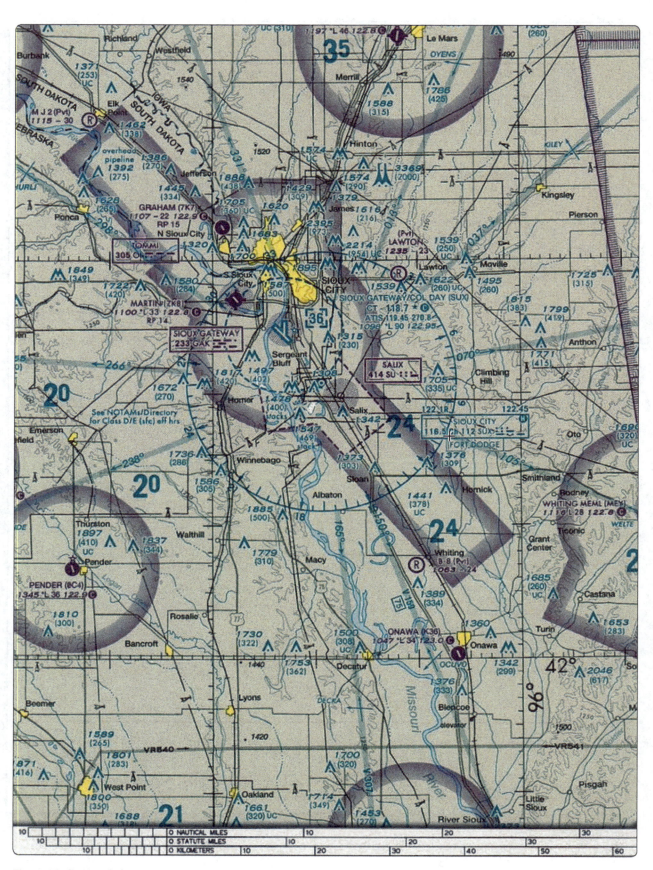

Figure 79. *Sectional chart excerpt.*

64   **IOWA**

SIOUX CITY   N42°20.67' W96°19.42'   NOTAM FILE SUX   **OMAHA**
  (L) VORTAC 116.5   SUX   Chan 112   313 ° 4.4 NM to Sioux Gateway/Col Bud Day Fld. 1087/9E.   **HIWAS.**   **L–12I**
  VOR unusable:
      280°–292° byd 25 NM   306°–350° byd 20 NM blo 3,000'
      293°–305° byd 20 NM blo 4,500'   350°–280° byd 30 NM blo 3,000'
      293°–305° byd 35 NM
  RCO 122.45 122.1R 116.5T (FORT DODGE RADIO)

SIOUX CITY

SIOUX GATEWAY/COL BUD DAY FLD   (SUX)   6 S   UTC −6(−5DT)   N42°24.16' W96°23.06'   **OMAHA**
  1098   B   S4   **FUEL** 100LL, 115, JET A   OX 1, 2, 3, 4   Class I, ARFF Index—See Remarks   **H–5C, L–12I**
  NOTAM FILE SUX   **IAP, AD**
  RWY 13–31: H9002X150 (CONC–GRVD)   S–100, D–120, 2S–152,
    2D–220   HIRL
    RWY 13: MALS. VASI(V4L)—GA 3.0 ° TCH 49'. Tree.
    RWY 31: MALSR. VASI(V4L)—GA 3.0 ° TCH 50'.
  RWY 17–35: H6600X150 (ASPH–PFC)   S–65, D–80, 2S–102,
    2D–130   MIRL
    RWY 17: REIL. VASI(V4R)—GA 3.0 ° TCH 50'. Trees.
    RWY 35: PAPI(P4L)—GA 3.0 ° TCH 54'. Pole.
  LAND AND HOLD SHORT OPERATIONS

LANDING	HOLD SHORT POINT	DIST AVBL
RWY 13	17–35	5400
RWY 17	13–31	5650

  ARRESTING GEAR/SYSTEM
    RWY 13 ←BAK–14 BAK–12B(B) (1392')
               BAK–14 BAK–12B(B) (1492') →RWY 31

  AIRPORT REMARKS: Attended continuously. PAEW 0330–1200Z ‡ during
  inclement weather Nov–Apr. AER 31–BAK–12/14 located (1492')
  from thld. Airfield surface conditions not monitored by arpt
  management between 0600–1000Z ‡ daily. Rwy 13–BAK–12/14
  located (1392') from thld. All A–gear avbl only during ANG flying ops. Twr has limited visibility southeast of
  ramp near ARFF bldg and northeast of Rwy 31 touchdown zone. Rwy 31 is calm wind rwy. Class I, ARFF Index
  B. ARFF Index E fire fighting equipment avbl on request. Twy F unlit, retro–reflective markers in place. Portions
  of Twy A SE of Twy B not visible by twr and is designated a non–movement area. Rwy 13–31 touchdown and
  rollout rwy visual range avbl. When twr clsd, ACTIVATE HIRL Rwy 13–31; MIRL Rwy 17–35; MALS Rwy 13;
  MALSR Rwy 31; and REIL Rwy 17—CTAF.
  WEATHER DATA SOURCES: ASOS (712) 255–6474. **HIWAS** 116.5 SUX. LAWRS.
  COMMUNICATIONS: CTAF 118.7   **ATIS** 119.45   **UNICOM** 122.95
    SIOUX CITY RCO 122.45 122.1R 116.5T (FORT DODGE RADIO)
  ⓡ **SIOUX CITY APP/DEP CON** 124.6 (1200–0330Z ‡)
  ⓡ **MINNEAPOLIS CENTER APP/DEP CON** 124.1 (0330–1200Z ‡)
    SIOUX CITY TOWER 118.7 (1200–0330Z ‡)   **GND CON** 121.9
  AIRSPACE: CLASS D svc 1200–0330Z ‡ other times CLASS E.
  RADIO AIDS TO NAVIGATION: NOTAM FILE SUX.
    SIOUX CITY (L) VORTAC 116.5   SUX   Chan 112   N42°20.67' W96°19.42'   313° 4.4 NM to fld. 1087/9E.
      HIWAS.
    NDB (MHW) 233   GAK   N42°24.49' W96°23.16'   at fld.
    SALIX NDB (MHW/LOM) 414   SU   N42°19.65' W96°17.43'   311° 6.1 NM to fld. Unmonitored.
    TOMMI NDB (MHW/LOM) 305   OI   N42°27.61' W96°27.73'   128° 4.9 NM to fld. Unmonitored.
    ILS 109.3   I–SUX   Rwy 31   Class IT.   LOM SALIX NDB. ILS Unmonitored when twr clsd. Glide path
      unusable coupled approach (CPD) blo 1805'.
    ILS 111.3   I–OIQ   Rwy 13   LOM TOMMI NDB. Localizer shutdown when twr clsd.
    ASR (1200–0330Z ‡)

SNORE   N43°13.96' W95°19.66'   NOTAM FILE SPW.   **OMAHA**
  NDB (LOM) 394   SP   121° 6.8 NM to Spencer Muni.

SOUTHEAST IOWA RGNL   (See BURLINGTON)

Figure 80. *Airport/facility directory excerpt.*

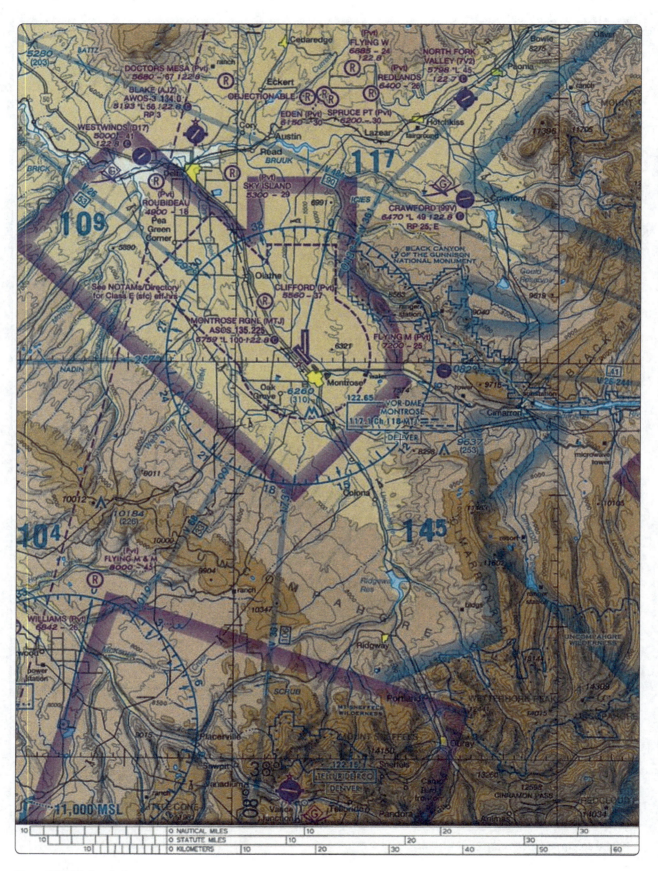

Figure 81. *Sectional chart excerpt.*

216   **COLORADO**

CRAWFORD (99V)   2 W   UTC −7(−6DT)   N38°42.25' W107°38.62'   DENVER
  6470   S2   OX 4   TPA−7470(1000)   NOTAM FILE DEN   L−9E
  RWY 07−25: H4900X20 (ASPH)   LIRL (NSTD)
    RWY 07: VASI (NSTD). Trees.   **RWY 25:** VASI (NSTD) Tank. Rgt tfc.
  RWY E−W: 2500X125 (TURF)
    RWY E: Rgt tfc.   **RWY W:** Trees.
  AIRPORT REMARKS: Attended continuously. Rwy 07−25 west 1300 ' only 25' wide. Heavy glider ops at arpt. Land to the
    east tkf to the west winds permitting. 100LL fuel avbl for emergency use only. Pedestrians, motor vehicles, deer
    and wildlife on and invof arpt. Unlimited vehicle use on arpt. Rwy West has +15 ' building 170' from thld 30' left,
    +10' road 100' from thld centerline. +45' tree 100' L of Rwy 07 extended centerline 414 ' from rwy end. −8' to
    −20' terrain off both sides of first 674 ' of Rwy 25 end. E−W rwy occasionally has 6 inch diameter irrigation
    pipes crossing rwy width in various places. Rwy 07 has 20 ' trees and −10' to 20' terrain 20' right of rwy first
    150'. E−W rwy consists of +12 inch alfalfa vegetation during various times of the year. Arpt lgts opr
    dusk−0800Z‡. Rwy 07 1 box VASI left side for local operators only or PPR call 970−921−7700 or
    970−921−3018. Rwy 07−25 LIRL on N side from Rwy 25 end W 3800 '. Rwy 07 1300 ' from end E 300 '. No thld
    lgts Rwy 07−25 3800 ' usable for ngt ops.
  COMMUNICATIONS: CTAF/UNICOM 122.8
  RADIO AIDS TO NAVIGATION: NOTAM FILE MTJ.
    MONTROSE (H) VORW/DME 117.1   MTJ   Chan 118   N38 °30.39' W107°53.96'   033° 16.9 NM to fld. 5713/12E.

CREEDE
  MINERAL CO MEM   (C24)   2 E   UTC −7(−6DT)   N37°49.33' W106°55.79'   DENVER
    8680   NOTAM FILE DEN   H−3E, L−9E
  RWY 07−25: H6880X60 (ASPH)   S−12.5, D−70, 2D−110
    RWY 07: Thld dsplcd 188 '.   **RWY 25:** Road.
  AIRPORT REMARKS: Unattended. Elk and deer on and invof arpt. Glider and hang glider activity on and in vicinity of
    arpt. Mountains in all directions. Departure to NE avoid over flight of trailers and resident homes, climb to 200 '
    above ground level on centerline extended prior to turn. Acft stay to right of valley on apch and/or departure
    route. 2' cable fence around apron.
  COMMUNICATIONS: CTAF 122.9
  RADIO AIDS TO NAVIGATION: NOTAM FILE DEN.
    BLUE MESA (H) VORW/DME 114.9   HBU   Chan 96   N38 °27.13' W107°02.39'   158° 38.1 NM to fld. 8730/14E.

  CUCHARA VALLEY AT LA VETA   (See LA VETA)

DEL NORTE
  ASTRONAUT KENT ROMINGER   (8V1)   3 N   UTC −7(−6DT)   N37°42.83' W106°21.11'   DENVER
    7949   NOTAM FILE DEN   H−3E, L−9E
  RWY 06−24: 6050X75 (ASPH)   1.1% up SW
  RWY 03−21: 4670X60 (TURF−DIRT)
    RWY 21: Mountain.
  AIRPORT REMARKS: Unattended. Wildlife on and invof arpt. Unlimited vehicle access on arpt. Mountainous terrain
    surrounds arpt in all directions.
  COMMUNICATIONS: CTAF 122.9
  RADIO AIDS TO NAVIGATION: NOTAM FILE ALS.
    ALAMOSA (H) VORTACW 113.9   ALS   Chan 86   N37 °20.95' W105°48.93'   298° 33.7 NM to fld. 7535/13E.

Figure 82. *Airport/facility directory excerpt.*

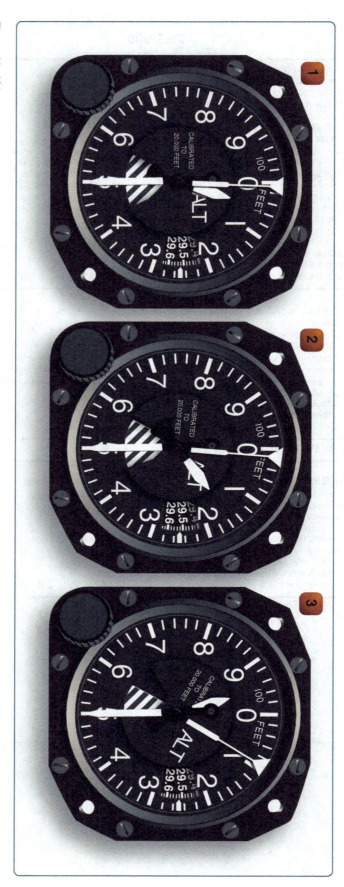

Figure 83. *Altimeter.*

LEARNING STATEMENT CODES AND LEARNING STATEMENTS

To determine the knowledge area in which a particular question was incorrectly answered, compare the learning statement code(s) on the Federal Aviation Administration Airmen Computer Test Report to the following learning statement outline. The total number of test items missed may differ from the number of learning statement codes shown on the test report, since you may have missed more than one question in a specific learning statement code.

Learning Statement Codes and Learning Statements for Pilots, Instructors, Flight Engineers, Dispatchers, Navigators, and Pilot Examiners Exams

Code	Learning Statement
PLT001	Calculate a course intercept
PLT002	Calculate aircraft performance—airspeed
PLT003	Calculate aircraft performance—center of gravity
PLT004	Calculate aircraft performance—climb / descent / maneuvering
PLT005	Calculate aircraft performance—density altitude
PLT006	Calculate aircraft performance—glide
PLT007	Calculate aircraft performance—IAS / EPR
PLT008	Calculate aircraft performance—landing
PLT009	Calculate aircraft performance—turbine temperatures (MGT, EGT, ITT, T4, etc) / torque / horsepower
PLT010	Calculate aircraft performance—STAB TRIM
PLT011	Calculate aircraft performance—takeoff
PLT012	Calculate aircraft performance—time/speed/distance/course/fuel/wind
PLT013	Calculate crosswind / headwind components
PLT014	Calculate distance / bearing from/to a station
PLT015	Calculate flight performance / planning—range
PLT016	Calculate fuel—dump time / weight / volume / quantity / consumption
PLT017	Calculate L/D ratio
PLT018	Calculate load factor / stall speed / velocity / angle of attack
PLT019	Calculate pressure altitude
PLT020	Calculate turbulent air penetration
PLT021	Calculate weight and balance
PLT022	Define Aeronautical Decision Making (ADM)
PLT023	Define altitude—absolute / true / indicated / density / pressure
PLT024	Define atmospheric adiabatic process
PLT025	Define Bernoulli`s principle
PLT026	Define ceiling
PLT027	Define coning
PLT028	Define crewmember

PLT029	Define critical phase of flight
PLT030	Define false lift
PLT031	Define isobars / associated winds
PLT032	Define MACH speed regimes
PLT033	Define MEA / MOCA / MRA
PLT034	Define stopway / clearway
PLT035	Define Vne / Vno
PLT036	Interpret a MACH meter reading
PLT037	Interpret a radar weather report
PLT038	Interpret aircraft Power Schedule Chart
PLT039	Interpret airport landing indicator
PLT040	Interpret airspace classes—charts / diagrams
PLT041	Interpret altimeter—readings / settings
PLT042	Interpret Constant Pressure charts / Isotachs Chart
PLT043	Interpret Analysis Heights / Temperature Chart
PLT044	Interpret ATC communications / instructions / terminology
PLT045	Interpret Descent Performance Chart
PLT046	Interpret drag ratio from charts
PLT047	Interpret/Program Flight Director/FMS/Automation—modes / operation / indications / errors
PLT048	Interpret Hovering Ceiling Chart
PLT049	Interpret ILS—charts / RMI / CDI / indications
PLT050	Interpret information on a Brake Energy Limit Chart
PLT051	Interpret information on a Convective Outlook
PLT052	Interpret information on a Departure Procedure Chart
PLT053	Interpret information on a Flight Plan
PLT054	Interpret information on a Glider Performance Graph
PLT055	Interpret information on a High Altitude Chart
PLT056	Interpret information on a Horizontal Situation Indicator (HSI)
PLT057	Interpret information on a Hot Air Balloon Performance Graph
PLT058	Interpret information on a Low Altitude Chart
PLT059	Interpret information on a METAR / SPECI report
PLT060	Interpret information on a Performance Curve Chart
PLT061	Interpret information on a PIREP
PLT062	Interpret information on a Pseudo-Adiabatic Chart
PLT063	Interpret information on a Radar Summary Chart
PLT064	Interpret information on a Sectional Chart
PLT065	Interpret information on a Service Ceiling Engine Inoperative Chart
PLT066	Interpret information on a Convective Outlook Chart
PLT067	Interpret information on a SIGMET
PLT068	Interpret information on a Significant Weather Prognostic Chart
PLT069	Interpret information on a Slush/Standing Water Takeoff Chart
PLT070	Interpret information on a Stability Chart
PLT071	Interpret information on a Surface Analysis Chart
PLT072	Interpret information on a Terminal Aerodrome Forecast (TAF)
PLT073	Interpret information on a Tower Enroute Control (TEC)
PLT074	Interpret information on a Velocity/Load Factor Chart

PLT075	Interpret information on a Weather Depiction Chart
PLT076	Interpret information on a Winds and Temperatures Aloft Forecast (FB)
PLT077	Interpret information on an Airport Diagram
PLT078	Interpret information in an Airport Facility Directory (AFD)
PLT079	Interpret information on an Airways Chart
PLT080	Interpret information on an Arrival Chart
PLT081	Interpret information on an Aviation Area Forecast (FA)
PLT082	Interpret information on an IFR Alternate Airport Minimums Chart
PLT083	Interpret information on an Instrument Approach Procedures (IAP)
PLT084	Interpret information on an Observed Winds Aloft Chart
PLT085	Interpret information on Takeoff Obstacle / Field / Climb Limit Charts
PLT086	Interpret readings on a Turn and Slip Indicator
PLT087	Interpret readings on an Aircraft Course and DME Indicator
PLT088	Interpret speed indicator readings
PLT089	Interpret Takeoff Speeds Chart
PLT090	Interpret VOR—charts / indications / CDI / ADF / NAV
PLT091	Interpret VOR / ADF / NDB / CDI / RMI—illustrations / indications / procedures
PLT092	Interpret weight and balance—diagram
PLT093	Recall administration of medical oxygen
PLT094	Recall aerodynamics—airfoil design / pressure distribution / effects of altitude
PLT095	Recall aerodynamics—longitudinal axis / lateral axis
PLT096	Recall aeromedical factors—effects of altitude
PLT097	Recall aeromedical factors—effects of carbon monoxide poisoning
PLT098	Recall aeromedical factors—fitness for flight
PLT099	Recall aeromedical factors—scanning procedures
PLT100	Recall aeronautical charts—IFR En Route Low Altitude
PLT101	Recall aeronautical charts—pilotage
PLT102	Recall aeronautical charts—terminal procedures
PLT103	Recall Aeronautical Decision Making (ADM)—hazardous attitudes
PLT104	Recall Aeronautical Decision Making (ADM)—human factors / CRM
PLT105	Recall airborne radar / thunderstorm detection equipment—use / limitations
PLT106	Recall aircraft air-cycle machine
PLT107	Recall aircraft alternator / generator system
PLT108	Recall aircraft anti-icing / deicing—methods / fluids
PLT109	Recall aircraft batteries—capacity / charging / types / storage / rating / precautions
PLT110	Recall aircraft brake system
PLT111	Recall aircraft circuitry—series / parallel
PLT112	Recall aircraft controls—proper use / techniques
PLT113	Recall aircraft design—categories / limitation factors
PLT114	Recall aircraft design—construction / function
PLT115	Recall aircraft engine—detonation/backfiring/after firing, cause/characteristics
PLT116	Recall aircraft general knowledge / publications / AIM / navigational aids
PLT117	Recall aircraft heated windshields
PLT118	Recall aircraft instruments—gyroscopic
PLT119	Recall aircraft lighting—anti-collision / landing / navigation
PLT120	Recall aircraft limitations—turbulent air penetration

PLT121　　Recall aircraft loading—computations
PLT122　　Recall aircraft operations—checklist usage
PLT123　　Recall aircraft performance—airspeed
PLT124　　Recall aircraft performance—atmospheric effects
PLT125　　Recall aircraft performance—climb / descent
PLT126　　Recall aircraft performance—cold weather operations
PLT127　　Recall aircraft performance—density altitude
PLT128　　Recall aircraft performance—effects of icing
PLT129　　Recall aircraft performance—effects of runway slope / slope landing
PLT130　　Recall aircraft performance—fuel
PLT131　　Recall aircraft performance—ground effect
PLT132　　Recall aircraft performance—instrument markings / airspeed / definitions / indications
PLT133　　Recall aircraft performance—normal climb / descent rates
PLT134　　Recall aircraft performance—takeoff
PLT135　　Recall aircraft pressurization—system / operation PLT136　　Recall aircraft systems—anti-icing / deicing
PLT137　　Recall aircraft systems—environmental control
PLT138　　Recall aircraft landing gear/tires—types / characteristics
PLT139　　Recall aircraft warning systems—stall / fire / retractable gear / terrain awareness
PLT140　　Recall airport operations—LAHSO
PLT141　　Recall airport operations—markings / signs / lighting
PLT142　　Recall airport operations—noise avoidance routes
PLT143　　Recall airport operations—rescue / fire fighting vehicles and types of agents
PLT144　　Recall airport operations—runway conditions
PLT145　　Recall airport operations—runway lighting
PLT146　　Recall airport operations—traffic pattern procedures / communication procedures
PLT147　　Recall airport operations—visual glideslope indicators
PLT148　　Recall airport operations lighting—MALS / ALSF / RCLS / TDZL
PLT149　　Recall airport preflight / taxi operations—procedures
PLT150　　Recall airport traffic patterns—entry procedures
PLT151　　Recall airship—buoyancy
PLT152　　Recall airship—flight characteristics / controllability
PLT153　　Recall airship—flight operations
PLT154　　Recall airship—ground weigh-off / static / trim condition
PLT155　　Recall airship—maintaining pressure
PLT156　　Recall airship—maximum headway / flight at equilibrium
PLT157　　Recall airship—pressure height / dampers / position
PLT158　　Recall airship—pressure height / manometers
PLT159　　Recall airship—pressure height / super heat / valving gas
PLT160　　Recall airship—stability / control / positive superheat
PLT161　　Recall airspace classes—limits / requirements / restrictions / airspeeds / equipment
PLT162　　Recall airspace requirements—operations
PLT163　　Recall airspace requirements—visibility / cloud clearance
PLT164　　Recall airspeed—effects during a turn
PLT165　　Recall altimeter—effect of temperature changes
PLT166　　Recall altimeter—settings / setting procedures

PLT167   Recall altimeters—characteristics / accuracy
PLT168   Recall angle of attack—characteristics / forces / principles
PLT169   Recall antitorque system—components / functions
PLT170   Recall approach / landing / taxiing techniques
PLT171   Recall ATC—reporting
PLT172   Recall ATC—system / services
PLT173   Recall atmospheric conditions—measurements / pressure / stability
PLT174   Recall autopilot / yaw damper—components / operating principles / characteristics / failure modes
PLT175   Recall autorotation
PLT176   Recall balance tab—purpose / operation
PLT177   Recall balloon—flight operations
PLT178   Recall balloon—flight operations / gas
PLT179   Recall balloon—ground weigh-off / static equilibrium / load
PLT180   Recall balloon gas/hot air—lift / false lift / characteristics
PLT181   Recall balloon—hot air / physics
PLT182   Recall balloon—inspecting the fabric
PLT183   Recall balloon flight operations—ascent / descent
PLT184   Recall balloon flight operations—launch / landing
PLT185   Recall basic instrument flying—fundamental skills
PLT186   Recall basic instrument flying—pitch instruments
PLT187   Recall basic instrument flying—turn coordinator / turn and slip indicator
PLT188   Recall cabin atmosphere control
PLT189   Recall carburetor—effects of carburetor heat / heat control
PLT190   Recall carburetor ice—factors affecting / causing
PLT191   Recall carburetors—types / components / operating principles / characteristics
PLT192   Recall clouds—types / formation / resulting weather
PLT193   Recall cockpit voice recorder (CVR)—operating principles / characteristics / testing
PLT194   Recall collision avoidance—scanning techniques
PLT195   Recall collision avoidance—TCAS
PLT196   Recall communications—ATIS broadcasts
PLT197   Recall Coriolis effect
PLT198   Recall course / heading—effects of wind
PLT199   Recall cyclic control pressure—characteristics
PLT200   Recall dead reckoning—calculations / charts
PLT201   Recall departure procedures—ODP / SID
PLT202   Recall DME—characteristics / accuracy / indications / Arc
PLT203   Recall earth's atmosphere—layers / characteristics / solar energy
PLT204   Recall effective communication—basic elements
PLT205   Recall effects of alcohol on the body
PLT206   Recall effects of temperature—density altitude / icing
PLT207   Recall electrical system—components / operating principles / characteristics / static bonding and shielding
PLT208   Recall emergency conditions / procedures
PLT209   Recall engine pressure ratio—EPR
PLT210   Recall engine shutdown—normal / abnormal / emergency / precautions

PLT211	Recall evaluation testing characteristics
PLT212	Recall fire extinguishing systems—components / operating principles / characteristics
PLT213	Recall flight characteristics—longitudinal stability / instability
PLT214	Recall flight characteristics—structural / wing design
PLT215	Recall flight instruments—magnetic compass
PLT216	Recall flight instruments—total energy compensators
PLT217	Recall flight maneuvers—quick stop
PLT218	Recall flight operations—common student errors
PLT219	Recall flight operations—maneuvers
PLT220	Recall flight operations—night and high altitude operations
PLT221	Recall flight operations—takeoff / landing maneuvers
PLT222	Recall flight operations—takeoff procedures
PLT223	Recall flight operations multiengine—engine inoperative procedures
PLT224	Recall flight plan—IFR
PLT225	Recall flight plan—requirements
PLT226	Recall fog—types / formation / resulting weather
PLT227	Recall FOI techniques—integrated flight instruction
PLT228	Recall FOI techniques—lesson plans
PLT229	Recall FOI techniques—professionalism
PLT230	Recall FOI techniques—responsibilities
PLT231	Recall FOI techniques / human behavior—anxiety / fear / stress
PLT232	Recall FOI techniques / human behavior—dangerous tendencies
PLT233	Recall FOI techniques / human behavior—defense mechanisms
PLT234	Recall forces acting on aircraft—3 axis intersect
PLT235	Recall forces acting on aircraft—aerodynamics
PLT236	Recall forces acting on aircraft—airfoil / center of pressure / mean camber line
PLT237	Recall forces acting on aircraft—airspeed / air density / lift / drag
PLT238	Recall forces acting on aircraft—aspect ratio
PLT239	Recall forces acting on aircraft—buoyancy / drag / gravity / thrust
PLT240	Recall forces acting on aircraft—CG / flight characteristics
PLT241	Recall forces acting on aircraft—drag / gravity / thrust / lift
PLT242	Recall forces acting on aircraft—lift / drag / thrust / weight / stall / limitations
PLT243	Recall forces acting on aircraft—propeller / torque
PLT244	Recall forces acting on aircraft—stability / controllability
PLT245	Recall forces acting on aircraft—stalls / spins
PLT246	Recall forces acting on aircraft—steady state climb / flight
PLT247	Recall forces acting on aircraft—thrust / drag / weight / lift
PLT248	Recall forces acting on aircraft—turns
PLT249	Recall fuel—air mixture
PLT250	Recall fuel—types / characteristics / contamination / fueling / defueling / precautions
PLT251	Recall fuel characteristics / contaminants / additives
PLT252	Recall fuel dump system—components / methods
PLT253	Recall fuel system—components / operating principles / characteristics / leaks
PLT254	Recall fuel tank—components / operating principles / characteristics
PLT255	Recall fueling procedures—safety / grounding / calculating volume
PLT256	Recall glider performance—effect of loading

PLT257   Recall glider performance—speed / distance / ballast / lift / drag
PLT258   Recall ground reference maneuvers—ground track diagram
PLT259   Recall ground resonance—conditions to occur
PLT260   Recall gyroplane—aerodynamics / rotor systems
PLT261   Recall hail—characteristics / hazards
PLT262   Recall helicopter hazards—dynamic rollover / Low G / LTE
PLT263   Recall hazardous weather—fog / icing / turbulence / visibility restriction
PLT264   Recall helicopter approach—settling with power
PLT265   Recall helicopter takeoff / landing—ground resonance action required
PLT266   Recall high lift devices—characteristics / functions
PLT267   Recall hot air balloon—weigh-off procedure
PLT268   Recall hovering—aircraft performance / tendencies
PLT269   Recall human behavior—defense mechanism
PLT270   Recall human behavior—social / self fulfillment / physical
PLT271   Recall human factors (ADM)—judgment
PLT272   Recall human factors—stress management
PLT273   Recall hydraulic systems—components / operating principles / characteristics
PLT274   Recall icing—formation / characteristics
PLT275   Recall ILS—indications / HSI
PLT276   Recall ILS—indications / OBS / CDI
PLT277   Recall ILS—marker beacon / indicator lights / codes
PLT278   Recall indicating systems—airspeed / angle of attack / attitude / heading /
          manifold pressure / synchro / EGT
PLT279   Recall Inertial/Doppler Navigation System principles / regulations / requirements / limitations
PLT280   Recall inflight illusions—causes / sources
PLT281   Recall information in an Airport Facility Directory
PLT282   Recall information in the certificate holder`s manual
PLT283   Recall information on a Constant Pressure Analysis Chart
PLT284   Recall information on a Forecast Winds and Temperatures Aloft (FB)
PLT285   Recall information on a Height Velocity Diagram
PLT286   Recall information on a Significant Weather Prognostic Chart
PLT287   Recall information on a Surface Analysis Chart
PLT288   Recall information on a Terminal Aerodrome Forecast (TAF)
PLT289   Recall information on a Weather Depiction Chart
PLT290   Recall information on AIRMETS / SIGMETS
PLT291   Recall information on an Aviation Area Forecast (FA)
PLT292   Recall information on an Instrument Approach Procedures (IAP)
PLT293   Recall information on an Instrument Departure Procedure Chart
PLT294   Recall information on Inflight Aviation Weather Advisories
PLT295   Recall instructor techniques—obstacles / planning / activities / outcome
PLT296   Recall instrument procedures—holding / circling
PLT297   Recall instrument procedures—unusual attitude / unusual attitude recovery
PLT298   Recall instrument procedures—VFR on top
PLT300   Recall instrument/navigation system checks/inspections—limits / tuning / identifying / logging
PLT301   Recall inversion layer—characteristics
PLT302   Recall jet stream—types / characteristics

PLT303	Recall L/D ratio
PLT304	Recall launch procedures
PLT305	Recall leading edge devices—types / effect / purpose / operation
PLT306	Recall learning process—levels of learning / transfer of learning / incidental learning
PLT307	Recall learning process—memory / fact / recall
PLT308	Recall learning process—laws of learning elements
PLT309	Recall load factor—angle of bank
PLT310	Recall load factor—characteristics
PLT311	Recall load factor—effect of airspeed
PLT312	Recall load factor—maneuvering / stall speed
PLT313	Recall loading – limitations / terminology
PLT314	Recall longitudinal axis—aerodynamics / center of gravity / direction of motion
PLT315	Recall Machmeter—principles / functions
PLT316	Recall meteorology—severe weather watch (WW)
PLT317	Recall microburst—characteristics / hazards
PLT318	Recall minimum fuel advisory
PLT319	Recall navigation – celestial / navigation chart / characteristics
PLT320	Recall navigation—true north / magnetic north
PLT321	Recall navigation—types of landing systems
PLT322	Recall navigation—VOR / NAV system
PLT323	Recall NOTAMS—classes / information / distribution
PLT324	Recall oil system—types / components / functions / oil specifications
PLT325	Recall operations manual—transportation of prisoner
PLT326	Recall oxygen system—components / operating principles / characteristics
PLT327	Recall oxygen system—install / inspect / repair / service / precautions / leaks
PLT328	Recall performance planning—aircraft loading
PLT329	Recall physiological factors—cabin pressure
PLT330	Recall physiological factors—cause / effects of hypoxia
PLT331	Recall physiological factors—effects of scuba diving / smoking
PLT332	Recall physiological factors—hyperventilation
PLT333	Recall physiological factors—night vision
PLT334	Recall physiological factors—spatial disorientation
PLT335	Recall pilotage—calculations
PLT336	Recall pitch control—collective / cyclic
PLT337	Recall pitot-static system—components / operating principles / characteristics
PLT338	Recall pneumatic system—operation
PLT340	Recall positive exchange of flight controls
PLT341	Recall power settling—characteristics
PLT342	Recall powerplant—controlling engine temperature
PLT343	Recall powerplant—operating principles / operational characteristics / inspecting
PLT344	Recall precipitation—types / characteristics
PLT345	Recall pressure altitude
PLT346	Recall primary / secondary flight controls—types / purpose / functionality / operation
PLT347	Recall principles of flight—critical engine
PLT348	Recall principles of flight—turns
PLT349	Recall procedures for confined areas

PLT350	Recall propeller operations—constant / variable speed
PLT351	Recall propeller system—types / components / operating principles / characteristics
PLT352	Recall purpose / operation of a stabilizer
PLT353	Recall Radar Summary Chart
PLT354	Recall radio—GPS / RNAV / RAIM
PLT355	Recall radio—HSI
PLT356	Recall radio—ILS / compass locator
PLT357	Recall radio—ILS / LDA
PLT358	Recall radio—LOC / ILS
PLT359	Deleted
PLT360	Recall radio—Microwave Landing System
PLT361	Recall radio—SDF / ILS
PLT362	Recall radio – VHF / Direction Finding
PLT363	Recall radio—VOR / VOT
PLT364	Recall radio system—licence requirements / frequencies
PLT365	Recall reciprocating engine—components / operating principles / characteristics
PLT366	Recall regulations—accident / incident reporting and preserving wreckage
PLT367	Recall regulations—additional equipment/operating requirements large transport aircraft
PLT368	Recall regulations—admission to flight deck
PLT369	Recall regulations—aerobatic flight requirements
PLT370	Recall regulations—Air Traffic Control authorization / clearances
PLT371	Recall regulations—Aircraft Category / Class
PLT372	Recall regulations—aircraft inspection / records / expiration
PLT373	Recall regulations—aircraft operating limitations
PLT374	Recall regulations—aircraft owner / operator responsibilities
PLT375	Recall regulations—aircraft return to service
PLT376	Recall regulations—airspace special use / TFRS
PLT377	Recall regulations—airworthiness certificates / requirements / responsibilities
PLT378	Recall regulations—Airworthiness Directives
PLT379	Recall regulations—alternate airport requirements
PLT380	Recall regulations—alternate airport weather minima
PLT381	Recall regulations—altimeter settings
PLT382	Recall regulations—approach minima
PLT383	Recall regulations—basic flight rules
PLT384	Recall regulations—briefing of passengers
PLT385	Recall regulations—cargo in passenger compartment
PLT386	Recall regulations—certificate issuance / renewal
PLT387	Recall regulations—change of address
PLT388	Recall regulations—cockpit voice / flight data recorder(s)
PLT389	Recall regulations—commercial operation requirements / conditions / OpSpecs
PLT390	Recall regulations—communications enroute
PLT391	Recall regulations—communications failure
PLT392	Recall regulations—compliance with local regulations
PLT393	Recall regulations—controlled / restricted airspace—requirements
PLT394	Recall regulations—declaration of an emergency
PLT395	Recall regulations—definitions

PLT396	Recall regulations—departure alternate airport
PLT397	Recall regulations—destination airport visibility
PLT398	Recall regulations—dispatch
PLT399	Recall regulations—display / inspection of licences and certificates
PLT400	Recall regulations—documents to be carried on aircraft during flight
PLT401	Recall regulations—dropping / aerial application / towing restrictions
PLT402	Recall regulations—ELT requirements
PLT403	Recall regulations—emergency deviation from regulations
PLT404	Recall regulations—emergency equipment
PLT405	Recall regulations—equipment / instrument / certificate requirements
PLT406	Recall regulations—equipment failure
PLT407	Recall regulations—experience / training requirements
PLT408	Recall regulations—fire extinguisher requirements
PLT409	Recall regulations—flight / duty time
PLT410	Recall regulations—flight engineer qualifications / privileges / responsibilities
PLT411	Recall regulations—flight instructor limitations / qualifications
PLT412	Recall regulations—flight release
PLT413	Recall regulations—fuel requirements
PLT414	Recall regulations—general right-of-way rules
PLT415	Recall regulations—IFR flying
PLT416	Recall regulations—immediate notification
PLT417	Recall regulations—individual flotation devices
PLT418	Recall regulations—instructor demonstrations / authorizations
PLT419	Recall regulations—instructor requirements / responsibilities
PLT420	Recall regulations—instrument approach procedures
PLT421	Recall regulations—instrument flight rules
PLT422	Recall regulations—intermediate airport authorizations
PLT423	Recall regulations—knowledge and skill test checks
PLT424	Recall regulations—limits on autopilot usage
PLT425	Recall regulations—maintenance reports / records / entries
PLT426	Recall regulations—maintenance requirements
PLT427	Recall regulations—medical certificate requirements / validity
PLT428	Recall regulations—minimum equipment list
PLT429	Recall regulations—minimum flight / navigation instruments
PLT430	Recall regulations—minimum safe / flight altitude
PLT431	Recall regulations—operating near other aircraft
PLT432	Recall regulations—operational control functions
PLT433	Recall regulations—operational flight plan requirements
PLT434	Recall regulations—operational procedures for a controlled airport
PLT435	Recall regulations—operational procedures for an uncontrolled airport
PLT436	Recall regulations—operations manual
PLT437	Recall regulations—overwater operations
PLT438	Recall regulations—oxygen requirements
PLT439	Recall regulations—persons authorized to perform maintenance
PLT440	Recall regulations—Pilot / Crew duties and responsibilities
PLT441	Recall regulations—pilot briefing

PLT442	Recall regulations—pilot currency requirements
PLT443	Recall regulations—pilot qualifications / privileges / responsibilities / crew complement
PLT444	Recall regulations—pilot-in-command authority / responsibility
PLT445	Recall regulations—preflight requirements
PLT446	Recall regulations—preventative maintenance
PLT447	Recall regulations—privileges / limitations of medical certificates
PLT448	Recall regulations—privileges / limitations of pilot certificates
PLT449	Recall regulations—proficiency check requirements
PLT450	Recall regulations—qualifications / duty time
PLT451	Recall regulations—ratings issued / experience requirements / limitations
PLT452	Recall regulations—re-dispatch
PLT453	Recall regulations—records retention for domestic / flag air carriers
PLT454	Recall regulations—required aircraft / equipment inspections
PLT455	Recall regulations—requirements of a flight plan release
PLT456	Recall regulations—runway requirements
PLT457	Recall regulations—student pilot endorsements / other endorsements
PLT458	Recall regulations—submission / revision of Policy and Procedure Manuals
PLT459	Recall regulations—takeoff procedures / minimums
PLT460	Recall regulations—training programs
PLT461	Recall regulations—use of aircraft lights
PLT462	Recall regulations—use of microphone / megaphone / interphone / public address system
PLT463	Recall regulations alcohol or drugs
PLT464	Recall regulations—use of safety belts / harnesses (crew member)
PLT465	Recall regulations—use of seats / safety belts / harnesses (passenger)
PLT466	Recall regulations—V speeds
PLT467	Recall regulations—visual flight rules and limitations
PLT468	Recall regulations—Visual Meteorological Conditions (VMC)
PLT469	Recall regulations—weather radar
PLT470	Recall rotor system—types / components / operating principles / characteristics
PLT471	Recall rotorcraft transmission—components / operating principles / characteristics
PLT472	Recall rotorcraft vibration—characteristics / sources
PLT473	Recall secondary flight controls—types / purpose / functionality
PLT474	Recall soaring—normal procedures
PLT475	Recall squall lines—formation / characteristics / resulting weather
PLT476	Recall stabilizer—purpose / operation
PLT477	Recall stalls—characteristics / factors / recovery / precautions
PLT478	Recall starter / ignition system—types / components / operating principles / characteristics
PLT479	Recall starter system—starting procedures
PLT480	Recall static/dynamic stability/instability—characteristics
PLT481	Recall student evaluation—learning process
PLT482	Recall student evaluation—written tests / oral quiz / critiques
PLT483	Recall supercharger—characteristics / operation
PLT484	Recall symbols—chart / navigation
PLT485	Recall taxiing / crosswind / techniques
PLT486	Recall taxiing / takeoff—techniques / procedures
PLT487	Recall teaching methods—demonstration / performance

PLT488	Recall teaching methods—group / guided discussion / lecture
PLT489	Recall teaching methods—known to unknown
PLT490	Recall teaching methods—motivation / student feelings of insecurity
PLT491	Recall teaching methods—organizing material / course of training
PLT492	Recall temperature—effects on weather formations
PLT493	Recall the dynamics of frost / ice / snow formation on an aircraft
PLT494	Recall thermals—types / characteristics / formation / locating / maneuvering / corrective actions
PLT495	Recall thunderstorms—types / characteristics / formation / hazards / precipitation static
PLT496	Recall towrope—strength / safety links / positioning
PLT497	Recall transponder—codes / operations / usage
PLT498	Recall Transportation Security Regulations
PLT499	Recall turbine engines—components / operational characteristics / associated instruments
PLT500	Recall turboprop engines—components / operational characteristics
PLT501	Recall turbulence—types / characteristics / reporting / corrective actions
PLT502	Recall universal signals—hand / light / visual
PLT503	Recall use of narcotics / drugs / intoxicating liquor
PLT504	Recall use of training aids—types / function / purpose
PLT505	Recall use of training aids—usefulness / simplicity / compatibility
PLT506	Recall V speeds—maneuvering / flap extended / gear extended / V1, V2, r, ne, mo, mc, mg, etc.
PLT507	Recall VOR—indications / VOR / VOT / CDI
PLT508	Recall VOR/altimeter/transponder checks—identification / tuning / identifying / logging
PLT509	Recall wake turbulence—characteristics / avoidance techniques
PLT510	Recall weather—causes / formation
PLT511	Recall weather associated with frontal activity / air masses
PLT512	Recall weather conditions—temperature / moisture / dewpoint
PLT513	Recall weather information—TWEB broadcasts / FAA Avcams
PLT514	Recall weather reporting systems—briefings / forecasts / reports / AWOS / ASOS
PLT515	Recall weather services—EFAS / TIBS / TPC / WFO / AFSS / HIWAS
PLT516	Recall winds—types / characteristics
PLT517	Recall winds associated with high / low-pressure systems
PLT518	Recall windshear—characteristics / hazards / power management
PLT519	Recall wing spoilers—purpose / operation
PLT520	Calculate density altitude
PLT521	Recall helicopter takeoff / landing – slope operations
PLT522	Recall helicopter – Pinnacle / Ridgeline operations
PLT523	Recall vortex generators – purpose / effects / aerodynamics
PLT524	Interpret / Program information on an avionics display
PLT525	Interpret table – oxygen / fuel / oil / accumulator / fire extinguisher
PLT526	Recall near midair collision report
PLT527	Recall BASIC VFR weather minimums